AF799849

CREDIT AND COMMUNITY

Credit and Community

Working-Class Debt in the UK Since 1880

SEAN O'CONNELL

OXFORD
UNIVERSITY PRESS

OXFORD
UNIVERSITY PRESS

Great Clarendon Street, Oxford OX2 6DP

Oxford University Press is a department of the University of Oxford.
It furthers the University's objective of excellence in research, scholarship,
and education by publishing worldwide in

Oxford New York

Auckland Cape Town Dar es Salaam Hong Kong Karachi
Kuala Lumpur Madrid Melbourne Mexico City Nairobi
New Delhi Shanghai Taipei Toronto

With offices in

Argentina Austria Brazil Chile Czech Republic France Greece
Guatemala Hungary Italy Japan Poland Portugal Singapore
South Korea Switzerland Thailand Turkey Ukraine Vietnam

Oxford is a registered trade mark of Oxford University Press
in the UK and in certain other countries

Published in the United States
by Oxford University Press Inc., New York

© Sean O'Connell 2009

The moral rights of the author have been asserted
Database right Oxford University Press (maker)

First published 2009

All rights reserved. No part of this publication may be reproduced,
stored in a retrieval system, or transmitted, in any form or by any means,
without the prior permission in writing of Oxford University Press,
or as expressly permitted by law, or under terms agreed with the appropriate
reprographics rights organization. Enquiries concerning reproduction
outside the scope of the above should be sent to the Rights Department,
Oxford University Press, at the address above

You must not circulate this book in any other binding or cover
and you must impose the same condition on any acquirer

British Library Cataloguing in Publication Data
Data available

Library of Congress Cataloging in Publication Data
Data available

Typeset by Laserwords Private Limited, Chennai, India
Printed on acid-free paper by
the MPG Books Group in the UK

ISBN 978–0–19–926331–8

1 3 5 7 9 10 8 6 4 2

Dedicated to the memory of my brother, Joe (1969–2006), and my mum, Bridie (1933–2007)

Preface and Acknowledgements

This monograph emerged out of one of the chance intellectual challenges and encounters that are amongst the advantages of the peripatetic academic lifestyle. Its origins lie in my time at the Business History Unit, at the London School of Economics, where I worked with Dil Porter and Richard Coopey to produce a business and social history of mail order retailing. Many of the arguments and conclusions expressed in this monograph have their origins in discussions with Dil and Richard. I became particularly interested in the role of catalogue agents as informal credit assessors and repayment enforcers in the working-class community. At the project's end I determined to explore working-class credit and community in a more holistic manner. Through the perseverance of the indefatigable Terry Gourvish at the Business History Unit, I made contact with Provident Financial and gained access to its extensive archive. The fruits of my labours therein first appeared in collaborative work with Chris Reid. As always, working with Chris provided a wonderful opportunity to reflect on my findings and immeasurably increased my chances of providing a coherent historical summary of working-class credit and debt. A move to Belfast, to take up a new academic post, placed me in an ideal location in which to include the unwritten history of the UK's credit union movement in my plans. The introduction explains how the research was enacted. In this preface, I wish to offer thanks to the many individuals and institutions that have provided assistance over the past eight years.

Practical and financial support was received from a variety of sources. Provident Financial agreed to grant unprecedented access to its archives and to host meetings of a Steering Committee that I established to oversee the research. Serving on that committee were Andy Davies and Dil Porter who provided numerous suggestions that benefited the shaping of my research and the analysis of its findings. I could not have asked for two finer colleagues to carry out this task and I am deeply indebted to both of them for their guidance and friendship. Provident's co-operation was secured after they were named, together with the pressure group Church Action on Poverty, as a User Group for the research findings from my ESRC funded project 'Credit, class and community' (ESRC award number R/000/22/3822). I am grateful for the assistance provided by Alan Thornton of Church Action on Poverty, who supplied many insightful references on the debate about consumer debt. At Provident David Rees and his colleagues kindly facilitated my access to the company's archive. I am delighted to recognize the ESRC for its financial support. In addition, the AHRC graciously funded the sabbatical in which this monograph was completed (AHRC award number 113004). I owe a debt of gratitude to David Hayton, at Queen's University, Belfast, for ensuring that the sabbatical ran smoothly, and to Alan Sharp at the University of Ulster who worked, in trying circumstances, to facilitate the earlier stages of the project.

I was granted access to historical material held by the Consumer Credit Association, and the five major mail order companies (Empire Stores, Freemans, Kays, Great Universal Stores, Littlewoods). Individuals who I particularly thank, for arranging this access, are Bill Oakes of RedCATS UK (formerly Empire Stores), Robert Blow at Freemans, and Martin Gilhooley at Grattan. Gillian Lonergan at the National Cooperative Archive courteously and professionally guided my research in that source. Staff at the National Archives (Kew), the Public Record Office of Northern Ireland, and the British Library were all extremely helpful.

Numerous individuals provided personal testimony on their experiences of consumer credit, from either side of the credit nexus. The thirty-two Belfast interviewees cannot be thanked by name (the names cited in the footnotes are pseudonyms), but I am extremely grateful to them for offering up their time. My thanks are also due to the staff of the various Belfast Day Centres that provided access to their clients, many of whom agreed to provide interviews. A number of individuals involved in the provision of consumer credit also provided interviews, but preferred to remain anonymous, whilst Peter Fattorini, Neville Greenwood, Michael Lilley, and Tom Chirnside all provided valuable testimony on the changing nature of credit and debt in the working-class community. Martin Logan and Harold Mangan provided valuable insights into the history of the credit union movement. Harold also provided testimony of his experiences of West Indian immigrants' uses of 'partners' in the 1950s and 1960s and a Birmingham woman, Toni, offered a perspective from a younger generation. Two groups of students registered with the University of Ulster experienced the joys of oral history under my supervision, by engaging in a project probing credit unions on either side of the Irish border. Their enthusiastic and professional approach produced important and original testimony, some of which is contained herein.

At Oxford University Press, Ruth Parr, Anne Gelling, Tim Saunders, Zoe Washford, Rupert Cousens, Seth Cayley, Mikki Choman, and Christine Ranft have professionally overseen my work. I hope the long list of names here is a function of the length of time I have been working on this project, rather than the difficulties of working with me. The two referees who first read the proposal for this monograph proffered several very valuable comments, as did the anonymous reader who read it when it arrived at OUP. I am extremely grateful to all three of these individuals. Numerous friends and colleagues provided assistance, advice, encouragement, or a boost to morale when it was required. Andy Davies and Dil Porter feature again in this category, as do Fidelma Ashe, Alan Bairner, Martin Burke, Michael Carter, Paul Corthorn, James Davis, Enda Delaney, Pete Donovan, Neil Fleming, Colin Harper, Keith Jeffery, Fearghal McGarry, Gillian McIntosh, Mike Willner, and the Cliftonville Redskins. Andy Davies, Jill Greenfield, and Chris Reid have all read drafts of various chapters and made suggestions that have greatly improved it. Jill, in particular, has worked tirelessly to support me over the last two difficult years, which have seen the deaths of my brother and mother. I have been fortunate indeed to have her love.

Contents

Abbreviations

ABCUL	Association of British Credit Unions Ltd
APR	Annual Percentage Rate
BDS	British Debt Services
CCA	Consumer Credit Association
CUNA	Credit Union National Association
CWS	Co-operative Wholesale Society
DTI	Department of Trade and Industry
GUS	Great Universal Stores
ILCU	Irish League of Credit Unions
NACUW	National Association of Credit Union Workers
NCC	National Consumer Council
NFCU	National Federation of Credit Unions
NFCCU	National Federation of Community Development Credit Unions
PSI	Policy Studies Institute
RCF	Retail Credit Federation
SLCU	Scottish League of Credit Unions
TSB	Trustee Savings Bank
UFCU	Ulster Federation of Credit Unions

Introduction

On easy terms? Borrowing and lending in the working-class community

THE STORIES OF JOHN AND ANNE-MARIE

John Moores was born in Eccles in 1896. He was one of the eight children of Louisa, a former mill girl. John's father was a bricklayer who, at one point, also part-owned a public house. However, this financial interest developed into a taste for the pub's chief product and alcoholism and violence made the marriage an unhappy one. Louisa separated from her husband, moving into her sister's home and taking in sewing to support the family. In 1907, they moved again when Louisa opened a confectionary shop. Her husband had returned by this point, but was unable to work due to injury. His drinking continued, however, and he financed it by taking money from the shop. Young John watched his mother secretly pawn her husband's gold watch to help with family finances. Eventually, debts forced her business to collapse and Louisa was compelled to take in washing to make ends meet, visibly tumbling down the social hierarchy in the process. Family fortunes improved again during the First World War, with John earning 18 shillings a week as a junior telegraphist, and Louisa opening another small business—a fish and chip shop—in 1918, a venture which was considered 'low' by some observers.[1] John's early life experience had provided a stark lesson in the hazards that faced the working-class family and of the difficulties of retaining respectable status in a world filled with economic uncertainties and judgemental onlookers. His mother's experience of debt, and the loss of personal autonomy that it brought her, left a deep imprint. Until

[1] Barbara Clegg, *The man who made Littlewoods: the story of John Moores* (Bury St Edmunds: Hodder & Stoughton, 1993), 11–23.

his death, in 1993, he constantly urged his family to take a cautious approach to consumer credit.[II]

Similar guidance was offered by her parents to Anne-Marie, who was born in Belfast in 1951. However, as a mother of seven children, she was unable to follow their advice. In the early 1980s, after separating from her husband, Anne-Marie found herself confronted on her doorstep by a debt collector. Recalling the episode over twenty years later, she remembered that the debt collector 'said to me that if I cooperated—sexually—that that would do instead of paying'. For Anne-Marie, this experience 'summarized all the fear that I had of debt. That you were in the clutches of other people, once you had debt.'[III]

Why does this study begin with the juxtaposition of these two stories? The answer is that Anne-Marie's debt had arisen through a sister-in-law's illicit use of her Littlewoods' catalogue. The debt was sold to a collection agency, leading to the arrival of her unwelcome and sleazy visitor. Littlewoods was founded by John Moores, who left his first employees in no doubt about his profound distrust of credit. Jim Wilson, appointed to Littlewoods Mail Order Stores in the late 1930s, recalled that: 'In the beginning, Mr John Moores—he wasn't keen on credit.'[IV] For this reason, Littlewoods catalogues did not offer credit in their first two decades of operation. Instead, catalogue organizers arranged groups of twenty customers to make weekly contributions to a 'shilling club'. The £1 collected each week was sent to the company and merchandise to that value was returned to one of the club's members. Lots were drawn to decide the order in which merchandise was to be received. The system was incredibly popular with working-class consumers who were familiar with the draw club principle. Many also shared Moores' practical and moral concerns about the dangers of indebtedness. Moores' conservative perspective also surfaced in relation to Littlewoods' retail stores, where, in the 1970s he intervened to scupper a plan to introduce store cards.[V]

Despite this outlook, Littlewoods was one of the main participants in the explosion of consumer credit in twentieth-century Britain. This monograph charts the cultural and economic turns and developments that produced outcomes that neither John Moores nor Anne-Marie

[II] Barbara Clegg, *The man who made Littlewoods: the story of John Moores*, 11–23.

[III] Interview with Anne-Marie (Mature student and mother. Born 1951. First husband a scaffolder; current husband a musician. Interviewed 20 May 2003).

[IV] Interview with Jim Wilson (retired Littlewoods Mail Order executive. Born 1908. Interviewed 12 November 1996).

[V] Clegg, *The man who made Littlewoods*, 141–2.

envisaged taking place. Anne-Marie's encounter with debt was the result of a chain of events that included marriage, the birth of seven children, a marriage breakdown, and the dishonest actions of her ex-husband's sister. She was caught up in a sequence of personal events that she struggled to control. In contrast, John Moores was a multi-millionaire, a patron of the arts, and owner of Everton Football Club, but he was also subject to events beyond his control. In his case, these included the rising demand for consumer credit that Littlewoods' competitors addressed aggressively. Reluctantly, Moores was forced to engage more fully with consumer credit.

The account that follows is a social and cultural history of borrowing and lending in working-class communities. It is also a business history of those who have advanced loans in those areas, examining the role of tallymen, check traders, mail order catalogues, legal and illegal neighbourhood moneylenders, and various forms of cooperative credit institutions. Working-class consumer credit is a subject where it is difficult to separate the social from the economic, the commercial from the cultural. For example, agents from within working-class communities made many business decisions on behalf of mail order catalogue companies or the large-scale moneylenders. Thus, on millions of occasions, the seemingly economic question of a customer's creditworthiness was influenced by culturally shaped factors such as an individual's respectability in the eyes of a neighbour.

A business history of this topic must detail this community-based form of credit assessment and juxtapose it with information on the internal workings of the consumer credit firms. Similarly, a social and cultural history must explore the details of business or legislative change and a central theme of this work is to assess the impact of such loaded concepts as 'usury' on commercial decisions and on the views of legislators. In taking this approach, this monograph employs a range of evidence including oral history, business archives, trade journals, and the masses of evidence presented to the Crowther Committee on Consumer Credit which sat between 1968 and 1971.

The concept of easy terms used in this introduction's subtitle is based on a phrase coined by some unknown credit company executive who, consciously or not, was engaged in a linguistic battle to overcome moral and economic qualms about the extension of consumer credit. Thus 'terms' refers in one respect to the contractual details involved in each transaction between customer and company (or its agent). It refers also to the powerful terms that illustrated society's suspicion of and hostility towards particular types of lending. Terms such as loan shark, and usurer, conjured up pungent images of powerless consumers in the clutches of rapacious creditors. This language heightened the sense of drama around the subject and made it difficult to reflect coldly on what was a matter of cultural and economic complexity. The terms were particularly evocative because they carried little precision. What was usury? What forms of credit transaction were harsh and unconscionable? When did the high costs associated with providing credit to working-class families with low and insecure incomes leave the realm of the acceptable and become exploitative? These are some of the questions driving this study. It is a study of the mundane everyday social relations enveloping the credit networks that were centred on and utilized within working-class communities. But in telling this story we encounter a far from mundane set of overlapping stories centred on race, religion, gender, and social hierarchy and a world where economic and cultural exchanges were influenced by a disparate range of factors. Some of these are easier to recognize than others. It is simpler to record changing government policy on consumer credit or to measure rising consumer demand than to ascertain the impact of residual anti-Semitism, of Christian social thought on usury, or of the impact of Islamic doctrine on credit use in the UK's Muslim communities, but each of the above is attempted.

AIMS AND ORIGINS

This monograph examines consumer borrowing in working-class communities since 1880. Its origins lie in an earlier collaborative project on the history of mail order retailing in the UK.[vi] This research examined the important role of credit in the success of the sector. Whereas home shopping companies in the USA, such as Montgomery Ward, and Sears, Roebuck & Co., achieved great success because of the geographical spread of their target market, which enabled them to undercut small town retailers on price, British mail order firms found a clientele amongst credit-dependent working-class consumers. In doing so, they became particularly reliant on the ready-made social networks of an army of female part-time agents who made catalogues available to

[vi] Richard Coopey, Sean O'Connell, Dilwyn Porter, *Mail order retailing in Britain: a business and social history* (Oxford: OUP, 2005).

family, friends, and neighbours and, in the process, assessed the credit risks involved in each potential catalogue loan.

On this basis, UK mail order was one of the retail success stories of the twentieth century, providing credit with low bad debt costs. Its significance within working-class families and communities, who had fewer credit options than their middle-class contemporaries, was even greater. From the 1970s, however, its influence slowly waned. The numbers of credit cards, store cards, and other forms of personal loan proliferated as financial institutions began to market money as a product in a fashion that they had not done previously. The best-paid and most educated working-class consumers were the first to move into these new credit channels. It was individuals from families in this group that the catalogue companies most valued as agents because they could be relied upon to carry out the transactions and form filling involved in mail order retailing. Alternative forms of credit, decreasing returns for acting as a mail order agent for small commission payments, and the decline of working-class neighbourliness, saw the number of customers per catalogue agent fall dramatically between the 1960s and 1990s. In 1960, for example, the average Littlewoods agent had 16 customers; by 1997 they served only 2.8 customers (two of whom were usually from within the agent's household). As a result, computerized credit scoring became more important to mail order companies than the tried and tested method of credit assessment, and payment enforcement, of one neighbour by another. An executive in one of the leading companies spoke, in 1999, of his belief that this was creating 'credit orphans' in low-income neighbourhoods.[vii] These 'orphans', who had previously received merchandise on credit through mail order agents, were forced to seek other credit channels. Many became customers of Provident Financial, Cattles, and London Scottish Bank, all of whom provided doorstep loans. Like the mail order sector, these companies had a long history of supplying credit through large armies of agents who built up personal relationships through their weekly visits to customers, and knowledge of individual communities that provided valuable information on levels of creditworthiness. The high costs associated with loans from these doorstep lenders were a key factor that motivated those who have promoted credit unions. These mutual savings and loans institutions, which first appeared in the UK

[vii] Anonymous mail order executive: interviewed by Sean O'Connell and Dilwyn Porter.

in the 1960s, were championed as a community-based and low-interest alternative to doorstep lenders.

This recurring link between credit and community is intriguing and worthy of renewed historical investigation. The aim of this study is to examine the separate but overlapping histories of those forms of moneylending that have utilized community networks in their operations. The forms of credit discussed herein have been most commonly associated with 'low income communities'; a term which at the starting point of our study—1880—could have been applied to virtually all working-class areas. Paul Johnson has outlined that in the early twentieth century 'many, perhaps most manual workers could expect at some time in their lives to face acute financial crisis'.[VIII] Hence there was a widespread familiarity with many of the forms of consumer credit that are the subject of this monograph, even if there was often a reluctance to acknowledge it.

The customers of the doorstep credit companies today have been left far behind financially, by more affluent skilled or semi-skilled workers. Many are still engaged in borrowing in order to finance the purchase of necessities, rather than the signature items of modern affluence. Rather than being labelled 'thriftless', as they might have been a century ago, in the age of computerized credit scoring and financial market segmentation, they have been redesignated as the 'sub-prime sector' or the 'financially excluded'. Their existence, in significant numbers, owes much to a number of factors. The first of these was the Thatcher government's reversal of the redistribution of income begun by the Edwardian Liberals. A related factor was the recession of the late 1970s and early 1980s and the widespread unemployment that followed, which reduced the creditworthiness of millions of families.[IX] Finally, the credit boom of the 1980s, followed by the crash of the late 1980s and early 1990s created significant numbers of credit-impaired consumers, with whom the mainstream financial companies are extremely reluctant to deal.[X]

As a result, there are now regular calls upon the government to intervene in the sub-prime credit market. The current controversy adds

[VIII] Paul Johnson, *Saving and spending: the working-class economy in Britain 1870–1939* (Oxford: Clarendon Press, 1985), 3.

[IX] David Vincent, *Poor citizens: the state and the poor in twentieth century Britain* (London: Longman, 1991), 193–204.

[X] E. Kempson and E. Whyley, *Kept out or forced out: understanding and combating financial exclusion* (Bristol: Joseph Rowntree Foundation, 1999).

a further element of significance to the history of earlier controversies involving creditors whose operations took them into working-class streets and homes. An analysis of the debates and legislation that emerged as a result has the potential to inform aspects of contemporary discussion. The companies who thrive today on their ability to offer loans to low-income families do so because of the quasi-monopolistic position that they enjoy with their customers. But they also succeed because their service is familiar and convenient for those customers and is based upon face-to-face relationships and community networks. These community networks do not take the more attractive form that is advocated by credit union supporters, which revolves around volunteers and emotional rather than fiscal reward: instead they mirror the type of commercialized relationship that has successfully existed between creditors and low-income communities for more than a century.

THE HISTORIOGRAPHY OF WORKING-CLASS CREDIT AND DEBT

Two recent contributions to the literature on working-class experiences of credit and debt provide the departure point for what follows. Work by Margot Finn and Avram Taylor has described how major sectors of the modern consumer credit market remained reliant on informally gathered personal information about customers. This informality entailed the continuance of a highly social relationship between credit providers (or their agents) and customers into the twentieth century; a period which is most frequently assumed to have witnessed the arrival of depersonalized shopping.[xi] Finn believes that the social nature of credit offered by the retailers she analysed is inadequately theorized by purely economic models. Borrowing from Mauss and Bourdieu, she argues that retail credit in the Victorian and Edwardian eras remained strikingly reliant on routine obligatory gifting patterns more commonly associated with traditional societies. Bourdieu's maxim that credit 'creates obligations . . . by creating people obliged to reciprocate' is highlighted

[xi] C. P. Hosgood, 'Knights of the road: commercial travellers and the culture of the commercial room in late-Victorian and Edwardian England', *Victorian Studies*, 37/4 (Summer 1994), 519–47; Margot Finn, *The character of credit: personal debt in English culture, 1740–1914* (Cambridge: Cambridge University Press, 2003); Avram Taylor, *Working class credit and community since 1918* (Basingstoke: Palgrave Macmillan, 2002).

in Finn's description of how credit retailers endeavoured to create reciprocation in the form of long-term loyalty from their customers.[xii] This resulted in a focus on the nature of personal ties with consumers, as much as on price considerations.[xiii] As shopkeepers had only imprecise information on the economic assets of credit applicants, they attempted to read 'personal worth and character from their clothing, their marital relations, their spending patterns and their perceived social status', as well as their religious connections.[xiv] This connection between character and creditworthiness placed a significant brake on the modernization of this area of the market. Finn shines a light on the cultural aspects of exchange and demonstrates that economic behaviour is not to be understood simply in the context of the modern contract economy.

Much of Finn's analysis concerns middle-class consumers and their involvement in highly personalized credit networks. However, she also deals with the relationship between tallymen, or Scotch drapers as they were also known, and the working-class women on whose doorsteps they contracted credit agreements. The present study develops the insights offered by Finn on Victorian and Edwardian credit networks and investigates those creditors whose *modus operandi* enabled them to capture elements of gifting, reciprocity, and obligation into what were, on the surface, economic relationships with working-class borrowers. They used highly socialized methods of sales and collection, which stood the test of time. A study of debt enforcement, published in 1973, described how creditors 'tend to impose structure on their uncertainty by transforming all data into significant symbols'. It noted that honesty, integrity, and sincerity are 'elusive social qualities, which are conventionally recognized by corresponding body, facial and interactional styles' and that it was in social encounters that the creditor or their agent could examine 'discernible and nameable properties of performance'.[xv] Significantly, in attempting to read the bodies, characters, and homes of potential debtors mail order companies, and the array of companies that provided doorstep credit, employed working-class agents whose own experience and connections were deployed to assess creditworthiness, reduce risk, and ensure long-term custom. Thus Finn's insights on the socialized nature of the credit nexus are used to probe those

[xii] Finn, *The character of credit*, 9.
[xiii] Ibid. 92
[xiv] Ibid. 21.
[xv] Paul Rock, *Making people pay* (London: Routledge and Kegan Paul, 1973), 41.

twentieth-century credit markets in which it was most fundamentally important.

Taylor's investigation of working-class credit on Tyneside since 1918 has already traversed some of this terrain. He develops sociological analyses by Philip Abrams and Anthony Giddens, to chart the operations of companies who provided credit on the doorsteps and in the front parlours of working-class homes. Taylor argues that companies specializing in this sector were 'ultimately somewhat anachronistic' and 'in a sense, a survival from a previous era' that was out of step with the 'highly bureaucratised methods employed in other sections of the credit industry'.[xvi] The agent's weekly call, to collect repayments, established a process of routinization that created a sense of 'trust or ontological security, which was psychologically relaxing for customers'.[xvii] Agents had, according to Taylor, both altruistic and instrumental motivations. This combination reflected the emotional and economic elements of the relationships that existed between creditors' agents and their customers. The hundreds of thousands of agents employed by the large mail order companies, and those of the myriad companies who supplied loans on the doorstep, enabled their employers to become embedded within local social networks and to exploit the 'norm of reciprocity'.[xviii] The commercial orchestration of reciprocity was an important weapon for these companies, particularly as they faced increased competition from more bureaucratized, and less expensive, modes of consumer lending as the twentieth century wore on.

A significant contribution of this monograph is that it extends and deepens Taylor's findings by addressing a lengthy list of credit institutions, sources, and themes that have not received previous historical assessment. Business records from a number of companies that advanced credit in working-class communities are examined, as are trade journals and a wide range of records held at the National Archives. These sources provide fresh insights into the activities of borrowers and creditors, and into the frequent critiques levelled at what were often viewed as 'unscrupulous' lenders and 'feckless' debtors. In addition, a number of mutual credit institutions receive their first systematic assessment. These include the doorstep credit offered by co-operative retailers, the credit union movement, and the large number of rotating credit societies formed

[xvi] Taylor, *Working class credit*, 177.
[xvii] Ibid. 133.
[xviii] Ibid. 34–5.

by a diverse range of consumers. The latter discussion encompasses the 'diddlum clubs' of Edwardian Salford and the 'partners' that were first organized by Jamaican immigrants in the 1950s. By amassing evidence from a wide variety of sources it has also been possible to build up the most comprehensive picture to date of illegal moneylending, from the 'she usurers' of Edwardian Liverpool through to the violent loan sharks of the late twentieth century who occasionally surfaced from murky waters to appear in newspaper exposés. Included in this evidence is oral testimony gathered in Belfast. The choice of Belfast as the location of the oral history research enabled a number of important questions to be addressed. It facilitated an investigation of the existence and importance of locality, neighbourhood, and community in the formation and maintenance of credit cultures. Belfast also has a particular significance for social policy debates. In the UK in general, credit unions provided 0.1 per cent of all personal loans in the early 1990s, but in Northern Ireland they provided 8 per cent and had operated widely since the 1960s.[xix] By exploring the respondents' experiences of credit unions, in a city where their history and membership lists are lengthy, the study probes the merits of what are frequently posited as a panacea to the financial problems of low-income families. It also facilitates the first historical account of UK credit unions.

Other sources include the numerous files relating to consumer credit at the National Archives, particularly the records of the Crowther Committee on Consumer Credit; the archives of Provident Financial (the UK's largest moneylending company); the archives of the Consumer Credit Association (the successor body to the tallymen's trade body and representative of the doorstep moneylenders); the records kept at all the major mail order companies (Empire Stores, Freemans, GUS, Littlewoods, Grattan, and Kays), and the biographies of leading mail order executives; periodicals such as *Credit World, Credit Trader*; and *Credit Union News;* as well as the co-operative movement's national archive.

This work also draws upon Melanie Tebbutt's important history of pawnbroking, which detailed the social and economic factors that lay behind its virtual disappearance in the post-war years.[xx] The following

[xix] R. Berthoud and E. Kempson, *Credit and debt: the PSI report* (London: Policy Studies Institute, 1992), 86.

[xx] Melanie Tebbutt, *Making ends meet: pawnbroking and working class credit* (Leicester: Leicester University Press, 1983).

chapters delineate the extent to which other methods of consumer lending used by working-class individuals adapted to the market conditions in which pawnbrokers struggled. Mail order boomed between the 1950s and late 1970s and is still of major importance as a form of working-class borrowing, particularly for those on limited incomes. Companies such as the Provident Clothing and Supply Company, who operated as check traders (selling checks or vouchers on instalment to customers in their homes who could then use the checks in the shops that agreed to accept them), found their traditional business declining slowly from the 1950s, but discovered fresh impetus by joining the new breed of doorstep moneylender that emerged in the 1960s. The tallymen or Scotch drapers, who had rebranded themselves in the early twentieth century as credit traders, also faced difficulties in the second half of the century and many businesses closed or were sold to major companies. A significant number also restyled themselves and became doorstep moneylenders. The new moneylenders drew upon the agency-based credit assessment skills developed over many decades in the working-class communities in which they operated. The 1960s also witnessed the emergence of credit unions in the UK. It is telling that these institutions, which were viewed as a mutual and equitable financial alternative to costly commercial forms of consumer lending, were also envisaged as vehicles through which to mobilize and re-energize community. Significantly, many credit union pioneers did not originate in the 'traditional' working class. They emanated from Irish and Afro-Caribbean immigrant communities.

Johnson's major contribution to the historiography also informs many aspects of the following discussion. Examining the period between 1850 and 1939, he argued that the moral and cultural uncertainties associated with particular forms of credit were partly dependent on the status of the products that were purchased through them. A distinction was not to be found between those who did or did not use credit, but between families who used it to buy 'luxury' goods and others who used it to 'fill their bellies and cover their nakedness'.[xxi] This created a hierarchy of credit channels, matching those that existed for merchandise and for social status. Thus, for example, the piano bought through hire purchase by the respectable working-class family was perceived more positively than the boots bought through a moneylender's loan by an unskilled worker's

[xxi] Paul Johnson, 'Credit and thrift and the British working class, 1870–1939', in J. Winter (ed.), *The working class in modern British history* (Cambridge: CUP, 1985), 153.

wife. This did not mean that the former method of credit was used unapologetically. As was reported by the Consumer Council's Elizabeth Ackroyd in 1967: before the war there was at least one 'furniture firm that advertised that its goods were delivered in plain vans' because 'certain people still felt that there was something discreditable about selling on tick'.[xxii] There were verbal concealments, also, with families describing how they had got merchandise 'on trust' rather than on credit, in order to neutralize stigma. In more affluent working-class districts, dependence on credit for non-luxuries was taken as a sign of reduced financial independence and respectability, whilst the successful negotiation of a hire purchase agreement in other circumstances was a sign of 'trust in your long term economic stability'.[xxiii] Johnson's work highlights the fact that households not only had to 'balance income and expenditure', but had to do so 'in an intensely competitive world in which position or status had to be constantly reasserted'.[xxiv]

Those engaged in the supply of consumer credit were in an equally competitive environment and subject to frequent scrutiny of their methods and practices. This was particularly true in Victorian and Edwardian county courts, where credit transactions between working-class housewives and tallymen were the subject of sustained critique. Gerry Rubin has described how many judges viewed them very much as 'fringe capitalists', whose business was at best misguided, at worst morally dubious.[xxv] Finn has provided the most recent analysis of how these creditors responded by forming status-enhancing trade associations and by laying claim to a place in modern economic practice.[xxvi] The following chapters will describe how those that followed the tallyman's path to the working-class doorstep created organizational structures designed to prevent the judicial chastisements their predecessors had received. The legal ambiguities and moral qualms associated with the provision of credit to working-class wives, which had been at the heart of the tallyman's troubles, continued to be an important issue

[xxii] *Credit Trader*, 6 May 1967.

[xxiii] Johnson, *Saving and spending*, 160–2.

[xxiv] Ibid. 4.

[xxv] G. R. Rubin, 'The County Courts and the tally trade, 1846–1914', in G. R. Rubin and David Sugarman (eds.), *Law, economy and society, 1750–1914: essays in the history of English law* (Abingdon: Professional Books, 1984), 346.

[xxvi] Margot Finn, 'Scotch drapers and the politics of modernity: gender, class and national identity in the Victorian tally trade', in M. Daunton and M. Hilton (eds.), *The politics of consumption: citizenship and material culture in Europe and America* (Oxford: OUP, 2001).

shaping the activities of creditors and consumers. For example, despite their regular association with the female consumer, most mail order catalogue companies did not appoint female agents in large numbers until the 1930s. Their conservatism in this regard initially limited their effectiveness amongst the cash-poor, credit-dependent, working-class women who became the mainstay of mail order retailing.

As numerous histories have made clear, the responsibility for making ends meet fell to the working-class housewife who was the 'household and financial manager'.[xxvii] The relationship between female borrowers and male creditors provided regular ammunition for critics. In Johnson's view, there were many who 'could not comprehend that a middle-class outlook might be inappropriate in working class economic circumstances', and the plebeian female financial experience was even further removed from their understanding.[xxviii] The question of annual interest rates, which was assumed to guide the rational middle-class consumer, rarely entered the mind of the harassed working-class wife. The costs she incurred in buying on credit, and having collectors come to her door, were viewed by critics as an unthrifty working-class attribute rather than an outcome of economic inequality.[xxix] Johnson has demonstrated that, aside from the expense, there were a number of advantages in weekly collected credit. Uppermost amongst them was the ability to bring some semblance of planning to limited budgets. An external discipline was imposed on the housewife by 'the power of contract' in circumstance where will power 'was seldom strong enough to permit accumulation in a week when money for food and rent was short'.[xxx]

This perspective allows the working-class woman more agency than she was granted by contemporary critics. Indeed, if Finn's reading of reports from a number of county court cases is accurate, then their agency sometimes extended to consciously dramatic court appearances that utilized gender stereotypes of the duped working-class woman and the smooth-talking tallyman in an attempt to escape financial liabilities.[xxxi]

[xxvii] Elizabeth Roberts, *A woman's place: an oral history of working class women* (Oxford: OUP, 1984), 124. See also Tebbutt, *Making ends meet;* Carl Chinn, *They worked all their lives: women of the urban poor in England, 1880–1939* (Manchester: Manchester University Press, 1988), 8.

[xxviii] Johnson, *Saving and spending*, 223.

[xxix] Ross McKibbin, 'Social class and social observation in Edwardian England', *Transactions of the Royal Historical Society*, 5th series, 28 (1978), 184.

[xxx] Johnson, *Saving and spending*, 22.

[xxxi] Margot Finn, 'Working-class women and the contest for consumer control in Victorian County Courts', *Past and Present*, 161/1 (1998), 152.

Finn's accounts of court activity provide a colourful illustration of the extent to which the modernization of economic relations was culturally mediated. Tensions were played out within the courts between classical liberal perspectives on personal autonomy, and market exchange, and moralized critiques of creditors' practices. The fact that tallymen were amongst the most regular litigants in the county courts established a reputation that they never quite shook off, even after they rebranded themselves as credit drapers and, later, credit traders. They learned, in practice, what Paul Rock's sociological study of debt enforcement noted, in 1973, that in popular perceptions the 'moral status of the vengeful creditor is even lower than that of the benign one'.[xxxii] The ultimate sanction of the county court was to imprison debtors for up to six weeks, if they were ruled in contempt of a court order to pay a debt. This occurred in only a tiny fraction of cases. In 1904, for example a high point was reached for the number of plaints (which registered a creditor's intent to sue for payment), when 1,338,732 were registered. Of these, 365,616 led to judgement summonses being issued, of which 227,061 eventually reached court. A committal order against the debtor arose in a massive 135,798 of these cases, but only 11,066 were enforced. Thus 0.8 per cent of all actions resulted in imprisonment for debt in that year, but a significant one in ten debtors had been threatened with this foreboding sanction.[xxxiii] The years 1904–6 were high points of county court activity and Johnson believes that this represented evidence of economic distress amongst large sections of the working class at that point. A sample of cases in West Hartlepool found that three out of four of those bringing debtors to court were local drapers, grocers, and bakers. Doctors and furnishers were also active litigants.[xxxiv]

Thus although the Victorian and Edwardian county courts were filled with a vast variety of plaintiffs and defendants, it was consumer credit debt with which they became most strongly associated. This link became ingrained in the popular imagination, even though imprisonment for debt became increasingly rare. The numbers incarcerated by the county courts in the 1920s and 1930s were between 1,000 and 4,000 per annum.[xxxv] A large proportion of these cases involved committals for

[xxxii] Rock, *Making people pay*, 56.

[xxxiii] Patrick Polden, *A history of the County Court, 1846–1971* (Cambridge: Cambridge University Press, 1999), Appendix 3, Table 1, and Table 5.

[xxxiv] Paul Johnson, 'Small debts and economic distress in England and Wales, 1857–1913', *Economic History Review*, 46/1 (1993), 68.

[xxxv] Polden, *A history of the County Court*, Table 5.

failure to pay maintenance orders, bastardy orders, and local rates.[xxxvi] However, rising numbers of hire purchase commitments led to greater concern about imprisonment for consumer debts in the swinging sixties than had been the case in the hungry thirties. The numbers committed by county courts reached a post-war peak of almost 8,000 in 1962. Following a recommendation by the Payne Committee on the Enforcement of Judgement Debts, the Administration of Justice Act in 1970 abolished imprisonment for commercial debt. It had by that point become accepted, as the Consumer Council's Elizabeth Ackroyd maintained, that 'it was only the feckless and inadequate who ended up in prison', not the 'hard-core debtors' who had set out with an intention to default.[xxxvii]

However, despite the rarity of imprisonment for debt, the 'collection sequence' that followed cases of default was 'a progress into controlled unpleasantness', in which a creditor could 'make a defaulter suffer a variety of pains: discomfort, stigma, repossession, intimidation, harassment by a debt-collector, and legal action'.[xxxviii] Anxiety about becoming the central character in such a drama provided a further reason for working-class consumers to fear indebtedness, which was added to the desire to retain respectable status. Debt was far removed from working-class conceptions of economic independence and 'the rigid perceptions of personal agency and responsibility . . . associated with modern individualism'.[xxxix] It was also deemed to signify a failure in rational household management. Those observing working-class families in the early twentieth century often identified credit use as 'feckless spending' and socialists lamented the failure of many workers to engage with thrifty consumerism in the form of the co-operative movement.[xl] Critics regularly failed to identify the key role of inadequate income. This was still the case later in the century. In the 1950s the poor were viewed as 'inadequate and even pathological in some way'.[xli] In the early 1970s notions of the 'fecklessness' of debtors were still very

[xxxvi] National Archives (hereafter NA): LCO 2/1145, 'Imprisonment for debt: statistics and costs, 1928–1935'; J. D. Unwin, *The scandal of imprisonment for debt* (London: Simpkin Marshall, 1935).

[xxxvii] NA: AJ 3/128, 'Payne Committee and Administration of Justice Bill: The Consumer Council press notice', 3 December 1969.

[xxxviii] Rock, *Making people pay*, 64.

[xxxix] Finn, *The character of credit*, 128.

[xl] Johnson, *Saving and spending*, 4.

[xli] Tebbutt, *Making ends meet*, 195.

much in circulation, carrying with them the implication of 'irrationality, impulsiveness and unpredictability'.[XLII]

With society so ready to censure the financial transactions of the working-class wife, it is unsurprising that her monetary juggling was frequently shrouded in secrecy. Pat Ayers and Jan Lambertz have delineated the extent to which this was the case in interwar Liverpool, where many women faced the task of managing on inadequate incomes, whilst also attempting not to draw attention to their husbands' frequently tarnished claims to 'breadwinner' status.[XLIII] Moreover, the stigma attached to credit use did not disappear simply, at some point in the 1950s, once the affluent society was born. Surveys on consumer credit demonstrate that its use was deprecated by a majority until much later in the century. One survey, carried out in 1969, found that a majority believed credit was wrong in principle.[XLIV] Only in 1979 did survey evidence indicate a 'substantial change in the public's attitude towards credit', with a majority accepting its use.[XLV]

This shift was matched by a gradual swing, at state level, away from concern over the principle of credit towards a new focus on its regulation. The 1927 Moneylenders Act, which created a nominal annual interest rate ceiling of 48 per cent, was arguably the last piece of legislation to be viewed by its supporters as a means of snuffing out a form of commerce that they viewed as inherently exploitative. After 1945, policy on consumer credit entered a period in which the principal desire was to manage its impact upon the economy rather than on individual consumers. As Matthew Hilton has demonstrated, the state and consumer bodies such as the Consumer Council increasingly identified consumer education as the key to limiting the excesses of the free market. The organized consumer movement in post-war Britain was awash with a discourse of rational and enlightened consumption that was best illustrated in the Consumers' Association's magazine *Which?*[XLVI] The 'ideal type' consumer at the centre of this discourse was male and middle class and far removed from the working-class

[XLII] Rock, *Making people pay*, 282.

[XLIII] Pat Ayers and Jan Lambertz, 'Marriage relations, money, and domestic violence in working-class Liverpool, 1919–1939', in J. Lewis (ed.), *Labour and love: women's experience of home and family, 1850–1940* (Oxford: Basil Blackwell), 1986.

[XLIV] Committee on Consumer Credit, *Consumer credit: report of the Committee* (London: HMSO, 1971).

[XLV] Office of Fair Trading, *Consumer credit* (London: HMSO, 1981).

[XLVI] Matthew Hilton, *Consumerism in 20th-century Britain* (Cambridge: Cambridge University Press, 2003), 205–9.

women who struck millions of credit bargains on doorsteps or in front parlours. State inquiries into aspects of consumer protection, such as the Moloney Committee on Consumer Protection in 1961, concluded that British businesses were unlikely to 'engage in practices for which consumer protection was necessary'.[XLVII] This perspective was echoed by the Crowther Committee on Consumer Credit, which had the unenviable task of investigating a market that, by the 1960s, had become extremely complex. Its report, published in 1971, informed the construction of the Consumer Credit Act of 1974. One of its measures was the requirement that creditors indicate the annual percentage rates (APR) associated with their products. The APR was intended to make consumers aware of the 'true cost' of borrowing and empower them to take their business elsewhere, should they decide that a loan was overpriced. The system proved extremely complex and surveys consistently revealed that most consumers failed to understand it. Their confusion was shared by many seasoned members of the credit trade.[XLVIII]

There was some evidence of a slight sea change in the focus on education in the 1980s. In 1985, Jacqui King of the Money Advice Association argued that post-war government's 'emphasis on consumer education' had produced 'limited results' and, in consequence, organizations such as her own were winning favour.[XLIX] The Money Advice Association emerged during the deepening recession of the early 1980s with the assistance of the National Consumer Council and took on the major task of dealing with mounting levels of consumer debt. In the same period there was also local government backing for consumer advice projects.[L]

As will be explained below, the 1980s also witnessed rising national and local government support for the credit union movement as a palliative for debt in low-income communities. The limited impact of credit unions in this regard produced a high-profile campaign, led by groups such as Church Action on Poverty and Debt on our Doorstep, which piled the pressure on government to introduce much greater levels of consumer protection in the sub-prime sector. Creditors, government, pressure groups, and low-income consumers stand currently at an interesting crossroad. It is hoped that the chapters that follow might

XLVII Ibid. 225.

XLVIII Tebbutt, *Making ends meet*, 202.

XLIX *Consumer Credit Association News*, November 1985.

L E. Kempson, *Money advice and debt counselling* (London: Policy Studies Institute, 1995), 3.

provide an enriched historical perspective on many of the issues with which they are concerned.

NARRATING DEBT

The morally charged discourses that have surrounded credit and debt create particular problems for historians seeking to explore this issue via oral testimony. In developing a strategy to analyse such problematic territory, the work of Judy Giles is particularly apposite.[11] Describing interviews with working-class women (born between 1900 and 1939) she noted the high levels of investment they made in adhering to 'respectable' values. They frequently articulated a 'good old days' version of the past that transformed a complex past into a simplified and acceptable form for narration in the present. As described by Giles, the attainment of 'respectable' womanhood involved a rejection of attributes identified with girlishness and immaturity. Success or failure was demarcated by the use of opposing terms. Thrift and the avoidance of credit were opposed to extravagance and indebtedness. However, Giles argues that there was a distance between what her interviewees actually did as young mothers, to manage family finances, and the way in which they remembered it. These contradictions arose in interviews, either through the detailed narration of examples from everyday life or at moments when silence became 'significant as articulation'. Her main point is that oral testimony not only provides 'facts' about people's lives, it also offers valuable information on how people interpret their past and their present. In developing Giles's approach, the intention is not to overstate the 'fictionality' of oral history. In the analysis that follows oral accounts are understood to be socially constructed, but so too are the scribbled notes of a civil servant on a National Archives file dealing with government policy on consumer credit, the report of a policeman who reluctantly set about an investigation of illegal moneylending amongst women in London's East End, or a newspaper exposé on extortionate credit written by a journalist with a tight copy deadline.

A theoretical aim of the project was to probe the nature of social memory in the oral narratives collected in Belfast and to analyse them within the particular problematic thrown up in the context of borrowing

[11] Judy Giles, '"Playing hard to get": working-class women, sexuality and respectability in Britain, 1918–1940', *Women's History Review*, 1/1 (1992).

and lending. Interviews with those associated with the consumer credit industry, including credit traders, mail order executives, moneylenders, and credit union volunteers were also treated in this fashion. Each sector has its own social memory and its own agendas. Like working-class women, they too wished to protect their status and project a respectable image of their activities. The subjectivities that emerge from the oral interviews are mined to explore the way in which the narratives are formed and to ask why they are shaped in particular ways and what this can say to us about credit and debt.

The majority of Belfast interviewees (27) were aged over 70 and were contacted at the day centres they attended, where the project was explained to them. A further three were aged between 42 and 52.[LII] Interviewees came from a range of working-class and religious backgrounds. The aim was to ascertain attitudes towards various forms of credit held by individuals whose life histories encompassed the spectrum of labouring class experiences. A further two interviews were conducted with moneylenders registered in Northern Ireland. In addition, sixteen interviews were conducted with credit union members and volunteers from both the Republic of Ireland and Northern Ireland and two with long-standing volunteers from English credit unions.[LIII] In addition a number of historical accounts written by pioneers of the British credit union movement were consulted in addition to other published material on credit unions. The project also draws upon testimony previously collected from a sample of mail order agents, as well as interviews with three former mail order executives. Two former credit traders agreed to be interviewed as did two moneylenders from the North of England. Also interviewed was a former chairman of the Retail Credit Federation and the Consumer Credit Association and representatives of two pressure groups, Debt on our Doorstep and Christians against Poverty.

An initial discovery when analysing the interviews with the Belfast consumers was that 'credit' and 'debt' were often defined differently by the interviewees and interviewer. The majority of female interviewees conformed to the 'respectable' womanhood model identified by Giles and maintained that they had never been in debt and had always paid cash. When talking about their own lives most female interviewees

[LII] Transcripts are available at the UK Data Archive: UKDA study number: 4993.

[LIII] Two of these were conducted by Sean O'Connell; the others were carried out under his supervision by students of the University of Ulster.

emphasized their successful role as household manager: 'It was tight, but I managed, I managed!' was the proud claim of Lily, a milkman's widow.[LIV] It was only at the conclusion of many interviews, when direct questions were asked about individual forms of credit, that its use was acknowledged. Frequently interviewees did not comprehend the weekly arrangements offered by Provident or the mail order companies as involving them in debt of any kind. Credit was associated with hire purchase for more expensive items, and one was only in debt when unable to make payments. This perspective was important because, as Johnson has previously noted, it provided a rationale for ignoring widespread familial and social pressures expressed in maxims such as 'neither a lender nor a borrower be'. A variety of creditors actively developed such thinking by labelling their systems 'clubs'. Thus 'members' made a payment to the club, rather than paying off a consumer debt.

The testimonies revealed a diverse pattern of economic relations within working-class marriages in Belfast. Many female interviewees professed ignorance of their husband's wages. Not surprisingly, the majority of this group reported usage of short-term or crisis credit. Others recalled that their husbands brought home an unopened pay packet each week: this cohort was least likely to mention first-hand experience of financial struggles. What was striking was the extent to which the choice of a spouse continued to dictate whether or not a working-class woman could expect to find herself struggling financially. Thus it was wrong to assume that a husband's skill or high wage level automatically translated to a life of financial simplicity for his wife. A husband's drinking or gambling habits could ensure that his wife found herself using short-term credit. Testimony of this nature arose in almost a third of the interviews: in two cases the information was from the lips of an alcoholic husband. In one of these cases, Seamus offered a disjointed interview in which he took pleasure in his account of drinking and leaving his wife to struggle with money management and the rearing of the eleven children from whom he was, by the time of the interview, estranged.[LV] Bridie, the mother of three children, was reduced to waiting outside the fire station where her husband worked,

[LIV] Interview with Lily (born 1920. Widow and retired shop assistant. Mother of two. Deceased husband was a milkman. Protestant. Interviewed 11 September 2002).

[LV] Interview with Johnny (born 1930. Retired docker. Father of four. Roman Catholic. Interviewed 15 April 2001); interview with Seamus (born 1930. Retired plumber. Father of eight. Roman Catholic. Interviewed 13 October 2002).

on payday, to ensure that money was not lost to his gambling habit.[LVI] Ethel's husband had a very well-paid job as an aircraft fitter, although finances were tight due to the eight children in the family. However, Ethel's task was made more difficult by her husband, who appears to have exploited the fact her Welsh origins meant that she was unfamiliar with Belfast practices. He gave Ethel a weekly allowance, rather than handing over his pay packet unopened, claiming that it was not the custom to do so in Belfast. His claim was undermined by the evidence of many other interviewees.[LVII]

Many of these Belfast narratives covered the post-1945 era, but resembled those described in histories of interwar working-class life. Penny was born in 1940 and was one of ten children. Despite the enormous task faced by her mother in raising such a large family, Penny believes her father handed in only half his modest wage to the family kitty. One outcome of this was her mother's routine use of pawning, which was done without her husband's knowledge. Penny recounted one story to illustrate this. Her father had returned from work and could be heard upstairs following an unusual routine:

> My mother says: 'What's he doing?' And I says til her: 'I don't know what he's doing.' And she says to me: 'Go to the bottom of the stairs and listen.' And I says: 'I think he's in the wardrobe.' And she says 'Oh my God, if he sees them trousers are away!' So the next thing the voice came down the stairs: 'Where the hell's my trousers!' And she had the dinner by that time set out and some of us was eating a wee bit of dinner . . . And my father came down screaming about the trousers, and he asked: 'Where's my bloody trousers?' And she says: 'I pawned them', she says. And he says til her: 'What you pawned the trousers!' 'Yes, and your children's eating it and you're eating it!' [said her mother].[LVIII]

This story was related with laughter by Penny, but her mother eventually had a psychological breakdown after amassing debts she could not repay with a variety of creditors.

Given the claims by significant numbers of husbands to inappropriate levels of personal leisure expenditure, it was unsurprising that male interviewees volunteered their testimony rather more reluctantly than

[LVI] Interview with Bridie (born 1923. Retired carer. Mother of three. Separated from her husband who had been a fireman. Interviewed 10 October 2002).

[LVII] Interview with Ethel (born 1920. Widow and mother of eight. Husband was an aircraft fitter. Protestant).

[LVIII] Interview with Penny (born 1940. Mother of four. Husband a labourer. Raised as a Protestant, converted to Catholicism on marriage).

females. It became clear that the gendered nature of social memory, upon which they had to build their own accounts and make sense of their personal histories, often left them struggling to compose a place and a role for themselves in the research project that was explained to them. As it dealt with making ends meet and domestic money management, many men were clearly unable to compose a narrative account in which they felt comfortable and able to articulate a meaningful account of their personal history and gendered self. In this respect, many of the male interviewees were in an analogous position to the former female members of the Home Guard who in interviews with Penny Summerfield found themselves discomposed because, unlike their male equivalents, they had no public discourses to draw upon through which to locate their own personal narratives. For example, women did not feature as members of *Dad's Army* in the perennially popular BBC comedy. Some of Summerfield's interviewees even became uncertain that there had been a women's Home Guard and had a strong sense that the organization's history was a 'male story'.[LIX] A number of male interviewees moved away from the 'female story' that seemed to dominate the question of domestic money management, providing testimony that was far removed from those offered by female interviewees. Several narrated tales about masculine activities away from the home that endangered their wife's efforts to keep the family 'respectable'. This oral testimony provided insights into aspects of working-class credit and debt that are often hidden from the historian's view, particularly illegal moneylending. The clearest example of this came from the retired docker, reformed alcoholic, and gambler, Johnny. He related the story of Jack, a docker. Jack was indebted to a number of dock-gate moneylenders, but had managed to avoid them for a number of weeks. Eventually, the moneylenders banded together and formulated a plan to intercept Jack—and his pay packet—as he left the docks one Thursday evening. Jack had been tipped off about their scheme, but had no means of avoiding them as they had each taken up position at a different exit. In desperation, Jack hailed a drinking buddy who, conveniently, was passing along the docks in a pilot boat. Having explained his situation, Jack was taken down the river Lagan and safely deposited. He was ensconced in a favourite bar before the moneylenders realized their quarry had slipped the net. Johnny concluded the tale by writing that 'people like Jack were something of folk heroes around the

[LIX] Penny Summerfield, 'Culture and composure: creating narratives of the gendered self in oral history interviews', *Cultural and Social History*, 1/1 (2004), 65–93.

docks, because in our eyes they had beaten the bloodsuckers at their own game'.[LX]

A number of questions arise from this story. The impecunious hero, Jack, escaped from his creditors on this occasion, but we do not learn what happened once the tale was told, in the rest of our hero's life. Did the moneylenders return the following week, and the week after? Did they not know where Jack lived or where he liked to drink? And crucially, of course, did Jack exist? Many of us might argue that whether or not Jack lived is the most fundamental point. If he did not then this story would be seen by some as proof of oral history's limited value, which led Eric Hobsbawm to write that it is simply 'personal memory which is a remarkably slippery medium for preserving facts'.[LXI] However, perhaps we need to move beyond this quixotic pursuit of empirical truth to ask ourselves whether or not what is believed in collective, social memory is not a 'truth' that is worthy of excavation. In this instance, such an approach involves asking what do the myths, if we want to call them that, tell us about working-class community or memory more broadly. In this case, the story of Jack could be read as a particularly male myth and one that involves a certain form of masculinity at that. For a start there is not much of the 'good old days' or the respectability found in the testimony from Belfast females or in Judy Giles interviews in what Johnny chose to relate. Jack the docker outwitted the hated moneylenders, but not in order to return home to his wife and family—but to a favourite pub. In a brilliant essay on masculinity in dockside Liverpool, Pat Ayers has revealed how the construction of dockside masculinity was historically, geographically, and culturally specific.[LXII] She described the lack of control these Liverpool dockers had over their workplace, which undermined the ability to build work-based cultural capital that provided the basis for masculine identity in many sections of the working class. Most obviously, dockers competed against each other for casual work. As a result, Ayers concludes, male bonding was underpinned by a highly developed understanding of 'a male community of interest'.[LXIII] We should, therefore, read the story told by Johnny as one in which the

[LX] Interview with Johnny (born 1930. Retired docker. Father of four. Roman Catholic. Interviewed 15 April 2001).

[LXI] Eric Hobsbawm, *On history* (London: New Press, 1997), 206.

[LXII] Pat Ayers, 'The making of men: masculinities in interwar Liverpool', in M. Walsh (ed.), *Working out gender: perspectives from labour history* (Aldershot: Ashgate, 2001), 66.

[LXIII] Ibid. 70.

narrator is seeking to send out a message about a social group of which he was a part. The colourful elements in the story may not have been matched by the daily practice of the docker's life, but Jack provides a symbol of resilient masculinity. Thus we should read the tale as a parable about overcoming the economic odds that were stacked against the unskilled working-class male in 1950s Belfast. Our analysis should be guided by the work of Luisa Passerini: 'When people talk about their lives, people lie sometimes, forget a little, exaggerate, become confused, get things wrong. Yet they are revealing truths . . . the guiding principle for [life histories] could be that all autobiographical memory is true: it is up to the interpreter to discover in which sense, where, and for what purpose.'[LXIV] In this case, the importance of this story for Johnny was that it gave agency to him and his male co-workers for the same reason that discourses of respectability proved strongly attractive to female interviewees. An attention to narrative structure, form, metaphor, and the silences, or 'not saids', of these oral texts by the historian enables interviews to be read on many levels. As Joan Sangster has argued, it should be possible to keep a keen materialist eye on an interview's context whilst also being informed by post-structuralist insights into language. The cultural construction of memory should be a focus of inquiry, to be placed in a framework of social and economic relations. As Sangster argues, 'while it is important to analyse *how* someone constructs an explanation for their life, ultimately there are patterns, structures, systemic reasons for those constructions which must be identified to understand historical causality'.[LXV]

The same logic and method has been applied herein to interviews with those who supplied credit to working-class communities. This testimony drew upon corporate collective memory. Those interviewed were all highly familiar with the critiques that have been launched against those involved in providing costly consumer credit within working-class communities. They were well prepared to provide an alternative vision in which their trade featured as paternalistic providers of a service that helped low-income families clothe their bodies and furnish their homes. Like Giles's female interviewees, who sought agency for themselves in the way they constructed their testimony, creditors also had an interest in declaring that their customers had agency, that they were not powerless.

[LXIV] Joan Sangster, 'Telling our stories: feminist debates and the use of oral history', *Women's History Review*, 3/1 (1994).

[LXV] Ibid. 25.

The extent to which this perspective is an accurate depiction of the relationship between low-income consumers and their creditors is at the centre of this book and facilitates an explanation of the endurance of such relationships in spite of persistent campaigns to ameliorate the plight of the financially excluded.

1

Credit on the doorstep: the tallymen

Nowhere did consumer credit resist the march of modernizing bureaucracy more than in the various forms of doorstep credit used by millions of working-class families. The tallymen, or credit drapers, who predominated initially in this respect, were well established by the late nineteenth century. They provided working-class housewives with the means by which to access cheap mass market merchandise in a period before the development of hire purchase. The analysis offered in this chapter builds upon the recent histories of consumer credit by Margot Finn and Avram Taylor that were delineated in our introduction. Both argue that major segments of the market relied extensively on high levels of sociability rather than bureaucratic and depersonalized systems. Their findings remind us of the social nature of credit and its reliance on the routine obligatory gifting patterns of pre-modern society. According to Finn, Victorian and Edwardian credit retailers endeavoured to create reciprocation in the form of long-term loyalty from customers, by paying as much heed to personal ties as to price considerations.[1] This chapter will begin our explanation of how creditors who dealt with twentieth-century working-class consumers brought such highly socialized relationships to new levels. It builds on Taylor's study of Tyneside, by examining the national picture. The chapter forms a link between the analysis by Finn, and others, of nineteenth-century tallymen, and Taylor's discussion of their role in the twentieth century. Like Finn, Taylor's work also highlights the 'somewhat anachronistic', personalized and highly social practices that were central to the business models of credit retailers.[2] Although Taylor identifies both altruistic and instrumental motives amongst credit agents, the system he describes was

[1] Margot Finn, *The character of credit: personal debt in English culture, 1740–1914* (Cambridge: Cambridge University Press, 2003), 92; Avram Taylor, *Working class credit and community since 1918* (Basingstoke: Palgrave Macmillan, 2002).

[2] Taylor, *Working class credit*, 133.

ultimately highly exploitative, involving elements of 'performance' and 'emotional manipulation'.[3] This assessment is rather more critical than Paul Johnson's view that 'poor families with many unfulfilled wants will not waste money on some type of saving or borrowing repeated week by week if they derive little or no advantage from it'.[4] Seen from this perspective, Taylor's assessment might appear to diminish the agency possessed by the millions of individuals who made use of the credit drapers over the course of the twentieth century.

Using a wider range of sources than have previously been deployed, including government papers, business records, and oral history interviews, this discussion reassesses this question. To do so, it borrows further from Finn, utilizing her insights on how credit, connection, and character were assessed by Victorian and Edwardian credit traders—often on the basis of qualitative judgements—to explore how the cultural capital of working-class consumers, which was frequently as limited as their economic capital, was measured by potential creditors and their agents. The street, home, and body were all scanned and assessed in this process, and were often as valuable as information on income, occupation, and family size. Whilst many of the cultural messages that could be read in this way were economically determined, there was considerable leeway for consumers to engage in an element of performance in order, for example, to ensure that they were deemed respectable and creditworthy. Thus performance, cynical or not, was a two-way process.

The sector was certainly economically significant. For example, in 1939 the government estimated the combined check and credit trading turnover to be £100m, representing almost 3 per cent of retail sales.[5] This chapter explains how credit drapers—or credit traders, as they styled themselves—acquired their share of this significant market. The next chapter examines the check traders. The two chapters probe the controversies that dogged both sectors and explain why large numbers of consumers continued to make use of such heavily criticized methods of expenditure. To the surprise of their critics, their use did not collapse in the affluent society of the 1950s and 1960s. Many of their traditional

[3] Ibid. 35.

[4] Paul Johnson, *Saving and spending: the working class economy in Britain 1870–1939* (Oxford: Clarendon Press, 1985), 5.

[5] London: National Archives/Public Record Office (hereafter NA). BT 64/3430—Official Committee on Post-War Employment, *Papers on social security contributions and hire purchase of consumer goods;* Provident Financial Group (PFG), PFG04/051, *Summary of returns.*

customers demonstrated a loyalty to these expensive forms of credit that baffled observers. However, we shall see that these sectors were ill-equipped to deal with the substantial challenges brought by factors such as the rapid growth of mail order catalogue sales in the 1950s and 1960s and the credit explosion of the 1970 and 1980s. By the 1970s, they were losing the 'cream' of their market to new financial products offered by the high street banks and others. Their response was to fall back on their core strengths, as providers of doorstep credit, by developing a new niche as doorstep moneylenders.

'FRINGE CAPITALISTS': FROM TALLYMEN TO CREDIT TRADERS

The tally trade was a business that was highly dependent on customary practice and personal association. The tallymen were widely envisaged in the popular imagination as providers of costly and low-quality clothing to customers living a hand to mouth existence. As a result, those involved in the business sought to divest themselves of the label, preferring credit draper in the nineteenth century and, from the 1920s, credit trader. Itinerant credit traders have operated since the sixteenth century, but it was in the nineteenth century that their presence became significant. Operating from an urban shop or warehouse, they dispatched 'packmen' to canvass door to door for buyers willing to pay by weekly instalments. In the second half of the nineteenth century demand for clothing and drapery grew markedly. Clothing accounted for an estimated 6 per cent of working-class household expenditure in 1845, a figure that doubled to around 12 per cent by 1904.[6] Ironically, given the controversy that enveloped their activities, there is minimal data on the scale and scope of credit traders' operations. In the early 1870s, Birmingham's credit drapers claimed over 50,000 customers. In Leeds, the figure was said to be over 70,000.[7] At the turn of the century, one estimate suggested that around 3,000 firms, with travellers operating either out of a central warehouse or a retail store, had a

[6] Margot Finn, 'Scotch drapers and the politics of modernity: gender, class and national identity in the Victorian tally trade', in M. Daunton and M. Hilton (eds.), *The politics of consumption: citizenship and material culture in Europe and America* (Oxford: OUP, 2001).

[7] Ibid.

combined annual turnover of £12.8m.[8] In 1909, *Woodhead's directory of the credit drapers of Great Britain* recorded a total of 4,255 credit drapers.[9] The following year, representatives of the trade reported that they allowed credit 'up to £6 or £7, and in exceptional cases up to £10'.[10] By the 1950s, the average customer was purchasing merchandise totalling £12 and paying for it over 24 weeks. The sector was then operating successfully, according to one account, in the areas where it had traditionally 'flourished'. These were said to be 'Scotland, the North-East, the Liverpool area, South Wales and London'.[11] However, this imprecise analysis does not indicate the extent of the trade and Woodhead's directory suggests a much more extensive nationwide trade. In 1909 Newcastle was saturated with 147 credit drapers, representing one for every 1,707 citizens. Elsewhere in the north, there were marked differences in diffusion rates that cannot be explained straightforwardly. Liverpool had only one credit draper per 11,476, which was a lower figure than that for the midlands boomtown Coventry, which had one for every 8,230 citizens. Uneven distribution may be explainable, in part, by the use of certain urban centres as bases for credit rounds that extended into their rural hinterland. This factor could explain Exeter's one credit draper per 2,560 citizens and Truro's one per 2,831. There was also an over-representation of credit drapers in Scotland in 1909, when it had 14.6 per cent of those recorded, but only 11.6 per cent of the total British population.[12]

Whilst the term 'tallyman' originated from the practice of marking each instalment on a stick, half of which was kept by each party to the agreement, 'Scotch draper' was also used due to the large numbers of Scots engaged in the system in England and Wales. Those advocating the abolition of imprisonment for petty debt in the late nineteenth century frequently suggested that these traders had been driven south by abolition in Scotland, which was enacted in 1835.[13] But, as we have seen the high incidence of credit drapers in Scotland does not support this theory. Moreover, the Scottish system of debt

[8] Judge Parry, 'The insolvent poor', *New Century Review*, January 1900.

[9] Geo Woodhead, *Woodhead's directory of the credit drapers of Great Britain* (Manchester: Geo Woodhead and Co. Ltd, 1909).

[10] *The Times*, 22 and 25 March 1910.

[11] L. C. Wright, 'Consumer credit and the tallyman', *Three Banks Review*, 44 (1959), 20.

[12] Geo Woodhead, *Woodhead's directory of the credit drapers of Great Britain.*

[13] Finn, 'Scotch drapers'.

administration did not eliminate hardship. In 1920, for example, the Scottish Trade Union Congress called for legislation forbidding tallymen to supply goods to a woman without her husband's explicit consent. It was claimed that large numbers of husbands only found out about debts on receipt of an arrestment order on their wages. For some of those involved, further injury followed via dismissal from employment.[14]

The involvement of tallymen in the recovery of debts in the English and Welsh county courts became notorious. The county courts operated from 1847, with the recovery of small debts being amongst their functions.[15] Critics were vexed by their ability to impose prison sentences of up to twenty-one days in cases where debtors were deemed to be in contempt of court, due to failure to act on the court's instructions. In reality, imprisonment was rare: 6,452 individuals fell foul of this sanction in 1890, in a year when the county courts dealt with just over one million cases.[16] However, the continuation of imprisonment of working-class debtors, and the fact that their liability was not expunged by incarceration as had been the case prior to the Debtors Act (1869), highlighted blatant legal inequalities. The Bankruptcy Act (1861) provided middle-class debtors with a vehicle through which to protect assets from seizure and negotiate a reduction in their debts.[17] As Johnson has argued, this implied they were essentially honest victims of economic misfortune, whilst working-class debtors had 'a fundamental lack of desire and intention to honour debts they had willingly entered into'.[18] Critics became concerned that the threat of imprisonment was used more frequently than the Act had anticipated, but in 1898 the *Credit Drapers' Gazette* argued that it was an ultimate deterrent against 'crafty and cunning parasites' that did not repay 'by cash, but by every excuse under the sun'.[19]

Creditors did not have it all their own way in the county courts, which often echoed to judicial critique of those credit businesses that were viewed as 'fringe capitalists'. Their actions were frequently viewed

[14] *The Times*, 18 February 1920.

[15] For a lengthy administrative history see Patrick Polden, *A history of the County Court, 1846–1971* (Cambridge: CUP, 1999).

[16] Paul Johnson, 'Small debts and economic distress in England and Wales, 1857–1913', *Economic History Review*, 46/1 (1993), 67.

[17] Paul Johnson, 'Class law in Victorian England', *Past and Present*, 141 (1993), 159–60.

[18] Ibid. 162–3.

[19] *Credit Drapers' Gazette*, 10 September 1898.

as ill-advised and, at worst, morally dubious.[20] Credit drapers were prominent in this respect, whilst grocers, shopkeepers, and others who frequented the courts equally regularly received far less censure.[21] The nature of this criticism centred on two culturally loaded issues: the definition of luxuries and necessities, and the role of the female consumer. A major issue was the ambivalent legal position of married women and their ability to enter credit agreements on their husband's behalf. The Married Women's Property Acts of 1870, 1882, and 1893, together with legal precedence established in the courts, recognized married women as property owners without making them fully liable for the debts they incurred.[22] Courtroom uncertainty often focused on whether or not a husband had clearly agreed that his wife should acquire credit on his behalf, and on whether the goods bought were 'luxuries' or 'necessaries' that were appropriate to the family's social station. Judges often ruled in favour of husbands who argued that they were ignorant of their wife's purchase of 'luxury' items. The fact that clothing was not always straightforwardly classifiable as luxury or necessity left credit drapers more exposed than other creditors.[23] Legal uncertainties facilitated copious debates on the dangers of offering credit to the working classes, and particularly on how female consumer aspiration could lead, in the worst cases, to the incarceration of unsuspecting husbands. In 1906, one *Reynolds News* columnist wrote that 'poor women are no less liable to attacks of female vanity than the women of the rich. The subtle tallyman brings his show of finery and insidiously points out how easy it is to pay for the goods at a trifle every week.' As a result, it argued, money was taken from elsewhere in the family's budget, concluding with the husband's appearance in court.[24] That credit traders penetrated the home to carry out their commercial seduction of female consumers also scandalized judicial morality and provided juicy copy for newspapers. The worst fears of some were compounded by Judge Parry, of the Manchester and Salford county court, who reported that a poor woman once told him that a Scotch draper had said to her 'If I canna

20 G. R. Rubin, 'The County Courts and the tally trade, 1846–1914', in G. R. Rubin and D. Sugarman (eds.), *Law, economy and society, 1750–1914: essays in the history of English law* (Abingdon: Professional Books, 1984); Finn, *The character of credit*, ch. 7.

21 Finn, 'Scotch drapers'.

22 Erika Rappaport, '"A husband and his wife's dresses": consumer credit and the debtor family in England, 1864–1914', in Victoria de Grazia (ed.), *The sex of things: gender and consumption in historical perspective* (Berkeley: University of California Press, 1996), 168.

23 Ibid. 168.

24 *Reynolds News*, 20 October 1906.

'ave yer brass I'll take yer body'.[25] In 1911 Parry extended his critique to the stage, authoring a play, *The Tallyman*, which featured 'amusing dialogue' and was performed in Manchester and London. It depicted an engine driver's wife who 'cannot resist or pay for the dresses the Tallyman brings round'. He, in turn, 'cannot resist the wife's smiles' and is only sent dashing away on the return of the 'strong, stern husband'.[26] In resurrecting the common theme of tallyman as sexual Lothario, Parry was echoing evidence heard by the Royal Commission on Divorce and its Administration, which a few months earlier had been told by one judge that 'it was common practice for tallymen to make improper suggestions to married women who were in debt for goods supplied'. The claims were angrily denied by a plethora of enraged credit traders who, it was made clear, included at least one Lord Mayor and numerous councillors who provided credit to 'respectable working men'.[27]

Whilst there was clearly a strong degree of antagonism towards credit traders in the courts, judicial responses to debtors were complex and motivated by various factors. Finn argues that some judges demonstrated 'an indulgent condescension for the foibles of the working class consumers in their district'. On other occasions, anxieties about the credit system's ability to smudge sartorial and class boundaries were exhibited. In one colourful example from Bow County Court in 1884, the judge observed how one credit draper had sold a shawl 'at 12s. 6d., fit for my wife to wear, to a woman whom I would not pick up off a dung-hill'.[28] Others, such as Parry, felt that young wives deserved criticism for being 'an easy prey for the travelling draper' and felt that many 'marry on credit to repent on Judgement Summonses'.[29] Another stream of thought lay the blame for indebtedness at the door of drunkenness. The paucity of this diagnosis is revealed by the close relationship between labour market fluctuations, income instability, and county court activity in the late nineteenth and early twentieth centuries. Crises in the family economy were clearly a more regular cause of insolvency than alcohol alone.[30]

The powerful mix of social relations involved in episodes of plebeian indebtedness enabled judges to become influential participants in the moral economy surrounding the issue. The judiciary frequently

[25] *Fortnightly Review*, May 1898. [26] *The Times*, 21 February 1911.

[27] Ibid., 22 and 25 March 1910.

[28] Margot Finn, 'Working-class women and the contest for consumer control in Victorian County Courts', *Past and Present*, 161 (1998), 152.

[29] Judge Parry, 'The insolvent poor', *New Century Review* (January 1900).

[30] Johnson, 'Small debts and economic distress', 65–87.

imposed what it felt were more equitable terms. Creditors were often frustrated by adjournments or repayment orders, set at deliberately low rates.[31] Courts operated with a remarkable degree of independence and idiosyncrasy.[32] Whilst some judges, such as H. T. Atkinson of Leeds, viewed imprisonment for debt 'as the last lingering relic of a barbarous age', others were reluctant to interfere in contracts between creditors and customers.[33] Creditors were sensitive to these differences, keeping records of the courts more likely to pass judgement in their favour.[34] On other occasions, local credit drapers associations, following the methods of the general trade protection societies, employed solicitors in their attempts to thwart particularly unhelpful legal precedents in various localities. A change of judge could alter local trends dramatically. Leeds, home to Atkinson in the late 1880s, was one of five courts responsible for jailing 28 per cent of all imprisoned debtors in England and Wales by the 1920s.[35]

Debtors were not completely powerless in this process. Finn has concluded that their engagement with prevailing judicial concerns 'allowed the weak to speak out and gain agency in their own defence'. Numerous strategies were essayed. Parry noted the regular appearance of debtors' wives in courts, complete with babes in arms, as an act designed to signal emotively the potential consequences of any punishment. Finn's analysis of cases from the 1890s suggests that there were a disproportionate number of reductions in the claims awarded when a wife represented her husband.[36] Other ploys were riskier, such as that adopted in 1906 by one debtor who received judicial commiserations on 'having an extravagant wife who pledged his credit with reckless traders', only to be discovered wearing the coat and vest of which he 'had previously sworn he had no knowledge'.[37] Archives do not allow for a full assessment of the extent of such occurrences, or the factors that lay behind them. Moreover, only a small proportion of cases were contested and proceedings took an average of only eighty-five seconds. No more than 2 per cent of judgements went in favour of the debtor.[38]

[31] Finn, *The character of credit*, 263. [32] Polden, *A history of the County Court*.
[33] Cited in Finn, *The character of credit*, 262.
[34] Polden, *A history of the County Court*.
[35] NA: LCO 2/1145, *Imprisonment for debt: statistics and costs*.
[36] Finn, 'Working-class women', 137; Finn, *The character of credit*, 257.
[37] *Credit Trader*, 20 January 1906.
[38] Johnson, 'Small debts and economic distress'.

The extent of such activity as a proportion of all cases is less important than the overriding images that emerged from the small minority reported in the press. These forged the tallyman as 'a stock figure in representations of plebeian consumer excess' and as an unscrupulous bloodsucker.[39] When the opportunity arose, judges in criminal courts also recorded their thoughts on the system. In 1900 a North London magistrate heard the case of a gold watch and chain, stolen by one servant girl from another. However, it was the method of its purchase rather than its theft that received attention. It had been bought from a tallyman for £4 15s, but was valued by a jeweller at only 25s. The magistrate took it upon himself to intervene in the contract between young woman and creditor, advising her to make no further payments, as 'he did not hesitate to describe the system as one method of robbery'. At that point she had repaid only 4 shillings and had obtained a bargain, if she took the judicial advice.[40] The loaded term 'tallyman' came to be a by-word for unscrupulous commerce and incessant bad publicity encouraged many credit drapers to seek 'status passage' for their trade via a modernization programme that enhanced their social standing and raised ethical standards.[41] This process began in the mid-nineteenth century and was to become a regular feature of the trade. Following a general trend amongst credit providers, they organized trade protection societies to record details of bad debtors and fraudsters from the 1830s. A journal, *Credit Drapers' Gazette*, was established in 1882. Ten years later, the growing connections between numerous local credit drapers' associations were formalized in the Credit Drapers' Federal Union, which in 1922 became the National Federation of Credit Traders (NFCT), and in 1962 the Retail Credit Federation (RCF).

The sector was aware that some within its ranks were capable of sharp practice. It was a form of business that had relatively low entry costs, encouraging significant numbers to become involved. Former travellers regularly set up businesses of their own, often obtaining goods on credit or sample stock from a wholesaler with central showrooms.[42] Disreputable practices were frequently disparaged in the trade press, in discussions that ranged from the anti-Semitic through to more logical expositions of the dynamics of high-pressure selling. In 1898 the

[39] Finn, *The character of credit*, 262. [40] *The Times*, 19 November 1900.

[41] G. R. Rubin, 'From packmen, tallymen and "perambulating Scotchmen" to credit drapers' associations, c.1840–1914', *Business* History, 28/9 (1986), 221.

[42] Wright, 'Consumer credit and the tally man', 18.

Credit Drapers' Gazette, revealing anxiety about the anti-Scottish tone of some critics, suggested that 'members of the Hebraic race', such as 'Mr Israel Isaacs' who might trade as 'McBlank', were amongst those responsible for questionable commercial practices.[43] Two years later it acknowledged, more thoughtfully, that pressure on young salesmen could lead them to sell to women without their husband's authority. The suggested remedy was to leave a 'paper for the signature of the head of the house', which would also 'kill the collusion and affected ignorance of many men when they come into court'.[44] Half a century later, the National President of the NFCT still found it necessary to address the 'unpleasant methods' of a 'disreputable minority'. These included using high-pressure sales to offload items that were clearly not wanted by customers; disguising the balance to pay by not marking it clearly in repayment books; and deliberately 'overloading' a customer with credit they could not comfortably repay. He condemned the 'get rich quick merchants' who used these methods as 'parasites battening on the gullibility of ignorant and unoffending housewives', but acknowledged that the 'line between sound and undesirable canvassing was a thin one'.[45] This thin line lay at the heart of outsiders' readiness to see potential peril in each doorstep credit transaction.

Protection registers were one of the credit traders' earliest initiatives to reduce bad debt. In 1914, the Registrar of Birmingham county court acknowledged that 'improved methods of status investigation have enabled creditors, especially in the drapery trades, to collect more accounts without recourse to the Court'. In some cases, this was achieved by blacklisting streets 'in which experience shows that a credit trade cannot be profitably conducted'. The system was not foolproof, however: one imaginative woman had 'succeeded in obtaining goods from the same firm under no fewer than thirty-nine different names'.[46] The key strategy for minimizing bad debt involved nurturing habitual customers. In 1910, a Manchester journalist shadowed a credit draper on his rounds. He described the personal relationships that laid the foundations for routinized credit transactions. The trader remembered 'the biographies of every family', asking in one home about 'William and Jane, and Tom's little girl who was ailing a fortnight ago'. This form

[43] *The Credit Drapers' Gazette*, 29 October 1898. [44] Ibid., 31 March 1900.
[45] *Credit Trader*, 10 March 1956.
[46] G. A. Whitelock, 'The industrial credit system and imprisonment for debt', *Economic Journal* (March 1914), 34–5.

of relationship made it easier for customers to broach the possibility of missing a payment because work had been 'scanty' or their husband had 'been out of a job for two or three weeks'. As they 'begged to be excused', the reporter noted that they 'were decent folks, and they looked ashamed, but not afraid. No dread of the County Court was in their eyes.' The trader maintained that he never knowingly did business without the man of the house knowing of it, although it was tricky to ask bluntly 'Does your husband know of this?' There was also a minority of customers who paid through a friend, as 'they don't want their neighbours to know they buy on credit'. He provided examples of customers who had been allowed to delay repayments due to unemployment and were grateful for the forbearance shown to them. This treatment produced a debt of gratitude that was 'demonstrated by the fact that [he] deals with the children and grandchildren of his older customers'.[47] Loyalty was one form of payment, but there were also financial costs: delayed repayments added further to the expense of instalment buying and home collection. In 1905, the credit traders James Stewart & Sons Ltd of Manchester had a mark-up of 75 per cent, as opposed to 50 per cent by cash retailers. At that time the company found that bad debt occurred in up to 15 per cent of sales, a result of high prices, combined with the regular economic crises that were part of life in the 'very poorest streets' in which it operated.[48] In the years following the First World War, as working-class economic fortunes improved, the company found that bad debts fell and that instalment sales were increasingly accepted.[49] The trade received less negative publicity than it once had, partly because the luxury/necessity debate was becoming more identified with consumer goods bought on hire purchase. The spectacle of repossession of goods sold in this fashion provided new modes of human tragedy for newspaper columns. Analysis of West Hartlepool county court demonstrates that debts arising from hire purchase or mail order sales had a more marked presence from the mid-1930s to 1951, reflecting the rise to prominence of those sectors.[50] Discussion of county courts in *Credit Trader* dwindled in the 1920s and 1930s and had disappeared by the 1940s and 1950s, suggesting declining use of the courts by the sector.

[47] *Manchester City News*, 19 March 1910.

[48] *Credit Trader*, 29 April 1950.

[49] Ibid., 29 April 1950.

[50] Teeside Archives Department: AK19/16, West Hartlepool county court, *Plaint and Minute Book C*, 1934–51.

Despite this, criticism of credit traders did not disappear. It was frequently centred, as before, on women's use of credit. These critiques do not always correspond with the recollections of credit traders' customers. Mavis Knight, born in London in 1917, described how she started working life with very few clothes: 'but as I went by, I managed to get meself something off the tallyman, sort of thing, and pay him sixpence a week, or something like that, you know. But gradually I was beginning to sort of dress meself. I was always trying to make meself look nice.' Mavis's use of this form of credit was instrumental in boosting her self-esteem, gaining the attentions of young men, and in allowing her to take her own small part in the glamorous world of consumption that she was introduced to at the local Astoria cinema. She married in 1936, aged 19, in a brown dress rather than a white one, as it had to be of subsequent practical use. It was bought, like her husband's suit, from the 'tallyman'. Mavis did not buy extravagantly on credit. She used it to achieve targets that she set for herself. Following her marriage furniture was bought on hire purchase and repaid at '15 bob a week'. She set up home outside the notorious Campbell Bunk in North London, where she and her husband had grown up and also determined to improve the material quality of life by having a small family. Mavis and her husband did not rise out of the unskilled working class, but they created a domestic environment that was a marked improvement on those they had experienced as children.[51]

However, whilst Mavis was dressing a family and building a home on credit, others were expressing concerns about its continuing dangers. A leading Charity Organization Society member opined, in 1937, that the 'tallyman' caused misery on new estates because few 'housewives can resist his wiles, and it is not until the wife has become entangled in many agreements that the husband has any knowledge of the extent to which his credit has been pledged'. The London County Council's Education Committee was told, in 1939, of the problems caused by the relocation of families to estates remote from traditional markets where budget clothing could be acquired. As a result, they were 'getting into the hands of the tallyman', which was also allegedly the result of their 'trying to live up to a higher standard' in their new surroundings.[52] Interwar economic turbulence ensured that the value of protection registers was

[51] Jerry White, *The worst street in North London: Campbell Bunk, Islington, between the wars* (London: Routledge and Kegan Paul, 1986), 212–15.

[52] *The Times*, 16 December 1937; 14 March 1939.

re-advocated, particularly from the late 1920s. In 1929 it was reported that irregularly employed Belfast workers, or 'swells', were being forced to use 'cheap credit as a solution for their financial problems'. The protection register should be used, it was argued, to differentiate the 'swells' from the 'rotters', who had no intention of paying. Belfast credit traders were urged to refer each application to the register and, thereby, identify customers applying for up to six credit deals at once. This would remove up to 20,000 court cases each year, many of which were 'issued against the same people time after time'. It would also facilitate reduced prices and attract customers put off by the 'disparity between the retail cash price and the price charged for credit terms'.[53]

Despite the existence of protection registers, many traders trusted their own ability to recognize future bad debtors by reading the bodies, homes, and social connections of potential customers. Tom Chirnside, who joined his family firm in 1930s Lancaster, recalled that 'for a time locally we did keep a record of rogues but we very rarely used any commercial organization'. He felt that they had 'enough knowledge' within the firm and that they 'were dealing with the sort of person who wanted to pay their bills, who wanted to keep a good name'. The first question asked of a prospective customer was 'Who recommended you?' If this was an existing customer related to the applicant, it was felt that 'if the family is good, they're good'. There were rare exceptions, including a Manchester family of twelve where 'the twelfth was a bit of a rogue'. If applicants had no familial links with the firm, Chirnside's father advised him to 'look at the curtains, look at the woman's shoes, look at the garden; if the garden's well cared for the chances are they're good payers'.[54]

In 1919, James Stewart & Sons provided its travellers with standing orders for careful credit control. In 'no case', they were told, 'must a pass book be made out to a married woman unless she is a widow'. They were also ordered not to 'sell goods to people with dirty houses, or who are themselves slatternly. If a woman is poorly shod she is hard up and should not be accepted as a customer.' Lodgers were also viewed as unacceptable, unless travellers personally guaranteed their purchases. Enquiries were 'made amongst other customers regarding the character' of prospective clients, as 'useful information can be obtained by keeping one's ears

[53] *Credit Trader*, 26 September 1929.

[54] Interview with Tom Chirnside (retired credit trader. Born 1916. Interviewed 16 August 2002).

and eyes open'.[55] Once a customer had been assessed as respectable, and honest, they embarked on a relationship with their collector/agent with strongly ingrained elements of performance and negotiation on both sides. In 1931, with the Whitsun festivities approaching and customer demand for new clothes at a peak, Stewart's logbook noted acerbically that customers were not complaining of money shortages. Travellers were told to insist on increased payments and not to appear 'too eager' to take orders.[56] In June, it reported that customers were raising the issue of money problems caused by short-time working and instructed travellers to remind them of their recent promises of increased payments.[57] On these occasions, customers had engaged in their own 'cynical performance', to adapt Taylor's perspective, to ensure their families were well dressed at Whitsun.

Passages of economic turbulence in this period brought renewed attention to the subterfuges that might be employed to outmanoeuvre any customer trying to employ the desperate or dishonest debtor's most cynical ploy: the 'moonlight flit'. The NFCT regularly advised on such matters. Collectors anticipating such an action were instructed to discover in advance precise details of where the customer's relatives lived, by pretending to have knowledge of the area concerned. Information solicited was to be 'jotted down in their notebook', as soon as they were out of sight. In cases where a flit had been accomplished successfully, local newsagents and insurance men were recommended as sources of information on the new address. As former neighbours were deemed unlikely to assist in debt collection, it was 'better to pose as an insurance agent' when seeking information from this source.[58] More routine encounters also included elements of performance. For customers this might occur when explaining missed payments to a sceptical collector, although on such occasions the housewife had the opportunity to remain off-stage, by moving out of sight at the sound of the dreaded knock on the door. Tales of not so well-drilled children informing collectors 'Me muvver says she's aht' are commonplace in folklore.[59] On the collector's

[55] Consumer Credit Association (hereafter CCA), *Year Book and Trade Directory*, 8 October 1919.

[56] Ibid., 31 March 1931. [57] Ibid., 6 June 1931.

[58] CCA: Stewart and Sons Logbook; The National Federation of Credit Traders and the Scottish Credit Traders' Federal Board, *Year Book and Trade Directory, 1930*, 409–12.

[59] For an example see the account of a Lambeth childhood, *The Times* 28 January 1957.

side, ritualized ploys included those calculated to foster a higher rating in the family's regard than others calling for payments. One Chester firm employed an effective traveller who 'used to take a packet of sweets round . . . [and] always the gate was opened for him by a child', who was rewarded with a sweet. His motto was: 'if you pleased the kids, you pleased the mum'.[60] It was in the traveller's interests to establish a ceremonial element to these visits, which culminated with the handover of the required sum. Punctuality was crucial in this respect. Chirnside had an average of two or three minutes for each of his 240 house calls in Lancaster during the late 1940s. A delayed arrival provided an excuse for non-payment. For related reasons a number of customers had the dubious privilege of receiving an early visit each Friday, as soon as they had been paid. Other customers were equally concerned that their own timetable was met by Chirnside: 'I had a cup of tea at four o'clock with Mrs Dobson [she] expected me at four o'clock—cup of tea and a scone. If I went in at two minutes to four, she said "You're early". If it was two minutes past: "Where have you been?" '[61]

The ritualized and routine nature of credit trading was also important in securing business from the families of established customers, on which the trade was highly reliant. Michael Lilley, who joined Kings of Chester in the 1950s, recalled how the generational cross-over operated:

> Well it was a matriarchal society without any doubt. The money was controlled by the mother . . . all the offspring, as they went out into the world, would be given to you as customers. The mother would say to you—'There's your customer. They're ready to pay now. They are going out into the wide world, but you look after them—control their credit. Don't let 'em have any more than such and such.' And you'd agree between you what they could have.[62]

This example suggests that whilst the collector enforced the traditional saving discipline on the new customer and benefited financially, they could also have their grounds for manoeuvre set out by the matriarch, in cases were she had long experience of this form of credit. Any attempt to overextend credit would jeopardize the trust relationship with the whole family. Thus there was always a delicate balance to be maintained in order to retain customers and ensure the repeat orders on which long-term profitability depended. In the 1950s an estimated 80 per cent

[60] Interview with Michael Lilley (veteran credit trader and former chairman of the Consumer Credit Association. Interviewed 18 November 2000).

[61] Interview with Tom Chirnside. [62] Interview with Michael Lilley.

of all customers were regulars.[63] Dealing with a familiar trader, who was expected not to exploit their position, was a strong factor from the family's perspective. On the other side of the relationship, personal connection was all important for the trader. Credit traders may have operated without elaborate, if any, written agreements, but there was a strong social contract between them and their clients. According to Lilley, there was a 'mutual understanding between the consumer and yourself', in which 'they had their rules, you had your rules'. If the traveller breached 'those rules—or any confidence or trust—there'd be an envelope on the door next week when you called [with] all the money in it and you'd know damn well that you'd never be able to see them again'. Lilley recalled occasions when customers had to be prevented from overextending their finances as difficult moments that could cause offence: 'If a customer said to you "I want a new coat please", you'd say "Mrs So and So you can have it in three weeks time. Get your account down a little bit first."' As Melanie Tebbutt has previously noted, 'a word out of place could always end an account'.[64] However, collectors more frequently used their weekly visits to encourage, rather than discourage, further spending. The issue of 'paid-up' customers were regularly featured in the trade press. One article in 1928 suggested that collectors be encouraged to look at 'paid-up accounts as a financial loss to themselves'.[65] The personal relationship established with a collector could make it difficult for customers to either end their dealings with a company or to miss a payment. Many felt that to do so would damage the agent's income or let them down in some way.[66]

Further strategies were developed by credit traders to deal with more fundamental disruption to business routines, such as those that arose during the Second World War. In 1942, Stewart & Sons' travellers were told to exploit the government's insistence on deposits of 2s 6d in the pound for all hire purchase agreements, by telling customers that credit traders were being pressed to do likewise.[67] Like all retailers, the company had to adhere to price controls and it was prohibited from adding credit

[63] Wright, 'Consumer credit and the tallyman', 21.

[64] Melanie Tebbutt, *Making ends meet: pawnbroking and working class credit* (Leicester: Leicester University Press, 1983), 176.

[65] *Retail Credit World*, October 1928. Cited in Avram Taylor, *Working class credit and community since 1918* (Basingstoke: Palgrave Macmillan, 2002), 123.

[66] See, for example, National Consumer Council, *Consumers and credit* (London: NCC, 1980), 320.

[67] CCA: Stewart's and Sons Logbook, 21 August 1942.

charges to customer's bills. This, along with evacuation and enlistment, helped reduce customer numbers during the war. Stewart's accounts fell by one quarter. Many credit traders subsequently concluded that they had only survived the war because 'money had been plentiful'.[68] The war did bring some positive outcomes for credit traders. Stewart's found that price control had shown them 'it was possible to sell on credit on a lower mark-up than they had believed possible'.[69] Meanwhile, meetings between the Board of Trade and the NFCT had 'given leading civil servants an entirely different view of the type of men engaged in the trade'. They had assumed that 'Scotch drapers' took extreme measures against customers and were reportedly surprised to learn that hundreds of NFCT members had never been inside a county court.[70]

'CHAMPAGNE APPETITES WITH GINGER-BEER POCKETS': CREDIT TRADERS AND THE LIMITS OF THE AFFLUENT SOCIETY

The NFCT's mood remained positive in the immediate post-war years. The need to take action for debt diminished in this period, and there was a debate about whether or not protection registers should be scrapped. One credit trader claimed, during 1946, that 'people have money now and also may have changed in character'.[71] This replicated the assessment made after the previous Great War that numerous 'bad payers' had become 'first class payers' as a result of higher wartime earnings.[72] This indicates the extent to which those cast by credit traders in the role of 'rotter' or 'rogue' were often driven by economic factors rather than dishonesty. Caution was still being urged on travellers by *Gusto*, the in-house magazine published by Great Universal Stores' (GUS) credit trading division. An issue in 1948 explained that the traveller's function 'is to see that the customer is never over-sold so that the customer is not worried as to whether he or she can pay the weekly instalment'.[73] The theme continued in the next issue, when it warned that some 'of the general public have champagne appetites with ginger-beer pockets'. It believed that 'one hundred accounts at 5s

[68] *Credit Trader*, 16 March 1946.
[69] Ibid., 29 April 1950.
[70] Ibid., 10 May 1947.
[71] Ibid., 30 November 1946.
[72] Tebbutt, *Making ends meet*, 184.
[73] *Gusto*, Spring 1948.

per week, £25 in all, are a better risk than twenty accounts at 25s per week'.[74]

That there was a need for this cautionary language is suggestive of strong demand in the sector, and the 1950s provided something of an Indian summer for credit traders. In 1950 one trade journal claimed that

> Our status is higher then ever before. We are serving a community which has a standard of living above that of its predecessors. Income levels have risen in the working class field; expenditure is being deviated into the essentials necessary to give better home conditions. Poorly dressed people, bare-footed children and ragged off-springs are things of the past. The people are better educated, more credit-minded and, taken as a whole, are more dependable than ever before.[75]

One economist suggested that hire purchase commitments reduced disposable income and created a demand for clothing and other necessities that was met by credit traders. He believed that 'the two forms of credit may be mildly complementary'.[76] However, growing competition and rising expenses were also a feature of life in the 1950s for credit traders. They faced additional costs, such as those associated with supplying travellers with cars. As one credit trader put it, the 'argument that cars are ideal for executives but a luxury for staff will not hold water in this nuclear fission age'.[77] There was also upward pressure on salaries in a period of low unemployment. GUS's credit trading division was offering travellers £5 a week in 1950, plus 8 per cent commission on collections over £50 per week. This did not prove overly attractive and staff recruitment was problematic, as the young men of the *Room at the top* generation resisted the lure of unglamorous, modestly remunerated employment.[78] During the 1950s the numbers using mail order for credit purchases rose tremendously. Credit traders could not compete with the range of merchandise attractively marketed in the 1,000-page catalogues of the early 1960s. The mail order giants exploited their growing economic muscle to secure branded goods and shake off, at least partially, their dowdy image. Credit traders were unable to do likewise. Although they prided themselves on their close relationship with clients, they could rarely match that between mail order agent and

[74] Ibid., Autumn 1948. [75] *Credit Trader*, 16 September 1950.
[76] Wright, 'Consumer credit and the tallyman', 20.
[77] *Credit Trader*, 2 April 1955.
[78] Interview with Michael Lilley; interview with Tom Chirnside; *Credit Trader*, 16 September 1950.

customer, whose ties were often familial. The credit trader's full-time traveller was frequently male; mail order agents were predominantly female and part-time. The fact that the latter was often motivated as much by the social side of agency as the financial one, allied to her closer proximity to the gendered and temporal patterns of the working-class home, were strong competitive advantages.[79] With incomes rising and employment rates high, many consumers also became increasingly aware of the cheaper prices and greater choice available from high street stores such as Marks and Spencer, C&A, and British Home Stores. One young Liverpool woman, interviewed in the late 1950s, thought that the clothes she had bought from what she called 'the Jew man' for £7 12s could have been obtained from C&A for £4.[80] Liverpool was one area where economic factors remained relatively depressed, reproducing the conditions that created the initial demand for credit trading. But a report published in 1959 found that the sector remained generally well represented in its traditional areas, even though the 'low-income' label no longer applied in many of them; 'particularly in mining districts'. Demand, it argued 'has been maintained largely through custom and goodwill, reflecting the personal element involved in credit trading'.[81] One credit trader, who began work in the 1950s, believed that half his customers used him out of need, the rest out of habit.[82] This is a further reminder of the association between credit and gifting. The sense of obligation felt by customers was an important source of repeat business in the post-war era when the prospect of using other forms of credit, or cash, grew significantly.

One of those competitors was hire purchase. But credit traders made little use of hire purchase, most preferring to operate without formal contracts.[83] One contributor to *Credit Trader* felt that this was a missed opportunity, because 'customers are frequently anxious to give the [hire purchase] order to her usual credit man. The monthly visit to a bank to pay instalments is often a confounded nuisance to her, whilst the purchase of postal orders may be even more unpopular.'[84] In practice, with the typical credit trader employing between one and ten travellers, their total turnover was insufficient to finance hire purchase

[79] Richard Coopey, Sean O'Connell, and Dilwyn Porter, *Mail order retailing in Britain: a business and social history* (Oxford: OUP, 2005), 120–1.

[80] M. Kerr, *The people of Ship Street* (London: Routledge and Kegan Paul, 1958), 92.

[81] Wright, 'Consumer credit and the tallyman', 20.

[82] Tebbutt, *Making ends meet*, 197.

[83] Interview with Michael Lilley.

[84] *Credit Trader*, 2 April 1955.

agreements.[85] More ambitious financing programmes were the province of the few multiple companies involved in credit trading, such as GUS. It had diversified into credit trading in the 1930s, with the purchase of established businesses such as Alexander, Sloan & Co. Ltd of Glasgow.[86]

Whilst traditional business routines remained effective, they were somewhat inflexible in the face of changes that occurred in many inner city areas during the 1950s. Stewart & Sons still advised collectors, as they had done in the 1920s, that customers must be 'natives of the district'.[87] This stricture took on new meaning in this period of renewed Irish immigration, in addition to the arrival of Asian and West Indian migrants. Established approaches to customer recruitment, centring on family connection, also raised barriers, particularly to Asian or West Indian customers who represented a total market of one million by 1966.[88] Moreover, cultural differences between these groups and credit traders may have led the latter to form harsher interpretations of slow payments than would have been made in cases involving 'natives'. It was found, in 1959, that there were few districts where 'reselling' by credit traders did not take place. Only 'poor credit low income districts', such as those hosting 'recent immigrants', were cited in this category.[89] *Up the junction* (1963), Nell Dunn's controversial series of short stories, depicted members of Brixton's black community as customers of Barny, a particularly unscrupulous tallyman with a van 'full of sheets, skirts and petticoats in cellophane'. Barny described his modus operandi as follows:

> You get a foot in the door, start off with a few soft goods . . . a couple of shirts for dad—shoes for Johnny, an underset for Mum—soon they're buying everything off of you—bedroom suites, curtains, kitchen sets, cardigans . . . Once you've got yer foot in the door, you keep it there . . . you hold on to 'em and you never let 'em go.

We learn that 'Sixty per cent of me calls are black—I'm like the white hunter, at the end of the street.' Barney reveals his low regard for the mental abilities of these customers and relishes the inability of many customers to keep track of the payments they have made to different

[85] Wright, 'Consumer credit and the tallyman'.

[86] *Credit Trader*, 11 June 1938.

[87] Ibid., 29 April 1950.

[88] James Cronin, *Labour and society in Britain, 1918–1979* (London: Batsford, 1984), 141.

[89] Wright, 'Consumer credit and the tally man', 20.

tallymen: 'you can go on collecting ten bob a week for a year'. The BBC adaptation of Dunn's book brought Barny to the TV screen, where he was depicted persuading a young West Indian man to buy a jacket so small that it cannot be buttoned up. The scene suggests Barny's racial preconceptions were broadly held.[90] It also reveals a willingness to assume that immigrant groups were likely victims of unscrupulous creditors, in the same way that earlier observers of working-class families had been sceptical of their ability to agree equitable credit contracts. Paul Rock's sociological study of debt, published in 1973, discovered that West Indians were often 'cast as defaulters by creditors assessing applicants'. One informant argued that 'It is no secret that eighty per cent of my hire purchase debts are coloured people.' His view was that they came from countries that were 'not sufficiently developed in character to manage their affairs'.[91] This view conflated allegedly quantifiable experience with racist stereotyping, to the obvious disadvantage of West Indian customers. Given that doorstep creditors were highly reliant on reading verbal and non-verbal cultural clues when assessing honesty in applicants, it is highly likely that cultural differences weighed against non-white applicants. Perhaps Dunn's depiction of Barny was accurate, and many West Indian migrants were exploited by unscrupulous credit traders. However, as will be relayed in the chapter on co-operative credit, this community demonstrated considerable agency by importing credit rotation societies from their homelands and by being instrumental in the creation of the British credit union movement. Others were themselves taking a role in commercial credit operations. From the late 1950s, door-to-door credit companies were employing 'coloured agents' to sell products, ranging from motorcycles to baby clothing, in Brixton. They included Miriam W., whose ambition, resourcefulness, and social origins—'on the borderline of the lower and the middle classes'—gave her characteristics valued by many credit companies when seeking new agents.[92]

Many of the dubious techniques depicted in *Up the junction* had been identified in a 1957 report, prepared for the National Citizen's Advice Bureaux Committee. The quality of salesmanship was one of the issues that most exercised the committee. Although the report commended the

[90] Nell Dunn, *Up the junction* (London: Virago Press, 1988).
[91] Paul Rock, *Making people pay* (London: Routledge and Kegan Paul, 1973), 30, 40.
[92] Sheila Patterson, *Dark strangers: a sociological study of the absorption of a recent West Indian migrant group in Brixton, south London* (London: Tavistock Publications, 1963), 241, 317.

NFCT for its co-operation and noted that the body, then representing 2,650 credit traders in England and Wales, had a 'principle of good trading', it also subjected it to a number of strong criticisms. Amongst these were reports that photographs of children were being 'sold at vastly inflated prices', and that the debt was sold on to other firms 'who thus gain an entry and push the sale of drapery'. Allegations were received about collectors confiscating family allowance books 'until the amount equaled the arrears'.[93] They were, however, unable to provide details of how commonplace such practices were or whether those involved were attached to any trade association. The report was more confident that inadequate payment cards were a fundamental problem and that they were often too small for the purpose required, or were left blank. The term 'goods' was often entered without further description, engendering confusion about which payments were for which item. They considered that 'this question requires more careful attention from traders generally than it has hitherto received'.[94] The issue was a pressing one, not least because they discovered evidence of dishonesty amongst some collectors. Although the NFCT stated that only 0.5 per cent of sales ended in bad debt, the report considered this figure to include only those cases where all other methods of collection had failed. It assumed that significant numbers of families experienced financial hardship in repaying debts that had been taken on inadvisably. Moreover, it felt that with collectors generally recompensed at the minimum wage levels set by the Retail Drapery, Outfitting and Footwear Trade Wages Council, but earning commission for high sales, that it was in the 'interest of the agent . . . to increase the amount of his sales'.[95] The fact that agents were not responsible for bad debt exacerbated any tendency towards risk taking. Keen to urge policing by the NFCT, the report advocated the issue of badges to agents related to the organization and also joined an increasing chorus calling for the licensing of door-to-door sellers.[96]

Post-war council estates were frequently the setting for the practices that caused concern. Tensions were also raised within families that echoed some of those that had featured in nineteenth-century courtrooms. One Glaswegian woman recalled her life on the Blackhill estate on either side of the Second World War and remembered

[93] National Citizens Advice Bureaux Committee, *Hire purchase and credit buying* (London: National Council of Social Service, 1957), 8–9.
[94] Ibid. 11. [95] Ibid. 10–13. [96] Ibid. 15.

tensions between her mother and father, over credit, being repeated in her marriage:

I think it was easier for women to get into debt in those days for there were lots of men coming round the doors selling things and for a woman who doesn't have very much she would say "Well it's only so much a week". It's the easiest thing in the world to do. The men would open up their big cases and we would all crowd round looking at the nylons and shiny scarves and things. Many a time I used to fall out with my own man over the same thing.[97]

The easily duped housewife also made continued appearances in the press. In 1964, one newspaper asked is 'the tallyman to blame because Mrs Freda Wales is in Holloway Prison, her four children are in a children's home and her husband is cooking his own dinner?' The Dagenham housewife had been found guilty of defrauding the National Assistance Board of £600. Her husband levelled the blame for her dishonesty on the firms who offered her fourteen separate credit accounts.[98] Credit traders felt the whole sector was stigmatized by press reports, such as this and others like one in the *Daily Express*, describing 'the social evil of doorstep "never-never" business'.[99] As we have seen, television's growing interest in working-class life resulted in a number of appearances of 'tallymen' that the trade felt were highly negative and unrepresentative. Ken Loach directed the BBC's adaptation of *Up the junction* in 1965. Watched by over ten million viewers, it shocked the nation with its depiction of casual sex and abortion. As well as concerns about exploitative creditors in a new multi-racial context setting, Barny also raised another perennial anxiety, by boasting of his exploits with female customers and ability to get them deeply indebted. The impact of his appearance was heightened by the striking manner of his depiction; sitting in the car and addressing the camera/audience directly about his dubious methods.[100] A year later, Granada TV's *Coronation Street* featured another profiteering tallyman, making what the RCF viewed as inaccurate statements about a credit trader's profits. In a letter of protest to Granada the RCF argued that the term 'tallyman . . . went out with the Ark' and that 'if there were

[97] Interview with Mrs P. cited in Anne McGuckin, 'Moving stories: working class women', in E. Breitenbach and E. Gordon (eds.), *Out of bounds: women in Scottish society 1800–1945* (Edinburgh: Edinburgh University Press, 1993), 211.

[98] *Daily Herald*, 24 July 1964. [99] *Credit Trader*, 23 November 1963.

[100] I am grateful to Professor John Hill for providing this insight into Loach's techniques and their impact.

such a type as you portrayed last night, it is doubtful if he would survive in business more than a few months'.[101]

The RCF continued to believe that media coverage of consumer credit issues was often ill-informed and dominated by eye-catching cases, involving a minority of disreputable traders. It was however, successful in lobbying the Consumer Council on a number of issues, particularly in getting it to drop its support for the licensing of doorstep sellers. The Council made doorstep selling one of its top three priorities in 1963.[102] It was a concern because, as the Crowther Committee reasoned, when 'an experienced salesman, dependent on commission, is facing an inexperienced housewife on her doorstep, or in her sitting room, there is hardly an equality of bargaining power'.[103] The Council argued that although doorstep credit trading was 'a perfectly reputable occupation of benefit to consumers', in the early 1960s there had been 'an infusion of. . . shady operators', bringing 'the whole practice of selling goods over the doorstep into disrepute'.[104] Disturbing cases included that of an elderly lady, forced to slash her food budget, after purchasing a set of encyclopaedias via thirty monthly instalments of 50 shillings.[105] The RCF wooed the Council in several meetings and won the approval of its Director, Elizabeth Ackroyd. It pointed out that given the small sums involved in each individual transaction, it was in their financial interests to secure continual business from a family.[106] It was in the RCF's favour that its message dovetailed with the Council's emphasis on empowering individual consumers in preference to interventionist consumerism.[107]

As the 1960s wore on, it was clear that increasing numbers of credit traders were struggling to survive. The sector faced a combination of rising prosperity, intense competition from cash and credit retailers, and significant changes in customer demands. The Crowther Committee estimated that in 1966 the 3,464 specialist itinerant credit traders had

101 *Credit Trader*, 5 February 1966.

102 NA: AJ/3/1O—Hire purchase legislation; AJ4/3 *Licensing of doorstep salesmen.* Meeting on doorstep selling, 20 February 1964.

103 Committee on Consumer Credit, *Report of the Committee* (London: HMSO, 1971), 2.5.18.

104 *Credit Trader*, 28 March 1964.

105 Elizabeth Ackroyd, 'Doorstep selling abuses', *Credit Trader*, 19 February 1966.

106 NA: AJ4/10 Consumer Council. *Doorstep Selling*, Minutes of meeting 21 July 1964.

107 On the Consumer Council and state attitudes towards consumerism at this point see Matthew Hilton, *Consumerism in 20th-century Britain* (Cambridge: CUP, 2003), 228–41.

combined instalment sales of £128m. Typical transactions ranged from £30 to £40.[108] This compared with figures of £374m for general mail order retailers, who provided strong competition in the credit traders' main market of clothing and footwear. These two lines still dominated the itinerant credit trade's turnover, with 56.4 per cent of all sales.[109] The fact that the RCF was not called to present evidence by the Crowther Committee seemed to suggest that the sector was in terminal decline and many within it were beginning to consider undertaking fundamental restructuring.

'CUSTOMERS NEVER COMPLAIN THAT A £5 NOTE IS THE WRONG SIZE OR COLOUR': THE SHIFT TO MONEYLENDING

As the swinging sixties unfurled credit traders attempted to affect economies of scale, pooling resources to fight multiple and mail order retailers. The Chirnsides did so by joining a buying group of independent stores in 1969. In the 1970s the firm moved into cash retailing, which subsequently became the mainstay of the company. By 2000, the company was taking only £300–400 per week on its credit rounds, whereas they had once been so concentrated that they included one Lancaster street of thirteen houses where ten houses were on its books. Of the other houses Tom Chirnside recalled: 'two didn't want me, one I didn't want'. The company's credit business 'gradually went away. The standard of living of the working man and his wife—there's no comparison whatsoever to what it used to be. I mean everybody went to Blackpool for their holiday, now they go to Florida.'[110]

Kings of Chester also joined a buying group with seventy members, but it lost its economic clout as members began to close down or sell out to larger companies in the choppy economic waters of the 1970s. New costs, incurred via the introduction of Value Added Tax in 1973, were the final straw for many businesses.[111] Further difficulties were encountered with soaring inflation in the late 1970s.[112] Even relatively large companies struggled to cope. Stirlings of Glasgow, which had 300

[108] Committee on Consumer Credit, *Report*, 12.5.16.
[109] Ibid., Table A12; Table A22; Table A16; Table A25.
[110] Interview with Tom Chirnside. [111] Interview with Michael Lilley.
[112] *Consumer Credit Association News*, September 1981.

travellers in the 1950s, employed fewer than half that number when the business was sold in 1983. Even Alexander, Sloan & Co. and Midorca House, owned respectively by GUS and Phillips Electrical, could not cope in these market conditions.[113] However, another GUS subsidiary, Morses Ltd, which had been acquired in 1947 at a time when its 200 travellers operated only in Southern England, began to buy out smaller credit traders.[114] GUS-produced merchandise and catalogues supported its subsequent growth, and it was able to achieve much greater competitiveness than its rivals. It covered the whole of the UK by the 1980s. At that point, the company had reached Belfast, where Anne-Marie, who had recently separated from her husband, made use of it:

> I wasn't working, I had a lot of children and I didn't think I'd get hire purchase anyway. Coz the hire purchase always tended to be on your income and your husband's income and at the time you would have been told there and then: "I'm sorry but you're not suitable for credit". I've been with friends and they got that [answer] and I thought—no, not for me. And, this man came round and it was Morse's catalogue... So I got my house carpeted from Morse and then I ordered the suite from Morse.[115]

Anne-Marie's story indicates that there was still a market for merchandising on the doorstep in the 1980s, although many credit traders had shifted into the moneylending sector. In 1978, the RCF merged with the National Personal Finance Association, to form the Consumer Credit Association (CCA). Its journal carried debates on the competing merits of moneylending and merchandising. It also carried more familiar discussions, such as one in 1983, featuring a trading standards officer's view that doorstep selling was 'an emotive subject' because some consumers were vulnerable to skilled sales people. He noted that 'a salesman, once inside a home, is looked upon as something akin to a guest, and most people find it difficult to be rude to guests by asking them to leave'.[116] His perspective once again raised the highly personal relationship that existed between doorstep credit traders and their customers, involving circularized elements of reciprocity and obligation. It was a relationship that was highly routinized and dependent upon habit and the credit trader who kept getting a foot in the door could

[113] Ibid., June 1985. [114] *The Times*, 13 September 1947.

[115] Interview with Anne-Marie (mature student and mother. Born 1951. First husband a scaffolder; second husband a musician. Interviewed 20 May 2003).

[116] *Consumer Credit Association News*, May–June 1983.

obtain regular orders. However, as Johnson has argued, although the habits developed by working-class consumers in their management of scarce monetary resources were not rapidly transformed, they were not immutable. Modification of habit when it did arrive often took place between, rather than within, generational groups. In addition, there were lags between economic and cultural change.[117] Thus, by the 1980s what one credit draper called the 'cream' of his traditional customers had fallen away.[118] With competition for their business having opened up significantly, first through mail order catalogues and then through credit cards, store cards, and bank loans, the 'cream' moved on. Their less affluent counterparts were left to deal increasingly with doorstep credit in the form of personal loans, as many credit traders sold their rounds to moneylenders. Others, such as Liverpool's Gerry Dunn, began combining both forms of doorstep credit. By 1991 his family business recorded 93 per cent of its turnover in personal loans. He dryly remarked that 'customers never complain that a £5 note is the wrong size or colour'.[119] Even Morses Ltd, with the financial backing of the GUS merchandising empire, moved into doorstep lending and was sold, in 2005, to London Scottish Bank Plc.[120] The shift from merchandising to moneylending caused controversy amongst the descendants of the tallymen. It did, however, ensure them a continuing place at the epicentre of new debates about debt and the low-income consumer with the pejorative label tallyman, replaced with the even more damning loan shark. The sector's shift into moneylending was mirrored by the check traders, who will be the subject of the next chapter.

CONCLUSION

This chapter has indicated the extent to which credit traders were able to maximize highly personalized and 'somewhat anachronistic' forms of business deep into the twentieth century. They did so under the critical gaze of the judiciary, the media, and consumer watchdogs. Their trade association, which had been highly active in the nineteenth century, continued to be so and had some successes in explaining the economics

117 Johnson, *Saving and spending*, 215.
118 Tebbutt, *Making ends meet,* 219–20.
119 *Consumer Credit Association News*, May/June 1991.
120 London Scottish Bank, *Report and Accounts 2005*, 4.

of credit provision in low-income communities. It argued, as it had long done, that examples of exploitative practice were to be found only on the fringe of credit trading and that customers appreciated the service that was offered. This appeared to be demonstrated during the 1950s when their turnover remained buoyant amidst rising incomes. But this was also the result of the sector reaping rewards from its creation of obligation through long-term dealings with its clientele. Credit had indeed obligated customers and many proved their willingness to reciprocate. Reciprocation implies an element of equality in a relationship and this is something that Taylor's analysis has questioned, in regards to various forms of doorstep credit. As the business histories of credit traders examined in this chapter reveal, the companies involved were 'cynical' in their dealings with customers in terms of seeking new orders or enforcing repayment. This is, however, the nature of any commercial relationship. What concerned outside observers was the extent to which the system was exploitative due to factors such as consumer ignorance, or high-pressure selling. Such concerns were exacerbated by individual cases that appeared in the media, such as the depressing tale of the Dagenham housewife Freda Wales, or the depiction of the fictional tallyman Barny in *Up the junction*. There is, however, minimal evidence to suggest that consumers were deliberately forced into debt by credit traders. Even amongst consumers with little economic or educational capital, there was, as Johnson explains, an ability to identify wasteful expenditure. The service offered by credit traders was expensive, but the fact that it did not decline more rapidly in the 1950s and 1960s indicates that a large number of consumers still found it useful. It is also true, however, that there was a great deal of customer inertia in this respect and changes in demand for different forms of credit appear to have occurred between, rather than within, generational groups. Once a line of credit had been established, consumers with few other options were loath to give it up. Moreover, they were content to deal with what had become a familiar form of provisioning the family home and credit traders worked hard on establishing themselves as part of the housewife's weekly routine. But the growing numbers of mail order users in the 1950s and 1960s suggests that those within the working classes who were still required to buy clothing and other household necessities on credit terms had found a more attractive alternative. Catalogue credit was also expensive, but it offered greater choice and the commercial exchanges involved were conducted even more informally than those with the credit trader, because the part-time catalogue agent was often a relative or friend. Significantly mail order agents were predominantly female and their economic dealings with customers were viewed with less suspicion by commentators. The tallyman never quite managed to disrobe himself of his Victorian image as a predator who commercially seduced housewives behind their husbands' backs. As we shall see in the next chapters—on check traders and mail order retailing—others involved in providing consumer credit to working-class consumers took valuable lessons from the credit trader's experiences in the courts and designed operational systems that minimized exposure of their business methods.

2

The rise of the Provident system: check trading

This chapter discusses a form of credit that bore operational similarities to that of the credit traders. Check traders occupied an unusual position, as the middle-men between consumers and retailers. The companies involved, led by the Provident Clothing and Supply Co. Ltd, sold checks to customers that were traded for merchandise sold by shops taking part in the scheme. Customers repaid the check trader on a weekly basis, with collection taking place over a nominal twenty weeks. A small sum, which became known as a poundage fee, of one shilling for every pound on the check's value was also paid to cover the costs incurred in the agent's weekly visits. For the customer, the system offered the possibility of discovering a greater range of goods than were to be had from the tallyman. Checks could be spent in a significant number and range of retail outlets: customers could acquire items ranging from their Sunday best outfit to a sack of coal, or even their false teeth. This flexibility was the key factor in the spread of check trading, and many retailers signed up to take part because it directed customers to them who would not otherwise have patronized their stores. It also enabled retailers to avoid the costs and risks associated with financing credit independently. They did not have to assess credit risk, pursue non-payers, or take them to court. But retailers did have to pay sizeable commissions to the check trader when redeeming the check and it was this aspect of the system, and the hidden charges that customers faced, that proved most controversial. However, critics found it impossible to land a clean punch on the check traders. The tripartite arrangement between credit trader, customer, and retailer created hurdles for anyone attempting to identify its real costs. The poundage charge, when calculated as an annual percentage rate, came in at under the 48 per cent figure that was suggested as harsh and unconscionable by the Moneylenders Act of 1927. Precise evidence that retailers raised prices to compensate for the discounts they had to offer to check traders was also difficult to locate. The companies involved, in attempting to set themselves apart from the tallymen, argued that check trading was about thrifty consumerism and not profligacy. The Provident's name indicates its engagement in moralized debates about consumer credit.

The check trading system proved popular with large numbers of customers. This is demonstrated below through a detailed examination of the records of the Provident. The company came to dwarf all other forms of doorstep credit supplied by the credit traders, other check traders, or by the co-operative movement's mutuality clubs. Data, mined below, reveals that in both the mid-1930s and the 1950s, Provident topped the one-million-customer mark. In the late 1960s it amassed 1.5 million customers. The popularity of Provident, and check trading, again demonstrates that price was not the top priority for working-class consumers operating limited weekly budgets. Check traders offered them an opportunity to make small weekly payments that were collected from their door in a fashion similar to other doorstep credit traders. The companies involved developed agency systems that penetrated working-class neighbourhoods and established personalized credit networks that had been the hallmark of the credit traders. They also engendered high levels of long-term customer loyalty, or dependency. Check traders also morphed into doorstep moneylenders in the 1960s. This was a logical step because check trading was effectively a substitute vehicle for moneylending, which emerged because of the latter's lack of respectability in the late nineteenth and early twentieth centuries.

'BRADFORD SHOULD BE THE MOST JOYOUS CITY IN THE KINGDOM': THE SPREAD OF CHECK TRADING 1880–1939

'Unlimited credit, a philosopher once declared, is the sovereign cure for all human ills and woes. If this is true, Bradford should be the most joyous city in the kingdom, for it has become within the past few years the centre of the greatest system of credit-buying ever known in England.' With these words, written in 1908, the *Daily Mail* began a series of articles on the Bradford-based Provident Clothing and Supply Company.[1]

[1] *Daily Mail*, 16 April 1908.

Check traders and their agents were, by then, familiar figures on the working-class landscape. Provident was founded in 1880, using a system which appeared to have a number of progenitors. In the view of the Crowther Committee on Consumer Credit, it evolved from check clubs, which were credit rotation societies in which consumers placed small weekly sums. The total collected each week was placed at the disposal of one member of the club, with a lottery deciding an individual's position in the 'turn'. The Crowther Committee believed that the system was commercialized in the 1870s by the arrival of check trading companies.[2] This had strong parallels with the emergence of mail order clubs that were also based on credit rotation within groups of working-class individuals. A further similarity was the employment of agents who operated within their own communities and enabled companies involved to maximize loyalty and obligation amongst customers. This effectively institutionalized elements of gifting within a commercial relationship. There were also similarities with the industrial insurance companies who also established doorstep collections by agents.[3] The links between sectors were often very visible to working-class households, as many agents worked simultaneously for industrial insurance companies and check traders.[4] The modest pay received by agents, around 20 shillings per week for part-timers and between 20 and 70 shillings for full-timers during the 1920s, encouraged this employment pattern.[5] Those who did combine the two roles amassed greater knowledge of their customers and created more deeply embedded relationships. Modest pay also brought a turnover of agents that created opportunities for the companies involved, as new appointees provided access to customers amongst their friends and neighbours.[6]

An internal Provident document, written in the late 1920s by an executive manager with several decades' experience, instructed agents on how to monitor the working-class family life cycle. Credit was to be 'kept low to the labourer with young children', because his disposable income would be at a low ebb. But agents should be ready to raise 'it in future

[2] Committee on Consumer Credit, *Report of the Committee*, Cmnd. 4596 (London: HMSO, 1971), 47.

[3] Laurie Dennett, *A sense of security: 150 years of Prudential* (Cambridge: Granta Editions, 1998), 310.

[4] *Daily Mail*, 16 April 1908.

[5] Bradford. Provident Financial Group (hereafter PFG): PFG/03/11: Agent's recruitment leaflet, *c*.1920s.

[6] PFG/01/156: Check and credit trade typescript for publication by H. Webb (1929), 49.

when [the children] work'. However, when these young workers set up their own home, depriving their parents of a financial contribution to the household exchequer, their parents' 'credit levels must be watched again and reduced'. The cycle began again, with a visit to the new home of the departed adult children, who were 'encouraged to take up credit'.[7] From a customer's perspective, the disciplinary function brought by the agent's weekly visits was not unwelcome. As Paul Johnson has observed of industrial insurance collectors, they imposed the external discipline of contract in working-class communities by applying 'pressure on the housewife in those weeks . . . when there was scarcely enough money to feed the family' and reminded customers of 'long-run goals when immediate financial pressures seemed overwhelming'.[8] Interviewed by the *Daily Mail* in 1908, the Provident's founder Joshua K. Waddilove argued that check trading 'promotes thrift'. He maintained that whilst it was 'easy enough to declare that the working man ought to save his shilling a week himself' and only go to the shop when he had put by the cash price, 'it is very difficult to keep the shilling untouched'. The agent's visit ensured that the shilling was kept for him and that this 'payment for clothes and boots [became] like rent'.[9]

Parallels with industrial insurance are unsurprising, given that Waddilove had worked in that industry as an inspector. Insights gained therein of working-class budgeting informed the check trading system. In christening his new company, he attempted to deflect moralized critiques about providing credit to working-class families. The Provident's nomenclature, like that of the dominant operator in industrial insurance—the Prudential—suggested both thriftiness and respectability, although both companies had their critics. In 1910, one county court judge offered a linguistic counterblast by suggesting that Waddilove's company be renamed 'The Improvident'.[10] Provident's foundation narrative also served a legitimizing function. Waddilove, an active Wesleyan Methodist, apparently developed 'grave objections' to the 'tallyman system', noting that its 'goods are usually dear, the stock is limited and

[7] H. Webb (1929).

[8] Paul Johnson, *Saving and spending: the working-class economy in Britain 1870–1939* (Oxford: Clarendon Press, 1985), 38–9.

[9] *Daily Mail*, 17 April 1908. On insurance agents see Johnson, *Saving and spending*, 221.

[10] PFG/03/007: Provident's ninety years of service, *Evening Chronicle*, 13 December 1910.

a housewife is tempted to indulge in many needless things'.[11] As a charitable action, he began issuing checks 'redeemable by special arrangement' at local shops for clothes, boots, and coal. Waddilove then paid the shops out of his own pocket.[12] His virtue was rewarded and women approached him, voicing their willingness to pay a small premium if he commercialized the system. The Provident was established and retailers were persuaded to accept its checks and pay a 'discount' (typically between 12 and 17 per cent) when settling bills with the company. In return, store owners were promised increased turnover and a reduction in the administrative or bad debt costs associated with credit. A typical check was for £1 and was repaid in twenty weekly instalments of one shilling. Customers could spend their check after eight weekly payments, or immediately, if they paid a 'poundage' fee of one shilling per pound. Around 95 per cent of customers favoured the latter option in 1908 and it subsequently became the standard method.[13]

The company's agents canvassed for customers and made weekly collections. They were tasked with remaining attuned to the socio-economic fortunes of the communities they covered. Agents provided the first level of credit assessment, with a hierarchy of inspectors and superintendents overseeing their decisions. A number of sources suggest that check traders operated relatively strict credit assessments. One credit retailer reported, in 1929, that the Provident did not take on a customer without obtaining one reference from a shopkeeper and two from householders.[14] A former agent for the Nottingham City and Suburban Check Trading Association remembered how, in 1924, he was directed to enquire of shopkeepers: 'Do you know Mr. So and so?' and 'Does he pay his way?' If they responded negatively 'you'd just turn them down'.[15] Waddilove claimed that his company could 'not give credit to the slums without losing a very large proportion of our money'. It sought out 'the better working classes, people in receipt

[11] *Daily Mail*, 17 April 1908.

[12] PFG/03/007: *Colonnade* (newspaper of the Provident Group) Special issue, *Provident's ninety years of service*, 1970.

[13] *Credit Draper*, 23 May 1908.

[14] Cited in Melanie Tebbutt, *Making ends meet: pawnbroking and working class credit* (Leicester: Leicester University Press, 1983), 186.

[15] Nottingham Local Studies Lifetimes Collection (NLSLC): A104 a–d. Interview with Mr Bert Tansley, former check trade agent conducted 21 August 1984). Thanks are due to Peter Scott for providing this reference.

of a weekly wage'. In 1908, the *Daily Mail* suggested that there were relatively affluent families earning between '£5 to £7 a week who make all their purchases of personal attire in this way'.[16] The fluidity of terms such as 'respectable' or 'better class' must be borne in mind: many of the Provident's 'better class' customers might have fallen close to one or more of the many poverty lines constructed by the social scientists busying themselves in early twentieth-century working-class districts. For example, a survey of Merseyside, in 1934, concluded that most families around the poverty line utilized clothing clubs, whilst less than half those above it did so.[17]

However, it is clear that Provident did not do business with those who could not repay, as its impressive growth demonstrates. By 1890 it employed 325 field staff throughout Lancashire and Yorkshire. In 1900, its only functioning offices outside these counties were in Birmingham, Glasgow, and Leicester, but the next decade witnessed UK-wide expansion. In 1910, 3,000 agents were employed in 91 branches, centred on areas of high urban density. In that year the company's turnover was over £1m.[18] Its heaviest concentration of offices, 38, was still in Yorkshire and Lancashire. However, the company was also well represented in the Midlands/Potteries and London with 14 and 15 offices respectively. Scotland, Wales, and Ireland had 6, 4, and 2 branches respectively. A small number of others were located in South-West England, the South-East, the North-East and Cumbria, and the South Coast.[19] Locations included areas with high levels of poverty, such as Dublin and Liverpool, as well as more prosperous Edwardian centres like Coventry, Crewe, and Swindon.[20] The phenomenal success of check trading prompted the series of feature articles in the *Daily Mail*, mentioned above, in which Provident was described as the 'poor man's banker' and the 'greatest system of credit-buying ever known in England'.[21] The Registrar of Birmingham County Court, W. H. Whitelock, writing in 1914, felt that check clubs were taking the 'place formerly occupied here by the Scotch draper'. He appeared content with this, because whereas the

16 *Daily Mail*, 16 April 1908.

17 D. Caradog Jones, *Social survey of Merseyside* (London: Hodder and Stoughton, 1934), 213.

18 PFG/03/136: *Provident Clothing and Supply Company Ltd: fifty years of progress*, 1930; *Daily Mail*, 17 April 1908;. PFG/04/076: *Dublin shopping guide*, 1910.

19 PFG/04/001: Dates of opening and closure of district offices.

20 Ibid.

21 *Daily Mail*, 16 April 1908.

latter gave unskilled labourers up to £12 in credit, checks traders offered only £2.[22]

However, the check trader did not escape the opprobrium attached to those offering credit in working-class communities. Arnold Bennett's best selling novel *The card* (1911) parodied the system and the 'philanthropic' motives of those behind it. The novel featured the coldly opportunistic Denry Machin, who establishes the Five Towns Universal Thrift Club after learning the intricacies of money management in the plebeian home during spells as a rent collector and unlicensed moneylender. Whilst Machin is depicted as a character with some redeeming qualities, Walter Greenwood's classic interwar novel *Love on the Dole* (1933) offered readers the less engaging entrepreneurialism of Mrs Nattle. Amongst other money-making schemes, she is an agent for the Good Samaritan Clothing Company. Mrs Hardcastle becomes indebted to the company as part of her family's spiral into economic meltdown that ends with her daughter, Sally, prostituting herself to the local street bookmaker.[23] The economic uncertainties that provided the backdrop to *Love on the dole* created challenges for check traders. The Provident lavished greater attention on areas where household income was less dependent on struggling traditional industries. In the 1920s offices were opened in towns such as Luton and Slough. Even Bournemouth, more usually associated with colonial retirees, was opened up. The 1930s saw the company's biggest expansion to date, with 128 new offices established. Almost half were in the South of England, in places such as Cambridge, Canterbury, Eastbourne, Salisbury, and Tunbridge Wells. Demographic shifts, ushered in by slum clearance and council house building, were reflected in the establishment of offices in places such as Huyton, near Liverpool, in 1938. Similar patterns followed in the 1950s when locations such as Basildon, Bracknell, and Brentwood were added to the company's list.[24]

Provident's early start meant that it dominated what was often referred to as the provident system. The operations of its rivals were much smaller and geographically circumscribed. When the Crowther

[22] W. H. Whitelock, 'The industrial credit system and imprisonment for debt' *Economic Journal*, 23 (March 1914), 34–5.

[23] Arnold Bennett, *The card* (London: Eyre Methuen, 1973 edn.); Walter Greenwood, *Love on the dole* (London: Cape, 1935).

[24] PFG/04/001: Dates of opening and closure.

Committee surveyed the sector in the late 1960s, it discovered that the total turnover of the 370 small and medium-size businesses that were members of the National Federation of Check Traders (NFCT) was only two-thirds that of the Provident.[25] Avram Taylor has described some of its initial rivals: retailers operating what was dubbed the ticket system. It was strongly embedded in the North-East of England and appears to have pre-dated Provident's formation. The latter only managed to establish itself in Newcastle from 1909 and in Sunderland from 1911, after earlier efforts failed.[26] Ticket clubs were established by department stores, such as Parrish's of Byker and Shephard's of Gateshead, to serve a working-class clientele, and were said to cost the retailer 50 per cent less to operate than choosing to accept Provident checks. However, unlike the check, a ticket could only be used at one store.[27]

A Provident check's portability was a major advantage over ticket schemes. The company's lists of retailers were substantial. It had agreements with 14,000 retailers during the 1930s, and 20,000 by the 1960s.[28] Efforts were made to secure the most significant retailers in any given location, often by accepting lower discounts than were demanded from smaller shops. A local hairdresser typically paid up to 20 per cent, whilst a department store might be asked for a discount of 8 per cent.[29] By 1908, checks could be used to buy anything from 'photographs to bassinettes and from barometers to artificial teeth'. In the mid-1930s, Provident's Wolverhampton customers could patronize nineteen shops selling boots and shoes, thirteen house furnishers, twelve retailing ready-made clothes, nine bespoke tailors, eleven opticians, nine purveyors of wireless sets, four jewellers and watchmakers, three wallpaper and paint retailers, two second-hand furniture shops, two second-hand clothes shops, and one coal merchant.

Customers were informed that the check's flexibility meant that it could be used in shops with 'competitive prices'. This facility, it was argued, was worth more than the dividend paid to the patrons of the co-operative movement's mutuality schemes, which were developed from 1923 as a response to the check system. Customers were also

[25] Committee on Consumer Credit, *Report*, 76.

[26] Avram Taylor, *Working class credit and community since 1918* (Basingstoke: Palgrave Macmillan, 2002), 127; *Daily Mail*, 12 May 1908.

[27] *Daily Mail*, 12 May 1908. Taylor, *Working class credit*, 31.

[28] PFG/01/067: *Memorandum upon Miss Ellen Wilkinson's Hire Purchase Bill;* Economist Intelligence Unit, 'Check trading', *Retail Business* (1964), 45.

[29] Economist Intelligence Unit, 'Check trading', 46.

informed that checks enabled them to get better value for money than mail order shoppers, who, it was alleged, paid high prices.[30] A check could be subdivided and used in more than one store; retailers were instructed to enter the amount spent in their premises on the back of what became known as a 'travelling check'. Responding to claims that retailers adopted 'special prices' when approached by his customers, Waddilove claimed that customers need not reveal their method of payment until the point of sale, thereby preventing a retailer from raising the cost.[31] Shopkeepers who opposed the system scoffed at this suggestion. They maintained that retailers accepting checks added the costs of the discounts to their cash price, and that 'the "club" customer is soon "spotted" as a rule'. One argued that 'a special line of rubbish' had to be kept for check customers.[32] Some evidence for the existence of such practices emanated from a female shopper who told one newspaper, in 1910, that she had produced a Provident check to pay for a jacket, which was priced at 16s 6d, and was then asked to pay a further 1s 6d.[33] Whilst it is impossible to assess the extent of these practices, it is clear that shopkeepers allotted check users second-class status. From the outset, retailers asked check traders to urge their clients to shop during quiet periods. In 1905, Provident customers were advised to 'shop as little as possible' on Saturdays because they would not receive 'the attention we wish you to have'. They were instructed to shop 'about the middle of the week', when tradesmen 'will highly appreciate your doing so' and would 'serve you far better'.[34]

Some retailers took concerted action to oppose the system. They included a group who paraded a donkey through Bury, in 1913, bearing a placard that read: 'I am an ass. I buy club checks and lose 3s 6d on every 20s.'[35] More generally, shopkeepers debated the merits of check clubs for themselves and their customers. In 1915, *Credit Draper* wondered how, charging discounts of up to 17.5 per cent, the check traders 'ever managed to get reputable shopkeepers to fall into their trap'. Yet it recorded 'that many excellent firms have been allured'.[36] They were attracted by the prospect of increased turnover. Check agents were said to be walking advertisements for retailers on their employer's

[30] PFG/O4/076: *Wolverhampton Shopping Guide*, 1935.
[31] *Daily Mail*, 17 April 1908.
[32] *Credit Draper*, 25 April 1915; *Daily Mail*, 4 May 1908.
[33] *Penny Illustrated Paper*, 15 October 1910.
[34] PFG/04/149: Slip advising customers not to shop on Saturdays, 1905.
[35] *Daily Sketch*, 1 December 1913.
[36] *Credit Draper*, 25 April 1915.

list. One Edwardian retailer reported that his annual turnover rose from £2,000 to £5,000 after he began accepting checks. Furthermore, his customers bought 'better goods with checks than they ever did with cash'. More misery, he felt, had 'been brought to homes by the packman [the tallyman] than by the club system'. Another shopkeeper commented that check shoppers 'invariably spend more than their check, thus considerably reducing the rate of discount on the purchase'. Manufacturers also began to see attractions in the scheme. One large footwear producer offered to enter into an agreement to stock a shop for one Manchester retailer, but only if he were to 'open an account with the Provident'.[37] A footwear retailer on the other side of the Pennines reported that 'my experience is that a large amount of business comes to me in this way that I would not otherwise get'. This was especially true at certain periods:

> everybody must have clothes and boots for the Whitsun holidays. The children must go barefoot and ragged for the rest of the year, but on Whit-Sunday they must be smart. I have many a mother come to me from the slums a few days before Whitsun, with perhaps half a dozen ragged children with her; she will pick out my most showy line . . . showy but not of much practical use. But the mother has half a dozen pairs, one for each child, and pays for them with her check. The transaction is over, so far as I am concerned, in a few minutes, and my money is sure. I am willing to pay the clubs for bringing me that kind of custom.[38]

Other retailers were less sanguine about the potential for increased business offered by check clubs. One claimed that he had been sold a vision of 'an army of canvassers around his district' that would 'double his trade'. After accepting checks, his turnover rose as promised. But when his rivals also began to accept checks the trade was 'shared between the shops as before', except that they paid the clothing clubs 3s 6d in the pound, for what he dismissed as 'their American business'.[39] A further source of complaint was the delay between selling merchandise and the receipt of payments from the Provident. A West of England trader, exercised by the retailer's wait of up to three months for reimbursement, dismissed Waddilove's core claim about check clubs:

[37] *Daily Mail*, 5 May 1908. [38] Ibid., 20 April 1908.

[39] Ibid., 4 May 1908. For the similar disapproving attitudes about credit, and its connections with American consumerism, amongst interwar motor dealers see Sean O'Connell, *The car in British society: class, gender and motoring 1896–1939* (Manchester: Manchester University Press, 1998), 28.

'The whole system is one of borrowing, not thrift, and any system that encourages the working classes to borrow must be demoralising.'[40] Watching from the sidelines, the *Credit Draper*, voice of the tallymen, enjoyed the spectacle, noting the acceptance of checks by retailers who had previously lambasted the 'extortionate prices' associated with credit trading. It described them as being like 'the Pharisees', who 'plume themselves on not being like other men' and scoffed at their continuing claim to be 'cash shopkeepers'.[41]

What did working-class consumers make of the various accusations made about the check traders? In 1908, one retailer claimed to have profited from placing a 'No club checks taken' sign in his window. He also related cases of cash customers leaving shops when they witnessed checks being produced as payment, because they suspected they would, as a result, be overcharged.[42] However, most of the available evidence suggests that consumers were more positive about the check trade. A Welsh worker argued in 1908 that the 'working man cannot afford to pay cash' and therefore 'had a choice between credit clubs or the Scotch packman'. He believed the latter 'cost us fifty per cent more and we had to order things before we saw them'.[43] His viewpoint echoed the impression that Lady Bell drew from her investigations in Middlesbrough, which concluded that check and ticket clubs were a popular choice for housewives. The shopper could 'get the goods that she sees at the prices marked in the windows, whereas by the other system she is at the mercy of tallymen, who may palm off on her at a given price something which is usually sold far below it'. Using the tallyman also meant buying 'the thing unseen from a sample shown her'.[44] A Manchester worker noted the 'great strides in respectability' made by the working classes: 'as soon as work is over, clogs and shawls are discarded and they don better attire and go out. The homes have improved. One of the great causes of this improvement' was, he felt, 'Mr Waddilove's idea, which has released us from the packman and helped us to get value for money.'[45]

Despite these approving voices, controversy continued to stalk the check trader. In 1938, the *Daily Express* claimed that annual profits of up to 1,700 per cent were made at the combined expense of retailers

[40] *Daily Mail*, 23 April 1908.
[41] *Credit Draper*, 13 June 1908.
[42] *Daily Mail*, 4 April 1908.
[43] Ibid., 29 April 1908.
[44] Florence Bell, *At the works: a study of a manufacturing town* (London: Virago, 1985), 71.
[45] *Daily Mail*, 29 April 1908.

and consumers. In reality, Provident's profits were just under 5 per cent of annual turnover. In 1934 a turnover of £5,729,463 produced profits of £284,751.[46] The cost of home collection and administration absorbed the vast majority of what the *Daily Express* assumed to be profit. The newspaper reported that retailers who did not accept checks were demanding 'that the activities of the check trading companies should be rigorously curtailed [and] that they be subjected to the Moneylenders Act of 1927'. That legislation cited annual interest rates over 48 per cent as 'harsh and unconscionable', unless demonstrated otherwise in the courts. Retailers' organizations were reportedly threatening to boycott manufacturers supplying those who accepted checks and had issued the public 'with leaflets exposing the check system'.[47]

That large sections of the public continued to ignore such advice is indicated by the growth of check trading. The system allowed users a greater flexibility in planning expenditure, and the potential to locate the keenest prices. If a customer repaid the cost of a check in the minimum twenty-week period the cost of credit was approximately 23.3 per cent APR, less than half the ceiling set by the Moneylenders Act.[48] Interest rates were reduced if the customer took the average twenty-four weeks to repay the check trader.[49] In any case, although check trading might have been viewed as a substitute for moneylending, the relationship with the customer differed: it was based on the sale of an item (the check) and not cash loans. Users were aware that there were extra costs associated with checks, although they calculated them imprecisely. They were encouraged to think in terms of their 'membership' of 'check clubs', which, together with the routine payment of a fixed weekly sum, served to mask the use of credit and the customer's indebtedness to the company. There was simply the prospect of paying something akin to 'cash prices' in return for a small collection charge. As one Belfast man put it: 'all you paid on these Provident checks was one shilling to the pound—five percent—so they weren't too bad, they weren't really extortive. But probably the shops who took the Provident checks were dearer to shop in than the shops that didn't.'[50] Unlike hire purchase,

[46] PFG/01/105: Shareholders meeting minutes, 23 April 1934.

[47] *Daily Express*, 27 August 1938, 25 August 1938.

[48] Committee on Consumer Credit, *Report*, 584.

[49] PFG/01/067 *Memorandum upon Miss Ellen Wilkinson's Hire Purchase Bill;* London, National Archive: BT 250/37, National Check Traders Federation.

[50] Interview with Johnny (born 1930. Retired docker. Father of four. Roman Catholic. Interviewed 15 April 2001).

there were no added interest costs for late payment and items bought by checks could not be repossessed. Taylor has charted the highly shameful symbolic ritual associated with the repossession of goods by hire purchase suppliers in 1930s Newcastle.[51] The experience was no less painful for Joan from Belfast, who failed to make her hire purchase payments in the 1980s: 'I was so ashamed, it was awful. I didn't want to be in the house when they came, but obviously me husband wasn't going to take responsibility for it . . . I wished they'd have come at night time to take it, but they didn't, they came during the day.'[52] This added to the attraction of checks for those who used them for higher priced items that might otherwise have been secured via hire purchase.

As with other credit providers employing personalized collection methods check traders had to present an empathetic persona when dealing with cases of ill-health, unemployment, or industrial action. In 1929, one Provident executive wrote that such cases 'are normal trade risks, and the only course open is to encourage payment of a small amount from such sources as unemployment pay, until employment is once more obtained'.[53] The company was hit hard by the miners' strike and General Strike of 1926; a sharp decline in the average overall value of checks sold continued into 1927 and 1928. Turnover diminished by an average 0.5 per cent per annum in these years.[54] A Provident report in 1931 noted that in the wake of 'the strike of 1926 the North and Midlands were at once in a sad plight'.[55] The strike was described as an 'economic blizzard' that bankrupted many smaller check traders because the smaller discounts they commanded from retailers meant they were less cushioned than their larger rivals.[56]

More mundane calls on family budgets explain why the average repayment time for checks was 24 rather than 20 weeks, suggesting

[51] Avram Taylor, '"Funny money", hidden charges and repossession: working-class experiences of consumption and credit in the inter-war years', in J. Benson and L. Ugolini (eds.), *Cultures of selling: perspectives on consumption and society since 1700* (Aldershot: Ashgate, 2006), 164.

[52] Interview with Joan (born 1960. Mature student, care home worker, and mother of three. First husband a labourer; current husband a taxi driver. Protestant. Interviewed 10 April 2003).

[53] PFG/03/156: Check and credit trade typescript for publication by H. Webb (1929), 11.

[54] Sean O'Connell and Chris Reid, 'Working class consumer credit in the UK, 1925–1960: the role of check trading', *Economic History Review*, 58 (2005), 386.

[55] PFG: uncatalogued document, *Report on the general situation and sundry suggestions*, 14 December 1931.

[56] *Credit Trader*, 23 August 1947.

that customers had some ability to exploit the reciprocity embedded in the relationship with their agent. One former agent recalled that many customers did not pay him in advance of holidays. In the lead-up to 'an August Bank Holiday', he found that 'half the people wouldn't pay you . . . they said "Oh, it's the holiday week . . . we want the extra money to spend." '[57] Writing in 1957, a journalist recalled his Lambeth boyhood and the methods used by his mother and others to excuse themselves from paying their check trade collector. As the agent knew 'something of human nature' and sympathized 'to an extent with his clients' problems', he 'almost invariably' took 'such rationalisations in good grace, for he knew if a person had not got the money, then he or she could not pay'. However, 'he could be really nasty' if 'he thought a client was wilfully misleading him and making no effort at all to pay'. In these cases 'slanderous remarks' were shouted, 'so that all the neighbours could hear'.[58]

Such incidents do not appear to have markedly affected the popularity of checks. The interwar period witnessed rapid expansion at Provident. It dealt with approximately 680,000 customers during 1925, when its turnover of £5 million was five times its level in 1910.[59] Customer numbers reached a highpoint of around 1.1 million in the middle and late 1930s. The routine nature of the check system is demonstrated by the fact that there was relatively little seasonal deviation in customer demand in the interwar period, with only a modest increase in the fourth quarter as Christmas loomed. Although Provident's customer numbers expanded between the wars, the average value of credit advanced to each customer fell in nominal terms from £18.61 per annum in 1925 to less than £14.74 in 1933, before recovering slightly to £16.37 in 1939.[60] These figures reflect a combination of factors. One of these was the growth of competition, particularly from the growing mail order catalogue sector. Provident's strong presence in many localities where the staple industries predominated was a further issue, exposing it to economic problems. Its efforts to extend into the English South and Midlands were an attempt to offset this, by diversifying its customer base.

The success of this diversification indicates that the check was deemed a useful financial tool by many early twentieth-century consumers. The Tyneside interviewees featured in Taylor's study felt that Provident

[57] Nottingham Local Studies, Interview with Bert Tansley.

[58] *The Times*, 25 January 1957.

[59] PFG/04/051: Summary of returns.

[60] O'Connell and Reid, 'Working class consumer credit', 389.

checks were the best form of credit available to them during the 1930s. One said: 'when the Provident came onto the scene it was ideal. That's how I brought up my family, with the help of the Provident.'[61] Melanie Tebbutt believes that greater acceptance of credit amongst interwar consumers forced retailers to grudgingly adopt instalment methods.[62] The complex mix of reactions to the growth of the check trade certainly supports her hypothesis. Despite the hidden costs associated with the check system, it was more empowering for working-class consumers than many of the commercial alternatives, particularly the tallyman. Shoppers were attracted particularly by the flexibility offered by checks, in a period when few other working-class credit channels offered such portability. Thus the sector finished the 1930s in a comparatively strong position. However, in the next two decades it was to face new challenges—brought on by war, growing competition, and affluence—that halted the check trades' advance.

'THE FECKLESS AND OFTEN THE STUPID POOR'? CHECK TRADING 1939–1962

Check traders experienced a bumpy ride during the Second World War, when they faced their first serious brush with government regulation. The imposition of purchase tax and price controls on utility goods led retailers to secure a reduction in discounts agreed with check traders, with the average amount falling from 17 to 12.5 per cent.[63] In February 1941, check traders responded by asking customers to pay a poundage charge of 1s 6d rather than 1s.[64] Their timing was inauspicious, as the sector was about to be subjected to a strong critique by the influential Women's Group on Public Welfare. Its study, *Our towns*, contained damaging sections on check trading that were made available to the Board of Trade before publication. One section explored 'wasteful spending' by that section of the working class 'whose economy is built on "tick" and who', it argued, 'have little idea of facing the hard discipline of "managing"'. It bracketed 'inferior types of clothing club' with burial insurance, football pools, excessive expenditure on drink and tobacco, pawning and using moneylenders, and 'extravagant hire-purchase arrangements'. In contrast, the report

[61] Taylor, '"Funny money"', 170.
[62] Tebbutt, *Making ends meet*, 170.
[63] *Credit Trader*, 27 February 1943.
[64] PFG/01/068: Poundage file.

cited the mutuality clubs operated by the co-operative movement as an alternative where it 'was difficult to see any drawbacks'.[65] These also charged a shilling in the pound collection fee, but any purchase made contributed to the quarterly dividends received by co-operative members. However, the report did not reveal that the mutuality clubs only extended credit to co-operators with healthy financial balances with their store, which excluded large numbers of poorer consumers.[66] Check traders also offered a mobility that the mutuality schemes did not. One Glaswegian woman recalled that this 'was a big advantage . . . it wasnae a case of one shop', the 'Co-op, they gave you 20 weeks or 38 weeks but then you only had the Co-op, whereas the Provident gave you a selection of different shops . . . you could spend it in Paisley and you could spend it in Glasgow, it wasnae as if you were constricted.'[67]

Our towns provided ammunition for the Board of Trade, at a time when it was seeking to control consumer spending. One internal memorandum drew on the report to refer to the 'wickedness of check trading'. It argued that customers paid 'heavily for the credit they are given and for the services of the agent', and that they were 'often fleeced by shops'.[68] The Board of Trade prohibited the poundage charge in 1941 and, despite legal challenges, it remained outlawed until 1949.[69] Its prohibition contributed to a drop in Provident customers; numbers slumped to 535,000 in 1944. Members of the public who lobbied the Board of Trade on the poundage issue were dismissed. One letter, from Mrs Othen of Poole praising check trading, was described as the 'third stock letter sent'.[70] Customers were clearly encouraged to lobby government: an organized petition in Leeds, for example, collected

[65] Women's Group on Public Welfare, *Our towns, close-up: a study made in 1939–42 with certain recommendations* (London: Oxford University Press, 1943), 10; Appendix VII.

[66] NA: BT 64/85, *Orders prohibiting poundage charges by check traders*. Representations by Newcastle and Tyneside chamber of trader.

[67] Interview with Mrs A, cited in Adam Gibson, 'Patterns of demand for working-class credit: the case of check trading 1918–1970', unpublished undergraduate project (Glasgow, 1999).

[68] NA: BT 64/81 *Credit and check trading: report by the War-time Social Survey on investigations into credit buying*.

[69] NA: BT64/81 Goods and Services (Price control). Parliamentary Secretary's Committee, Report by Sub-Committee on Hire Purchase. *Hire Purchase and Credit Sale Agreements* (Control) Order (S.R. and O. 1943, No. 321).

[70] NA: BT64/85 Check Trading. *Appeal by housewife in connection with Order prohibiting poundage charges by Check Traders*, 1942.

30,000 signatures.[71] However, with the system serving as many as 1.8 million regular patrons, the concerns from Mrs Othen, and others, were not entirely manufactured.[72] Her disquiet was too easily dismissed because the price she paid for credit did not equate with ideas of rational consumption held by civil servants, and the Women's Group on Public Welfare. But, as we have seen, check trading was valued by many consumers who viewed it as the best credit option available to them. Customer reaction to the poundage ban may also have been influenced by the understanding that this payment represented the agent's wage, and many subsequently agreed to compensate agents directly for their collections during the prohibition of poundage.[73]

As was the case with the credit traders, high wartime wages helped keep check traders afloat despite falling customer numbers. Between 1940 and 1944 the rise in value on the average check was more than double the increase in weekly wage earnings, and it was equal to it between 1945 and 1949.[74] One explanation for this is that many customers invested wartime cash surpluses in checks, in anticipation of future purchasing requirements. Checks could be kept to hand, along with the appropriate coupons, to quickly purchase any item in short supply that might appear in a store in the scheme, or be set aside for post-war requirements. Whilst this theory must remain in the realm of conjecture, it suggests an element of rationality amongst check users that was denied them in the *Our towns* study.

Although Provident's customer numbers returned to their pre-war levels of just over one million in 1951, growth was more sluggish thereafter and it stalled in the late 1950s. Data from the company's archives also reveals that demand for checks became more seasonal in the late 1950s, with customer numbers rising by between 80,000 and 100,000 from the third to the fourth quarter. The average value of checks taken out grew at a substantially slower rate than average earnings during the 1950s, rising barely at all between 1955 and 1959.[75] This suggests that for increasing numbers of customers, checks were becoming less a part of their weekly routine and more of an additional option, at Christmas.

[71] *Credit Trader*, 12 September 1942.

[72] This figure is calculated on the 1.1m regular Provident customers in 1939 plus the regularly expressed view that other companies had a market that was two-thirds that size.

[73] *New Dawn* (official organ of the National Union of Distributors and Allied Workers), May 1946.

[74] O'Connell and Reid, 'Working class consumer credit', 387.

[75] Ibid. 389.

The check traders did, however, continue to report their successes in keeping levels of bad debt at minimal levels. In the mid-1930s Provident claimed levels of just 0.75 per cent, and thirty years later the Economist Intelligence Unit reported similar levels for the entire sector.[76] It is likely that paying the 'Provy' was a higher priority for the financially pressed housewife than paying either its check trading rivals or the credit trader, because being blacklisted by the company closed a greater number of shop doors. The effective use of agents to assess creditworthiness, police borrowing, and establish long-standing personal and lucrative relationships with customers also kept debt low; as did the fact that many check customers struggled to access other forms of credit. In 1981 Compass Paget Limited, of Sheffield, outlined both points. It explained that a significant number of customers 'might not be accepted as creditworthy by other credit systems that do not follow Paget's method of careful control and weekly collection'. This imposed 'a discipline that enables many customers to keep their account up-to-date and keep their credit-worthy status when they might find difficulty in doing so under a less controlled system'.[77] By proudly declaring their low levels of bad debt, check traders were—like other creditors who dealt with the working classes—involved in an exercise designed to head off critiques about indebtedness. Bad debt was effectively that proportion of business that the companies had entirely written off. Alongside that were many slow payers of various types, whose experience of check trading was often uncomfortable. For these customers, the agent's disciplinary function became transparent. Agents were instructed to place 'extensive pressure' on slow payers.[78] Tardy payers who became non-payers might receive a visit from a branch manager, and legal action was often threatened even though the threat was seldom carried forward.[79] In 1964, the Economist Intelligence Unit noted that informal pressure was preferred to the use of county courts.[80] The manager's appearance marked a break with routine, and was calculated to elicit a more deferential response from customers who were confronted by an unfamiliar individual, whose

[76] PFG/01/105, Shareholders' meeting minutes, 23 April 1934; Economist Intelligence Unit, 'Check trading', 44.

[77] Monopolies and Mergers Commission, *Great Universal Stores PLC and Empire Stores (Bradford) PLC: a report on the proposed mergers* (London: HMSO, 1983), 49.

[78] PFG/01/156: Check and credit trade typescript, for publication by H. Webb (1929), 79.

[79] Taylor, *Working class credit*, 156.

[80] Economist Intelligence Unit, 'Check trading', 44.

presence signalled a change in their relationship with the company. It formed part of the debt collection sequence, described by sociologist Paul Rock as 'a progress into controlled unpleasantness'.[81] The agency system afforded check traders the opportunity to make frequent calls aimed at recovering debt over an extended period. If this failed they would, as Provident's biggest rival Cattles explained in 1981, put the 'most important cases' in the hands of collection agencies or solicitors, and take a small number of cases to courts.[82]

Checks continued to be used by a variety of individuals in the 1950s and 1960s. One survey of 1960s London found that 'affluent' workers with large families were still buying most clothing with checks.[83] But income and family size were not the only factors. Ethel, who had grown up as one of two children in the interwar Rhonda Valley, was a Belfast mother of eight in the early 1960s. Despite her husband's skilled job as an aircraft fitter, she reluctantly made use of checks 'when we were really hard pushed'. Her upbringing had been 'grounded in don't have it if you can't afford it . . . but there was times when you had to do things that you didn't want to do, it went against the grain, but you had to do it'. Looming in the background of her narrative was the stereotype of the bad manager. She was keen to point out that she faced tougher circumstances, and 'a different way of life', than her mother: 'there were only two of us—whereas there were eight of mine'. Ethel felt that had her marital home been in the Rhonda she 'could have gone to mother or even sometimes your Aunts for help. But, I had nobody here [in Belfast].' A further important factor was that Ethel's husband did not hand over an unopened pay packet to her: 'I used to think it odd, because my father always came home and handed his pay packet intact, nothing taken out. But it's different here—every man gives their wife housekeeping money and sometimes, I suppose it was adequate, sometimes it wasn't.' Her husband may well have portrayed his behaviour as a Belfast tradition, but, in contrast to Ethel, many Belfast housewives received an unopened pay packet.[84]

The Economist Intelligence Unit also discovered families with comparatively high incomes 'who could well afford to pay cash' using checks

[81] Paul Rock, *Making people pay* (London: Routledge and Kegan Paul, 1973), 64.

[82] Monopolies and Mergers Commission, *Great Universal Stores*.

[83] Hilary Land, *Large families in London: a study of 86 families* (London: Bell, 1969), 50.

[84] Interview with Ethel (born 1920. Widow and mother of eight. Husband was an aircraft fitter. Protestant).

and paying in instalments, in order 'to maintain a high level of cash in hand from the weekly wage'.[85] Many such families may have been habitual check users, conditioned by a process of 'routinisation', as described by Taylor. A lengthy personal relationship with their agent and the creation of gifting and obligation, established through the credit nexus, helps explain the prolonged use of checks by some. Surveys have also indicated the propensity of low-income consumers to utilize forms of credit they have seen used by family members.[86] Joan, from Belfast, began using Provident checks in the 1980s after she was introduced to them by her mother-in-law. Doris, who was thirty years older, recalled using the same check agent as her mother 'year after year, till he died, the poor man died'. At this point, 'they sent a girl but by then I was able to manage better you know? My family had grown up.' The termination of the relationship with her long-term agent may have been at least as significant as her changing family circumstances, as his departure removed a cross-generational sense of obligation from the family.[87]

For those dealing with financial emergencies, checks could be used to buy merchandise that was immediately pawned to raise cash. This practice embarrassed the check traders. On other occasions, the agent, or others, bought the check from a customer, at a discount. A notorious example was rehearsed in a West Hartlepool courtroom in 1953, and led to it being dubbed 'tick town' by journalist Keith Waterhouse. He described it as a 'fantastic town' where seven out of ten people live on credit and 'pink vouchers that are the legal tender'.[88] In the week in which the local Odeon screened Glen Ford in *Lust for gold*, three women were charged with offences against the Check Trading Control Order of 1948. They were implicated in the 'wholesale illicit trading in Trading Checks . . . taking place at West Hartlepool and suburbs', buying checks, at a discount, either for their own use or to sell them on. A £1 check was typically purchased for fifteen shillings and resold for sixteen. The case had emerged after a local independent check trader reported sixteen women. Police enquiries revealed that one woman had committed suicide, having become heavily indebted by the process. A police report stated that the 'illicit traffickers were making a very

[85] Economist Intelligence Unit, 'Check trading', 44–5.

[86] Janet Ford, *Consuming credit: debt and poverty in the UK* (London: Child Poverty Action Group, 1991), 38.

[87] Interview with Joan. Interview with Doris (born 1934. A retired cleaner. Husband was a labourer. Protestant. Interviewed 24 March 2003).

[88] *Daily Mirror*, 6 March 1953.

profitable business and living in luxury by bleeding women who could ill afford to re-pay the check traders weekly for checks they receive'. An officer who had visited the homes of some of the women who had sold checks was shocked at the poverty he found and believed that 'the slavery of debt' had prevented an improvement in their home conditions. They were said to be involved in a cycle of check buying, without their husband's knowledge, in an attempt to pay off previous debts. One of those involved in the trafficking, Mrs Hartley, a widow aged 51, claimed that she had been approached and persuaded to buy the checks by customers who 'wanted to go to Blackpool' or were 'in difficulties over the payment of a particular debt'. Police had observed 'women queuing outside Mrs Hartley's house either to sell or buy checks from her'. She maintained that she was of assistance to these women. Her co-accused Mrs Hurst admitted that she had been involved in the activity for twelve years and did not know that it had been prohibited. Both Hurst and Hartley were said to be well known throughout West Hartlepool as women who would buy and sell checks. All three received fines.[89] It appears that there was a ready market for second-hand checks in the town at this time. Speaking fifty years later, Dorothy, the wife of a retired second-hand car dealer, recalled how the system worked from the perspective of some of the town's more affluent residents. Dorothy was one of the recipients of the second-hand checks. When using them at one of the local department stores, she always made sure that the shop assistant knew that she had acquired the check at a knock-down rate—rather than out of necessity—to ensure that her status did not dip in their eyes. Dorothy's daughter added: 'If you were offered a club [check] and did not need it, you still took it if you had the cash because there would be someone in the family, or circle of acquaintances, saving for something, who could use it. And so you passed it on, at cost, and the favour would be returned. I can recall using them without ever actually understanding the background to them.'[90]

Concern about the Hartlepool incident led the Board of Trade to launch a wider investigation. The NFCT believed that the case was due to the unusually large numbers of non-affiliated small check traders in Hartlepool, together with the nature of the town's port

[89] *Northern Daily Mail*, 27 February 1953; NA: BT 258/172. *Control of check trading Order 1948: evidence of contravention of the Order by those trafficking in checks.*

[90] Interview with Dorothy (born 1923. Mother of two. Husband a retired second-hand car salesman. Interviewed 10 May 2001). Interview with Dianne (born 1954. Lecturer. Interviewed 10 May 2001).

economy. NFCT members had access to national and local blacklists of the non-creditworthy and it maintained that 'the backbone of check trading' was 'the respectable working class and not the feckless poor'.[91] The NFCT's President had argued earlier that the difficulties endured during the 'no poundage' period had produced 'a cleaner and more respectable check trade'.[92] This view was largely borne out by investigations into the sector. They indicated that the resale of checks was not unheard of in other areas, particularly North-East England, but that it appeared to be a declining phenomenon. In Stoke, for example, it had been prevalent in the 1930s, but had become less so. It was still not unknown, however, in Belfast and Birmingham as late as the 1980s.[93]

Although the resale of checks was a minority practice that was in decline, the West Hartlepool investigation was one of those moments that reactivated moralized views on the use of doorstep credit. Stupidity, rather than necessity, was often seen to be the driving force behind its use, as is indicated by the view of check customers held by one civil servant. He described them as 'the feckless and often the stupid poor'.[94] Material factors, such as family size, economic misfortune, or limited alternative credit channels, had little place in such a world-view. The West Hartlepool case caused embarrassment at the Board of Trade and the Home Office, with both departments suggesting that the other should oversee check trading. The Home Office already had responsibility for moneylending and pawnbroking, and had no wish to extend its duties. The issue arose at a difficult juncture because the remaining controls on check trading, including one setting a maximum poundage charge, were about to be lifted. One civil servant noted that their object 'has always been predominantly social—to control check traders' charges so as to prevent them taking too much money out of the poor—rather than as a support to price control'.[95] The NFCT told the Board of Trade that many members would be happy to keep the

[91] NA/PRO, BT 258/172, *Control of check trading Order 1948: evidence of contravention of the Order by those trafficking in checks.* Minutes of meeting with National Federation of Check Traders, 10 September 1953.

[92] *Credit Trader,* 12 April 1952.

[93] NA: BT 258/172, *Control of check trading Order 1948:* evidence of contravention of the Order by those trafficking in checks. Summary of information from Chief Constables; interview with Joan; Gillian Parker, *Getting and spending: credit and debt in Britain* (Aldershot: Avebury, 1990), 33.

[94] NA: BT 258/172, *Control of check trading Order 1948.* Memo by G. H. Andrew, 12 December 1952.

[95] NA: BT 258/17, *Control of check trading Order 1948.*

controls, to prevent bad practice. It was also mindful of a renewal of press criticism about high costs.[96] Thus, like the tallyman before them, check traders were keen to engage in a process of status passage that brought higher social standing to the trade. In the 1960s, the sector began a move to shed itself of the 'clothing and supply image', as it attempted to disrobe itself of its connections with necessitous consumption and engage with affluence.

TRYING TO LOSE 'THE CLOTHING AND SUPPLY IMAGE': RESPONDING TO THE AFFLUENT SOCIETY

The most pressing problem check traders encountered in the post-war years was not dealing with embarrassing scandals associated with some of the more desperate check users. Instead, they faced twin challenges emanating from increasing spending power and growing competition, particularly from mail order. However, the sector received an unexpected fillip as a result of government economic policy. In 1952 the first in a series of Hire Purchase and Credit Sale Agreement (Control) Orders focused sharply on credit controls. The first Order instigated a compulsory one-third deposit, and a maximum repayment period of eighteen months, on a range of consumer goods. Terms control, as it became known, was in force between 1952 and July 1954, then again from February 1955 to October 1958, and once more from April 1960 until September 1971. Further credit controls operated between 1973 and 1982 when they were finally removed from the government's economic armoury.[97] The merchandise covered by the controls was very much extended in 1955, at which point 'all consumer durables on which extended credit was normally advanced' were included, from motor cars to household furniture and electrical goods. Additional measures were taken to deal with what the Board of Trade described as 'bogus rental schemes' that had been established in an attempt to evade the controls. Most significant was the Control of Hiring Order of February 1956, which included the requirement

96 Ibid. Evidence from National Federation of Check Traders.

97 NA: BT 250/14, Committee on Consumer Credit. Hire purchase controls. Note by the Board of Trade and Treasury; Richard Berthoud and Elaine Kempson, *Credit and debt: the PSI report* (London: Policy Studies Institute, 1992), 44–5.

that consumers pay nine months' rental in advance before receiving a rented television.[98] These requirements remained in place until 1970. Consumers involved in deals that broke the terms of these controls risked prosecution, alongside the retailers or finance houses involved. The impact of the controls tended to be marked, at least in the short term. One of the leading credit reference agencies found that the number of enquiries it received from clients about the credit history of individual consumers fell 'by up to 50 per cent overnight' in the wake of their reimposition.[99] In 1968, the Board of Trade agreed that credit controls generally had had an immediate impact on the markets, but admitted that their long-term effects were less readily identifiable.[100]

A further effect was to provide opportunities for check traders to engage with new areas of consumption, by developing a product that was not subject to terms control. The sector introduced vouchers, with higher values than checks. Provident introduced them in 1962. They assisted the purchase of more expensive consumer durables. Initially they were for sums of up to £100, rising to £200 by 1970. The collection charges for vouchers were between 7.5 and 15 per cent of their value, and they were repaid over 40- to 100-week periods.[101] The larger value vouchers became a means by which consumers and retailers could sidestep terms control. The Treasury described this development as 'a serious gap in credit controls at those times when it is needed'. It also drew in companies described as 'refugees from hire-purchase' and added to the rising complexity of the consumer credit market that led to the establishment of the Crowther Committee on Consumer Credit in 1968.[102] GUS and Philips Electrical were amongst companies who became involved in voucher trading.[103] Thus, in a period of rising affluence, a much maligned credit method secured an unlikely second wind. By 1966, £25 million worth of business was being done by clothing and footwear retailers and department stores, offering their

[98] NA: BT 240/14, Hire Purchase controls; *The Times*, 28 July 1958.

[99] C. McNeil Greig, *The growth of credit information: a history of UAPT-Infolink plc* (Blackwell: London, 1992), 206.

[100] NA: BT 250/14. Hire purchase controls.

[101] Economist Intelligence Unit, 'Check Trading', 47: NA: BT 250/37, National Check Traders Federation. Evidence to the Committee on consumer credit.

[102] NA: BT 258/2544 Hire Purchase, Avoidance of HP restriction by check trading and personal loans schemes. Memo by E. L. K. Sinclair, 22 December 1966; Committee on Consumer Credit, *Report*, 75.

[103] *Credit Trader*, 2 May 1970.

own checks and vouchers.[104] For Provident, vouchers opened the door to agreements with a number of major retailers. British Home Stores, Foster Menswear, Halfords, Woolworth, Rumbelows Ltd, H. Samuel Ltd, John Collier, Burtons, Hepworths Ltd, Boots, W. H. Smith, and Debenhams were amongst names on Provident's list by the early 1970s.[105] It was reported that 'customers using vouchers do not do so instead of checks, but in addition, since the two are used to fund essentially different types of purchase'.[106]

The boost that vouchers brought to check trading led to the emergence of the first serious rival to Provident. Numerous imitators had followed its lead in the early twentieth century, when many small companies were established across Yorkshire and Lancashire by an assortment of former mill hands, insurance collectors, or ex-Provident employees. These included the Practical Clothing and Supply Company Limited. Founded in St Helens in 1910, it had 63 branches, 324 staff, and an annual turnover of £7m by the early 1970s.[107] The vast majority of businesses remained modest in scale, often being run by a single owner-collector. In 1964, a third of NFCT members had an annual turnover below £5,000.[108]

But in the 1960s, a significant competitor emerged. It originated in 1927 under the direction of Joseph R. Cattle, as the Hull Clothing and Supply Company Limited, and traded as a draper and gentlemen's outfitter. In 1966, as Cattle's (Holdings) Limited, it began an aggressive geographical expansion, taking control of Leeds-based Crescent Premier Supply Co. Ltd. This was the first in a series of acquisitions of established check trading companies.[109] Easy Purchase Services Limited of Sheffield (1968) and Grimbsy Supply Co. Ltd (1969) followed. In 1970 all check trading activities were rationalized as Shopacheck Limited, which had agreements with 2,500 retail outlets. By 1973, Cattles had added the National Clothing & Supply Co. Ltd of Wolverhampton, the Equitable Clothing & General Supply Co. Ltd, of Bradford, the Progressive Group (based in Derby), and the Caledonian Group (based

104 Committee on Consumer Credit, *Report*, 432.

105 PFG/04/076, Provident shopping guide, Southampton-Hythe, 1974.

106 *Investors Review*, 7 September 1973.

107 *Daily Mail*, 16 April 1908. London: PFG/03/007 *Colonnade*, May 1971. Dun and Bradstreet Ltd, *Guide to key British enterprises* (London: Dun and Bradstreet, 7th edn., 1973).

108 Economist Intelligence Unit, 'Check trading', 46.

109 PFG/5/43, Cattle's (Holdings) Limited, Chairman's statement 31 March 1967.

in Glasgow and Northern Ireland) to its portfolio. Its sights were 'firmly fixed on a national network of check trading branch offices coupled with complementary services', including motor insurance sold through checks.[110] Between 1968 and 1980 its turnover rose from £1.7 to £64 million and it had secured a 10.4 per cent share of the check/voucher sector, compared to Provident's 65.7 per cent.[111]

Following a move into public ownership in 1962, Provident also went through a period of reorganization and diversification under a new team of executives with experience in other areas of consumer credit. These included Richard Davenport, who had gained hire purchase expertise at Bowmaker and Lombard Banking, and Alan Edgar, a marketing specialist from Littlewoods Mail Order. Davenport was struck by the access Provident had to customers' homes via its 10,000 agents, remarking: 'Who on earth else had that sort of lever?' Initiatives were taken to exploit this relationship further: the new management felt that Provident was still seen as a means through which 'to buy coal and shoes' and that it was time for modernization. Edgar revamped the company's image, improving marketing and communications with both staff and customers. Promotional literature was rethought and redesigned. A newspaper, *Colonnade*, was launched as the means through which to provide agents with information and a marketing magazine, *Arcade*, which resembled a mail order catalogue, was circulated to customers. Television advertisements were used to introduce the Provident to potential new customers.[112] This was an attempt to update its traditional socially embedded agency network, borrowing from an approach that had proved successful at Littlewoods. Provident's objective was to accompany some of its traditional customers into a more affluent world.

Three in four check trade agents were female by the late 1950s, representing a further parallel with mail order where nine in ten agents were women.[113] Feminization of mail order agency networks, which began in the 1930s, paid dividends to the companies involved because part-time female agents demonstrated greater interest in the

[110] PFG/5/43, Cattle's (Holdings) Limited, 1970.

[111] Monopolies and Mergers Commission, *Trading check franchise and financial services: a report into the supply of trading checks in the United Kingdom* (London: HMSO, 1981), 37, 87.

[112] PFG/03/007, *Colonnade* 90th anniversary issue.

[113] NA: IR 40/16045, *Income tax treatment of check trading in credit industry,* B250/66 Provident Clothing and Supply Company Ltd., 1968–1971.

social aspect of the job, which facilitated higher levels of customer satisfaction.[114] Check traders appear to have reaped a similar harvest from female agents. Full-time male collectors on Tyneside 'had to work harder to build up a relationship as they would not usually have an existing connection with their customers'. According to Taylor, they were driven by financial motivations, whereas 'the social interaction that goes with the job has an entirely different meaning' for part-time agents.[115] Provident also believed that female agents possessed budgeting knowledge and 'a native ability to appraise the creditworthiness of the men and women around them'.[116] A related factor was that the post-war decline in industrial insurance reduced economic opportunities for the more financially motivated agents, reducing numbers of male agents.[117]

Provident's overhaul produced success over the course of the following decade when it achieved a steady growth in profits that was 'increasingly vertical'. An annual profit of £1.25 million in 1962 rose to £3 million in 1968, £4.25 million in 1971, and almost £7 million by 1972.[118] It further extended its branch networks, from 340 in 1962 to 600 by 1972. This growth was assisted by the acquisition of Practical Credit Services Limited and Bristol Clothing and Supply Company Limited, giving it greater coverage of Wales and the West of England and raising customer numbers to 1.5 million. The renewed business and increased clientele brought by the introduction of vouchers convinced check traders that the sector could shift further upmarket. The Provident's Davenport declared, in 1972, that it wished to stick 'firmly to the C1/C2 market'. The company envisaged an expansion to meet both the saving and borrowing requirements of these groups and noted that half the population remained without bank accounts. Provident purchased the People's Bank in 1971 and Davenport felt that the company could compete with the Trustee Savings Bank, offering interest on savings accounts and cheque books to customers. It intended to operate the People's Bank from the 600 local offices that co-ordinated Provident's army of agents. The offices could be enlarged or 'even moved to better sites than they have at the moment', although Davenport did not anticipate a 'marble halls' approach'. Overall, the policy was to 'move

[114] See Chapter 3. [115] Taylor, *Working class credit*, 155.

[116] PFG/01/044: Annual Report, 1963.

[117] Nottingham Local Studies: Interview with Bert Tansley; Dennett, *A sense of security*, 310.

[118] Investors' Review, 7 September 1973.

away from the Clothing and Supply image more and more into the People's Bank'.[119]

However, the fillip given to the check trade by the introduction of vouchers proved short-lived. By the mid-1970s, it was clear that the sector was struggling to remain buoyant in uneven economic seas. Provident's individual problems were exacerbated by large financial losses incurred by a senior employee's 'unauthorised' trading in hedge funds.[120] Its check customer numbers fell by a third, from their peak of 1.5 million in 1968 to one million in 1975. By 1979, one million represented the combined check customer figure for Provident, Cattles, and the third largest company, Sheffield-based Compass Paget Ltd.[121] An internal Provident survey, from 1975, recorded the company's concern at the loss of some of its key customer groups. Those turning their backs on check trading were most commonly under 25, were more likely to be owner-occupiers, and to have higher usage rates of retail credit and credit cards than retained customers.[122] The Monopolies and Mergers Commission (MMC) calculated that the total check and voucher business had declined in real terms, to a third of its 1971 level by the decade's end.[123] Its 1978 survey of check customers—together with internal Provident market research from 1975—represent the most detailed insight available into users, as the sector did not receive the sort of regular attention given to the flourishing mail order sector.

Only 8 per cent of those in the MMC survey of check/voucher users were from the A/B/C1 groups (the professional, managerial, and white collar occupational groups). Those from the C2 (skilled manual workers), D (semi-skilled manual workers) and E (unskilled workers, the unemployed, and pensioners), categories represented 36, 33, and 23 per cent respectively. When these figures are compared to the latter three groups' representation in the general population, which was 32, 22, and 9 per cent, they paint a plebeian portrait of users. Voucher use predominated amongst the younger and higher-status social groups captured in the survey.[124] Those with young families were most heavily represented. Of those interviewed 41 per cent

[119] *Evening Standard*, 20 May 1972.
[120] PFG/03/007: *Colonnade*, September 1974.
[121] Monopolies and Mergers Commission, *Trading check franchise*, 46.
[122] PFG, Provident customer survey 1975.
[123] Monopolies and Mergers Commission, *Trading check franchise*, 88.
[124] Ibid. 59.

were under 34, and Provident told the MMC that the majority of its customers had at least one child under 16.[125] This factor was made apparent by the list of items checks were used for, which was topped by children's clothing mentioned by 59 per cent of those surveyed.[126] A greater proportion of check clients lived in rented accommodation than the general population, contributing to high customer levels in Scotland where owner-occupation was below the UK average. Provident's own data indicated that 71.3 per cent of customers were council tenants, while 20.3 per cent of its market were owner-occupiers.[127] Mail order was used by 40 per cent of check customers, whilst 41 per cent utilized no other credit method. Hire purchase, bank loans, and retailers' credit were used by 5, 7, and 7 per cent respectively. Approximately 50 per cent of customers held bank accounts, but it appears that nine out of ten customers were paid on a weekly cycle.[128] The major companies instructed their agents that new customers must come from the ranks of the employed, and check traders were also wary of those in privately rented accommodation.[129]

The MMC discovered that many users were not aware of the APR payable on borrowing. Most focused on their weekly payment figure, which was typically below £2. Less than a third of those surveyed identified a disadvantage of using the system, with only 4 per cent described as dissatisfied. This was despite the fact that costs rose appreciably in the 1970s. The poundage charge, by then termed the service charge, had risen from 5 to 15 pence for each pound of credit. This produced typical APRs for a £100 check from Cattles of 77 per cent in 1980, where the nominal repayment period was 25 weeks. It was higher still at Provident (97 per cent) because collections were made over 23 weeks. Compass Paget charged 10 pence over 22 weeks, producing an APR of 55 per cent. The extended repayments for vouchers, which ranged up to 110 weeks, produced lower APRs, varying from 44 to 58 per cent.[130] Check traders argued that APRs were a clumsy system for measuring the small-scale, short-term credit in which they dealt. They also highlighted the costly nature of home collection, which, nonetheless, met with customer approval. Another complaint was that

[125] Ibid. 30. [126] Ibid. 60.
[127] PFG, Provident customer survey 1975.
[128] Monopolies and Mergers Commission, *Trading check franchise*, 58, 30.
[129] Ibid. 27. [130] Ibid. 40, 23, 50, 40, 23.

the APR did not always make the cost of credit transparent, and that mail order companies were able to continue headlining their service as interest free credit, whilst concealing instalment payment costs in the headline prices. The MMC noted the rising APR figures associated with checks, but having compared the check traders' gross profits with those of other finance companies it opined that these were not extortionate.[131]

Increased service charges were blamed on the economic difficulties the check traders faced. These included higher interest rates on their own borrowing, rising staff costs, and diminishing discounts from retailers. Growing reluctance to pay discounts to check traders saw many retailers leave check schemes: Provident maintained agreements with 25,377 retailers in 1973, but only 19,530 by 1979.[132] Even those who remained on the lists expressed little enthusiasm for the system. One ladies fashion retailer, with 164 branches throughout the UK, reported that the proportion of its turnover financed by checks was 23 per cent in certain areas. It considered this aspect of business to be the least 'attractive type of transaction taking place' in its shops, but its removal would mean the withdrawal of its 'representation entirely from some areas'. Provident market research, conducted in 1975, suggested that the falling number of shops available to its customers caused more complaint than rising charges: over half its customers complained about the former, compared with one in six for the latter.[133] Whilst some patrons grumbled that the service was not as flexible as it had been, more affluent customers were beginning to explore more sophisticated financial products. Check traders identified a 'tendency towards monthly as opposed to weekly pay' as a factor in 'the penetration of banking into social groups C2 and D'. The Trustee Savings Bank emerged as a particularly serious threat, increasing its lending from £3 million in 1975 to £166m by 1979. The latter figure was greater than the £141 million checks and vouchers sold that year.[134] Between 1975 and 1978 the proportion of total British personal borrowing made up of checks and vouchers fell from 1.9 to 1.2 per cent.[135] Check trading was becoming increasingly marginal, but its decline did not signal the demise of the major companies involved in the sector.

[131] Monopolies and Mergers Commission, 77–80, 95.
[132] Ibid. 29.
[133] PFG, Provident customer survey 1975.
[134] Monopolies and Mergers Commission, *Trading check franchise*, 6.
[135] Ibid. 6.

CONCLUSION

This chapter demonstrates that check traders' customers, like those of the credit traders, demonstrated either ignorance and myopia or an appreciation of other aspects of what was clearly a costly system. Findings, ranging from the Belfast oral testimony through to the survey of the MMC, indicate that check users had, at best, a vague concept of the true costs of the system, even after the Consumer Credit Act of 1974 forced credit companies to provide more information about them. In any event, the APR attached to a check or voucher transaction could not indicate any costs that the retailer might add at their end of the transaction. This was one of many areas where the calculation of interest rates was incapable of providing transparency for consumers. It is clear that factors such as the number of retailers to which checks or vouchers provided access, weekly collection, and the fact some leeway was granted for missed payments, received higher priority in customers' calculations. The fact that the true costs of using check traders were masked by the complexity involved in the tripartite nature of the system also appears to have deterred the government from interfering. It was described by the Crowther Committee on Consumer Credit as a 'hybrid transaction' that existed in a legal limbo.[136] The Treasury, and the Board of Trade, only became exercised about check trading when it appeared to be operating against their efforts to control consumer credit and consumer demand. This was the case during the Second World War, and in the 1960s, when vouchers became a method for the evasion of hire purchase controls. Their interest in the potential social consequences of check trading was less marked and seems to have been used as a flag of convenience in the 1940s, in an effort to reduce the sale of checks and contribute to the control of consumption. In the long run, it was not government action, or better consumer education, that reduced the economic and social significance of check trading. That was achieved by the increased spending power of the sector's traditional customers, together with the arrival of a range of alternatives to the check trader. As some of those alternatives, such as credit and store cards, proved more attractive to retailers the check traders lost their patronage. However,

136 Committee on Consumer Credit, *Report*, 174.

this only occurred in the 1970s, following check trading's last hurrah, which was brought about by vouchers and the evasion of hire purchase in the 1960s.

As the MMC noted, check traders also benefited from the fact that 'some customers may be unaccustomed to using other forms of credit (except mail order) or may have formed a strong habit . . . reinforced by the visit of the agent'.[137] Higher levels of disposable income in the 1950s and 1960s 'did not go immediately into new forms of thrift—habits developed over many years of low income were not changed over night'.[138] Thus, once again, cultural practices lagged behind economic improvements. The introduction of higher value vouchers at once assisted the continuation of habitual behaviour, and kept the relationship with the agent/company that had provided financial resources when they were thin on the ground. Although the Provident was a much more significant enterprise than the credit traders we observed in the last chapter, it was also unable to continue its traditional business in the face of the multiplying competitors who began dealing with a more affluent working class. As was the case with credit traders, check traders retained a grip on some customers for longer than might have been anticipated. But as the Provident's internal market research demonstrates, like the credit traders, it was losing the 'cream' of its customers by the 1970s. Habit was not 'immutable'.[139] At the outset of the 1970s, the plans of the check trading sector were posited on increasing affluence and diminishing poverty, but they were thwarted. Finding the affluent workers that they had hoped to connect with through new financial products escaping their embrace, check traders found a fresh niche on familiar terrain. By the end of the 1970s, it was apparent that their future was tied up with doorstep moneylending and with customers who were soon to be branded the financially excluded. Close personalized relationships were to remain at the core of this business, but with much higher interest rates. Chapter 5 will deal with the check traders' rebirth as major moneylenders in the last four decades of the twentieth century. Surveying check trading, at the dawn of the Thatcher revolution, the MMC concluded that the sector's profit was not 'excessive', although it was slightly above those of other finance

[137] Monopolies and Mergers Commission, *Trading check franchise*, 94.
[138] Johnson, *Saving and spending*, 215.
[139] Ibid. 215.

companies.[140] As retailers departed check schemes in large numbers, to be replaced by personal loans, the transparent costs to the consumers who were excluded, or excluded themselves, from cheaper financial products were set to become clearer and the level of controversy was set to grow.

140 Monopolies and Mergers Commission, *Trading check franchise*, 95.

3

Retail capitalism in the parlour: mail order catalogues

This chapter examines the position of the mail order catalogue in the working-class family economy, outlining its role as a major source of consumer borrowing. In both its reliance on instalment sales and its use of massive numbers of part-time agents, UK mail order stood apart from its European and North American counterparts for whom price competition and personal shopping were much greater factors.[1] UK catalogue retailing's success was not anticipated by analysts in the 1930s, who were oblivious to the market for credit-based home shopping. They felt that catalogue shopping had gained enormous popularity in North America 'for the obvious reason that distances are greater' and because economies of scale and scope enabled mail order retailers to undercut the prices offered by small town stores. As these possibilities did not present themselves so readily to UK catalogue retailers, it was assumed that mail order would be 'a declining factor in the distributive trade'.[2] By the time this forecast was essayed, a thriving British mail order sector had operated for three decades and was about to enter a further period of rapid expansion. It will be demonstrated here that catalogues had a significant function as a conduit for an enormous volume of consumer credit. In addition, the formats catalogue retailers devised to extend instalment sales to millions of consumers were highly instrumental in eroding both pragmatic and moral barriers against consumer borrowing in general.

[1] For a detailed analysis of this see Richard Coopey, Sean O'Connell, and Dilwyn Porter, *Mail order retailing in Britain: a business and social history* (Oxford: Oxford University Press, 2005), Introduction.

[2] D. Braithwaite and S. P. Dobbs, *The distribution of consumer goods* (London: George Allen and Unwin, 1932), 200; L. E. Neal, *Retailing and the public* (London: George Allen and Unwin, 1932), 65.

The first credit mail order catalogues appeared in the late nineteenth century and quickly established a firm foothold. The sector had already attracted tens of thousands of agents by the end of the 1930s, who serviced over one million customers on behalf of the leading companies—Empire Stores, Freemans, Grattan Warehouses, Littlewoods, and Great Universal Stores (GUS). The latter was the market leader and a favourite of city investors.[3] But it was in the years of rapid economic growth following the Second World War that the sector made its greatest mark, regularly leading the way in retail growth. Becoming increasingly lavish and weighty, at 1,000 pages in length by the 1960s, the catalogue became one of the signature items of the affluent society and featured in millions of homes. Like others dealing with the working-class consumer, mail order companies developed an agency system to penetrate this market. Most agents were part-time and served a relatively small number of customers. Estimates suggest the average number of customers per agent was sixteen in 1960, and twelve in 1970. By late 1980s and 1990s the average number of customers per agent had fallen to two or three because the majority of traditional agents had been replaced by the personal shopper, using the catalogue for their own family.[4]

The ascent of mail order was due to the appointment of agents in droves. By the time the sector's rapid post-1945 growth prompted the first detailed investigation of the phenomenon, in 1961, agents numbered an estimated 800,000–900,000. A decade later, the Crowther Committee on Consumer Credit calculated that the figure was between 3 and 4 million. The numbers rose further to around 4.8m in 1981. By the 1990s there was an estimated 7.4 million agents, but the majority were personal shoppers. Only 2.5 million were operating as traditional agents.[5] The vast numbers recorded at various points explain why, in 1980, 46 per cent of all women were believed to have had

[3] *The Times*, 19 June 1939.

[4] H. S. Crawshaw, 'Does mail order fit the retail life cycle?', MBA Thesis, (Bradford, 1980), 211; Monopolies and Mergers Commission, *The Littlewoods Organisation PLC and Freemans PLC* (London: HMSO, 1997), 123, 130, 167 n.

[5] Mass Observation Ltd/Economic Intelligence Unit, Retail Business Survey, 'Mail order', November (1961), 16; Consumer Credit, *Report of the Committee*, Cmnd. 4596 (London: HMSO, 1961), vol. ii, appendices, 97 n. Monopolies and Mergers Commission, *Great Universal Stores PLC and Empire Stores (Bradford) PLC: a report on the proposed mergers* (London: HMSO, 1983), 8–9; Monopolies and Mergers Commission, *The Littlewoods Organisation PLC and Freemans PLC* (London: HMSO, 1997), paras. 226–7, 12.

experience of overseeing an agency.[6] This represented a mighty sales force, particularly in the working-class groups in which mail order customers predominated. In 1961, 76 per cent of customers were from the C2 (skilled manual), D (semi- and unskilled manual) and E (casual workers, unemployed, widows, and pensioners) social groups. Their over-representation is indicated by the fact that these groups made up only 67 per cent of the adult population. Twenty years later the figures were 67 and 61 per cent respectively.[7]

The relationship between mail order agent and customer was based on the existing social networks formed through familial, neighbourhood, or workplace connections. They were centred predominantly on female agents, who, by the mid-1960s, made up 87 per cent of the total.[8] The agency system, and weekly collections, bore comparison with aspects of the structures evolved by check and credit traders. But mail order retailers had advantages in terms of credit control, marketing, and sales that were reflected in the increased turnover that the sector recorded year on year until the late 1970s, at which point its advance faltered. In 1950, mail order turnover was estimated at 0.9 per cent of retail sales by value. The figure rose to 2.5 per cent in 1961, 4.1 per cent in 1970, and 5.3 per cent in 1979. The statistics are more impressive still if the sector's share of non-food retail sales is probed: it was 5.7 per cent in 1965 and 9.2 per cent in 1979.[9] As these figures indicate, between 1950 and 1980 the mail order sector experienced significantly higher sales growth than other retailers.

This achievement was due largely to mail order's development of instalment sales, and it was in the field of consumer lending that it made its greatest impact. By 1969, the sector's credit sales of £448m represented an estimated 48 per cent of all instalment sales financed by retailers.[10] This proportion rose to 75 per cent in 1983.[11] There was a steep decline thereafter, to 24 per cent in 1996, as an 'explosion in the availability of credit . . . greatly diminished customer reliance on agency catalogues'. According to the MMC, much of this 'explosion' was due

[6] Monopolies and Mergers Commission, *Great Universal Stores*, 9.

[7] Mass Observation Ltd/Economic Intelligence Unit, 'Mail order', 20.

[8] J. Mann, 'The pattern of mail order', *British Journal of Marketing*, 1 (1967), 44.

[9] Coopey, O'Connell, and Porter, *Mail order retailing*, Table 2.1, 53; Crawshaw, 'Does mail order fit the retail life cycle?', Appendix C, 276.

[10] It is not clear how each of these figures was calculated and, as such, they are indicative only of broad trends.

[11] Committee on Consumer Credit, *Report*, vol ii, Table A18, 437.

to 'a continued growth in credit cards usage', as well as the development of doorstep lending by Cattles, Provident, and London Scottish Bank.[12]

By this point, the wheel had turned full circle. In the 1950s and 1960s mail order was the beneficiary of restrictions on hire purchase, as governments sought to exercise a degree of economic control by managing consumer demand and expenditure. In the 1980s, the reverse was true. In 1982, credit controls were eliminated and the bank 'corset' released, as the Thatcher government deregulated financial markets and encouraged a swelling demand for unsecured lending that was met by credit cards, store cards, and personal loans.[13] Mail order was particularly vulnerable in respect of the more economically comfortable members of the working class who had played a pivotal role in its earlier success. These groups became increasingly detached from catalogue shopping, choosing to consume elsewhere or turning to mail order for personal use only—rather than acting, as many of them had in the past, as agents who recruited customers. The gradual reduction in the numbers of traditional agents has also been explained in terms of a decline of working-class community, social networks, and trust, in the final decades of the twentieth century. This chapter will conclude by probing this issue. It also analyses the extent to which the traditional agent's decline, and the emergence of computerized credit scoring to replace the agent's informal assessment, led to the exclusion of those described by one industry insider as 'credit orphans'. But it begins by examining the original methods employed to offer credit by post, and the relationships formed between catalogue retailers, agents, and customers that enabled the mail order catalogue to become a familiar item in countless working-class homes.

FROM WATCH CLUBS TO DEFERRED PAYMENTS: THE ORIGINS OF CATALOGUE CREDIT

The introduction of postal orders in 1881, as a method of payment for those without bank accounts, swiftly followed by the arrival of an improved parcel delivery service the next year, set the logistical

[12] Monopolies and Mergers Commission, *Great Universal Stores PLC*, 6. Monopolies and Mergers Commission, *The Littlewoods Organisation*, 134.

[13] Janet Ford, *Consuming credit: debt and poverty in the UK* (London: Child Poverty Action Group, 1991), 18.

foundations for mail order retailing. The sector's arrival was neatly juxtaposed with important economic trends. From the 1870s, rising real wages and the stabilization of food prices enabled a number of pioneers to democratize mail order retailing, which had previously been associated with middle-class shoppers.[14] The first of the pioneers was Fattorini & Sons of Bradford (who became Empire Stores Ltd in 1910). In 1853, this jewellery retailer met a growing demand for timepieces amongst working-class men by founding 'watch clubs'.[15] Club members agreed a small weekly amount, between 6d or 1s, which was to be paid for a fixed period. They then drew lots, to decide the order in which each would receive their individual merchandise. This represented the commercialization of credit rotation societies, or 'draw clubs', that were familiar to the working classes. Credit was financed within the club, eliminating any element of risk for the Fattorinis. The system allowed relatively well-paid workers—such as the railwaymen who were prominent amongst early customers—to acquire merchandise that was well beyond the scope of their weekly disposable income. The clubs imposed their own discipline by fining members for late payments. The respectability of the clubs was signalled by the status of those involved, the fact that the system did not produce debtors before the county courts, and by the relatively high status of the merchandise being acquired. It has been argued that the moral uncertainties associated with particular forms of credit may have been partly dependent on the status of products that were purchased through them. Thus the distinction was not to be found between those who did or did not use credit, but between families who used it to buy 'luxury' goods and others who used it to 'fill their bellies and cover their nakedness'.[16] Watch club members covered their bellies with the luxury time pieces which hung from their fob chains. By 1875 modest illustrated catalogues contained merchandise such as gold watches, priced from £3 to £25, wedding rings from 7/6 to £2, knives and forks from 3/6 per half dozen, metal tea pots from 3s to 14s, and writing desks from 3/6 to 40s.[17] Although

[14] Coopey, O'Connell, and Porter, *Mail order retailing*, 14–17. T. R. Gourvish, 'The standard of living, 1890–1914' in A. O'Day (ed.), *The Edwardian age: conflict and stability 1900–1914* (London: Macmillan, 1979).

[15] Patrick Beaver, *A pedlar's legacy: the origins and history of Empire Stores 1831–1981* (London: Henry Melland, 1981), 32.

[16] Paul Johnson, *Saving and spending: the working- class economy in Britain 1870–1939* (Oxford: Clarendon Press, 1985), 153.

[17] Bradford: Empire Stores, 'Fattorini's fourth watch club for Carleton', 1875.

respectable, those involved were not always abstemious: the clubs often met in pubs. But Empire Stores recorded, in 1912, that it sought out the 'better class of public house' in which to establish clubs.[18]

By 1900, 1,000 clubs were in operation. At this point both Fattorini & Sons, and Kays of Worcester (another jeweller turned catalogue retailer), were edging towards the operational structures that became the bedrock of the credit mail order industry. In 1899, Kays deployed a 'deferred payment system', operated through part-time agents recruited by a team of travellers.[19] However, those approached to act as agents frequently reacted negatively to the suggestion that they become involved in the morally hazardous world of consumer borrowing. In 1907, travellers received instruction from the company on overcoming the objections of reluctant potential agents. In 'trying to appoint a good man' and to 'remove from him any prejudice he may feel against the system', they were told to remind him that 'councils, railway companies and all other public bodies do their business upon the "instalment system" '.[20] Kays had effectively introduced the modern mail order system, with its twin dependency on agents and credit. Customers no longer had to wait their 'turn' in the draw. Instead, once the first instalment was paid, their goods were dispatched and the agent made further collections over the ensuing nineteen weeks. The agent was paid a small commission, usually 10 per cent if taken in cash, or 12.5 per cent off their own catalogue purchases. As the system developed its final feature emerged: the cost of credit was bundled into the catalogue price, which was the same whether paid by cash or instalment. Either by accident or design, this removed any possibility that the system could be attacked on the controversial territory of interest rates. It also allowed some consumers to maintain the fiction that they were not using credit.

The Kays' model was utilized by the second wave of mail order companies that emerged early in the twentieth century. Foremost amongst them were Freemans, formed in London in 1905; and J. E. Fattorini & Co. (later Grattan Warehouses), a company established in 1912 by John Enrico Fattorini following a family dispute.[21] In the years on either side of the Great War, each company produced

[18] Empire Stores, Departmental Minute Book 1912–1916, section meeting 14 November 1912.

[19] Worcester: Kays Heritage Centre (Henceforth Kays), Kay & Co., *Board of Directors*, 24 July 1899.

[20] Kays: *Letter to travellers*, 1907.

[21] Beaver, *A pedlar's legacy*, 53.

substantial catalogues, of 200 to 300 pages, that were distributed to several thousand agents. Grattan Warehouses, for example, had 4,000 agents by the early 1920s. The 1912 Freemans' catalogue featured gramophone players, pianos, bicycles, and watches, together with the draperies and clothing that had become, and would remain, the staple merchandise of the catalogue. On offer were 'Freemans' celebrated suits' accompanied by suggestive copy: 'Don't lie awake at night wondering why you can't get a situation. Buy a Freemans' suit and you will soon be suited.'[22] Freemans consistently attempted to establish itself as the most glamorous of the catalogues by exploiting its London base and highlighting its proximity to metropolitan style. The capital often featured on its colourful catalogue covers.

By the 1920s mail order was attracting serious attention from retail rivals, including the co-operative movement, who were concerned about its growing threat.[23] But the mail order sector was yet to take the steps that established the strong relationship with female consumers that secured its position as a major force in British retailing. Its early concentration on watch clubs, and on items associated with the respectable working man, enabled it to utilize the associational culture that was such an important feature of Victorian and Edwardian masculine identity.[24] Dealing with male club organizers distanced mail order retailing from close association with female consumption and side-stepped the damaging critique that was directed at the tallyman and his doorstep dealings with working-class wives. Mail order firms were reluctant to appoint female agents, despite the fact that their catalogues were teeming with clothing, household items, and merchandise most often purchased by women. This created an obstacle to growth. The cautious approach that the companies had to adopt in extending credit to consumers with whom they had no face-to-face contact, and who were often in distant locations, was a further factor limiting growth in the early twentieth century. Both these obstacles were overcome in the late 1920s by developments that set the foundations for a tremendous expansion of catalogue sales.

[22] London, Freemans, Freemans Catalogue 1912.

[23] W. R. Blair, *National retail price fixing for co-operative productions and the desirability of the mail order business for co-operators* (Manchester: Co-operative Union Ltd, 1925), 9–11.

[24] John Tosh, 'What should historians do with masculinity? Reflections on nineteenth century Britain', *History Workshop Journal*, 38 (Autumn 1994), 179–202. Keith McClelland, 'Some thoughts on masculinity and the "representative artisan", in Britain, 1850–1880', *Gender and History*, 1, (1989), 164–77.

'ORGANIZE A LITTLEWOODS CLUB AND MAKE FRIENDS!' THE FEMINIZATION OF MAIL ORDER

During the late 1920s and early 1930s, GUS and Littlewoods returned to the draw club system as the inspiration for what were marketed as 'shilling clubs'. Groups of twenty customers paid a shilling each per week to an 'organizer', who submitted the £1 collected to the company in return for merchandise of that price. Lots were drawn to arrange the order in which goods were delivered to club members. The organizer would invariably 'not put her name into the hat at all', tacitly accepting the last turn.[25] This method of selling determined catalogue prices, which were generally set at 10, 20, or 30 shillings. For £1, for example, a GUS customer could acquire 'a fourteen piece stainless steel set of knives and forks with carvers to match', a 'gentleman's suit, or even a fur stole'.[26] GUS was founded in Manchester during 1900 and initially operated an agency mail order system similar to that of Kays. In the late 1920s it experimented with a 'turn club system', discovering rapidly that it 'eased the company's potential cash flow and credit problems'.[27] It also generated brisk growth, which led to GUS's flotation on the stock market in 1931. Potential investors were advised that 'as the business is conducted mainly on a cash basis, debtors and in particular bad debts are almost eliminated'.[28] Removing bad debt, and credit costs, from the balance sheet made capital available for expenditure on 'extensive advertising' to recruit club organizers.[29]

In 1932, John Moores, the entrepreneur behind Littlewoods Pools Ltd, decided to enter the mail order market. The company's new venture was viewed with concern by credit traders. One journal noted that 'football pool promoters seem to realise what a remarkable mailing list they have'. On the list were 'hundreds of thousands of addresses . . . all of clients who pay regularly each week—it is easy to appreciate what a sound nucleus they must have of any mail order business'.[30] In developing its catalogue operation, Littlewoods mimicked the GUS turn club system. It approached a number of its trusted football pools' customers to act as the first cohort of club organizers and, thereafter, advertised extensively.

25 Littlewoods, *Littlewoods Mail Order Stores Ltd* (Liverpool: Littlewoods, 1955).
26 *Credit Trader*, 24 February 1968. 27 *Mail on Sunday*, 30 June 1991.
28 *The Times*, 11 July 1931. 29 Ibid., 11 July 1931.
30 *Credit World*, December 1935.

The combination of advertising and the club system had dramatic effects, establishing Littlewoods and GUS as the two largest catalogue retailers. In 1930 Empire Stores distributed 8,000 catalogues to its agents, but even if we assume that each agent was dealing with twenty customers, their total number was dwarfed by the one million customers claimed the following year by GUS.[31] Comparisons of trading data also indicate the impact made by GUS's clubs. Grattan Warehouse's annual trading profits during the mid-1930s averaged £82,000, whilst at GUS they were £306,000.[32] Data on Littlewoods' immediate impact was also impressive. By 1937, when the well-established Freemans had 30,000 agents, Littlewoods claimed 700,000 club members, suggesting it had signed up 35,000 organizers by its fourth year of operations.[33] High street retailers were quick to offer caustic comment on the advances being made by their new competitors. In 1936, Littlewoods' catalogue was described as 'a wonderful business and actuated by the highest ideals of philanthropy—except, of course, towards the retail trader, who pays the local rates but whose customers are being urged to set up shop "without capital" and to "make profits without risk"'.[34]

Their financial success allowed GUS and Littlewoods to diversify. Both opened high street stores. GUS also diversified within mail order, acquiring rival companies John England Ltd and Kay & Co. Ltd in 1933 and 1937 respectively. Littlewoods retained a much more cautious approach to credit. Its main catalogue remained wedded to the club system into the 1950s. In 1952 John Moores—or Mr John as he was styled—used one of his regular catalogue homilies to define the company's customers as he saw them. Although they were not always in a position to pay 'cash down', they did 'like the idea of weekly payments'. However, they did not want credit 'with all its extra charges, formalities, personal enquiries, obligations and other irritants'. A Littlewoods club 'is NOT Credit . . . it is a dignified, convenient and thrifty way of Cash buying'.[35] Moores clearly felt that his company had struck a chord with the value systems of substantial numbers of consumers. That his catalogue functioned as a credit rotation society, financed by the club members, made its structure both familiar and

[31] Beaver, *A pedlar's legacy*, 64; *The Times*, 9 June 1932.

[32] *The Times*, 25 April 1934; 1 April 1935; 26 September 1935; 19 May 1936.

[33] Freemans: Untitled notes on the company history, 7; Littlewoods: Littlewoods Mail Order Stores catalogue, Spring 1936.

[34] *Credit World*, February 1936.

[35] Littlewoods, Littlewoods Autumn and Winter catalogue 1952.

respectable to those who might have been wary of the stigma that still loomed over consumer credit deep into the second half of the century. Close social ties were a precursor to a club's creation, enabling the trust on which the system was dependent. The massive success of Littlewoods Pools had indicated to the company that respectability and gambling were not incompatible: ten million people speculated on the football pools each week by 1939.[36] Its mail order division, by using draw clubs, added similar elements of chance and excitement to household consumption. Catalogues carried pages dedicated to the 'thrill of being a club member' and illustrated this point with photographs, such as one in 1937 that featured a smiling group eagerly watching a respectably attired woman making the draw from a man's hat.[37] Gladys Thomas, from Birmingham, ran a Littlewoods club at this point and, together with her husband George, fondly remembered the sense of anticipation that the 'draw' brought to their home and George's workplace. George explained how 'I took my hat and put the twenty numbers in it and there'd be maybe eight people in the house and they'd all pick a number out. Then I'd take it to work and another twelve would pick their numbers out.'[38]

Moores claimed that a survey of 20,000 football pools' customers, carried out by Littlewoods prior to its plunge into mail order, discovered that they 'overwhelmingly' preferred the draw club system over a credit-based catalogue.[39] Perhaps this was the case, and Moores' customers shared his conservative views on credit. It is also possible that when faced with a survey asking them this question they gave the 'respectable' answer, or that in voting for the club system they affirmed a method that had long been acceptable to the 'prosperous artisan . . . who saw nothing improvident about their wives paying weekly into a . . . club and, if they were lucky in the draw, making purchases in advance of their saving'.[40] Littlewoods' catalogue explicitly championed its methods over those of instalment payments, arguing that amongst 'those whose

[36] Mark Clapson, *A bit of a flutter: popular gambling and English society, c.1823–1961* (Manchester: Manchester University Press, 1992), 162.

[37] Littlewoods: Littlewoods Autumn 1936 catalogue; March 1937 catalogue.

[38] Interview with Gladys and George Thomas (both born in Birmingham, in 1912 and 1910 respectively. Gladys was a home maker and George a bread delivery man. They had four children).

[39] Barbara Clegg, *The man who made Littlewoods: the story of John Moores* (Bury St Edmunds: Hodder & Stoughton, 1993), 5.

[40] R. Harris, M. Naylor, and A. Seldon, *Hire purchase in a free society* (London: Hutchinson, 1961), 21.

incomes are restricted, the "Club" system of buying is particularly appreciated because, besides offering practically all the advantages of the Hire Purchase system—it has none of its disadvantages'.[41] There was, of course, the disadvantage of having to wait up to twenty weeks for one's merchandise. But it is clear that many consumers, schooled in maxims that lauded thrift, deferred gratification, and the avoidance of indebtedness, were very much at home with the club system.

By the 1950s, however, this option was becoming less attractive. Post-war austerity and rationing arguably diminished the patience of some consumers. This group included women like Beryl Ratcliffe, who became an agent for the GUS subsidiary Trafford Warehouses, which offered credit terms. She found that her 'neighbours were interested in the catalogue as one did not have to "wait your turn"—as was the idea with Littlewoods at that time'.[42] The 'thrill of the draw' had also subsided for the Birmingham couple, Gladys and George. Following the war, they welcomed a Grattan Warehouses' catalogue into their home. They considered its approach to credit 'more modern' and came to view Littlewoods' as 'old fashioned'.[43] Credit terms were introduced only gradually in Littlewoods' range of catalogues during the 1950s, with the draw club system finally meeting its demise in 1959.

It is possible that a contributory factor in the club system's interwar success was that many more consumers were aware of it than of the credit mail order companies, as the latter were not as extensively advertised as GUS and Littlewoods. Female organizers were targeted by Littlewoods from the outset, women's weekly publications being the main advertising forum.[44] Its conservative policy on credit enabled Littlewoods to be innovative in this respect and the appointment of vast numbers of female club organizers explains its growth, and that of GUS, more than any other factor. The credit-based companies had shown no great enthusiasm for female agents, particularly married ones. Like others in the consumer credit industry, they were concerned about the legal status of goods sold on instalments to married women. Before 1939, Empire Stores only signed up male agents.[45] Freemans operated a similar policy. One traveller recalled that before the Second World War,

[41] Littlewoods: Littlewoods Mail Order Stores, Autumn 1936.

[42] Beryl Ratcliffe: Questionnaire, 11 June 1997.

[43] Interview with Gladys and George Thomas.

[44] Robert Brandon, 'The origin and development of mail order in the United Kingdom', *Journal of Advertising History*, 8 (March 1984), 6–11.

[45] Beaver, *A pedlar's legacy*, 46.

'I was not allowed to appoint women.'[46] This was the case even though mail order executives realized that provisioning the home with mail order merchandise was a highly gendered activity that 'essentially . . . was done by the wife'.[47] The anticipated gender of the agent shaped publicity material issued by the credit-based companies. A perennial theme was that an agency provided financial rewards for the resourceful. In 1935, Freemans promised to show the 'ambitious' the way to turn 'spare time into money—to convert all the hours and minutes which would otherwise be wasted into cash'.[48] Examples of existing agents who had bought desirable consumer durables with their commission, or, in the most successful cases their own homes, were deployed to rouse acquisitive urges. Freemans was, in effect, offering a modified form of penny capitalism, one in which the working-class entrepreneur did not have to speculate to accumulate. Their only commitment was their spare time.[49] Freemans offered the highest commission available to the mail order agent at that time, 25 per cent on cash sales or 20 per cent for credit sales, compared to the 20 per cent or 15 per cent offered by Grattan Warehouses and the 10 per cent paid by Littlewoods to the organizers of its shilling clubs. This was enough to attract agents such as Alf Yeo, who was lured from a rival company by the high commission and earned £40 in his first year with Freemans.[50] These commission levels came at a cost and GUS told its own customers that buying from Freemans meant they would receive 'inferior goods of cheaper quality'.[51]

It is highly likely that the higher commissions being paid by the credit mail order companies had a knock-on effect on merchandise quality, providing a competitive advantage for GUS and Littlewoods. However, it was their recruitment of female agents and the discovery of a means through which to tap into the temporal patterns and varied aspirations of female consumers that enabled Littlewoods and GUS to advance rapidly. The motives of most female agents differed somewhat from those of the ideal agent envisaged by Freemans' advertising. Women were often drawn to catalogue shopping by factors other than straightforwardly financial ones. The language employed in Freemans' literature was highly

46 Freemans: transcript of interview with Alf Yeo, 1985.

47 Freemans: transcript of interview with Tony Rampton, 1982.

48 Freemans: 'Freemans' Spare Time Savings Bank', 1935.

49 On penny capitalism see John Benson, *The penny capitalists: a study of nineteenth-century working class entrepreneurs* (London: MacMillan, 1979).

50 Freemans: transcript of interview with Alf Yeo.

51 Manchester, Great Universal Stores: Letter to customers, n.d, *c.*1930s.

gendered, as were the notions of time that implied a clear demarcation between the hours of waged labour and those available for rest and leisure. Whilst this was the pattern for many men, it was not the case for most married women, for whom spare time existed as a secondary consideration, to be fitted around demanding domestic routines. The priorities of 'other family members took precedence over their own use of time'.[52] Significantly, the catalogue provided an opportunity to take a break from the housewife's busy schedule, without arousing too much self-guilt about leaving other household chores to one side. Littlewoods worked hard to foster the overlap between work and leisure that was offered by the catalogue. In 1936, catalogue readers were reminded that it was 'a glorious thrill to choose periodically something for the home, for the children, your husband or yourself'.[53] Littlewoods' early catalogues bore similarities to women's magazines, such as *Woman* and *Woman's Own*, which were simultaneously targeting the more affluent sectors of the interwar working classes.[54] These magazines also carried a 'work' element, in the advice they offered readers on consumer issues. Increasing use of colourful illustrations gave the catalogue a degree of physical resemblance to popular magazines. In its spring 1936 catalogue, Littlewoods inserted a number of articles that would not have been out of place in *Woman's Own*, including one that answered questions on etiquette. This demonstrated the aspirational nature of the market that the company was courting, as did its catalogue covers, which like magazines attempted to signal to and construct an ideal readership. The cover for the autumn 1935 catalogue featured a smartly dressed young couple in a well-furnished home. Whilst the man smoked his pipe and read a book, his wife busied herself putting up new curtains.[55] Littlewoods attempted to eschew any guilt that might be felt about expenditure with the company by praising customers for thriftiness: 'the unconsidered shilling that would have been spent and forgotten goes for goods of value—economy—quality—comfort'.[56]

[52] Claire Langhammer, *Women's leisure in England, 1920–1960* (Manchester: Manchester University Press, 2000), 133.

[53] Littlewoods: Littlewoods Mail Order Stores Catalogue, September 1934, Autumn 1936; Autumn 1935.

[54] On *Woman's Own* see Jill Greenfield and Chris Reid, 'Women's magazines and the commercial orchestration of femininity in the 1930s: evidence from *Woman's Own*', *Media History*, 4/2 (1998), 161–74.

[55] Littlewoods, Autumn 1935 catalogue.

[56] Littlewoods: September 1934 catalogue.

The feminization of mail order enabled the companies to exploit female sociability. Whilst the original watch clubs had given access to masculine networks, female consumers proved most lucrative for mail order retailers. This was due to women's role in marshalling family finances and because, as Judy Giles and others have argued, the interwar working-class female had a vision of how the burgeoning consumer society could offer her 'something that little bit better' than her mother had experienced.[57] Another aspect of the working-class women's 'leisure' which was to prove extremely useful for the mail order companies was their role in neighbourhood socialization and information exchange.[58] This aspect of their lives provided many women with insights into neighbours' lifestyles and budgets that were priceless for the catalogue companies. Moreover, opportunities that the catalogue provided for socializing were discovered to have a strong attraction for many women. John Moores realized this two years after launching Littlewoods' first catalogue, when he met a group of organizers. One of them, a council worker's wife, told him that 'my door bell seldom used to ring, but it goes constantly these days. I've made scores of new friends, and we've always got something to talk about. People who passed my house before and never glanced at it, are now my friends.' The company acted on this discovery, altering its advertising copy from 'Form a Littlewoods Club and Make Money' to 'Organise a Littlewoods Club and Make Friends!'[59]

Those mail order companies operating on a more straightforward credit system began to recruit female agents in 1939. This development must have been influenced by the successes achieved by GUS and Littlewoods. Furthermore, anxieties about appointing female agents were diminished, if not entirely removed, by the Law Reform (Married Women and Tortfeasors) Act, 1935. It removed a husband's liabilities for his wife's debts, which had been widely viewed by creditors as an obstacle to suing married females in the county courts. Finally, surviving information from the companies involved suggests that the removal of male agents at the outset of the Second World War was at least as big

[57] Judy Giles, '"Playing hard to get": working-class women, sexuality and respectability in Britain, 1918–1940', *Women's History Review*, 1/1 (1992); Jerry White, *The worst street in North London: Campbell Bunk, Islington, between the wars* (London: Routledge and Kegan Paul, 1986).

[58] Melanie Tebbutt, *Women's talk? A social history of gossip in working-class neighbourhoods, 1880–1960* (Aldershot: Scholar Press, 1995).

[59] *Empire News*, 30 October 1955.

a contributor as either of the above factors.[60] Whatever the motivation was, female agents rapidly came to predominate. By the 1950s and 1960s they represented almost 90 per cent of all agents.[61] Their roles as organizers of their own family budgets and within female-centred social networks were vital in the expansion of credit-based mail order in the age of affluence, as it had been in the 1930s for the draw clubs. The shilling clubs marked a significant moment for the development of mail order and for consumer credit, creating a vehicle for the mass commercialization of credit rotation societies. Importantly, they did so by incorporating female consumers who were responsible for domestic budgeting in millions of homes. The draw club format also attracted consumers to the catalogue who were wary of the credit-based catalogues. They provided a half-way house through which credit-averse consumers passed on their journey towards credit-based mail order and the post-Second World War explosion of consumer credit, which was channelled through the mail order companies.

SPOTTING GAY CURTAINS AND AVOIDING WINDOW CLEANERS: EXTENDING CREDIT BY POST

Credit sales presented mail order retailers with particular difficulties. The first experiments with it, which occurred around 1900, greatly increased turnover but introduced new operational demands. Providing credit for thousands of geographically dispersed working-class customers was a daunting task, with the potential for much greater risk than that faced by those offering credit on the doorstep. Possible hazards included the financial losses associated with defaulting customers, as well as potential for damage to the reputation and status of any company that came to be widely associated with working-class debtors: the tarnished reputation of the tallyman hovered over the whole consumer credit industry. Whilst pragmatically setting aside funds to meet 'bad and doubtful debts', mail order companies relied on notions of respectability in seeking out agents and customers. Occupation and income were frequently the signals used in assessing this concept. In 1908, for example, it was

[60] Coopey, O'Connell, and Porter, *Mail order retailing*, 101.
[61] Mann, 'The pattern of mail order', 44.

noted that most Kays customers belonged to 'the artisan classes'. In case appearances—or occupations—were deceptive, the company took the precaution of exchanging monthly lists of 'agents who are undesirable' with Empire Stores. This was occurring in 1913, but this form of relationship broke down at some point in the 1930s and the mail order sector became renowned for the extent to which each company jealously guarded business information.[62] According to one executive, interviewed in the early 1970s, this was because one company chose to exploit a reciprocal arrangement: 'There was a gentleman's agreement before the war on this sort of interchange . . . Then somebody had a naughty idea and put the names of their good agents into this blacklist so that they knew that no competitor would ever take their agents away. So it broke down . . . We were very upset about this . . . but nobody trusts anybody else in this game.'[63]

Even before this breakdown in trust between commercial competitors, local knowledge was the key to expansion. Bridgeheads into working-class neighbourhoods were established by travellers who were tasked to appoint part-time agents. The travellers were instructed to solicit information on the financial probity of prospective agents from their local shopkeepers. They were also detailed to inspect houses for clues about desirable agents. In 1907, Kays told its travellers that only by gaining entrance to a candidate's home could telling cultural signifiers be garnered: 'get inside and have an actual sight of the place . . . you won't expect to see a palace, but at the same time if the house is dirty, it shows a man's lack of interest in his own home'.[64] Forty years later, Freemans' travellers were informed that promising indications included 'gay curtains' or 'an announcement posted in a window in connection with Church festivities'.[65] Ideas about respectability and honesty varied and were often idiosyncratic. It was logical that a Freemans' traveller advised his colleagues, in 1947, to appoint 'working men in safe jobs', citing the example of bus company employees. The same can be said of Joseph Fattorini's view, articulated in 1940, that some people 'invariably turn wrong'; he illustrated his point with the example of

[62] Worcester Record Office: Kay & Co., Board of Directors, 1 January 1900; Annual General Meeting, 28 February 1908; Empire Stores, Departmental Minute Book 1912–1916, section meeting 2 January 1913.

[63] Paul Rock, *Making people pay* (London: Routledge and Kegan Paul, 1973), 39.

[64] Worcester Record Office: BA/5496/3 Kay & Co., 'Advice to travellers', 27 September 1907.

[65] Freemans: *Freemans Staff Sentinel*, 4 (October 1947).

window cleaners, whose income was episodic. More puzzling, however, was his suspicion of 'people in cathedral towns'.[66]

Once travellers had appointed an agent they usually saw no more of them, much to the concern of those responsible for agency administration. Bad debts did not become apparent until an agent had been with the company for six months, long after the traveller had moved on. In 1940, Joseph Fattorini confirmed that the company's section heads blamed the travellers for bad debts. He noted that 'we never admit this. It is the supervisor's job to keep the section straight and stop bad agents. (But actually there may be truth in it.)'[67] Perhaps as a result of this realization, credit mail order companies were using credit reference agencies to augment their travellers' judgements by the 1930s, checking potential agents' names against county court records.[68] However, Empire Stores continued to use travellers until the 1970s.[69] Continuing the well-established association between credit and personal connection, the best source of reliable agents was through introductions by those already established in the role. Kays noted this in 1912 and offered agents a bonus for each successful introduction. By 1936, Grattan Warehouses were offering up to 35 shillings for this function.[70] This process was important in the steady expansion of credit mail order in the interwar period.

Mail order retailers relied on their agents to gather information on their customers. Local social networks were highly effective in identifying levels of creditworthiness and in ensuring repayment. The draw clubs, from which the first mail order agencies evolved, existed on the basis of a high level of 'social connectedness'. This enforced repayment, as those involved valued their 'social collateral' within the group and strove to maintain it and to avoid the shaming process that would ensue from a failure to pay one's contributions.[71] This

[66] Freemans: transcript of interview with Alf Yeo, 1985; Empire Stores: Joseph Fattorini's 'Red Book', 10.

[67] Empire Stores: Joseph Fattorini's 'Red Book', 13.

[68] Freemans: transcript of interview with Alf Yeo, 1985.

[69] Interview with Peter Fattorini (former Empire Stores' executive) conducted by Sean O'Connell and Dilwyn Porter on 22 July 1998.

[70] Worcester Record Office: 5496/2 Kay & Co., draft letter to agents, 1912; Grattan: *Grattan News*, October 1936: cited in Dyson, 'The Fattorini family and its contribution to mail-order trading in the United Kingdom', unpublished undergraduate dissertation (Bradford, 1977), 45.

[71] Timothy Besley and Stephen Coate, 'The economics of rotating credit and savings associations', *American Economic Review*, 83/4 (September 1993), 805.

remained a strong aspect of mail order agencies, ensuing low levels of bad debt. Speaking in 1968, one mail order executive revealed how the system had worked since its inception. As his company's customers had to make payments to someone who was 'invariably a neighbour or a friend, they are afraid that the agent may talk about [debts] . . . to other customers'.[72] However, mail order retailers did not place blind faith in their agents' innate ability to establish high levels of trust amongst communal networks. Agents received guidance in this task. Empire Stores, for example, warned them to be 'very cautious as to the amount of business [to accept] in one house or in one family', and to 'keep first orders small until experience is gained'.[73] Agents' accounts were closely monitored and they were reined in if the company felt they were being overly ambitious. Limits were commonly imposed on the amount of credit allowed in each agency. In 1968, for example, Trafford Warehouses, a GUS company, allowed new agents between £30 and £40 credit to extend amongst their customers.[74] The emphasis on respectability in agent recruitment produced an unexpected dividend, as it was discovered that embarrassment led some to secretly pay the debts incurred by errant customers.[75] In these circumstances, the fear of being shamed that was an important factor in maintaining the dynamics of traditional credit rotation societies took on a new form, with the agent fearing a loss of their own status with the company due to a defaulting customer. The full extent of this behaviour is not known, but evidence given to the Crowther Committee in 1970, by GUS, suggests that it was exploited. It was explained that although GUS's army of 1.25m agents were not responsible for their customers payments 'they had a moral responsibility to see that customers paid the requisite amount required'.[76]

This moral imperative ensured that in the normal course of events it was the mail order customer who was financially disciplined, through their relationship with the agent. In 1910 Kays instructed its agents that when customers missed a payment agents were not to 'leave them until the next week', they were to 'call upon them again and again the same week until you *do* get a payment'. These 'black calls' were to be made in the evenings 'when you are most likely to find the husband and

[72] *Credit Trader*, 24 February 1968. [73] Beaver, *A pedlar's legacy*, 64–5.
[74] *Credit Trader*, 24 February 1968. [75] Mann, 'The pattern of mail order', 48.
[76] National Archives (Henceforth NA) BT 250/88: *Mail order 1968–1970 Evidence from GUS*, 19 March 1970.

wife at home'.[77] Given the careful selection of customers, this factor did not arise for many mail order agents, but when it did it created awkwardness between individuals with close social connections. Several veteran agents report that a customer not paying, for whatever reason, was the only negative experience of running an agency. Reflecting on her many years as an agent, Anne from Merseyside reported, in 1997, that disadvantages 'have been few, but I have had the odd bad payer—but have learnt from experience not to allow this type of customer to become in deep debt'.[78]

Mail order firms discovered that some customers were prepared to gain advantage from mail order's on-approval system, through which customers returned items that did not meet with their satisfaction. According to mail order company lore, wedding dresses or men's suits were often swiftly returned with the tell-tale addition of a smattering of confetti. More serious were the 'deliberate "twisters"' who made 'a living going from one mail-order company to another, obtaining the maximum amount of credit available and then doing a "moonlight flit"'.[79] By the early 1970s, the firms felt that they could spot a 'professional debtor' by the type and quantity of merchandise that they ordered: 'We can tell very often when they're trying to do us. They buy watches, they buy jewellery, they buy negotiable items, consumer durables. If we get an agent who just starts ordering watches and typewriters, you put the clamps on them pretty quickly.'[80]

Such customers, however, were in a minority. Most agents carefully selected only those from amongst their family or associates whose economic circumstances meant they would be able to make repayments. We have seen that Margot Finn has demonstrated how retail credit in the nineteenth century bore the characteristics of gifting patterns of traditional societies; the mail order agency brought a similar relationship into what became the most common form of credit retailing in the twentieth century. The agent was usually well known to the customer with strong social or familial ties. There was the weekly ritual of visits to collect payments and to interact socially. The catalogue provided a focal point for discussions about a customer's growing family or rites of

[77] Worcester Record Office: Kays, Kay to Mr G Blank, 19 August 1910. Emphases in original.

[78] Anne. Questionnaire returned June 1997.

[79] *Credit Trader*, 25 December 1965; 24 February 1968.

[80] Rock, *Making people pay*, 64.

passage, such as a significant birthday or arrangements for Christmas. As the representative of the mail order company, the agent was the gatekeeper to a convenient credit facility, as well as the world of goods presented in the catalogue. The successful operation of credit control by agents was demonstrated, ironically, by the fact that agents consistently recorded higher average levels of bad debt than their customers. A study conducted in 1989, for instance, found that levels of bad debt amongst agents were around 5.4 per cent, but for customers they stood at only 1.5 per cent. The authors observed that 'the indications are that local and personal arrangements for collecting instalments provide a valuable control on arrears'.[81] From the outset, the weekly call of the mail order agent served a disciplinary function. One personal account demonstrates its importance. As a young housewife in 1980s Belfast, Joan found that weekly payments through a catalogue helped her eke out a limited income: 'We got clothes out of catalogues and things like that . . . I mean [my husband] was only a labourer and life was tough.' Her agent was a neighbour and a former schoolmate: 'everybody knew her, she was the catalogue lady . . . who catered for the whole estate and she was able to get her holiday every year out of all us lot'. Joan then decided to run her own catalogue, but, with the personalized credit control of the agent replaced by a more bureaucratic relationship with the catalogue company, she fell into arrears and her agency was closed.[82]

Eric, from Sheffield, had been a Grattan's agent for fifty years when he was interviewed in 1999. His testimony reflected the agent's effectiveness in restricting bad debt. The character and connections of his customers were a key starting point: 'The first customers . . . which is only natural, was me mother, and there was me sister, there were her husband, there was a chap called Stubbins—that had a printing shop, business down there—that me father knew. But then . . . there were some of me relations in.' Eric ran the agency, assisted by his wife, and neighbours and workmates were subsequently recruited as customers. In five decades there had been only one customer whom Eric classed a 'bad payer'. He was a cinema manager and 'he ordered a typewriter off me—about twenty quid—and he absconded. He went and he took

[81] Richard Berthoud and Elaine Kempson, *Credit and debt: the PSI report* (London: Policy Studies Institute, 1992), 154.

[82] Interview with Joan (born 1960. Mature student, care home worker, and mother of three. First husband a labourer; current husband a taxi driver. Protestant. Interviewed 10 April 2003).

the takings from the cinema as well and I wrote up about it and they said don't worry about it.' On another occasion he was able to use his local knowledge to prevent Grattan's jeopardizing its relationship with a customer who had not paid for several weeks:

I had a chap at work as one of me first customers, and he had to go in hospital and he missed about two weeks I think, three weeks and . . . they sent me a letter saying that he'd missed two weeks and they were going to get in touch with him . . . I wrote back to them and told them—I said to them—'you don't do that'! Because, I said, 'this man's been in my club ever since I started', and I'd been running it then I think about ten years, fifteen years, and I said 'and he's a good payer, and he's in the hospital'.

Eric did recall one further occasion when fulfilling his disciplinary function placed him in the middle of a marital financial squabble. Pursuing a slow payer, he and his wife visited her at home. Her husband was in and the woman told Eric 'Oh you've no need to worry, I'll put it up, you'll get your money.' Her husband subsequently appeared at Eric's door with the money, 'but he played hell with me . . . He said: "You shouldn't have let my wife have that stuff!" He said: "If I'd have known, she wouldn't have had it because", he said "she's a bad payer".'[83] In other interviews, conducted with former mail order agents, stories of default were rare. Agnes, who ran a Freemans' catalogue in Belfast from the 1950s to the 1990s, was emphatic in her view that she could automatically trust a neighbour with credit: 'Oh yes. Oh, I never would have refused anybody and I never had anybody that didn't pay.'[84]

However, the small proportion of turnover classified as bad debt represented a significant number of indebted individuals and, as mail order grew in scale and scope, they contributed to a rising proportion of county court cases.[85] This was despite the fact that mail order firms sought to avoid the negative exposure that had been the fate of the tallymen. Any system involving instalment payments inevitably created debtors, but the prospect of heavy county court loads was not one that the companies looked at with eagerness. A number of policies emerged to alleviate potential problems. As was the case with other creditors, mail order retailers made allowances for increased debt during periods

[83] Interview with Eric (born 1934. A retired factory worker who had raised three children with his wife. Interviewed 3 March 1998).

[84] Interview with Agnes (born 1923. A retired shop worker and mother of five. Her husband had been an electrician. Interviewed 22 February 2003).

[85] Committee on Consumer Credit, *Report*, 139.

of economic hardship. This was the case for Empire Stores, and Kays, during the miners' strike in 1926 when they accepted late payments and recorded significant financial setbacks in Yorkshire, the North-East, and South Wales.[86] Even London-based Freemans had to make a similar gesture during the General Strike, doing so in the anticipation that it 'would boost the reputation of the firm'.[87] During normal passages of business, recourse to the county courts was considered, but often ruled out. In 1940, management at Empire Stores noted that 'county court work is not very profitable if at all' and that it was 'advisable to cut losses unless it is a very bad case'.[88] Thirty years later a mail order executive revealed that 'we would write off a debt sooner than collect. It's just not worth our while.' This was, he argued, because 'mail order is desperately trying to become respectable. It is respectable, in fact, but there's a dodgy image sticking to it.' Despite this claim large numbers of mail order debtors did come before the county courts, but research conducted in 1969 revealed that 70 per cent of cases were dropped by the companies if a defence was filed. This was not only due to the expense of having to fight a case, but because, like other creditors, mail order firms wished to 'refrain from acts which jar with the presentation of a clean front'. However, it was revealed that despite a wish to avoid the bad publicity that might result from a contested court case that was drawn to the public's attention, there was a willingness to exploit 'these modes of enforcement' in other ways, by threatening 'the debtor with a sanction they have no intention of using'.[89] Mail order companies did so through the use of letters. In the early 1950s, payment arrears at Freemans were 'dealt with in a small way by Mr Leonard Tostavin', with 'one girl assisting him'. Debtors received missives from this duo under the 'name of T. Leonard', encouraging them to believe that their debt 'had been passed on to a real debt collector'. By the mid-1950s, with business expanding dramatically, Freemans' bad debt department employed a staff of twenty.[90] In the early 1970s, one mail order firm explained to the sociologist Paul Rock that it had 'designed a standard letter with a solicitor' to be sent to debtors. Any money received in response was divided 75 : 25 between the company and its legal adviser.

[86] Empire Stores: Board of Directors, 24 October 1927; Worcester Record Office: Kays, Kay & Co. Annual General Meeting, 10 July 1926.
[87] Freemans: Transcript of interview with Marjorie Grainger, 1985.
[88] Bradford: Empire Stores: Joseph Fattorini's 'Red Book', 23.
[89] Rock, *Making people* pay, 65–6.
[90] Freemans: Transcript of interview with Arthur Holgate, 1985.

A company executive explained: 'We'll probably use this for all debts under five pounds, where we have no real intention of suing . . . but the debtor doesn't know this. And it may be a means of picking up a certain amount of money. It costs us nothing to try it.' As Rock explained, the courts, prisons, and debt collectors all provided symbolic ammunition for creditors. The threat of action was more important than action itself, because the latter was expensive and executed in only a minority of cases. These stock letters were part of a series of methods used by a variety of creditors to create 'controlled anxiety' amongst debtors.[91] This methodology remained standard practice. The Policy Studies Institute's (PSI) survey of debtors, published in 1992, found that mail order firms rarely did more than write to those in arrears, although these letters took a firm line and threatened legal action.[92]

Another response to debt was to sell it on to specialist companies. Mail order firms amassed sizeable customer numbers, making the sale of parcels of debt commercially viable. This was the case at Empire Stores from 1916, and at Freemans from at least the 1950s.[93] Freemans took this course of action because rapidly expanding business produced levels of bad debt that it struggled to manage. Initially, the company found it difficult to pinpoint local specialists to whom it could offload its bad debts and a member of staff embarked on a tour of county courts to identify likely candidates. Freemans discovered great variations in the prices debt collectors were willing to pay; prices ranged from 2.5 to 25 per cent of the total debt.[94] If debts were sold, the customers concerned found themselves in the hands of companies for whom creating 'controlled anxiety' was a speciality. In 1980s Belfast, Anne-Marie found herself confronted by a debt collector. She had moved out of her marital home, following the breakdown of her marriage, but her Littlewoods catalogue subsequently arrived there and Anne-Marie later recalled that 'my sister-in-law had taken it and ordered stuff for her children in my name, right, and then didn't pay it'. Anne-Marie 'spent two and a half years paying off her debts . . . I don't know whether it was a hundred and ninety or two hundred and forty'. The debt had been sold to an agency 'who then charge you more to pay the debt off. So the debt just accelerates. But the man that came at the time had said

[91] Rock, *Making people pay*, 70.

[92] Berthoud and Kempson, *Credit and debt*, 163–4.

[93] Empire Stores, General Minute Book 1910–1930. Special Directors' Meeting 13 November 1916.

[94] Freemans: transcript of interview with Arthur Holgate, 1985.

to me that if I co-operated—sexually [nervous laugh]—that that would do instead of paying.' For Anne-Marie this

> summarized all the fear that I had of debt. That you were in the clutches of other people, once you had debt . . . you're in the clutches of people like that . . . even now it makes me feel sick, it upsets me to think. It upsets me because somebody more vulnerable than me has agreed to that. Now I'm not saying that all debt-collecting agencies—[but] people who would collect debt off working-class people tend to be sleazes anyway—but this one was a particularly unpleasant person. And I always made sure I had the money and I never forgive Lillian for putting me in that position. And I never ever said it to her that she done it. I never spoke about it because I know that she had five children of her own and she was married to a serious alcoholic and I know that she had her own problems, but she put me in that position and I never forgave her for it. Although I speak to her, I never mention it; I still hold it against her. I don't hold it against her that I paid that debt off for her, I hold it against her because of him standing at my doorstep that night. And what he said to me, I found so, so offensive.[95]

The tale of this particular debt collector is reminiscent of Judge Parry's remarks on lecherous tallymen. It demonstrates the lived reality of the powerful metaphorical link between debt and the loss of personal autonomy. In the most distressing cases this disempowerment left female debtors vulnerable to sexual advances. Anne-Marie's account also reveals that social networks were not only exploited by mail order companies; in this case her desperate sister-in-law made use of a dissolving social connection to amass debts for which she would not be held accountable. The story also indicates that the commercial orchestration of kinship and communal ties by mail order companies was not foolproof. Partly for this reason, as information technology became more advanced, the sector began to investigate less socialized methods of credit control.

'WE TRIED TO HIDE THE COMPUTER AS MUCH AS POSSIBLE': NEW TECHNOLOGY AND ITS IMPACT ON THE AGENT–COMPANY RELATIONSHIP

By the 1960s, the scale and scope of mail order retailing was so vast that it created massive logistical problems for the companies involved.

[95] Interview with Anne-Marie (born 1951. Mature student and mother of seven. First husband a scaffolder; current husband a musician. Interviewed 20 May 2003).

Information about agents had to be collected, stored, and continually reassessed. One outcome of this was the emergence, in the 1960s, of British Debt Services (BDS). It was a debt collection agency and credit reference bureau, dealing extensively with the mail order sector. GUS, its first and most important customer, sold its debts to BDS from the mid-1960s. By 1968 BDS had pursued almost 230,000 mail order debtors and responded to 4 million credit reference enquiries. Like other credit reference bureaux, it faced criticism for stockpiling black information rather than white data. In other words, it compiled records of problem debts rather than episodes of successful repayment. It did so by collating data from *Stubbs Gazette*, which reported all county court judgements over £30. Records of all cases for sums between £10 and £30 were bought from the Lord Chancellor's Office. This was added to information held in its own debt recovery department.[96]

Despite its use of BDS, mail order's methods did not always meet with the approval of outsiders. In 1968, the Consumers' Association criticized what it felt was a lax approach to credit checking.[97] In its defence, the sector maintained that the system's effectiveness was demonstrated by low levels of bad debt. In 1970, these were reported to be between 1.2 and 2.5 per cent across all catalogue companies. GUS told the Crowther Committee that after the recovery of some outstanding debts—through a series of letters, the group's own debt collecting agency and, finally, court action—its net bad debt ratio was 0.84 per cent of total turnover.[98] The Committee was not told, however, that the proportion of bad debt could be massaged, using annual price inflation. One former mail order executive explained: 'bad debt is based on last year's prices. As long as inflation is in the system it covers a lot of bad smells in the bad debt department.'[99]

The National Citizens' Advice Bureaux (NCAB) was not convinced that mail order companies' administrative functions were coping with the massive demand that their glossy catalogues created. It told the Crowther Committee of communication problems within mail order

[96] NA: HO 264/261. Compilation and maintenance of records: Finance houses, including credit rating. Consumer Association evidence, March 1971; *The Times*, 2 January 1969; NA: AJ 3/139—Credit bureaux, 1965–1971. Note for the file by Susan Mardsen-Smedley, 1970.

[97] NA: HO 264/261. Compilation and maintenance of records: finance houses, including credit rating. Consumer Association evidence, March 1971.

[98] NA: BT 250/88. Mail order 1968–1970. Evidence of GUS, 19 March 1970; Evidence of MOTA 20 March 1970.

[99] Interview with anonymous former mail order employee.

companies, which had resulted in customers receiving, simultaneously, one letter acknowledging that their catalogue bill was in the black and another threatening legal action for the recovery of debt. The NCAB suggested that these errors 'may result in part from the introduction of computers into some large companies'.[100] Mail order companies were amongst businesses that pioneered the use of computers. Freemans was at the forefront of this development, taking the plunge in the early 1960s. Computerization fundamentally transformed the company's relationship with agents and customers, together with its approach to credit. The process was nerve wracking for company executives who feared that it might destabilize the key relationship that lay at the heart of the business.[101] Where once a mail order clerk might have added a few words of felicitation at the end of a letter to a long-term agent whose daughter or son was about to be married, the computer heralded the arrival of more depersonalized communication. Managers across the mail order sector were aware that this development carried risk and, as a result, the computer's role was often hidden from consumers. Empire Stores, according to Peter Fattorini, 'would always say there had been a clerical error not that the computer had made a mistake . . . we tried to hide the computer as much as possible'.[102]

Freemans' 200,000 agents were placed on its computer system in 1966. Initially, this was a vehicle through which to save clerical time. Computerization was also introduced in order to eliminate the mistakes made when handling the vast amounts of paperwork associated with the £1m worth of stock that was out 'on approval' in each week; a facility that made an important contribution to mail order's post-war growth. It was introduced to reassure customers with doubts about the quality of catalogue merchandise, and allowed them to return merchandise free of charge if it did not meet their requirements. Established agents were offered the service initially, and it was extended generally during the 1950s. However, there were enormous costs associated with the system; in 1960, for instance, Kays anticipated the return of 18 per cent of merchandise.[103] Freemans found that the computer offered

[100] NA: BT 250/49. Committee on Consumer Credit. National Citizens' Advice Bureaux Council.

[101] M. Jackson, 'Freemans mail order', in David Caminer, John Airs, Peter Hermon, and Frank Land, *User-driven innovation: the world's first business computer* (London: McGraw-Hill Book Company, 1998), 263.

[102] Interview with Peter Fattorini.

[103] *Credit Trader*, 30 August 1958. *The Economist*, 27 February 1960.

savings in this area, by providing 'impartial' information on transactions and returns per agent that enabled the company to reduce 'appro [on approval] stock as a percentage of sales'. The company then developed a scoring system for agents, based on their length of service, sales, bad debts, and the amount of merchandise they returned. Agents deemed to be 'uneconomic' were then removed from the roster and received no more expensive catalogues. Others, who were assessed as underperforming agents, were targeted with promotional literature. The system depersonalized relationships between administrative staff and long-standing agents, who, in some cases, received a catalogue despite the fact that their agency operated at a loss.[104]

As this example demonstrates, computerization provided new opportunities for data analysis and prepared the way for credit-scoring systems. Access to the electoral register was an important early stage in this process. Littlewoods bought the register in 1971 and downloaded 16 million names from it.[105] From that moment, an applicant's absence from the register was a key factor in credit refusals. The companies also began to assess levels of credit risk through analysis of their previous experience of a number of factors. Based on a computer package acquired from the American firm Fair Isaac Corporation, each prospective agent was allocated a credit score. A mark was attached to information provided on marital status, age, occupation, spouse's occupation, length of service with current employer, number of children, type of accommodation, length of residence, and bank/credit card details.[106] Empire Stores operated this system from 1978. Factors treated negatively in creating individual credit scores included 'the existence of a court judgement' on an applicant's file, whilst spending 'long periods at an address' and being an owner-occupier rather than a tenant were viewed positively. Initially, Empire Stores included a 'proximity factor' in its credit scoring package. If an applicant 'lived at 14 Acacia Avenue, we'd check . . . whether anyone at numbers 15 to 20, or 13 to 9 had any record of bad debt and if they had, it would count against you'. However, this practice was subsequently outlawed by consumer credit legislation.[107]

[104] M. Jackson, 'Freemans mail order', 265–6.

[105] *The Times,* 26 January 1971.

[106] Economic Intelligence Unit, *The UK mail order industry* (London: Economist Intelligence Unit Ltd, 1983), 36; Monopolies and Mergers Commission, *Great Universal Stores PLC,* 24.

[107] Interview with Peter Fattorini.

A major outcome of credit scoring was the emergence of GUS's subsidiary CCN (later Experian), as the market leader in the credit referencing industry. From the early 1980s, it provided credit referencing information for GUS's catalogue and made a handsome figure selling data to its catalogue rivals.[108] Mail order's interest in the benefits of computerized credit referencing was not simply the result of technological innovation. The economic chill of the late 1970s and early 1980s was sharply felt by many of mail order's core customers. At that point, bad debt levels rose to between 2 and 4.5 per cent of sales and credit controls were tightened.[109]

However, despite the powerful tools that were presented by computerization, only the creditworthiness of agents was assessed by credit-scoring programmes. Customers remained predominantly the responsibility of agents, who were left to 'form their own view' about which of their kin, neighbours, or workmates should be given credit and to what degree. Even in the 1990s, credit checks were only carried out on customers applying for high-value extended credit.[110] Thus, even in an era of technological and bureaucratic sophistication, with vast amounts of information captured by computer, personalized relationships between agents and customers remained at the heart of mail order and it is to this that we now return.

'COMFORTABLE AND UNWORRIED AMATEURS': MAIL ORDER AGENTS AND THEIR CUSTOMERS

A remarkable number of individuals acted as mail order agents during the course of the twentieth century. By the 1930s, their numbers were in the tens of thousands, but it was in the post-war era when the catalogue became a mainstay of working-class budgets that the figures soared. Where once a rather limited range of clothing and household goods had predominated in the catalogue, by 1961 *The Times* opined that it offered 'a riot of consumer goods' that provided 'an index to the affluent

[108] Monopolies and Mergers Commission, *Great Universal Stores PLC*, 8; Interview with Peter Fattorini; *The Times*, 1 August 1981.

[109] Monopolies and Mergers Commission, *Trading check franchise and financial services: a report on the supply of trading check franchise and financial services in the United Kingdom* (London: HMSO, 1981), 7.

[110] Monopolies and Mergers Commission, *The Littlewoods Organisation PLC*, 51, 61, and 90.

society'.[111] Mail order was the fastest growing sector of British retailing during the so-called long boom between the 1950s and early 1970s. The sector's annual turnover growth was around 15 per cent between 1950 and 1957, and it increased by a total of 87 per cent in the following four years.[112] This rapid extension of business demonstrated the attraction of home shopping, based on weekly payments and part-time agents. Various estimates suggested that total agent numbers stood between 2.5 and 4 million during the 1960s.[113] The number of customers per agent at this time, according to Littlewoods and Grattan's was 16.[114] It is clear, however, that these figures included a great deal of double counting. Many agents operated more than one catalogue, and unknown numbers of dormant agents were invariably included in the statistics.

The feminization of agency, which began in the 1930s, continued after the war and by 1960 an estimated 85 per cent of catalogue organizers were women.[115] A survey, compiled in 1961, suggested that mail order users were drawn heavily from groups categorized as C2, D, and E. At that point, these groups made up 76 per cent of mail order customers, but only 67 per cent of the population. There was a strong over-representation of those from the C2 category, who provided 42 per cent of mail order's customers although they accounted for only 32 per cent of the population. The D/E categories represented a combined figure of 34 per cent of mail order users and 35 per cent of the population. Those from middle-class classifications A/B and C1 were under-represented amongst mail order users, the former markedly so. They equated, respectively, to 8 and 16 per cent of mail order users and 13.5 and 18.6 per cent of the population.[116]

One explanation of the greater involvement of C2s in mail order is their relative spending power. They had higher levels of discretionary income, greater security of employment, and greater financial wherewithal with which to maintain repayments, when compared to their D and E contemporaries. They were, therefore, targeted specifically

[111] *The Times*, 3 April 1961.

[112] *Board of Trade Journal*, 31 May 1963, pp. 1249–50; *The Economist*, 27 February 1960.

[113] Mann, 'Pattern of mail order'; Committee on Consumer Credit, *Report*, vol. ii appendices, 443.

[114] Monopolies and Mergers Commission, *The Littlewoods Organisation PLC*, 131; Avram Taylor, *Working class credit and community since 1918* (Basingstoke: Palgrave Macmillan, 2002), 153.

[115] *Economist*, 27 February 1960.

[116] Mass Observation Ltd/Economic Intelligence Unit, 'Mail order', 21.

by mail order companies. From a crude marketing perspective, this group were the inheritors of the 'respectable working class' mantle. The involvement of C2s was revealed in later surveys that explored the social backgrounds of agents. In 1981, for example, 43 per cent of mail order agents were believed to be from this group, as opposed to 12 per cent from the A/B categories, 22 per cent from the C1 group, and 23 per cent from the D/E classifications. At least one company gave agents advice on customer selection that clearly militated against taking on many from the E category. An agent's instruction booklet, issued by Kays in the mid-1960s, advised them to 'satisfy yourself that' prospective customers, or their family members, were 'in permanent employment'. Agents were also instructed to exercise caution in accepting orders from 'Widows and Pensioners' and they were told it was only 'fair to [Kays] that you supply us with facts to show their ability to pay the weekly instalment agreed upon, without difficulty'.[117]

Those in the C2 category were also valued for their relatively high levels of literacy and numeracy. Peter Fattorini, of Empire Stores, recalled his father's view that 'it was amazing how the mail order business carried on when basically a group of people who had no formal business education—a lot of them not much education anyway—took credit decisions, collected the money, filled in your paperwork for you'.[118] This point was also highlighted by the presenter of BBC radio's *Home this afternoon* programme in January 1966: 'As I talked to all these people involved in the mail-order business, I think this was the most astonishing fact of all which emerged: that a business, organised at head quarters with stark efficiency, depends, at the end of the line, on a whole lot of comfortable and unworried amateurs.'[119] Handwriting became one of the formal assessments of a potential agent. Stanley Cooke, who was an executive first at Littlewoods and later at John Myers, recalled in his autobiography how, during the 1950s, an application could be rejected due to the 'type and style of handwriting'. It was considered important 'because we certainly did not want agents who could not write'. For that reason 'printed names instead of written were always suspect, as was immature or childish writing'. Applicants from 'bad credit areas' or 'doubtful credit roads in good areas' were also

117 Worcester Record Office: Kay & Co., 'How to establish and conduct a successful spare time agency', *c.*1964: 8.

118 Interview with Peter Fattorini.

119 *Credit Trader*, 5 March 1966.

routinely rejected.[120] In the 1970s, Empire Stores weaved many of these judgement criteria into its new computerized credit-scoring scheme, awarding points on the basis of whether an applicant had used a pen or pencil to fill in the appropriate forms.[121]

Once they had surmounted the hurdles that the mail order companies placed in their path, aspiring agents received instruction on the cautious development of an agency. They were directed to draw their first customers from family and close friends and to gradually build up their credit limits. The companies also published agents' newspapers to develop loyalty, by building upon the elements of sociability that were important to many agents. One of these was *The Littlewoods Organiser*, which fostered a paternalistic climate. In its first issue, in 1955, John Moores told readers that it was 'your own paper' through which to 'meet together in the great Littlewoods' family circle'. It represented one of many attempts to commercially orchestrate working-class mores, turning concepts of reciprocity and thrift to the company's advantage. For example, readers were exhorted to promote 'the thrifty Littlewoods Club idea amongst the young'.[122] The company even had its own Little Woody club for children, fostering links to the next generation of catalogue shoppers. In 1960 a rival company issued 30,000 birthday cards to agents' children, in its own effort to 'cement a strong relationship' with customers.[123] The firms had come to realize that agent loyalty and retention rates were raised by personalized communication.[124] In the mid-1960s, the average life span of an agency was around fifteen months and there were regular advertising campaigns aimed at agent recruitment.[125] Creating a sense of loyalty and belonging amongst agents was important because for many running a catalogue presented opportunities to reinforce social contacts, or to build new ones, and was a more appealing factor than earning small sums of commission. In the early 1960s, the average agent's annual turnover stood at £150, providing £15 commission.[126] Research published in 1967 found that 82 per cent of agents were stimulated primarily by the social attractions of operating a catalogue, 11 per cent acted mainly from financial motives, and a further 7 per cent utilized the catalogue

[120] Stanley G. Cooke, *It wasn't all work* (London: Regency Press, 1983), 156.
[121] Interview with Peter Fattorini.
[122] Littlewoods: *Littlewoods Organiser*, 1 (September 1955).
[123] *Credit Trader*, 4 June 1960.
[124] Interview with Peter Fattorini.
[125] Mann, 'Pattern of mail order', 44.
[126] Mass Observation Ltd/Economic Intelligence Unit, 'Mail order', 16.

only to serve their nuclear family.[127] It found that agents attracted by the sociability associated with running a catalogue offered greater levels of customer care, engendering loyalty and higher sales to their customers, than agents whose primary motivation was financial. The majority of customers viewed the agent as *their* representative rather than the company's, providing the mail order sector with a clear advantage over its competitors, particularly when agents offered encouragement in merchandise selection. These relationships ensured that catalogue shopping became strongly habitual, or part of a process of routinization as Avram Taylor has described it.[128] Habituation was greatly facilitated by the introduction of open-ended revolving credit facilities from the 1950s, which finessed the purchase of further goods before the initial payments were completed. These schemes encouraged home shoppers to convert a one-off twenty-week commitment into a constant feature of their budget. The presence of an agent who was a friend or relative could also benefit the companies by limiting the proportion of merchandise customers returned via the 'on approval' system, because to do so was to inconvenience a friend. For related reasons, customers often selected an alternative purchase when their first choice was out of stock, so as not to deprive their agent of commission.[129] The cultural exchanges involved often dovetailed into a system of informal economics. Florence from North Wales first bought catalogue merchandise in 1922, to help a friend in 'getting the benefit' of the commission.[130] Half a century later, a study of female factory workers discovered that a primary motive in catalogue use was to 'help a mate'.[131] One commentator, writing in 1976, went as far as to suggest that an agent with a strong personality could create a 'Mafia-like atmosphere' in which customers 'dare not refuse' to buy further merchandise.[132] Less melodramatically, a more detailed investigation suggested that a strong degree of 'normative compliance' could exist in such incidences, or when 'a group collectively spends time "going through" the catalogue together'.[133] It is clear that the frequently close relationship between agents and customers, together with the availability of credit, did provide the companies with

127 Mann, 'Pattern of mail order', 46–8.

128 Taylor, *Working class credit*, 133.

129 Mann, 'Pattern of mail order', 44.

130 Florence: questionnaire returned June 1997.

131 Sallie Westwood, *All day everyday* (London: Pluto Press, 1984), 97.

132 Rosemary Scott, *The female consumer* (London: Associated Business Programmes, 1976), 25.

133 Crawshaw, 'Does mail order fit the retail life cycle?', 79.

the opportunity to tie in many shoppers. But Florence was not alone in appreciating the opportunity catalogue shopping presented 'to spread payments as money [was] very short'.[134] Paying a neighbour or relative, perhaps over a cup of tea and as part of a social visit, offered a more congenial and discrete prospect than the weekly call of the Provident agent or credit trader: no one need know that a female friend was your agent and that consumer credit was being used to acquire household merchandise. In 1955 Littlewoods began slowly phasing out its draw clubs and moving all its catalogues to a credit mail order format. In advertisements for its new system, it described its modus operandi as 'dignified credit' and emphasized the fact that 'people did not care for collectors knocking on their doors'.[135]

The post-war expansion of mail order was also testimony of the continuation of key aspects of working-class community and culture. The agency system allowed firms to embed themselves in both traditional neighbourhoods and new housing estates. Although sociologists suggested that the latter had weaker social networks than the former, the mail order agent and her catalogue was one source of potential neighbourliness. Beryl from Hemel Hempstead built up a circle of friends through her catalogue, following her family's move to a new estate in 1953. Her home became a centre of social activity: 'Every Friday evening my neighbours and friends would come and sit in my kitchen, drink tea, look at the catalogue again—pay their cash.'[136] The big five companies began targeting agents on council estates in the 1950s.[137] Their success in this endeavour led to objections from local traders whose profits were threatened. In 1961, the local Chamber of Trade on Manchester's enormous Wythenshawe estate compiled a blacklist of mail order agents. It promised to report them to the council for running a 'business' from their homes and, thereby, breaking their tenancy agreements.[138] In 1967, the National Union of Small Shopkeepers urged that tenants acting as agents should pay higher rates to their local council, and that the mail order companies take out a licence for each of them.[139]

The catalogue offered convenience: a factor that was also identified as a source of mail order's startling growth in the 1950s and 1960s. In the case of the Wythenshawe women, it represented an alternative to city

134 Florence: questionnaire. 135 *Credit Trader*, 5 February 1955.
136 Beryl: questionnaire returned 10 June 1997.
137 Mann, 'The pattern of mail order', 48.
138 *Wythenshawe County Express*, 5 October 1961.
139 *Credit Trader*, 26 August 1967.

centre shops, which were a forty-minute bus journey away. Convenience, along with credit, was the factor that arose most in discussions of mail order's attractions and in this respect it did have many advantages over other retailers and credit providers. Women surveyed in 1961 indicated their appreciation of the 'on approval' system, which enabled clothing to be tried on in the privacy of their own home, once merchandise had been selected at leisure from the catalogue, rather than in the communal changing rooms of town centre shops. The companies attempted to minimize the amount of unwanted merchandise that was returned to them by instructing agents to take customers' measurements.[140] The increasing numbers of married women going out to work also heightened appreciation of mail order's convenience. In 1956, a mail order executive argued that 'the tremendous number of married women now employed in industry and commerce meant, in the aggregate, that millions of personal shopping hours per annum had been surrendered'. Mail order, he argued, removed the need for 'frantic selection in the lunch hour' and provided 'delivery to the home'.[141] This viewpoint was reflected in many subsequent surveys. However, this method of retailing and its credit provision was also appreciated by housewives who did not go out to work. Kathy from Merseyside remembered that when 'I first got married and stopped work I found I got things for the house which otherwise I couldn't afford and you could buy the best . . . I love to "home shop".'[142] Catherine from Wallasey became a Kays agent in the 1960s, after giving up paid employment to raise her family. She felt that for herself and other agents it helped 'eke out the small wages our husbands brought in'. Catherine could clothe 'all the children, myself and my husband and buy toys at Christmas for my children with a small payment due every week, instead of having to find the cash we didn't have'. She felt home shopping also had advantages over high street shops 'which might not have the required garment in the right size or colour and, of course, there was no need to take tired and bored little children round the shops, in the hope of finding just what you wanted for them'.[143] Whilst the convenience of mail order was acknowledged widely, there were social fissures amongst consumers in their relationship to consumption. Many middle-class housewives did not make use of mail order because they did not need to buy

140 Mass Observation Ltd/Economic Intelligence Unit, 'Mail order', 12–21.
141 *Credit Trader*, 7 April 1956.
142 Kathy: questionnaire 10 June 1997.
143 Catherine: questionnaire returned 16 June 1997.

clothing on credit. Many registered a preference for local shops and the 'personal touch'. The deference they appreciated when shopping was not anticipated by working-class women. In fact, the alleged snootiness of sales assistants towards the latter was posited as a factor in mail order's advance.[144]

A further attraction for many was the catalogue itself. Mail order's 'shop window' had reached a thousand pages in size by the early 1960s, representing a significant marketing tool. Many consumers, such as Anne from Merseyside, were attracted by it: 'as a child, in the 1950s, I was fascinated by all the merchandise in my mother's catalogue'.[145] The catalogue contained a greater variety of goods than were available from all but the biggest high street retailers and it dwarfed the range of goods on offer from even the largest itinerant credit traders. Before the 1950s 'well-known companies' did not sell their goods to the mail order companies 'because of the credit trade's reputation'. Later, recalled one mail order employee, 'companies could not afford not to sell to us'.[146] The sector was ordering merchandise in such large quantities by the late 1950s that it was able to negotiate prices that undercut those paid by smaller retailers by as much as 15 per cent.[147] This growing economic muscle also ensured increased supplies of branded goods from manufacturers, despite the opposition of conventional retailers. These included the National Association of Toy Retailers, which threatened, in 1963, to boycott manufacturers who supplied mail order companies. Its concern was that once the agent's discount was taken into consideration, catalogue prices fell below those on offer in its members' stores. Although catalogue charges were often higher than consumers paid elsewhere, mail order companies were keen to compete on price in key markets, such as that for children's Christmas presents. As was the case for others involved in supplying credit to working-class consumers, Christmas was a particularly significant period in the mail order calendar. The Census of Distribution in 1966 indicated that a third of all sales were realized in the fourth quarter of the year, between October and December.[148]

[144] Mass Observation Ltd/Economic Intelligence Unit, 'Mail order', 9; 'Mail and female', *New Statesmen*, 5 April 1968.

[145] Anne: questionnaire returned 20 June 1997.

[146] Freemans: transcript of interview with Arthur Holgate, 1985.

[147] Christina Fulop, *Competition for consumers: a study of the changing channels of distribution* (London: Institute of Economic Affairs, Andre Deutsch, 1964), 124.

[148] *Census of distribution and other services* (London: HMSO, 1966); *Credit Trader*, 19 October 1963.

The increasing proportion of branded goods in the catalogues, which was 35 per cent of all items by the mid-1960s, assuaged lingering concerns about the quality of mail order merchandise and helped swell the growing minority of middle-class users. In 1962, for instance, a marked increase was noted in numbers of 'branded electric shavers, typewriters, knitting machines, tape recorders, stereo record players, cine cameras and projectors, car seat covers and motor tyres, sailing dinghies and outboard motors, greenhouses and luxury garden furniture, washing machines and refrigerators'.[149] The formerly dowdy image of the catalogue was also diminished via the increasing appearance of star endorsements in the catalogues. One GUS-owned catalogue claimed to be 'top of the league in fashion for young men', as was signified by soccer star George Best modelling its clothes. The copy writers won no awards for originality in urging readers to see 'how spectacularly George scores on pages 407 to 412'.[150]

The expense of catalogue production (around 30 shillings each in 1961), advertising, credit and bad debt, and distribution costs, all contributed to the relatively high prices that mail order customers encountered. In 1964, the Consumers' Association estimated that prices for non-branded goods were between 10 and 15 per cent higher than their high street equivalents. In 1970, GUS concurred with the latter figure.[151] Agents reduced the cost of their own purchases by discounting their commission, which was typically between 10 and 12.5 per cent. However, price did not top the list of the typical catalogue shopper's considerations. More importantly, the small weekly instalments dovetailed with the budgeting constraints of the working-class purse. Even in the affluent society, such avenues of credit were important. The Crowther Committee heard that 97 per cent of mail order business conducted in 1966 was on credit terms, usually over twenty weeks, and that the 'characteristic transaction' was for £5 or £6.[152] These sums reflected the fact that the mainstay of catalogue credit continued to be utilized on household linens, textiles, clothing and footwear, which amounted to 60 per cent of all sales in 1951 and 51 per cent in 1978.[153]

149 *Credit Trader*, 7 April 1962; *The Economist*, 27 February 1960.

150 Manchester, Great Universal Stores. Trafford, Autumn/Winter, 1970.

151 *Which?* (June 1964) NA: BT250/88, *Mail order 1968–1970* Evidence from GUS, 19 March 1970.

152 Committee on Consumer Credit, *Report*, 97–8.

153 Crawshaw, 'Does mail order fit the retail cycle?', 65.

The high turnover of these items demonstrated the particular importance of mail order credit for low-income consumers and those operating tight budgets. It was noted above that agents from social groups D and E were not at the top of the agent recruitment agenda, but as customers who were vetted by a local agent they were well represented amongst mail order shoppers. In 1981 these groups made up 29 per cent of users, a figure that broadly equated to their representation in the general population.[154] Shortly afterwards, it was estimated that the catalogue was one of the two most frequently used forms of credit for low-income borrowers.[155] A survey conducted by the PSI, in 1989, suggested that whereas one in three mail order users accessed a catalogue via an agent, the figure rose to one in two for the poorest groups.[156] It was clear that a large number of mail order agents still operated as gatekeepers to others whose access to consumer credit was limited. However, the gatekeepers were a declining breed.

PERSONAL SHOPPERS AND CREDIT ORPHANS: MAIL ORDER SINCE THE 1980S

Agency mail order stagnated between the late 1970s and the century's end. It remained extremely significant, however in terms of merchandise turnover and in the amount of consumer credit it advanced. A major investigation of the sector by the MMC, published in 1997, revealed that its turnover totalled £3.25 billion, or 4.7 per cent of all UK non-food retail sales.[157] It continued to be a particularly important source of credit for working-class households, with 65 per cent of mail order customers emanating from the C2, D, and E social groupings, at a time when they made up only 51 per cent of the adult population.[158] Those described by the MMC as lower-income groups accounted for 70 per cent of agency mail order takings.[159] The MMC was advised that up to 35 per cent of mail order users were dependent on this form of credit. Grattan explained that up to 50 per cent of its agents were likely to be rejected by mainstream credit providers.[160] These

[154] Monopolies and Mergers Commission, *Great Universal Stores PLC*, 9.
[155] Ford, *Consuming credit*, 42.
[156] Berthoud and Kempson, *Credit and debt*, 82.
[157] Monopolies and Mergers Commission, *The Littlewoods Organisation PLC*, 10.
[158] Ibid. 168. [159] Ibid. 4. [160] Ibid. 93–5, 115.

findings tallied with the earlier PSI study, which estimated 24 per cent of catalogues were used by shoppers who had no other source of credit. It discovered that despite the credit explosion of the 1980s, the catalogue remained the most common source of credit, being used by 31 per cent of households.[161] Even in the mid-1990s, 60 per cent of agency mail order users did not have a credit card.[162] The catalogue's significance for the less affluent was highlighted further by the finding that households reporting only one credit commitment utilized mail order most commonly. The persistence of highly gendered patterns of catalogue shopping and money management in low-income families was made apparent by the fact that amongst married couples two-thirds of catalogues were used solely by the female, whilst only 3 per cent were used solely by the male.[163] It also became clear that low-income families from ethnic minorities had been added to mail order's customer rosters. Those from Afro-Caribbean backgrounds used it 'extensively for children's clothing and baby equipment'. One factor in this was claimed to be the pressure they faced, like other families, to buy the 'right clothes' for their brand-conscious older children.[164] Muslims from the UK's Bangladeshi communities also used catalogues, but less extensively. They appreciated the fact that it made no interest charge for credit and, therefore, satisfied Islamic prohibitions on usury.[165] Their motivations echoed those of the mid-twentieth century consumers who were drawn to catalogues because of their ambivalent status in relation to credit.

Mail order's role in providing a rare source of credit to the low-income family was also noted in 1992 by the PSI. It described the catalogue's complex position in the consumer credit market, explaining that it was the only means of borrowing that straddled the mainstream credit market (bank overdrafts, credit and store cards, hire purchase, bank and finance house loans) and the secondary market (moneylenders, credit traders, check traders, pawnbrokers, and the Social Fund).[166] This unique position became increasingly transparent due to significant shifts in the relationship between the catalogue companies and their customers from the late 1970s. Factors lying behind these changes

[161] Berthoud and Kempson, *Credit and debt*, 53.

[162] Monopolies and Mergers Commission, *The Littlewoods Organisation PLC*, 23.

[163] Berthoud and Kempson, *Credit and debt*, 53, 82–3.

[164] Alicia Herbert and Elaine Kempson, *Credit use and ethnic minorities* (London: Policy Studies Institute, 1996), 21.

[165] Ibid. 82–3. [166] Berthoud and Kempson, *Credit and debt*, 85.

included the return of high levels of unemployment, further rises in the number of women in paid employment, growing home ownership, the increased social and financial exclusion of low-income consumers, together with competition from credit cards, store cards, and other forms of lending. The most marked alteration in the mail order sector was the rise of the personal shopper and a concomitant decline of the traditional agent. Mail order companies became increasingly eager to cater for the more affluent direct mail market as opposed to their traditional credit-dependent patrons. In 1996, it was estimated that only a third of mail order agents (2.5 million) had customers outside their own home, the rest being personal shoppers. The average number of customers had fallen to between 2 and 3. It was also revealed that most agents paid their instalments on a monthly rather than a weekly basis, although the companies were not certain about how agents' customers arranged payments.[167]

The declining availability of the traditional agent left many customers with two options. They could turn elsewhere for credit or apply to run an agency themselves. The total number of agents, standing at 7.4 million in 1996, suggested that many took the latter option. The overall proportion of agents from the D and E social categories rose from an estimated 29 to 33 per cent between 1981 and 1996, with the figures in the C2 grouping falling from 36 to 29 per cent.[168] A combination of necessity—in the face of falling customer numbers per agent—and new opportunities presented by computerized credit scoring enabled the companies to pursue this course. It was also the case that many former C2 agents, recruited during agency mail order's golden years, had reached retirement age and entered the E classification. The former centrality of the agent as an informal assessor of creditworthiness and payments' collector diminished, as the companies adapted to the shift towards personal shopping. The appearance of telephone ordering in the 1980s assisted this factor.

The traditional agent's decreasing importance went hand in hand with evidence that the mail order companies were 'becoming reluctant to deal with people in deprived areas', particularly those 'with a lot of high-rise flats'.[169] As profitability was curtailed and sales' growth

[167] Monopolies and Mergers Commission, *The Littlewoods Organisation PLC*, 123, 121.

[168] Coopey, O'Connell and Porter, *Mail order retailing*, Table 4.2 and 4.3; 113.

[169] Ford, *Consuming credit*, 35.

sharply diminished, bad debt became more problematic for mail order companies. They tightened their credit regimes accordingly. In 1997, Freemans told the MMC that around 20 per cent of its sales were to long-established agents who would not have met its credit approval criteria had they applied to be agents at that point.[170] Meanwhile agents were demonstrating heightened circumspection towards their neighbours and were increasingly unlikely to entrust them with credit. This trend has been linked, by Avram Taylor, to Philip Abrams' concept of 'modern neighbourhoodism'. The suggestion is that late twentieth-century communities did not 'constrain their inhabitants into strongly bonded relationships with one another' and that the 'diffuse trust and reciprocity of traditional neighbourhoods' had 'collapsed in the face of new social patterns'.[171] Taylor illustrates this analysis through the case of Mrs Ford, who actively hid the fact that she operated a catalogue from her Tyneside neighbours because she was not prepared to trust them with credit.[172] Those without access to either a mail order agent whose trust they had won or a credit rating that would empower them to take up the role themselves, faced financial exclusion. One mail order executive, interviewed in 1999, described this group as 'credit orphans'.[173] He felt that in the past those in this category might have been taken under the wing of a mail order agent, often a neighbour or a relative by marriage. By the 1990s, however, high divorce/relationship breakdowns reduced the number of the latter associations. Meanwhile the Right to Buy scheme, which allowed sitting tenants to purchase their council houses, led to the polarization of neighbourhoods, creating an estimated 2,000 'sink estates' by the early 1990s, and increasing social divisions within the working classes.[174] One result of these trends was an increased potential market for doorstep lenders. In 1996, Littlewoods told the MMC that agents for Cattles, Provident, and London Scottish Bank provided credit 'on a local basis which used to be provided by agency mail order companies'.[175] For low-income consumers who did secure credit from one of the big mail order companies, there was the prospect of paying higher than average prices for merchandise. For example, the

[170] Monopolies and Mergers Commission, *The Littlewoods Organisation PLC*, 147.

[171] Taylor, *Working class credit*, 43. [172] Ibid. 174.

[173] Anonymous mail order executive. Interviewed by Sean O'Connell and Dilwyn Porter.

[174] Herbert and Kempson, *Credit use and ethnic minorities*, 21.

[175] Monopolies and Mergers Commission, *The Littlewoods Organisation PLC*, 135.

MMC received evidence that Littlewoods placed its highest mark-ups on items that were bought in large numbers by consumers with few credit alternatives. In 1990, the Social Service Advisory Committee reported that this was the case with 'people who were too poor to purchase major items like beds and furniture' through a loan from the government's Social Fund.[176]

By the late 1990s the agency mail order sector's profitability was far removed from the halcyon days of the 1950s and 1960s and the companies involved were each the subject of takeovers. The object of this restructuring was principally based on what the companies could offer their new owners in terms of direct mail order, rather than credit-based agency mail order.[177] In 1998, the *Observer* noted that 'lifestyles have changed dramatically. Credit is freely available, most women have at least part-time jobs and it is far less common to live in a community close-knit enough for catalogues to be passed among neighbours.'[178] Increased access to credit, through bank accounts and credit cards, certainly presented cheaper alternatives to catalogues for many working-class consumers. Meanwhile the proportion of female mail order agents in paid employment rose from around 40 to 60 per cent between the 1970s and 1990s.[179] The mounting pressures on women's time, and the financial rewards offered through employment, together with the relationships formed thereby, replaced many of the economic and social impulses that had launched so many agencies in the past. In doing so, it also reduced one of the strongest commercialized links between the family economy and community that had existed in the twentieth century.

CONCLUSION

Mail order proved to be the most successful form of commercial credit in terms of its expropriation of working-class social networks. It evolved from its origins as commercialized draw clubs into a billion-pound industry. The catalogue became a mainstay of the working-class family economy and an artefact around which established social relationships were maintained and new ones constructed. The amount of work

[176] Monopolies and Mergers Commission, *The Littlewoods Organisation PLC*, 172.
[177] Coopey, O'Connell, and Porter, *Mail order retailing*, 70–1.
[178] *Observer*, 28 July 1998.
[179] Coopey, O'Connell, and Porter, *Mail order retailing*, 134.

carried out by agents, for so little commission, was notable. Their most significant role was in assisting the companies to overcome the asymmetry of information that was a barrier to the extension of the large sums of credit to faceless shoppers throughout the UK. By the 1960s, the agency mail order sector was the single biggest provider of retail credit. It achieved this role because it was capable of straddling the divide between income groups. In so doing, it established a system that enabled it to play a significant role in providing credit to consumers who had few other sources of mainstream lending. Like the service offered by the credit traders and the check trade companies, catalogue borrowing was costly. But this was something that customers weighed against factors such as mail order's convenience, or the ability to return goods if they did not meet their satisfaction.

The customer's relationship with the agent acted as a further motivation to buy and was often part of complex layers of familial or neighbourhood obligation. Agents provided firm footholds in the community and enabled the gifting, reciprocity, and exchange that Finn has identified with nineteenth-century credit retailing to chime strongly in twentieth-century mail order. Significantly, these exchanges were often based around female sociability. The deeply embedded relationship of the mail order agent was one that credit traders and check companies could aspire to, but rarely match. Mail order was thus provided with a further non-price advantage over other creditors who were often relegated to the doorstep, whilst the mail order agent and her catalogue took up a place in the parlour or at the kitchen table. This greater informality ensured that the disciplinary role of the mail order agent was usually less transparent. Awkward knocks on the door were less common when the agent's customer was a sister, mother-in-law, or next-door neighbour. Mail order consistently had low levels of bad debt: a study of credit and debt in 1992 found the sector had the lowest level of default for all types of credit. It was just 3.3 per cent.[180] This was a significant achievement, in which the agent's role was central. Rock's study of debtors noted that 'many people are prepared to default on contracts made with large bureaucratic creditors because the contracts are not "personalised"'. It argued that 'debtors sometimes deny the moral force of arrangements which are not made on a face-to-face level or enforced on this level'.[181] Each of the forms of credit that have been

180 Berthoud and Kempson, *Credit and debt*, 153.
181 Rock, *Making people pay*, 103.

examined thus far sought to personalize credit relations to avoid the pitfalls described by Rock, but mail order was the most successful in this exercise.

The average mail order agent was of slightly higher social status than the typical customer and they, therefore, had the potential to act as a gatekeeper to credit. For many working-class customers informal credit referencing by an agent was preferred to form filling and the fear of rejection in the high street. This was particularly true of women who often had barriers placed in their way by conventional retailers. When applying for hire purchase, for example, women were often faced with the embarrassment of the 'male guarantor syndrome', being asked for a male relative's signature on credit agreements.[182] This provided mail order with a significant advantage that lasted until agents began to evolve in large numbers into personal shoppers, leaving many potential customers without an important source of borrowing. In the past three decades, computerized credit application systems have substituted increasingly for the informal role of the agent, allowing companies to cherry-pick those low-income customers they think will meet credit repayments. For those excluded in this process, substitutes had to be found. Doorstep moneylenders were one alternative and in the next two chapters our attention turns to their controversial history.

[182] Coopey, O'Connell and Porter, *Mail order retailing*, 130.

4

The moneylender unmasked

Every form of consumer credit associated with the working class has proved controversial, but none more so than moneylending. Its mention conjures up lurid images of 'shylocks', 'blood suckers', 'usurers', and 'loan sharks'. The next two chapters examine the use of moneylenders by working-class families, probing the role of illegal and legal lenders and their frequently ambivalent relationships with customers. They represent the most comprehensive historical discussion of this subject to date; one which provides the first analysis of the emergence of large-scale doorstep moneylending in the second half of the twentieth century. Disparate forms of evidence employed include oral evidence gathered in Belfast from moneylenders and their customers, the records of the UK's largest moneylending concern, and the material produced by a century of government and media attention on the topic.

The first of the two chapters examines evolving attitudes towards usury in the nineteenth century and the efforts made to construct a legislative architecture around moneylending in the twentieth century. It takes the story of moneylending through to the 1950s; the second chapter will take the narrative beyond that point. The Moneylenders Act 1900 introduced a requirement that moneylenders register with a magistrate. The relatively modest costs of the system encouraged large numbers of female street lenders to take this course of action. Their activities were then, in principle, subject to state surveillance. However, in the 1920s, controversies arose over the very different types of lending taking place in such diverse environments as the West End of London and the back streets of Liverpool. The ensuing debate was not assisted by the lack of knowledge about 'slum lending'. There was a complete lack of fit between the ambition of some campaigners to completely eliminate moneylenders and the day-to-day monetary crises encountered by many working-class women. With one eye on those lenders who were accused of exploiting the profligate sons of the aristocracy and another on the back street 'she usurers', legislators were unable to find a workable model through which to cater for the short-term lending of small sums by working-class borrowers. The increased licence fees introduced by the Moneylenders Act, 1927, and the nominal annual interest rates ceiling of 48 per cent led thousands of moneylenders to return to the subterranean world of illegal lending. The decline in registered moneylenders was a victory for anti-usury campaigners, but back-street lending continued. This chapter delineates the moral economy of back-street lending, exploring the extent to which repayments were enforced by norms of reciprocity and obligation. It explains who used moneylenders and why they did so. This discussion is assisted by oral evidence, gathered in Belfast, which demonstrates the ambivalent position of moneylenders in the community. This evidence also suggests that Catholic priests intervened, by instructing moneylenders on types of loans and rates that could be considered usurious. This involvement prefigured the Church's later strong support for credit unions as a source of low-cost loans. The chapter also probes the role of harassment or violence in the illegal moneylender's armoury, questioning whether attempts to reduce the misery caused by high-cost moneylending had the unintended consequence of increasing the incidence of intimidation. This issue is particularly salient given the regular assertions by contemporary moneylenders that any cap on interest rates would lead them to reduce lending to riskier customers, leaving the latter prey to loan sharks.

THE MONEYLENDERS ACT OF 1900

To introduce the term Shylock to this discussion is something of a cliché, but the powerful and negative imagery that reached its zenith in the form of Shakespeare's character from *The Merchant of Venice* enveloped moneylending, consistently colouring views of this wing of the consumer credit industry. The usury laws that operated throughout Europe into the nineteenth century have been described as 'among the last vestiges of the moral economies of the ancient and medieval eras'.[1] In the late eighteenth century, political economists began to contend that these laws were 'injurious to legitimate trade and commerce, and ineffectual in checking or preventing usurious and unconscionable

[1] H. H. L. Bellot and R. J. Willis, *The law relating to unconscionable bargains with moneylenders* (London: Stevens, 1897), 29.

bargains with moneylenders'.[2] Both David Hume and Adam Smith argued that interest rates were fixed by 'the economic laws of supply and demand'. In 1787, utilitarian philosopher Jeremy Bentham challenged the applicability of these laws for a modernizing economy:

> Usury is a bad thing, and as such ought to be prevented: usurers are a bad sort of men, a very bad sort of men, and as such ought to be punished and suppressed. These are among the string of propositions which every man finds handed down to him from his progenitors: which most men are disposed to accede to without examination.[3]

Bentham attacked the rich seam of anti-Semitism found in defences of the usury laws and argued for the 'liberty of making one's own terms in money-bargains'.[4] Bentham's viewpoint was widely enough diffused by 1854 for Parliament, in the spirit of laissez-faire, to repeal the laws. The typical patron of moneylenders was then assumed to be a middle-class businessman or trader; a market in which it was assumed that laissez-faire could reign unchecked.[5] However, as R. H. Tawney identified, moneylending had long gone on amongst the lower orders, often being 'intertwined with, and concealed by, other economic transactions'.[6] Loans raised by pledging property with a pawnbroker were viewed differently and were regulated by new legislation in 1800 and 1872. Interest charges on secured loans under £2 were restricted to 25 per cent per annum and 20 per cent for sums over £2. However, these were nominal figures and real rates of interest accrued by customers depended on the length of time an item was in pawn and how often it was pledged during the course of a year: an item that was redeemed on the same day on which it was pledged attracted charges that equated to annual interest rates of 3,000 per cent. Despite these nominally exorbitant figures, pawnbrokers found small pledges unprofitable, unless the transaction was repeated routinely.[7]

The removal of usury as a legal concept did not prevent the term's use in the moral economy that operated within many county courts. Moneylenders, like tallymen, were regular recipients of judicial critiques. In 1886, one judge advised a debtor to be 'an honest man' and pay

[2] Ibid. 29.

[3] Jeremy Bentham, *Defence of usury* (London: T. Payne and son, 1787).

[4] Ibid.

[5] Melanie Tebbutt, *Making ends meet: pawnbroking and working class credit* (Leicester: Leicester University Press, 1983), 101.

[6] William Thomas, *A discourse upon usury*—with an introduction by R. H. Tawney (New York: Harcourt, Brace & Co, 1925).

[7] Tebbutt, *Making ends meet*, 8–9.

all his creditors except the 'moneylender and Scotchman'.[8] When they did enforce moneylender's contracts, county court judges frequently set 'very small instalment payments', particularly in cases involving 'usurious interest' and notorious representatives of the trade such as Isaac Gordon.[9] Gordon's Jewishness added a powerful stereotype to his negative media image, as a lobby for the reimposition of legislative controls developed in the 1890s. The campaign was fronted by Thomas Farrow, Honorary Secretary of the Agricultural Banks Association, and a champion of the German Raiffeisen co-operative credit banks.[10] In 1895 he carried out research into 'the system of usury and the practices of money-lenders', publishing his findings in *The moneylender unmasked* and selling over 100,000 copies.[11] Farrow was the major witness before the Select Committee of the House of Commons that probed moneylending in 1897 and 1898, where he accused moneylenders of charging usurious rates of interest and of questionable practices. Amongst these was their habit of trading under assumed names. The origins of this lay with the 'survival of attitudes engendered by the usury laws, under which it had been necessary to disguise lending transactions'.[12] The desire for discretion was as much a function of borrowers' as lenders' preferences. Thus, newspaper advertisements directing borrowers to a 'philanthropic gentleman or widow' invariably led to a professional moneylender. A related concern surrounded the adoption of multiple trading identities. One moneylender—Baron Cohen—operated under eight different names, Mrs Vincent being one alias. Whilst borrowers appreciated secrecy, it put them in danger of exploitation if a lender approached them in a different persona offering further loans.[13] For the moneylenders, the pugnacious Gordon argued that a business had a right to trade under any name.[14] Recognizing

[8] *Credit Drapers' Gazette*, 1 July 1886 cited in Margot Finn, *The character of credit: personal debt in English culture, 1740–1914* (Cambridge: Cambridge University Press, 2003), 258.

[9] London: Parliamentary Papers. Monetary Policy, General, [12] 1897–8. *Select committee on moneylending*, evidence of Judge Owen, 20 July 1897.

[10] See the chapter on credit unions for their history and of Farrow's ultimately disastrous experimentation in this respect.

[11] *The Times*, 26 June 1895. Select committee on moneylending (1897–8), evidence of Thomas Farrow 18 May 1987.

[12] Dororthy Johnson Orchard and Geoffrey May, *Moneylending in Great Britain* (New York: Russell Sage Foundation, 1933), 61.

[13] Select Committee on Moneylending (1897–8), evidence of Thomas Farrow 18, 20 May 1897.

[14] Ibid., evidence of Isaac Gordon, 25 May 1897.

the issue of anti-Semitism, some Edwardian judges appreciated that 'it would be prejudicial to many lenders to have to do business under foreign-sounding names'.[15] Despite one of the Committee's tasks being to investigate the relationship between 'the poorer classes and the professional Money Lender' the majority of its attention was centred on loans to farmers, the clergy, civil servants, or 'the young son of the aristocracy who in the course of sowing his wild oats ran up large debts'.[16] In their case, it was suggested that moneylenders used their customers' dread of courtroom disclosure to enforce substantial interest repayments. This matter was satirically treated in the 1905 musical *The talk of the town*, which featured two 'Hebraic' moneylenders—'the brothers English'—who were amongst a ruined gentleman's creditors.[17]

When attention shifted towards the working class, concerns were raised that this category of borrower was misled by advertisements offering interest rates of 5 per cent that did not make it clear that this was a monthly, rather than an annual, figure. Further disquiet centred on exploitative contracts and the vulnerability of working-class applicants to 'fee snatchers' who placed loan advertisements solely to levy status enquiry charges on prospective borrowers to whom they had no intention of lending money.[18] The potential market for these scams was discovered by Farrow, who placed three dummy advertisements in 'a weekly journal largely read by the working classes' and received 450 loan applications.[19]

The misuse of bills of sale by moneylenders also surfaced before the Select Committee in 1898. Borrowers provided security for loans by signing over items of furniture to the moneylender through a bill of sale. The furniture was then leased back, at a price, which added an additional cost to that of the interest on the loan. The Committee also probed the imposition of harsh surcharges for missed payments.[20] However, the problems encountered by working-class borrowers featured infrequently

[15] Orchard and May, *Moneylending in Great Britain*, 84.

[16] Committee on consumer credit, *Report of the committee* (London: HMSO, 1971), 37.

[17] *The Times*, 6 January 1905.

[18] A potential borrower would pay a sum to cover the costs faced by the supposed lender in verifying the former's employment and income details. But once this sum was received no action was taken, leaving the applicant out of pocket.

[19] Thomas Farrow, *The money-lender unmasked* (London: Roxburghe Press, 1895), 133.

[20] Select Committee on Moneylending (1897–8), evidence of Sir Henry Hawkins, 15 March 1898; evidence of Sir J. C. Mathew, 22 March 1898.

before the Committee and Farrow's investigations provided limited insights into their dealings with moneylenders. The examples Farrow presented were not contextualized and their applicability to the broad spectrum of working-class experiences cannot be ascertained. It is clear, however, that his appeal for information uncorked a bottle filled to the neck with despair. One example featured the 'wife of a struggling mechanic', who had borrowed £5 to pay her child's funeral costs. After missing a payment—'the usurer harassed her, sent her a letter stating that he would have no excuses and that the exposure would not be pleasant before her neighbours'. The woman's letter to Farrow stated: 'I am afraid they will take proceedings. It worries me nearly to death.' The link between suicide and debt was also raised by the sister of 'a working man', who explained that her brother 'has gone away for a week or two to see if a change will do him good, for the poor fellow was driven almost to destroy himself'. A 'London cabman' claimed that he had been 'tricked into giving a Bill of Sale' and 'paying exorbitant interest'. He feared that 'after working so many years to get a comfortable home together, and also the means of a livelihood' that he was about to lose both. He begged Farrow: 'Please do not let the Money Lender know I have told you this, because I am afraid if it came to his ears he would crush us altogether.'[21]

Despite these disturbing vignettes, it is clear that a growing number of moneylending firms were attracting working-class custom, and that below that level there was a large subterranean market for very small loans that was transacted in the back streets of working-class districts. The Select Committee received very limited information on this category of lending. Judge Collier of Liverpool county court introduced committee members to the existence of 'the female usurer, who deals with the poor', but he noted that the authorities had 'no statistics about them'. Although there had been 'a great deal written' in Liverpool, 'about the halfpenny in a shilling a week' lenders the non-contractual and small-scale nature of their trade meant that he did not encounter them in his court. One further, rather utopian, perspective was offered on the poorest borrowers. The solicitor Sir G. H. Lewis opined that moneylending should be abolished and that, in such circumstances, the working-class borrower 'would find some brother or friend to help him' and that there would be 'self-help amongst these men themselves'. Moreover, he observed

[21] Farrow, *The moneylender unmasked*, 171–5.

that there were 'also many charitable societies who help people in difficulties'.[22] Lewis appeared oblivious to the fact that many working-class borrowers proudly valued their independence and preferred dealing with the moneylender, rather than face the probing questions of gatekeepers to charitable funds. No working-class voices were heard by the committee, testimony was garnered from moneylenders and their critics, the legal profession, and a small number of bourgeois borrowers.

Those, like Lewis, that hoped for the prohibition of moneylending were dissatisfied with the Moneylenders Act of 1900, although it was innovative in several ways. This was particularly true of a clause giving the courts the power to reopen and redraft moneylenders' contracts in cases where interest was judged excessive and the transaction 'harsh and unconscionable'. The Act also stipulated that a moneylender could trade under one name only and required them to register their details with the authorities. In the years that followed, moneylending firms were joined on the registration lists by appreciable numbers of back-street lenders, the relatively modest registration fees assisting this development. Registration ensured that small-scale lenders retained the right to bring defaulters before the county courts, although it did not always guarantee success. In 1910, the Judge at Lambeth county court regretted that 'a lot of lower class moneylenders had sprung up since the Act' and registered themselves. He believed that a 'large proportion of their business seemed to be transacted with the wives of working men behind the backs of their husbands', and threw out the case he was dealing with because the woman being sued had no authority, in his judgement, to pledge her husband's credit.[23] The next section of the chapter outlines the appearance of a new breed of significant small-scale moneylenders in the wake of the Act of 1900. Licensing provided them with a greater visibility, and allowed the courts, social workers, and the press greater insights into their existence and, in some cases, into their activities. Increased knowledge of their numbers and of their practices made a significant contribution to renewed agitation for further legislation on moneylending in the 1920s and provided the raw material for a much clearer historical understanding of the role of the 'slum lender' in the early twentieth century.

[22] Select Committee on Moneylending (1897–8), evidence of Judge Collier, 10 March 1898; evidence of Sir G. H. Lewis, 15 March 1898.

[23] *The Times*, 23 September 1910.

'SLUM LENDERS', 'SHYLOCKISM', AND THE MONEYLENDERS ACT, 1927

Insights into the numbers of registered moneylenders in the early twentieth century are limited because records were not centrally retained by the Inland Revenue. Registration fees collected in 1912 and 1925, of £7,728 and £7,773 respectively, suggest fairly steady numbers. However, it is not possible to make a simple calculation based on these sums, as those registering paid either a three-year sum of £1 or an annual fee of 6s 8d.[24] Moreover, there is circumstantial evidence suggesting numbers may have risen on either side of the Great War. The short-lived Federation of Moneylenders published details of the 7,896 lenders registered in 1913. Amongst them were the appositely named Edward and Alice Cashman of Walthamstow, Moore and Drain of Ancoats, and Sophia Borrows of Liverpool.[25] One source claimed that there were 9,173 registered moneylenders in England and Wales in 1926.[26] Surprisingly, none of the moneylenders' organizations were able to offer the Joint Committee of the Lords and Commons that investigated moneylending in 1925 any accurate figures for registered lenders in their districts. One Glasgow lender agreed, rather vaguely, that there were probably 1,000 in the city; stating that there were 'no statistics'.[27]

In contrast, Dorothy Keeling, the General Secretary of the Liverpool Personal Service Society, carefully researched the situation in that city in the early 1920s. Her findings were first highlighted, during 1924, in a report published by the National Council of Social Service, which was also influential in lobbying for new legislation on moneylending.[28] The Standing Council on Social Work, which represented over 100 voluntary organizations, was also part of a growing swell of opinion urging reform of moneylending, 'especially among the wage earning classes'.[29] As a result, Keeling was one of a number of witnesses from the voluntary sector who gave evidence to the committee, throwing greater light on lending

[24] Orchard and May, *Moneylending in Great Britain*, 82–3.

[25] M. Morgan (ed.), *Moneylenders' Federation Manual* (London: The Moneylender's Federation, 1913).

[26] James A. Dunnage, *The modern Shylock* (London: E. J. Larby, 1926), 6.

[27] Select Committee of the House of Lords and House of Commons: *Report on the Moneylenders Bill and the Moneylenders (Amendment) Bill*, Parliamentary Papers 1924–5 (153) viii. 31, evidence of George MacDonald, 18 June 1925.

[28] *The Times*, 23 August 1925. [29] Ibid., 18 March 1925.

amongst the poorest classes of borrowers than had been the case with the Select Committee of 1897–8. When Keeling's findings are compared with information published in 1913 they indicate a rise in the numbers of Liverpool moneylenders. In 1913 758 were registered in the city compared to 1,380 in 1925. The latter total included 1,100 women, the vast majority of whom lent small sums to their neighbours.[30] Keeling's research was prompted by concerns about the financial distress caused by small-scale borrowing in Liverpool. She familiarized herself with the back-street lenders and meticulously probed the registration records for Liverpool and Birkenhead. Keeling's work brought heightened attention to 'slum lending' and she assisted in drafting a parliamentary Bill that was one of the factors underlying the Select Committee's formation in 1925. Her evidence included sombre stories, such as that of a mother of five who became heavily indebted over the five-year period prior to her suicide.[31] The astronomical rates of interest associated with slum lenders were highlighted. A common charge of a penny a week for each shilling borrowed represented an annual interest rate of 433 per cent. Such calculations were not designed to place those providing small advances over very short periods in a favourable light and, as Melanie Tebbutt has noted, the practices of even the 'least avaricious' neighbourhood lender appeared extortionate from this perspective.[32] The reliance on annual interest rates as a measuring tool was based on the credit arrangements of more affluent consumers. Similarly, many of the assumptions that informed the Select Committee's views reflected a top-down perspective posited on concepts of the rational middle-class consumer that included limited insight into money management amongst the working classes. Away from Whitehall, the slum lender's customers frequently refused to join in the critique that was offered by many witnesses to the Select Committee: their choice of lender was not dictated by nominal interest rates but by the harsh economics of survival on a low income.

Those calling for fresh legislation were not united in their agendas. In launching his Moneylenders Bill in 1925, Lord Carson argued that annual interest rates should be capped at 15 per cent. However, Keeling advocated a figure of 60 per cent for unsecured loans.[33] Her suggestion was founded on an awareness of the greater administrative costs and

[30] Morgan (ed.), *Moneylenders' Federation Manual*, Select Committee on Moneylending (1924–5) evidence of Dorothy Keeling, 19 June 1925.

[31] Ibid., 18 June.

[32] Tebbutt, *Making ends meet*, 56.

[33] Select Committee on Moneylending (1924–5), evidence of Dorothy Keeling, col. 912.

risks associated with providing small loans to working-class borrowers. This rate was also advocated by moneylending firms involved in lending small sums, whist the Select Committee heard that one county court judge felt that a rate of 220 per cent was reasonable on high-risk loans.[34] H. T. Greenwood, of the Lancashire and Cheshire Moneylenders' Association, outlined the expenses incurred on the more modest loans that were repaid on a weekly basis at his company's offices. Interest rates of 40 per cent per annum were necessary, he maintained, simply to cover expenses. He argued that rather than including interest rates on agreements, moneylenders should be directed to stipulate the amount charged for credit. Greenwood claimed that invariably 'the would be borrower enquires: "If I borrow £10 what will it cost me, and how shall I repay it?" It is not once in six months that a borrower is concerned to enquire what the rate of interest is.'[35]

As well as having information on the situation in Liverpool, Keeling had explored moneylending in the USA, where, by 1924, a strong anti-loan shark lobby had secured the adoption of a Uniform Small Loans Law in twenty states. This capped interest rates at 3.5 per cent per month, or 42 per cent per annum. To sit alongside such legislation, Keeling noted that 'America recognises the need for the establishment of well organised Loan Societies to take the place of the loan sharks'.[36] Lending agencies, based on philanthropic principles, operated in America from the 1850s, becoming more numerous after 1880.[37] Acting on what she had discovered of the American experience, Keeling helped found the Liverpool Loan Fund Committee, which charged annual interest rates of 5 per cent on secured loans and 9 per cent if they were unsecured. Running costs were underwritten by the Personal Service Society.[38] However, as Lendol Calder has argued, the American lending agencies admired by Keeling eventually failed in their aim because they 'neither drove interest rates down through the force of competition, nor reached the neediest, and hence riskiest borrowers'.[39] In the same year that Keeling addressed the Select Committee, the Russell Sage Foundation, from which she

[34] Ibid. col. 113. [35] Ibid., evidence of H. T. Greenwood, 13 June 1925.

[36] Ibid., evidence of Dorothy Keeling, col. 905.

[37] Lendol Calder, *Financing the American dream: a cultural history of consumer credit* (Princeton: Princeton University Press, 1999), 120.

[38] Select Committee on Moneylending (1924–5), evidence of Dorothy Keeling, col. 905, 921.

[39] Lendol Caldor, *Financing the American dream* (Princeton: Princeton University Press, 1999), 122.

had sought advice, sold its loan society to a former 'loan shark', the Household Finance Corporation, which was itself climbing the ladder of respectability.[40] The Liverpool Loan Fund had a limited effect in the city, although it assisted 1,098 borrowers between 1925 and 1936.[41] It could not, however, eradicate the widespread deprivation that existed. High levels of unemployment and casual working, alongside factors such as above-average family size, created a strong demand for small cash loans. Moreover, as Pat Ayers has compellingly demonstrated in her study of Liverpool's docklands, a particular form of working-class masculinity was dominant in the area. Despite the fact that the family breadwinner model was effectively a fiction for most dockland families, local concepts of masculinity allowed men the status and privilege of 'provider' without any necessary fulfilment of the role. Furthermore, a strong male community of interest existed, which was underpinned by male conspicuous consumption, particularly by networking and reciprocity centred on drink. The form of masculinity taken up by many in Liverpool 'bolstered self-image and ensured that low and irregular earnings were primarily a problem for those women whose credibility was dependent on their being able to manage on what they were given'.[42] These factors ensured that Liverpool was tailor-made for back-street lending. The city was home to 9.6 per cent of all registered moneylenders in England and Wales in 1913, a proportion that appears to have risen to 15 per cent by 1925. The 1913 figure indicates that Liverpool had one registered lender for every 984 persons. The significance of this figure is revealed when contrasted with that for economically buoyant Coventry, where there was one moneylender for every 16,460 persons. Liverpool was also home to the third largest number of pawnbrokers—behind Manchester and London—making its relative deprivation abundantly clear.[43]

As well as championing philanthropic alternatives to commercial moneylending, Keeling also advocated a licence fee of £10, which she hoped would 'eliminate those moneylenders who are a danger to the public and unwanted by their profession'.[44] Moneylenders' representatives

[40] Ibid. 135.

[41] Select Committee on Moneylending (1924–5), evidence of Dorothy Keeling, col. 58.

[42] Pat Ayers, 'The making of men: masculinities in interwar Liverpool', in M. Walsh (ed.), *Working out gender: perspectives from labour history* (Aldershot: Ashgate, 2001), 74.

[43] Tebbutt, *Making ends meet*, 2.

[44] Select Committee on Moneylending (1924–5), evidence of Dorothy Keeling, col. 905, 92l.

favoured £25; a sum more likely to force out those neighbourhood lenders who presented an element of competition at the margins of their market. H. T. Greenwood also advocated that registered lenders should have to demonstrate a capital of £1,000; a measure, he claimed, that would stop 'the evil' described by Keeling. He cited Cardiff as another city in which 'women sharks are going about touting for lending from 5s to 10s'. He also provided one explanation for the over-representation of Liverpool among registered moneylenders, by suggesting that many of them were in fact not 'actual lenders', but 'mediums through whom a would-be borrower might come into contact with a lender'.[45] Despite her measured approach, Keeling's views stirred up strong passions in Liverpool. She was subsequently 'attacked by a money-lender when visiting in a back street', the only time such a thing occurred 'during all my twenty-two years as Secretary of the Personal Service Society'.[46]

The debate was complicated because other reformers approached the issue from a different perspective by targeting the activities of 'West End lenders'. It was in this respect that anti-Semitic elements of the debate surfaced. Newspaper coverage of the launch of Lord Carson's Bill described him as 'a crusader', and the moneylenders as 'a tribe'.[47] Similar sentiment also surfaced outside the capital. In 1927, in a Glaswegian court, Bailie Munroe asked Daniel Abrahams, the managing director of Robert MacLeod Ltd: 'Why do you people adopt these very Scots names? Is it to gull people?'[48] Those who labelled themselves 'provincial' or 'industrial' lenders were prepared to offer up the West End lender as a scapegoat. Greenwood supported the prohibition of the circulars that were extensively used by the latter group and which were claimed to be frequently disingenuous. He maintained that moneylenders in this category included a 'great many' who were 'aliens or foreigners', who used English names because their own name might be 'unsavoury'. Greenwood felt that if a moneylender was 'called Isaacs he should be registered as Isaacs and not as Curzon'.[49] The Anti-Moneylending Association Limited claimed that the West End lenders paid 'enormous sums' to the Press for advertising and had 'powerful friends behind the scenes' who invested in their businesses.

[45] Ibid., col. 961, 991.

[46] Dorothy Keeling, *The crowded stairs: recollections of social work in Liverpool* (London: National Council of Social Service, 1961), 112.

[47] *The Times*, 18 March 1925.

[48] Ibid., 2 December 1927.

[49] Select Committee on Moneylending (1924–5), evidence of H. T. Greenwood, 13 June 1925, cols. 519, 543–4, 551.

Their 'favourite victims' were still said to be 'expectant heirs, doctors, teachers, farmers, officers in the services, civil servants, bank clerks'.[50] The Association described the dubious methods of lenders who produced misleading advertising and veiled the true cost of borrowing from the unwary. Tactics to enforce repayment included threatening to inform employers of a borrower's debts, which was said to be achieved by the use of an 'objectionable and noisy type' of person who would visit the borrower's workplace to 'dun him'.[51] Particular courts, with arcane procedures familiar to the moneylenders and their legal representatives, but not debtors, also came under the campaigners' scrutiny. The *Daily Mail* described Derby Court of Record as 'the money-lenders paradise' because 80 per cent of its business involved this class of creditor.[52]

Potential legislation was debated again in 1926 and 1927, resulting in the Moneylenders Act, 1927. The Act introduced annual licensing at a cost of £15 and applicants had to convince magistrates of their good character. Courts were instructed to assume that, unless proved otherwise, loans attracting annual interest rates over 48 per cent were harsh and unconscionable. Moneylenders' circulars were prohibited and their newspaper advertisements were restricted to a simple statement indicating that loans were available, the amounts offered, and the moneylender's address. Debates preceding the Act were heated with a number of MPs arguing against key proposals. The Bill had received the backing of the Conservative government, but it was clear that the issue produced competing perspectives from individuals within all parties. It is important to note, however, that those taking a sceptical approach to the proposed legislation represented industrial districts where small-scale moneylenders were most prevalent. Josiah Wedgewood (Labour, Newcastle under Lyne) feared that the legislation would decrease competition and increase borrower's expenses. Increased

50 H. H. Kelsey, *3000% or the borrowers' book on moneylending* (London: Anti-moneylending Association Ltd, 1926), 9.

51 Ibid., 20 Particular courts, with arcane procedures familiar to the moneylenders and their legal representatives, but not debtors, also came under the campaigners' scrutiny. The *Daily Mail* described Derby Court of Record as 'the money-lenders paradise' because 80 per cent of its business involved this class of creditor.

52 *Daily Mail*, 18 January 1928, Kelsey, *3000% or the borrowers' book*, 11. NA: HO 45/18460 Moneylenders. Liverpool Court of Passage. Letter to Major Glynn MP from Sir Claude Schuster 1 December 1927. Other courts used in this respect included the Mayors and City of London Court, the Court of Passage, Liverpool, and the Salford Hundred Court of Record.

licensing costs would be 'borne, not by the moneylenders, but by people who have to borrow from them'. He felt that the debate was 'handicapped by the knowledge that most people consider those of the working class who are improvident or foolish enough to borrow money from moneylenders to be not worthy of any sympathy'. He advocated a licence fee of £5, to remove the 'very small lenders, often women', whilst being modest enough to transfer unregistered lenders of 'good character' into the legal sector. The more moneylenders 'practicing their trade and legally getting their remuneration the better it will be', he opined.[53] Many extra-parliamentary observers were bemused and Wedgewood later revealed that he received more critical letters on his stance on this issue than on any other matter.[54] One journalist believed 'Socialists have been the warmest friends of Shylockism. It is apparently the one form of Capitalism which they like.' The writer was equally surprised to learn that social workers had urged Parliament to consider the proposed legislation from the point of view of the poor: 'I was under the impression that social workers generally desire to put every possible obstacle in the way of the Shylocks of the slums, but apparently I was mistaken. Nothing should be done that will make it more difficult for usurers of this class—mostly she-usurers—to prey upon their poorer or less thrifty neighbours.'[55] The social work body concerned was the Charity Organization Society. Speaking on its behalf, A. R. Kennedy (Unionist, Preston) expressed the anxiety that a high licence fee would mean 'that there would be more unregistered moneylenders' and explained that 'it is so frightfully difficult to find out those carrying it on if they are not registered'. Others offered less complex perspectives. Robert Dennison (Labour, King's Norton) believed 'it should be made as difficult as possible for people to borrow who cannot afford to borrow money'. He wanted to 'eliminate completely the shilling a week woman with 1d or 2d a week interest, and the liability that accrues in consequence'.[56]

When the legislation was finally passed in 1927, its sponsor in the House of Commons, J. B. Burman (Unionist, Duddeston) said that one aim was 'to protect the unfortunate and unskilled against the

[53] Hansard, Parliamentary Debates, House of Commons. Standing Comm A. Moneylenders Bill. Official Rpt Wed 28 July 1926. Second Days proceedings, 54, 61.

[54] Hansard, Parliamentary Debates, House of Commons, 4 March 1927, col. 744.

[55] Cutting from *Truth,* 4 August 1926 in NA/PRO. BT 58/1084 *Moneylenders Bill 1926 to amend law in respect of persons carrying on business as moneylenders.*

[56] Hansard, Standing Committee A. 28 July 1926, 54, 59–61.

shrewd experienced and often rapacious moneylender.'[57] But sceptics remained. Joseph Kenworthy (Labour, Central Hull) asked how the recommended interest rate of 48 per cent could be applied to unregistered small loans, repaid at weekly interest.[58] On a more philosophical level, he wondered why the gross profits of moneylenders were being singled out when wholesalers and retailers marked up merchandise prices by over 48 per cent. This was a defence subsequently essayed by moneylenders, such as Harry Livingstone, of the Refuge Lending Society, who bemoaned the fact that his was 'the only type of business where—by law—we have to state our gross profit in a rate per annum. Many retailers and wholesalers would be astounded if they calculated their profits on this basis. . . . [O]ur profit, based on turnover, is less than 10%: most multiple stores show a return of over 13%.'[59]

On the other side of the argument, Sir Robert Thomas (Liberal, Anglesey) denied that moneylending could be called an industry. It was, he felt, an 'iniquitous system'. He told Parliament that 'the great majority' of registered moneylenders were 'the scum of the earth'. He claimed to have 'met some of these people who have been imposing their iniquitous system upon the downtrodden slums' and said that in looking 'into the face of one of these moneylenders', one saw 'the picture of the devil incarnate. Their trade is stamped upon their countenance.'[60] Other, more temperate voices, also suggested that there was a difference between moneylending and other market transactions. T. E. Naylor (Labour, Southwark) said 'one must realise that the moneylending business is not exactly the same kind of commercial business as is carried on by an ordinary company'.[61] R. J. Davies (Labour, Westhoughton) felt that if he lent £100 to another man that 'man is in bondage to me until he has paid that sum', and therefore, 'lending money is an entirely different business from an ordinary transaction'.[62] A leading supporter of the Bill, Sydney Wells (Unionist, Bedford) concluded that it was a 'comprehensive measure of social reform, and it is an honest attempt to relieve what has been a public scandal'.[63]

[57] Hansard, Parliamentary Debates, House of Commons, 4 March 1927, col. 728.

[58] Ibid., col. 740.

[59] Consumer Credit Association (Henceforth CA). Harry Livingstone, *Refuge Securities Limited 1895–1970: 75 years of money lending*, 13.

[60] Hansard, Parliamentary Debates, House of Commons Debates, 4 March 1927, cols. 791–2.

[61] Ibid., 1 July 1927, col. 796. [62] Ibid., col. 804. [63] Ibid., col. 837.

The immediate impact of the legislation was measurable in one way. As predicted, large numbers of lenders failed to apply for the £15 licences and recorded moneylenders fell to under 4,000 in 1928.[64] In 1930 numbers dropped to 3,759, and by 1949 that figure had more than halved and stood at 1,588.[65] It was believed that amongst those who had 'ceased to trade' were the notorious 1,100 female lenders in Liverpool. Whether such lenders had ended their activities is a moot point. Bodies such as the London and Provincial Legal and Commercial Aid Association were certainly sceptical. It reported, in 1929, that 'not a penny has ever been lent in the East end of London, or anywhere else at that rate [under 48 per cent], by any Money lender on unsecured loans'. They also produced a copy of an IOU note that was available at local stationers.[66] A woman applying for a licence at Tower Bridge Police Court, the following year, bemoaned the fact that her rivals did not pay the £15 fee and, thereby, also saved the cost of advertising their application in the local press.[67] During the Second World War it was stated that 'recourse to moneylenders is frequent and illegal moneylending by unregistered persons still prevalent in defiance of the law'.[68]

As will be seen shortly, legislation returned a subsector of moneylenders whose actions had been legitimated by the 1900 Act to the illegal category. It is possible that the 1927 Act had implications in two associated markets. During the 1930s legislative focus shifted to abuses in hire purchase transactions. It was reported that some of those involved had transferred from moneylending after 1927.[69] Others relocated to Dublin or Belfast to evade the legislation, and used the sanctuary of the Emerald Isle to continue lending to British borrowers.[70] As a result, the governments of Northern Ireland and the Irish Free State passed their own legislation on moneylending in 1933.

[64] NA: IR 40/3555 Registration of moneylenders, 1929–1931. Memo from Chief Inspector of Taxes Office, 28 November 1929; Cust 49/3299 *Transfer to local authorities of licenses and duties of hawkers, pawnbrokers, money lenders and refreshment housekeepers.* Memo dated 20 November 1947.

[65] *The Times*, 17 February 1950.

[66] NA: IR 40/3555 Registration of moneylenders, 1929–1931. Letter (28 June 1929) from B. J. Hyde of the London and Provincial Legal and Commercial Aid Association.

[67] *The Times*, 13 August 1930.

[68] Women's Group on Public Welfare, *Our towns, close-up: a study made in 1939–42 with certain recommendations* (London: Oxford University Press, 1943), 18.

[69] Peter Scott, 'The twilight world of interwar British hire purchase', *Economic History Review*, 56/2 (May 2003).

[70] *The Scotsman*, 8 February 1929. London: NA/PRO, HO 45/21053. Ireland: Moneylenders Bill (Northern Ireland), 1933.

Amongst those who crossed the Irish Sea was Moses Herman. He was recorded as a Sunderland-based moneylender in 1913, but moved to Belfast after 1927, where he regularly came to the attention of the Northern Irish authorities. Described by a judge in 1941 as a 'harsh, grasping and exorbitant moneylender', Herman had arrived in England from Lithuania in 1888 at the age of 18. In 1915 he collected the first of his thirteen convictions. Amongst his offences in Belfast was one for trading as a moneylender without a licence. On that occasion, in 1938, he had persuaded his clerk to set up a company in his own name and traded as Kane Limited. He was also found to be in illegal possession of a pension voucher as a security for debt. He was fined £100. However, he continued to be resourceful in his money-making schemes and was imprisoned for three months in 1943 for an attempt to defraud the War Damages Commission with a deceitful claim about damaged property.[71] The legal authorities were not alone in inflicting discomfort on Herman, he was defrauded by Belfast's borrowers on at least one occasion.[72] Herman represented the disreputable fringe of the commercial lenders. The available evidence suggests that he was part of a minority and that the majority operated within the law. The story of their dealings with working-class borrowers will be told shortly. But in order to fully understand the nature of moneylending within working-class neighbourhoods we must start by probing the nature of back-street lending.

'I THINK HIS TRADE IS HONEST': WORKING-CLASS LENDERS AND BORROWERS

In the late nineteenth and early twentieth centuries most borrowing by working-class individuals involved crisis loans, secured from lenders within the local community. For most of this period much of this lending was carried out illegally, although a large number of small-scale operators entered the ranks of registered lenders between 1900 and 1927. Much of this activity was based on gendered networks and borrowers were differently motivated. Female networks were centred on the neighbourhood and involved loans to cover financial crises, such

[71] *Belfast Telegraph,* 3 December 1940. *Irish News,* 15 January 1941.

[72] *Belfast Telegraph,* 10 April 1930: Public Record Office, Northern Ireland: FIN18/20/302, Moneylenders Prosecution Case A. Kane Ltd and Moses Herman.

as the inability to pay rent, or a doctor's bill. Male networks were centred on the workplace or pub, where debts were often associated with gambling or drink and, in this respect, small-scale borrowing by men was often for 'treats'. This mirrored male pawning patterns, as delineated by Tebbutt.[73]

In Belfast, for example, male moneylenders operated in centres of large-scale employment, such as the docks or gasworks. Women operated mostly in domestic environments, although the large numbers of females employed in the city's linen mills produced some work-based lenders. A smaller number of women acted as agents for licensed Jewish moneylenders.

Across the UK, the scale and scope of small loan activity was clearly significant. Its precise configuration was masked from investigators by factors that included customers' unwillingness to be the cause of an illegal moneylender's prosecution, or the exposure of the borrower's financial plight to her husband or neighbours. For that reason, research has failed to chart fully the complex networks that surrounded moneylending. Historically, informants have been more reluctant to talk about moneylending than other forms of credit and in interviews detail has emerged gradually, if at all. Sociological investigators in probing the extent of moneylending in London's Limehouse district, in 1917, 'conversed with one woman on the subject of moneylending for a whole hour' before discovering that she was herself active in the business.[74] Over eighty years later, a Belfast interview was quickly curtailed when the informant sensed my keen interest in her account of time she had spent acting as a moneylender's unofficial agent.[75] Avram Taylor also reported that many of his oral history interviewees, in the Newcastle area, 'flatly refused to divulge what they knew about money lending'.[76] The moneylender occupied a position at the bottom of the credit hierarchy. As a result, it is difficult for oral interviewees to weave accounts of visits to the moneylender into the sort of narrative of feminine respectability and accomplishment that Judy Giles has identified as central to

[73] V. Vesselitsky and M. E. Bulkley, 'Money-lending among the London poor', *Sociological Review*, 9 (Autumn 1917), 132; Avram Taylor, *Working class credit and community since 1918* (Basingstoke: Palgrave Macmillan, 2002); 52; Tebbutt, *Making ends meet*, 34.

[74] Vesselitsky and Bulkley, 'Money-lending among the London poor', 130.

[75] Interview with Rebecca (born 1913. Retired waitress. First husband a docker; second husband was a builder's foreman. She had four children. Roman Catholic. Interviewed 5 November 2002).

[76] Taylor, *Working class credit*, 46–7.

working-class women's historical identities.[77] In contrast, several Belfast male interviewees were prepared to talk openly about workplace or pub lenders. This testimony was far removed from the tales of aspiration, achievement, and respectability reported by Giles. In fact, the activities described—centring on drink and gambling—undermined women's attempts to manage the home in a respectable fashion. Perhaps surprisingly, a small number of Belfast women also provided testimony about moneylenders; although two of these three were more guarded in their comments than were the men. All these accounts help construct our understanding of both illegal and legal lending in working-class communities on either side of the Second World War.

The most detailed early twentieth-century investigation of street lending was that carried out in Limehouse in 1917. Visits to 100 'fairly respectable' female householders suggested that 47 had used a moneylender, largely as a result of the casual nature of employment in the local job market.[78] The survey identified a distinction between 'loans', which were generally for sums over £1, and 'borrowed' money for lesser amounts. Interest rates in both cases were high, but in the case of 'loans' the interest was deducted from the sum handed over. Thereafter, several weekly payments made good the debt. This arrangement was available only to those who could provide some indication of ability to pay, such as a rent book without arrears. In the case of 'borrowed' money a weekly charge was made for interest, but these repayments were not knocked off the principal amount. The common rate of interest was a penny in the shilling per week, equating to a nominal annual rate of 433 per cent.[79] This type of lending was known in Belfast as 'penny money'.[80] Interest rates were less important from the borrower's perspective than the affordability of weekly payments. Problems arose regularly, however, when loans were renewed for larger sums. This increased interest payments and lessened the likelihood that the principal would be repaid swiftly. It was common for a debtor, who was unable to pay off the principal out of their weekly income, to continue paying interest for months or years. Many of

[77] Judy Giles, '"Playing hard to get": working-class women, sexuality and respectability in Britain, 1918–1940', *Women's History Review*, 1/1 (1992).

[78] Vesselitsky and Bulkley, 'Money-lending among the London poor', 130.

[79] Maude Pember Reeves, *Round about a pound a week* (London: G. Bell and sons, 1913), 73.

[80] Interview with Johnny (born 1930. Retired docker. Father of four. Roman Catholic. Interviewed 15 April 2001).

the small-scale female lenders who had registered after the 1900 Act used this system and had the option of recourse to the courts when borrowers defaulted. In 1925, Mrs Harriet Freeman of Rotherhithe in South London sued three defaulters at Southwark county court. One, who had borrowed £4 and paid back over £15 in interest, but still owed the principal, was described by the judge as 'an extremely silly woman'; he also expressed his wish that all moneylenders would lose their money.[81] However, the fact that the courts did not dwell overly long on the particulars of these cases left the complete details of the financial relationship involved unexplained. Thus we do not know what circumstances induced Mrs Freeman to become a moneylender, or what events led customers to her door to acquiesce in a system that sapped their limited economic resources.

It is clear that numerous routes could lead an individual to the role of street moneylender. The impetus was regularly provided through a neighbour's approach to someone they knew had a little ready cash. A loan was requested and customary interest rates were often suggested by the prospective borrower rather than the lender.[82] Such encounters presumably arose once the borrower had eliminated the possibility of an interest free loan from a family member.[83] In other cases, borrowers were unwilling to make relatives aware of their financial problems. Jerry White's study of interwar Campbell Bunk provides a number of perceptive insights into lending in one of North London's poorest districts. Amongst the area's female lenders were a number of shopkeepers' wives. Others involved were women who rented rooms to the poorest of the local lumpenproletariat. These ladies were dubbed the 'lodging house sharks' by one critic.[84] Campbell Bunk's male lenders included the 'few regular earners on the railway or bus services'.[85] Their relative good fortune created local inequalities that could be turned to further advantage. This was potentially the case in a more general sense throughout the UK for skilled workers or foremen, such as the LNER engine driver who successfully applied for a moneylender's licence at Stratford Police Court in 1936.[86] Some skilled workers took measures to avoid the embarrassment of being approached for a loan. One

81 *London Evening News*, 18 June 1925. 82 Tebbutt, *Making ends meet*, 54.

83 Jerry White, *The worst street in North London: Campbell Bunk, Islington, between the wars* (London: Routledge and Kegan Paul, 1986), 74.

84 Dunnage, *The modern Shylock*, 11.

85 White, *The worst street in North London*, 17, 73.

86 *The Times*, 13 August 1936.

electrician and foreman at Belfast's Harland and Woolf shipyard in the 1930s 'never carried money to the shipyard. For his policy was if you loaned money you lost a friend.' This caution extended to his home life. As the recipient of 10s a week pension for naval service, he took care to collect it from a post office in a Catholic district some distance from his Protestant neighbourhood.[87] Money was also borrowed from individuals whose work took them into working-class neighbourhoods to collect cash. Such cases only entered the historical record when the police or social workers discovered them. In 1954, a Sheffield insurance collector was prosecuted for unlicensed moneylending, having accumulated over £100 on a loan of £4, collected at 16s a week interest for three years.[88] Seven years later a Bedford milkman was fined £25 for lending customers amounts between £10 and £40. His solicitor claimed this activity had 'snowballed', because 'satisfied customers came along and asked to borrow money'.[89]

Pensions, and other benefits, financed many moneylending enterprises. The Limehouse sample included three soldiers' wives who were financing their activities via separation allowances.[90] The registration of 4,088 new moneylenders between 1914 and 1920 suggests that these Limehouse ladies were not alone.[91] Moreover, the *Pawnbrokers' Gazette* believed that increasing numbers turned to street lenders in 1914 because pawnbrokers had lowered the sums they were willing to advance, as well as reducing their opening hours.[92] The tragic death tolls on the Western Front arguably produced an incentive (widowhood) to engage in moneylending and some capital (a widow's pension) to utilize in the activity. A Glasgow woman who applied for a moneylender's licence in 1927 was in receipt of a widow's pension from the War Office in respect of her first husband. This, together with proceeds from moneylending, was sufficient for her to proceed with her application despite a warning that it would jeopardize her second husband's parish relief.[93] Other penny capitalists financed this entrepreneurial activity with proceeds from another one. Hawkers were prominent amongst

[87] Interview with Lily (born 1920. Widow and retired shop assistant. Mother of two. Deceased husband was a milkman. Protestant).

[88] *The Times*, 27 July 1954. [89] Ibid., 13 December 1961.

[90] Vesselitsky and Bulkley, 'Money-lending among the London poor', 132.

[91] NA: IR 40/2736—Board of Inland Revenue: Stamps and Taxes Division: Registered Files. Registrations under Moneylenders Act 1900.

[92] *Pawnbrokers' Gazette*, 10 October 1914. Cited in Tebbutt, *Making ends meet*, 139.

[93] *Glasgow Evening Times*, 20 and 21 December 1927.

Liverpool's small-scale lenders throughout the early twentieth century. According to Pat O'Mara's autobiographical account, the 'fish and money' women of Edwardian Liverpool forced borrowers to take two shillings of 'putrid fish' with each loan of four shillings. The system was still active in the 1930s.[94] More generally, women who charged a small commission for taking neighbours' property to the pawnbroker often used their earnings 'to dabble in a little money lending': a point made in Walter Greenwood's semi-autobiographical novel *Love on the dole*, in which Mrs Nattle's window is adorned with the message 'Neighbours obliged'.[95] A sudden windfall could also spark involvement, particularly as it could draw borrowers' attention. One Belfast interviewee recalled how a neighbour got 'a big claim, worth about £100' after being shot accidentally in the mouth by a British soldier in the 1920s. Before this point she had been 'like ourselves, robbing Peter to pay Paul', but, subsequently, 'she would lend out money'. Thereafter, her husband was also to be seen 'standing outside the docks on a Friday evening collecting the money off the boys as they come out'. It appears that the family became licensed lenders in 1935.[96] Even a woman whose husband was paid earlier in the week than others could turn that to her advantage, by lending small sums.[97] The more ambitious financed their business via loans from commercial moneylenders. A police campaign against 'slum lenders' in Liverpool in 1909 culminated in a number receiving court summonses when they defaulted on their own loans from city centre lenders.[98]

Women lenders outnumbered men in the small loans sector, which catered extensively for female borrowers. They were very much part of the communities in which they operated. One newspaper reporting on Glasgow's 'East-End Shylocks' in 1927 expressed surprise that 'women living in single-apartments in the East-end of the city eking out their husband's income' were 'lending out small sums of money to their less

[94] Pat O'Mara, *The autobiography of a Liverpool Irish slummy* (Liverpool: The Blue Coat Press, 1998), 48; Pat Ayers, 'The hidden economy of dockland families: Liverpool in the 1930s', in W. R. Lee and P. Hudson, *Women's work in historical perspective* (Manchester: Manchester University Press), 282. On penny capitalism and moneylending see John Benson, *The penny capitalists: a study of nineteenth century working-class entrepreneurs* (London: Gill and Macmillan, 1983), 90.

[95] Tebbutt, *Making ends meet*, 51. Walter Greenwood, *Love on the dole* (London: Florin Books, 1934), 62.

[96] Interview with Mrs R. (born 1904. A Gallagher's tobacco factory employee, mother of eight and wife of a carter. Roman Catholic. Interviewed 13 October 2002). Interview with anonymous Northern Ireland moneylender, 2.

[97] Tebbutt, *Making ends meet*, 51. [98] *The Times*, 4 June 1909.

fortunate neighbours'. However, when such activities succeeded, their home and consumption levels often stood out. The Glaswegian women described above included several with 'capital running well into three figures'.[99] In 1936 a Glaswegian lender applied for a new licence, having moved from a one-bedroom house to a four-bedroom home.[100] Kathleen Dayus's account of Edwardian Birmingham describes the arrival in her street of Miss Vulcan, an elderly Jewish moneylender. Neighbourhood interest was stirred by the unusual sight of a painter preparing an empty house for a new occupant. That this was 'someone special' was confirmed by the arrival of 'a succession of beautiful old pieces of furniture', including a 'straw mattress and brass bedsteads on which the morning sun glittered like gold . . . real carpets . . . a leather armchair and kitchen chairs which matched and brass firedogs and a fender' and 'a highly polished harmonium'. Young Kathleen was befriended by Miss Vulcan, who asked her to 'spread the word around and tell people what my business is, and that if they need me I'll be able to help and charge only a little interest'. This offer was taken up by many local women. However, the episode ended unhappily, with Kathleen's mother owing Miss Vulcan £5. The glamour of the latter's entry into the narrative is matched by her unattractive exit, complete with an anti-Semitic undertone; Kathleen seeing an 'evil . . . side of her nature that she'd kept hidden from me.'[101] Another Kathleen, this one raised in the Markets area of Belfast in the 1920s, remembered the local moneylender 'because she used to go up in a jaunting car and I thought that was great. She used to have big gold earrings and fancy dresses.' Kathleen believed that the local moneylenders also had 'wee country houses out in the country somewhere for their summer holidays' and recalled, with laughter, that as a child she viewed them as 'the rich people; they were rich!'[102]

Another Belfast interview compared her granny's home in the 1960s with that of her moneylending aunt:

> My Aunt Sarah—the thing I remember most about her was—that she loved brasses, her whole wall had all these brasses—looked like she had a lot of money—you know. Cos my granny had very, very little. My granny had the

[99] *Glasgow Evening Times*, 21 December 1927.

[100] *The Scotsman*, 9 July 1936.

[101] Kathleen Dayus, *Where there's life* (London: Virago Press, 1985), 43–4, 67.

[102] Interview with Kathy (born 1920. Retired auxiliary nurse, mother of three children and wife of a flourmill worker. Roman Catholic. Interviewed 9 January 2003); Interview with Anne-Marie (born 1951. Mature student and mother. First husband a scaffolder; current husband a musician. Interviewed 20 May 2003).

barest necessities in her house and my Aunt Sarah had big silk cushions, you know, and there was always jam and chocolate biscuits. She'd always got all the goodies in the house. She made herself comfortable with her profits, very, very comfortable with her profit, and surrounded herself with things that she really liked.[103]

Whilst this relative affluence was significant in neighbours' eyes, profits made by registered small-scale lenders appear to have been too modest to attract income tax. One tax inspector recalled the situation in Peckham before the 1927 Act:

most of the registered moneylenders were women, the wives of workmen, who were in the habit of lending small sums periodically to neighbours. These cases produced practically no Income Tax, any profit realised from the moneylending operations when added to the joint other income of the husband and wife proving insufficient in most cases to alter a liability to Income Tax.[104]

What factors created the market in which this small-scale lending took place? There were numerous reasons why people used street lenders, despite their charging annual interest rates that rose into three figures. Most obvious was the inability to obtain cheaper forms of credit; in particular the absence of items that could be pawned to raise a secured loan.[105] In such an event, family or friends might be approached for an interest free cash loan or, failing that, an item that could be borrowed and taken to the pawn shop. Mrs R recalled helping out a teenage neighbour during the 1930s. The young woman had been left to manage her home on the wages of two casually employed dockers—her father and brother—following her mother's death. During a financial crisis and at her wit's end, she approached Mrs R and asked to borrow a pair of shoes that she then pawned. They remained in pawn for six months and Mrs R eventually had to remind the girl to redeem them:

Her Da got a week's work that week and she went up and lifted the pawn—and I was sitting in the house and she come down and she threw the parcel down and walked out—never said 'Thank-you', 'Kiss me arse!' or one thing or the other [laughter]—walked out. I was raging . . . my man would've killed me about that—for everybody got the lend of that. Oh God bless us! God help her too, she was tortured, tortured.[106]

103 Interview with Anne-Marie.

104 NA: IR 40/3555, Board of Inland Revenue: Stamps and Taxes Division: Registered Files. Registration of moneylenders 1929–1931, Memorandum 28 November 1929.

105 Paul Johnson, *Saving and spending: the working-class economy in Britain 1870–1939* (Oxford: Clarendon Press, 1985), 188.

106 Interview with Mrs R.

For obvious reasons, borrowers in such a precarious financial state, seeking very small loans, were not attractive to commercial lenders. One of them told the Select Committee in 1897 that this class of business was 'too much trouble; they keep moving about from one place to another'.[107] The working-class wife frequently turned to street moneylenders when, for example, she 'found herself "broke" in the middle of the week, and the grocer or baker refusing to give further credit'. Or, as in cases described by a Glasgow journalist in 1927, 'a husband may have borrowed money which, in a weak moment, he used for betting or for a "spree" with his pals, the result being that the wife does not get her "pay" at the end of the week, and has to follow her husband's example as far as "raising the wind" is concerned'.[108] Such accounts of working-class marriage were reported to be 'not uncommon' in Glasgow's courts. In Campbell Bunk, it was often their lodger's inability to pay the rent that offered landladies the opportunity to turn their entrepreneurial talents to moneylending.[109] Other loans originated, initially at least, in attempts to maintain 'customary standards of behaviour', or in related efforts to avoid the stigma of having to appeal for charity or state aid.[110] An investigation carried out during the Second World War found that one or more wage earner falling ill within a family generally ushered in a financial crisis. The same report suggested that publicly financed support for the unemployed during the 1930s had not been sufficient to prevent wide-scale recourse to moneylenders.[111]

Not all loans, particularly those taken out by men, were to deal with immediate crises, although the repayment costs could induce financial problems. There was often an association between lending and betting. The Select Committee of 1925 was told that in 'every factory and workshop' in the Midlands, 'there is some person ready to lend money to his fellow man from a penny to two pence in the shilling per week' and that this capital was usually used for gambling.[112] As was the case with female lenders, involvement in workplace moneylending did not automatically make a man unpopular. The case of George

[107] Select committee on moneylending (1897–8), col. 4201.

[108] *Glasgow Evening Citizen*, 21 December 1927.

[109] White, *The worst street in North London*, 74.

[110] Johnson, *Saving and spending*, 189–92; Veselitsky and Bulkley, 'Money-lending and the London poor', 131–3.

[111] Women's Group on Public Welfare, *Our towns*, 19.

[112] Select Committee on Moneylending (1924–5), evidence of Albert Hunt, 18 June 1925, col. 720.

Carter, who was lending money at his workplace, the Royal Small Arm factory, Enfield, in 1903, further illustrates the complex place of those involved. Carter was arrested outside the factory and accused of taking bets illegally. The damning evidence of a slip, reading 'Venus 1/- win' was allegedly found on his person and he was fined on his appearance in court. This was despite the testimony of friends who disputed the police evidence and claimed that the officers involved had committed perjury. The court heard that Carter was one of several moneylenders at the factory and that he was registered for this purpose. Arthur Vince admitted assisting Carter with his business, but denied that it included bookmaking and argued that he 'would not be seen in his company if he were a betting man'. The magistrate asked him 'Do you think one trade is infamous and the other is not?' He replied: 'I think his trade is honest.' A public meeting was subsequently attended by 500 to 'protest against the unjust conviction of Mr G Carter'. The campaign continued with a night of 'Grand Variety Entertainment' for the 'Carter Defence Fund', chaired by a local councillor, and a further meeting addressed by a Congregationalist Minister, Reverend Stanley Tape. What is interesting about all of this is the fact that so many were willing to support a moneylender. Clearly, Carter was not universally unpopular and appears to have been defended because he was likely to lose his job due to his conviction for illegal bookmaking.[113] The eventual outcome of the case is unclear, but Carter was still a registered moneylender in 1912.[114]

Aside from gambling there were other motives for borrowing that were driven by a variety of factors other than household necessity. In interwar Campbell Bunk, costermongers of both sexes regularly used moneylenders to buy stock for their day's work.[115] Johnny, a former Belfast docker, used a moneylender in the 1940s to buy his first tailored suit. It cost £10, a sum he would have found it 'very, very hard to save'. When asked why he didn't use an alternative, such as a Provident check, he replied:

> If I got a Provident check I couldn't go to certain shops that I wanted to. You started to get a little bit trendy [and] to get interested in the female anatomy,

113 NA: MEP0 2/637 Betting—appeal against conviction under guise of moneylending (15 November 1903–27 January 1904): *Weekly Telegraph for Waltham*, 4 December 1903.

114 Morgan, *The Moneylenders' Federation Manual*, 32.

115 White, *The worst street in North London*, 58.

you know. And you want to dress in the trendiest gear and you couldn't get the trendiest gear in a shop that took Provident checks.[116]

Two decades later, street moneylenders were still common in Belfast; a sign of affluence's tentative embrace of large sections of the UK economy. Pat recalled how, as a teenager in the 1960s, he used moneylenders:

My mates and me we used to be standing at the corner—maybe on a Saturday night—skint. And we would borrow three quid between us and that meant we owed three pounds and twelve shillings the following week. But we always paid the next week, so we'd meet on Friday night put twenty-four shillings in each and paid the money. So it suited us, although it was exorbitant. We were borrowing to go down town to the dance.[117]

Despite using the moneylenders, he also recalled shouting abuse at one, because she was one of the 'sinister shark types' who took benefit books as security for loans. His actions suggest a moral economy in operation amongst borrowers that identified some practices as beyond the pale:

One woman in particular—who was known as the Pension Book Queen—we used to shout it at her on the street. This woman used to come up the street, this very ugly woman who owned a shop and we used to—from the darkness—my two mates and me used to shout at her—'The pension book queen!' Which she fucking hated, she absolutely hated anybody knowing. She thought that people didn't know; the whole district knew.[118]

As will be explained shortly, some working-class borrowers approached commercial lenders for larger loans. By presenting some form of security or demonstrating stable earnings they could take advantage of the greater capital and less onerous terms on offer from these lenders. However, for those dependent upon the small-scale lenders, transactions attracted extremely high rates of interest that consistently shocked outside observers. Why did they tolerate such high rates, often over long periods?

The vast majority of street lenders, particularly after 1927, did not register their activities with the authorities. They could not, therefore, dangle the threat of a court summons over defaulters. Other methods of enforcement were required. Obligation, connection, and locality were the key factors in this respect. Carl Chinn suggests that working-class

[116] Interview with Johnny.

[117] Interview with Pat (born 1948. Boilerman. Three children—one deceased. Roman Catholic. Interviewed 10 September 2002).

[118] Ibid.

individuals felt duty bound to repay debts to neighbours and Taylor maintains that street lenders skilfully manipulated this norm of reciprocity for 'instrumental purposes'. Like the most successful agents of the check traders and mail order companies, neighbourhood lenders instilled a sense of obligation amongst their customers through the credit nexus, and were able to utilize the instrumental element that existed within the 'solidarity relationships within the working class'.[119] Obligation was heightened by proximity and connection. Ayers has argued that male workplace lenders were 'very well placed to ensure repayment' and the same point should be made for street-based female lenders.[120] Whenever an outsider counselled that a working-class borrower terminate their repayments, because their loans were not legally enforceable, the latter was generally shocked 'at any suggestion of repudiation' of a trust-based relationship. Significantly, 'the inescapable fact of poverty itself' meant that street moneylenders were 'actually held in esteem' and 'as friends who are kind enough to oblige the unfortunate'.[121] A Liverpool court that was investigating the suicide of an indebted woman in 1908 heard that female moneylenders were popularly known as 'Aunty'; a nomenclature that twinned them with 'Uncle'—the local pawnbroker.[122] In the same city two decades later, female borrowers with little understanding of the interest rates being charged were usually very grateful to their lender. '"She is very kind"', they would say of moneylenders demanding a penny in the shilling interest a week, 'little realising that this amounted to 433 per cent per annum,' wrote one exasperated observer.[123] One 'old woman wearing a shawl', who applied for a moneylender's certificate in Liverpool in 1927, could neither read nor write, but made a living by lending to dock labourers £1 on Mondays and receiving £1 2s in return on Fridays. The magistrate believed that this was 520 per cent per annum, but was told that customers were willing to pay and that her neighbours 'gave the woman a good character'.[124] Thirty years later, Madeline Kerr's study of one Liverpool district discovered that street moneylenders were 'not regarded as an exploiter but rather as a saviour'. The moneylender was

[119] Carl Chinn, *They worked all their lives: women of the urban poor in England, 1880–1939* (Manchester: Manchester University Press, 1988), 78; Taylor, *Working class credit*, 64–7.

[120] Ayers, 'The hidden economy of dockland Liverpool', 275.

[121] Women's Group on Public Welfare, *Our towns*, 19–20.

[122] *People's Bank Gazette*, October 1908.

[123] Keeling, *The crowded stairs*, 111.

[124] *The Times*, 21 December 1927.

'usually a "Gran", at any rate always an elderly woman'. The regular interest charged was '2s in the pound per week . . . but on the other hand a moneylender will lend neighbours money in times of great distress and refuse interest.' One woman described how when she was unable to meet the costs of her baby's funeral a moneylender, who was known to her family, told her 'to find out how much it would cost' and then 'she gave me the money. She took no interest. I gave her money back so much a week. I will never forget that.'[125] This was either very skilful manipulation of an emotional exchange or a genuine act of compassion. In either case, it did no damage to the lender's illicit business.

However, not all street lenders were viewed as positively. The relationship was frequently ambiguous: a factor demonstrated by Johnny. Asked what Belfast people thought of moneylenders, he proffered a definite reply:

> They despised them. The moneylenders then—and I mean without exception—seemed to have a superior attitude about them. They seemed to believe that they helped a lot of people out. I actually heard a moneylender saying that: 'I'm sick helping you out.' They actually came to believe that they were helping these poor people by lending them money. And that was the attitude. You had to be nice to them, and you couldn't go round and ask them in an abrupt manner to: 'lend me a loan'. You had to be cringing and whining. You had to humiliate yourself at times for to get the loan off them. For they liked you to battle for a loan, you know. They got that feeling of power over you, like a serial killer would get over another one of his victims. They had that power over you and sometimes they made you beg. I remember going around to one of them, who was a cousin of my father, for a loan and she'd tell you to come back, because she was saying her rosary or she was listening to The Archers on the radio [mimicking a posh English accent]. And this is the kind of thing that wasn't very good for the self-esteem, let's put it that way, you know. You felt humiliated. And you had to go back to her and then sometimes when you're back: 'Oh she's gone out—she's away over the chapel or the mission.' Now some of these were the pillars of society. They were regular church attenders. I actually don't believe that they were aware that they were committing the sin of usury.[126]

Note Johnny's familial link with the moneylender. Only later in the interview did it become clear that his father had acted as an agent for his moneylending cousin, that Johnny had himself carried out collections for her as a child, and that his mother later acted as an agent for another

[125] M. Kerr, *The people of Ship Street* (London: Routledge and Kegan Paul, 1958), 95.
[126] Interview with Johnny.

female moneylender. In all these instances, according to Johnny, they were not paid. From this viewpoint, they were doing favours for neighbours. This was a regular feature of the Belfast testimony.[127] Further ambivalence emerged in Johnny's testimony about another moneylender:

Anne F.—she was a lovely woman. I used to get a loan on Anne and pay her back the following week. I think she was charging 1/6 to the £ or something. Say I got a fiver off Anne—what happened was I was going with the wife, then I was out with the boys on the Saturday night—maybe playing poker. You're skint and you need to get a loan. Come Monday night I sent round to loan [from] Anne [and] she sent the money round.

A further level of complexity was added to the relationship through the role of the Catholic Church. Johnny wanted to repay one loan the following week, but Anne would only take repayments over nine or ten weeks. When he questioned her on this 'she was very hesitant about telling me and then she finally told me. The priest told her she was committing a sin' by arranging one-week loans. The priest had told her she could lend over the longer period (with fixed interest payments of 1s in the £ rather than 1s in the £ per week) and 'that's what she done to avoid committing a sin. As long as you worked within the bounds you didn't go to the flames of hell, you know. You could make as much money as you wanted (laughter).'[128] The longer repayment period had significantly reduced the annual interest rates associated with the loan. A licensed Belfast moneylender revealed that a now deceased illegal lender from the Markets area had also consulted his parish priest about his interest charges.[129] It is clear that kin, community, and religion intertwined to establish the social codes through which street moneylenders could operate within Catholic Belfast on either side of the Second World War. The Church's intervention in these local credit networks anticipated its involvement, from the 1950s, in the rapid growth of the Irish credit union movement.

Obligation and community links were not always enough to guarantee repayment. In 1936, a newspaper article on the ' "Sharks" who prey on Glasgow women', explained how Mrs X operated. Borrowers thought initially that they had 'encountered a female relation of Santa Claus', but soon realized she had been 'picking up a few tips from Shylock'.

127 Interview with Rebecca; interview with Anne-Marie.
128 Interview with Johnny.
129 Interview with Anonymous Northern Ireland moneylender 2.

These included threats to inform a borrower's husband, which was 'sufficient to set her trembling'.[130] The relative wealth of street lenders made them 'influential' and capable of making 'life very unpleasant for defaulters'.[131] Mary, who set up home in Belfast's Ardoyne district in 1938 described the area as

> terrible for moneylenders. I saw women that lent out money going to people's houses and standing outside their door 'til their husbands came. There was one woman—her husband worked up at the tramway depot—and the woman that lent the money used to go up and stand at payday at the tramway depot, which must have been very embarrassing for the man.[132]

The consequences for his wife are likely to have been even more unpleasant. In the most tragic cases, it was reported that suicide had resulted from indebtedness to moneylenders.[133] Embarrassing debtors was an effective weapon because resorting to a moneylender represented the ultimate sign of bad household management. Taylor's study reveals that similar harassment was also a common tactic in Tyneside.[134] Whilst lending within female street networks provided borrowers with an important financial tool, it was also a last resort. Women strove hard to portray themselves as good managers to their husbands and local community.[135] Using a moneylender severely weakened male authority within the family and implicitly questioned the adequacy of a husband's earning power. Domestic violence was, potentially, his explicit response.[136] Fear of shame and/or violence kept moneylending very much within a female 'shadow economy'. This was despite the fact that in the 'more specifically "male" shadow economy'—in places such as Campbell Bunk, or the Liverpool or Belfast docklands—workplace or pub moneylenders were also active. Their use, however, involved 'separate standards and value judgements' set by the men themselves.[137]

If shaming rituals did not work, violence, or its threat, could follow. Violence does not appear to have crossed gender boundaries. Female

[130] *Sunday Post*, 17 May 1936.

[131] Women's Group on Public Welfare, *Our towns*, 19.

[132] Interview with Mary (born 1913. Retired library assistant/shop worker, mother of seven and wife of a slater. Roman Catholic. Interviewed 2 December 2002).

[133] Keeling, *The crowded stairs*, 60; Vesselitsky and Bulkley, 'Money-lending among the London poor', 134.

[134] Taylor, *Working class credit*, 53.

[135] Giles, '"Playing hard to get"'.

[136] White, *The worst street in North London*, 143.

[137] Ayers and Lambertz, 'Marriage, money and domestic violence in working-class Liverpool', 208, 202.

lenders assaulted their female borrowers, or vandalized their property. In other cases, 'hard men' were recruited to threaten, or assault, the unfortunate woman's male relatives. The initially friendly Glaswegian lender 'Mrs X' was reported to use 'terrorism': '"Have you heard about poor Mrs Brown?" She will say to Mrs Smith suggestively. "She refused to pay me the money she owed me last week. Funny her son should be set upon by four men and beaten up so badly isn't it?"'[138] In 1933 a columnist in the *Sunday Mail* had urged the police to deal with Glasgow's 'new gangster money-lenders', a grouping he described as 'a crude form of syndicate . . . supported by gangs of young hooligans.' In the system the 'money-lender needs no security. He has the security of a gang of young corner boys who will beat up his victim if there is the slightest indication of rebellion.' Male relatives of female borrowers were prospective targets. Defaulters were told that the gang would 'tell the husband' and 'threaten to maul him over if he won't pay up'. A social worker claimed that 'there is scarcely a close in some of the poorer districts . . . which does not contain at least one victim of the unlicensed gangster money-lender'.[139] It is tempting to suggest that this Glaswegian development was an unintended consequence of the 1927 Act. As we have seen, in 1925 it was estimated that there were as many as 1,000 registered lenders in the city. In 1930 there were 172, and in 1936 there were 145.[140] The removal of large numbers of registered moneylenders, which ended the possibility that they could sue for small debts in the courts, must have increased the use of violence as a means of debt enforcement. It is possible that this was a localized phenomenon, associated with the profusion of violent gangs in interwar Glasgow; a development that saw it labelled 'the Scottish Chicago'. Andrew Davies has described how long-term high unemployment in the city led a number of street gangs to 'mutate into organized criminal gangs, operating protection rackets and forming networks of thieves'.[141] Illegal moneylending presented such individuals with further opportunities. However, the connection between violence and moneylending did not begin in Glasgow in the 1930s. In 1909 it was reported that large numbers of assault

138 *Sunday Post*, 17 May 1936. 139 *Sunday Mail*, 4 June 1933.

140 *The Scotsman*, 18 June 1930, 17 June 1936.

141 Andrew Davies, 'Street gangs, crime and policing in Glasgow during the 1930s: the case of the Beehive Boys', *Social History*, 23/3 (1998), 253; also Andrew Davies, 'Glasgow's "reign of terror": street gangs, racketeering and intimidation in the 1920s and 1930s', *Contemporary British History*, 21/4 (December 2007).

cases in Liverpool arose out of 'slum money lending', and that the 1900 Act did not protect customers in such incidences because even those of 'infamous character' could receive a moneylender's certificate. A terrifying portrait of one Liverpool female lender was presented. She was described as 'a notorious virago, a wrecker of homes' and as a 'big stout woman of about 50' who could 'fight like a man'. She was 'continually in rows owing to her money transactions and bears the scars of many a street battle on her face'. Combining 'the cunning of the fox with the tenacity of the tiger', she managed 'to keep out of the clutches of the law' and when 'collared, can always pay for legal advice'. If repayments were not forthcoming she did not 'sue her debtors' but 'thumps it out of them'. The toughness of some borrowers is indicated by the fact that she occasionally had to be reinforced by 'a gang of bullies, men and women, ready to help in assaulting a recalcitrant debtor or in smashing up her house'.[142] O'Mara's autobiography also describes the violence of the 'fish and money' women who relied 'upon their reputation for administering physical beatings to recalcitrant debtors'. He describes one woman who ended repayments to a moneylender on her priest's advice, only to be rewarded by being beaten 'into unconsciousness' and having all her 'furniture and prized religious pictures' broken up.[143] Reports of violence associated with 'slum lending' in Glasgow and Liverpool are a further reminder of the harsh economic conditions in both cities. In areas with high levels of unemployment, irregular earnings and families of above average size, street lenders faced greater difficulties in extracting payments from desperate borrowers, increasing the likelihood of violence.

The Belfast interviewees maintained that violence was not a regular tool in the moneylender's armoury, but close analysis of their narratives suggests that it did underpin the system. Johnny recalled a female moneylender, whose brother 'was a bit of a hard man, a leg breaker'. She asked him to 'go round to people who owed her money and more or less demand, with menaces, that they paid'.[144] Another informant explained how his grandmother, a moneylender, smashed the windows of bad debtors.[145] This evidence appears to tally with the view essayed by the Limehouse study that a successful moneylender had to be

[142] *The Times*, 4 June 1909. [143] O'Mara, *Liverpool Irish slummy*, 48–9.
[144] Interview with Johnny.
[145] Unrecorded interview with anonymous respondent.

'capable of administering a "hiding" '.[146] In the case of male debtors, a threat to inform their wife was unlikely to be an intimidating prospect, so violence was a more regular outcome. It is notable that during the 1950s Belfast's dock-gate moneylenders included a number of ex-boxers, whilst others employed 'hard men' as 'minders'.[147] The city's gasworks also attracted moneylenders, who either worked there or offered their services at its gates. Rates were 5s in the £ and one interviewee recalled a moneylender with a 'very nasty disposition', who was employed on the site, beating up one elderly alcoholic co-worker who owed him money.[148]

A factor that militated, potentially, against the use of violence was the possibility of an illegal lender being reported to the authorities. This happened on a very limited basis; often as the result of a husband discovering his wife's debts or after a borrower developed a grudge against a lender. Mrs Kate Skillett was fined £5, in 1939, for lending without a licence. She secured a capital advance from Staddon's Mutual Loan and Investment Society and began lending to neighbours in her flat complex at Milner Road, West Ham. Mrs Allen, a mother of six, initially borrowed 5s, at a cost of 5d interest per week. She increased the principal over the months to £3 15s and the weekly payment climbed to 6s 3d. She paid this between June and December 1938, at which point she was unable to continue, but still owed the principal. Other residents of the flats gave statements about Skillet's activities to police investigators who were prompted by an anonymous tip-off from a male informant. It is possible that he was the husband of Mrs Viney, who had 'found that she had borrowed money from Mrs Skillett and paid the total amount of money to his wife who thereupon paid off the debt'. Another possible motive for the tip-off was Skillet's move to a new address, on the leafy Byron Avenue, which may have engendered jealousy or a heightened sense of exploitation amongst her former neighbours. Her departure from the community must also have served to weaken any sense of obligation felt towards her.[149]

[146] Vesselitsky and Bulkley, 'Money-lending among the London poor', 136.

[147] Interview with Johnny.

[148] Interview with Benny (born 1930. Retired gasworks employee. Married with one son. Protestant. Interviewed 11 February 2003).

[149] NA: MEPO 2/4180, Unlicensed woman moneylender and her penny in-the-shilling interest: reward offered by Customs and Excise Department to Detective Sergeant.

A further method through which to bring a relationship with a moneylender to an end was by violence on the borrower's part. The Limehouse researchers learned that the conclusion to a transaction could depend on which party 'can offer the greater physical force or possesses the more lurid vocabulary'.[150] This appears to be what happened in the case of Frank Gillam, a 26-year-old labourer who, in 1927, attacked the husband of a woman to whom his wife was indebted.[151] Alternatively, a moneylender's bluff could be called, as was the case with one Limehouse woman, who 'repudiated the balance of her debt', after she was 'sworn at and abused by the money-lender in the street'. She calculated that it 'was not worth her while trying to sustain her reputation after she had been publicly insulted'. Another woman had paid £5 10s interest on a loan of £3 before the death of the moneylender brought an end to the payments.[152] A less dramatic conclusion could be arranged via the renegotiation of the loan, so that the principal was refunded in instalments. This was a course taken by some ' "conscientious" but "less long suffering" borrowers' in Limehouse, although the 'money-lender frequently objects to this course'.[153] Johnny, was able to use familial connections in Belfast in this respect. Following his wedding, in the early 1950s, he found himself with debts of £120 and with weekly interest payments higher than his earnings. Eventually he got his 'mother to go around' to arrange 'to pay this money back at so much a week, at a lower rate over a period of about three years'. This suggestion 'went down very, very badly', but the moneylender had no 'legal way of getting money back off me'. Although Johnny was aware that he could have repudiated the loan, he still felt 'a wee bit of sort of moral obligation' to the moneylender.[154]

Johnny was fortunate to have connections that enabled him to end the crippling interest-only repayments that prevented him addressing the repayment of the principal. Many other working-class borrowers avoided this excessive cost by dealing with commercial moneylenders and it is their story that is told next. The emergence of a new breed of doorstep moneylending, in the 1960s, is also probed as is the creation of several of the leading players in what became known at the end of the twentieth century as the 'sub-prime' sector.

150 Vesselitsky and Bulkley, 'Money-lending among the London poor', 137, 151; White, *The worst street in North London*, 91.

151 White, The worst street in North London, 91.

152 Vesselitsky and Bulkley, 'Money-lending among the London poor', 137, 134.

153 Ibid. 136.

154 Interview with Johnny.

CONCLUSION

This chapter has examined the underlying issues that motivated legislation surrounding moneylending in the early twentieth century. Deeply ingrained animosity to usury informed the attitudes of many taking part in efforts to diminish the role of moneylending in working-class communities. Knowledge of the factors that created demand for small, short-term loans was incomplete, as was that on borrowers' motives. Some of those driving the legislation in the 1920s were motivated by a desire to eliminate the metropolitan lenders who profited from the sons of the elite; their knowledge of the small loans market was non-existent. This is clear from their perplexed response to those MPs, usually from inner city constituencies, who spoke pragmatically about the impossibility of removing street lenders. The latter's presence was a function of the inequalities of the capitalist economy. It was also the result of a lack of low-cost alternatives for those borrowers with the most pressing financial needs. Schemes like Keeling's loan society were thin on the ground, and of assistance only to limited numbers. For those without the ability to save or without goods to pawn, an expensive unsecured loan, from the street lender, was the only option. An alternative source did arrive from the 1960s, in the form of Provident Financial, Cattles, and others who formed a new breed of controversial doorstep lenders in the final decades of the twentieth century. This development is related in our next chapter.

5

Doorstep moneylending since the 1950s

Moneylending is one branch of the consumer credit industry that might have been expected to wither on the vine of the affluent society. Instead, its fortunes, which had dipped in the wake of the Moneylenders Act, 1927, recovered from the late 1950s. This revival eventually created several of the biggest financial companies of the late twentieth century. In a process of commercialization, business formerly conducted by street lenders was absorbed by the large army of agents employed by Provident Financial, Cattles, and others. The elements of reciprocity and obligation that had once been transacted with the female street moneylender were transferred to these agents, two-thirds of whom, in the 1960s, were married women.[1] Provident agents, who had previously traded in checks, brought their own connections and community knowledge with them into this new doorstep loans market. The personalized nature of doorstep lending, the convenience of home collection, and the lack of alternative credit options have all been cited as explanations for the high levels of use of this sector. To the chagrin of anti-debt campaigners customers often expressed satisfaction with aspects of doorstep moneylending, despite the startling APRs that were associated with this form of borrowing. As had previously been the case with check and credit trading, perspectives on this form of lending were often very different on the low-income doorstep than they were from the office of the journalist, politician, or anti-debt campaigner.

The analysis herein demonstrates that moneylenders had anxieties about respectability and status and that similar concerns were exhibited amongst the many credit traders who contemplated the option of transferring into the expanding doorstep lending market in the 1960s and 1970s. Their unease was fed by the continuing widespread distaste for moneylenders. This angst was heightened on the frequent occasions

[1] London: National Archives/Public Record Office (hereafter NA), BT 250/60, Committee on Consumer Credit. Provident Clothing and Supply.

when investigators turned a spotlight towards the high APRs associated with the sector. The scale of these rates was one factor that led to doorstep lenders receiving the label 'loan shark', a term which was widely used from the 1980s. This appellation caused great discomfort to legal lenders, who campaigned to locate the label firmly on the shoulders of unlicensed lenders and with the harassment and violence associated with the illegal sector. This chapter provides the first comprehensive discussion of the new style moneylending sector that burgeoned from the late 1950s. It places the growth of commercial lenders within the context of wider developments in the working-class consumer credit market. The analysis of these legal lenders is also situated alongside the first detailed historical discussion of the illegal, often violent loan sharks who emerged in the last four decades of the twentieth century. Their methods and markets are contrasted with those of the 'slum lenders' and 'she usurers' of the early twentieth century. Whilst the doorstep lenders formed part of what came to be known as the sub-prime sector, the illegal lenders effectively serviced a sub-sub-prime sector. Despite the limited scale and scope of the latter it had great cultural and legislative significance. Images of the violent loan shark replaced the earlier figure of Shylock in popular understandings of moneylending. More significantly, however, the existence of illegal lenders and the harassment and violence associated with them provided a major stumbling block for those campaigning for a ceiling rate cap on moneylenders' interest rates, such as those that exist in Europe and in the USA. Since the 1990s many social policy analysts who have investigated this sector have come to the conclusion that a rate cap would result in the legal moneylenders abandoning their most risky customers, leaving them to the unregulated mercies of the illegal lenders. This was a perspective that the government came to accept.

The first section of this chapter examines the relationship between working-class borrowers and legal lenders before the 1950s. It examines the impact of the Moneylenders Act, 1927, noting the immediate and appreciable decline in registered moneylenders that ensued. It explains that the inability to use 'touts' or agents to find borrowers was perhaps the most significant aspect of the Act in terms of moneylenders and working-class customers. Oral evidence from Belfast demonstrates the importance of agents for moneylenders who did not have strong communal ties within working-class neighbourhoods; a factor that was particularly true for Jewish moneylenders. The next two elements of this analysis probe the issues that lay behind the arrival of the dynamic new doorstep lending industry, such as the decline in pawnbroking, in the late 1950s and 1960s. Check traders and credit traders predominated in this sector, using their long-established customer networks, which were based on home collection carried out by their agents. The final two sections of the chapter probe the increasing controversies that arose as the doorstep lending industry became more extensive and visible from the early 1980s and its juxtaposition with the much smaller but nonetheless symbolic illegal sector.

'SHY CREATURES LURKING IN ANONYMOUS OFFICES': TRADITIONAL MONEYLENDING FIRMS AND WORKING-CLASS BORROWERS

Street lenders, whether registered or not, were not alone in dealing with working-class borrowers in the late nineteenth and early twentieth century Britain. Neville Greenwood, whose family first became involved in moneylending in the nineteenth century, stated that it became 'a major business in the 1850s but [that] it was entirely operated from office premises'.[2] In 1914, the Registrar of Birmingham county court thought that there was 'probably no greater misconception about any trade than that of the moneylender' and that 'from the accounts appearing in the paper from time to time one would be led to suppose that the trade was entirely composed of rapacious harpies'. In his experience, it was possible for a working man to borrow small sums from moneylending companies at annual interest rates as low as 10 or 20 per cent. To secure this rate of interest a promissory note and written sureties from two other individuals were required. The largest moneylenders reportedly dealt with 10,000 transactions a year, which varied from £3 to £10 in value. The fact that these moneylenders were the borrower's last (legal) resort and that the risks associated with these loans were high was reflected in Birmingham county court. Whereas the average trader brought between 5 and 12 per cent of their credit transactions before the court, the figures for moneylenders were between 15 and 20 per cent.[3]

A number of the companies that specialized in lending to the 'sub-prime' market of the late twentieth century traced their roots

[2] *Consumer Credit Association News*, June 1985.

[3] W. H. Whitelock, 'The industrial credit system and imprisonment for debt' *Economic Journal*, 24 (March 1914), 37.

back over a century to a period in which they, or their current subsidiaries, operated as moneylenders or in closely associated sectors. Lewis Livingstone, a Jewish émigré, began trading in Wigan, initially as an itinerant credit trader, before he switched to moneylending in 1895. His business evolved into London Scottish Bank, which by 2005 had 190,000 customers in its home-collected credit section.[4] Livingstone's first 'office' was the front parlour of a Mrs Robinson, who was paid 10 shillings a week to receive applications and payments in her home. On her retirement in 1923, the bridge between the company and local community was perpetuated through the employment of her daughter.[5] Although the Moneylending Act of 1927 (and the Act that extended its regulations to Northern Ireland in 1933) prohibited the use of agents to tout for loans, they continued to be deployed unofficially in Belfast (and—we must assume—elsewhere). These individuals proved invaluable for lenders who had no organic stake in the networks of obligation and reciprocity operating within the neighbourhoods they trawled for customers and who were, as a result, less well placed to enforce repayment than local street lenders. In addition, the use of an agent with local knowledge was a safeguard against fraud. A retired Gasworks' employee, Benny, recalled how the unwary moneylender could be duped in 1930s Belfast. It was possible to buy 'a rent book out of Woolworths', which 'you filled in for yourself [laughs] and you had a clean rent book'. It could then be shown to the moneylender who then asked, 'Right, how much do you want?' The practised fraudster completed the transaction by using a fictitious name.[6] Moneylenders without agents could also become embroiled in unpopular forms of debt collection. One Jewish moneylender who lent door-to-door in Belfast's New Lodge district was tagged 'Dirty Coat' by local women: 'they were always ridiculing oul Dirty Coat', despite the fact that the 'whole district was into him'. Johnny, a retired docker, remembered that when not paid he would 'kick up a terrible stink', although he thought no woman was 'brought to court over not paying him. I think eventually he did get paid, because he pestered you so much he was paid.'[7]

[4] London Scottish Bank, *Report and Accounts 2005*, 6.

[5] Chester: Consumer Credit Association, (Henceforth CCA), Harry Livingstone, *Refuge Securities Limited 1895–1970: 75 years of money lending*, 2–11.

[6] Interview with Benny (born 1930. Retired gasworks employee. Married with one son. Protestant. Interviewed 11 February 2003).

[7] Interview with Johnny (born 1930. Retired docker. Father of four. Roman Catholic. Interviewed 15 April 2001).

Other lenders in the city avoided unseemly scenes by using agents, such as Rebecca, who was interviewed for this project. Her testimony was punctured by tensions arising from the competing strains of respectability and reciprocity. In arguing that 'I never had to go near moneylenders', it became clear that Rebecca meant she did not take loans herself. However, in the years following the Second World War, she acted as an intermediary for a Jewish moneylender. They met whilst Rebecca was working as a waitress in the city centre, and she subsequently introduced him to 'tons of customers'. They 'would have came with the money to me and I went down to Mr G. He never came near my house. My [husband] wouldn't have liked me to do that.' She explained how she recruited 'good customers', people who 'wouldn't steal on me. I knew what I was doing.' Asked how she selected people for loans, Rebecca explained that she chose 'people that you're friendly with'. Somewhat confusingly, she then said: 'There's some people I wouldn't lend a shilling to—I wouldn't—I don't believe in borrowing or lending.' Again she was referring to her own financial actions, detaching herself from the moneylending process. This was reinforced when she was asked if she received any payment for her role: 'No, no! No, no, no way would I want any. Oh I'd be insulted! I was only doing people good turns—no!'[8] Anne-Marie reported a similar pattern of behaviour in her childhood in the 1950s. Her grandmother 'had a friend who was a moneylender and he was Jewish'. He 'operated through sort of agents. So granny never actually made any money out of it, to my knowledge.' But if she knew that 'your father had died, you'd no money to bury him or something like that, she would've said: "Lend Sean the money". And he would've lent you the money.' She explained that he 'was very, very careful about' lending 'because he didn't have any clout in the district to make you pay it back'.[9] It appears that because these Jewish lenders were outsiders—in terms of class, locality, and religion—that agents proved most useful for them. It is impossible to ascertain if these agents did actually receive any form of payment in kind. Certainly, straightforward payment would have contravened the legislation on moneylenders' canvassers and touts. As only one of the three sources of this particular line of testimony

[8] Interview with Rebecca (born 1913. Retired waitress. First husband a docker; second husband was a builder's foreman. She had four children. Roman Catholic. Interviewed 5 November 2002).

[9] Interview with Anne-Marie (born 1951. Mature student and mother. First husband a scaffolder; current husband a musician. Interviewed 20 May 2003).

was directly involved—the others were recalling the involvement of family members—it is impossible to formulate a definitive statement on their motives. But it would seem highly unlikely that there was no financial recompense for their work: perhaps interest free loans or other perks were offered. In Rebecca's case she did indicate that the moneylender offered to 'buy me a house, because I got him so many customers [and] I would have paid him rent on that house'.[10] Rebecca turned down this offer. However, it was not possible to unravel the exact nature of the offer. There is a possibility that the moneylender hoped to turn their relationship into something more than a business relationship, but Rebecca ended the interview shortly after making these statements when, I suspect, she felt that too many questions were being asked about her role as a moneylender's agent. This consistent denial of a financial motive by those who offered testimony in this area provides further evidence of the ambivalence and duplicity surrounding moneylending.

Between 1927 and the early 1960s, moneylenders who did not use unofficial agents traded with borrowers at their offices. Many, such as H. T. Greenwood Ltd, had done so before 1927. Lewis Livingstone had opened a company HQ in Manchester's Market Street in 1903. Trading under the name Lewis's, it attracted complaints from the neighbouring department store of the same name when the latter began to receive enquiries about its 'loan department'. Potential borrowers were attracted by newspaper advertisements offering loans from £5 to £1,000, with repayments from two shillings per week.[11] Livingstone, or one of his sons, visited applicants to assess their circumstances and if 'a house was furnished with a side board, a table and 4 chairs (rickety)' they would lend the minimum £5. The Livingstones subsequently learned from one of their employees that before the First World War her grandmother had realized a little cash by renting out a sideboard to allow neighbours to pass such tests, charging '10/- per night, the borrower to arrange cartage both ways'.[12] This practice indicates that many customers were in straitened circumstances. It also reveals the potential resourcefulness and duplicity of working-class borrowers. However, customers' ultimate ability to repay was witnessed in the expansion of Livingstone's company. In 1936, when seven branches operated throughout Lancashire, the company became Refuge Lending Society.

[10] Interview with Rebecca.
[11] *Manchester Evening Chronicle*, 13 July 1909.
[12] Livingstone, *Refuge Securities Limited*, 11–12.

Philip Morris told the Select Committee of 1925 that he had been lending to Pontypridd's miners for two decades, charging annual interest rates of 60 per cent. He claimed that this was a nominal rate because, although a loan might be arranged over twelve months, often 'something happens, and he does not pay, it may drag on for two years or two and a half years, but eventually you get your money'. Morris explained that for a £10 loan he charged 10s a week for six months. This represented a total cost of £13 and it was this figure that interested borrowers. This remained the amount they repaid, whether they completed payment in good time, over six months, or took much longer to end the transaction. During the miners' strike of 1921 Morris claimed that he 'did not decline to do business with a single old client who came along. They all got pretty much what they asked for.' His loans started at £5 and averaged £30, although £10 to £20 was the limit during the strike. Loans were advanced on an unsecured basis and Morris maintained that he did 'business with people that I knew, old clients that had passed through my hands . . . I knew their characters, which is the chief thing in money lending. It was not a question of security; it was a question of character.'[13]

As with all those involved in supplying credit to the working class, Morris laid claim to respectable status for his clients as a means of legitimizing his activities. However, evidence from a number of moneylenders reveals their consistent status insecurities. The history of the Greenwood family, who were first engaged in moneylending in 1877, demonstrates the longevity of these status concerns. Neville Greenwood recalled how family members masked their occupation over several generations. When his grandfather stood as a Liberal candidate in the 1924 General Election, he purchased two shops and listed his occupation as shopkeeper. On Neville's birth certificate, his father was recorded as an accountant. When Neville entered local politics he was described as 'branch manager of a finance company', although in later years he was happy to explain that he was a moneylender.[14] However, a Northern Ireland moneylender indicated that the uneasiness continued with many businesses being wound up in the late twentieth century due to the status issue: 'moneylending gives people who are in it a fairly respectable living, they educate their family but their family don't want [to be] involved in

[13] Select Committee of the House of Lords and House of Commons, *Report on the Moneylenders Bill and the Moneylenders (Amendment) Bill*, Parliamentary Papers 1924–5 (153) viii. 31 (1925), cols. 1953, 1898, 1918–19, 1923.

[14] Interview with Neville Greenwood (veteran moneylender and member of the Consumer Credit Association. Interviewed 4 July 2003).

going out around. They see it as a bit of come down to go out and knock doors.'[15] Customers also desired discretion and Greenwood recalled the blacked-out window of his company's offices. Until the 1960s, the company operated on the basis of collecting repayments at the office and on providing invisibility for customers. This modus operandi fitted a 1964 *Sunday Times* description of moneylenders as 'shy creatures . . . lurking in anonymous offices'.[16] When a number of moneylenders met in 1965 to form the National Association of Moneylenders, it was agreed that there 'should be no interviews with any newspapers, as this would be dangerous'. Press releases were to be handled by 'agents appointed by the national committee'.[17] It is also noticeable that the term moneylending has not been commonly used by those engaged in the sector since the 1960s, with terms such as home-collected credit being regularly adopted. Borrowers were equally happy to deploy elliptical terms such as 'agent', 'caller', or even 'tallyman' to describe those with whom they dealt.[18] The use of such terminology may help to explain the apparent under-reporting of moneylending in national surveys of consumer credit. The 1989 Policy Studies Institute report, *Credit and debt*, suggested that only 500,000 households were using doorstep lenders. In the mid-1990s, the estimate was 3 million; by 2006 it was 2.3m.[19] Confusion over terminology may have been exacerbated by unwillingness to report the use of a much-vilified wing of the credit industry.

H. T. Greenwood Ltd illustrates the history of the class of money-lender that the Select Committee of 1925 called the 'provincial lenders'. The prohibition on agents and the restrictions on advertising ensured that businesses such as this were fairly static between the late 1920s and 1960s. Greenwood's Oldham branch lent just under £25,000 in 1927, but throughout the 1930s the figure hovered around £19,000. Only in the late 1950s did borrowing rise to £30,000, some of which met the extra demands experienced by families during the town's Wakes' Week. The company took up extra advertising space in the *Oldham Chronicle* in advance of these festivities.[20] However, there was clearly a limit to the

[15] Interview with anonymous Northern Ireland moneylender 1.

[16] *The Sunday Times*, 2 February 1964. [17] *Credit Trader*, 22 May 1965.

[18] Karen Rowlingson, *Moneylenders and their customers* (London: Policy Studies Institute, 1994), 23.

[19] Ibid. 3; Department of Trade and industry (DTI), *Illegal lending in the UK*, 77. <http://www.dti.gov.uk/files/file35171.pdf>, accessed 6 December 2006.

[20] Bradford: Provident Financial Group (henceforth PFG). Box marked 'to be catalogued', Greenwood's Oldham branch statistics; Greenwood's Minute book—18 July 1957.

business that the company could secure by operating to its traditional formula and under the restrictions of the 1927 Act. It was to be in the 1960s, as academics busied themselves in the 'rediscovery of poverty' that the moneylenders were themselves identifying new markets for their product.[21]

SECURED VERSUS UNSECURED LENDING: THE DECLINE OF PAWNBROKING AND THE RISE OF DOORSTEP LENDERS

Based on his own family's business experience, Neville Greenwood believed that between 1927 and the late 1950s there was no doorstep lending by licensed moneylenders. However, during the late 1950s a number of small companies realized that there was 'no enforcement authority for the 1927 Act', and began to offer doorstep loans at 'collected credit rates' that were well above the 48 per cent maximum annual interest rate established in 1927.[22] The agreements for these loans followed the classic working-class credit arrangement, in that they simply stated the length of the agreement and the weekly repayment rate. The 'home collection business' burgeoned, 'stealing customers and travellers from the retail credit business' in the process.[23] Observing those companies experimenting in doorstep lending 'met by incredible demand', the Greenwoods entered doorstep lending by purchasing a small Manchester-based business in 1966. The total cost of a £100 loan was then £125, repaid at £5 per week.[24] In the subsequent two decades the company expanded from 4 to 17 offices and increased employee numbers from 50 to 750. Its book debts rose from £100,000 to £10 million.[25]

In 1970, when Livingstone's Refuge Securities Ltd became a public company, it was described as the largest business of its kind in the UK. It had also experienced rapid development in the 1960s, extending its Lancashire branch network from 15 in 1961, to 42 offices in Northern

[21] See Peter Townsend and Brian Abel Smith, *The poor and the poorest* (London: Blackwell Publishers, 1965).

[22] *Consumer Credit Association News*, June 1985. Interview with Neville Greenwood and Michael Lilley of the Consumer Credit Association.

[23] Interview with Lilley and Greenwood.

[24] Neville Greenwood, 'The future of collected credit', *Consumer Credit Association News*, June 1985, 13. Interview with Neville Greenwood.

[25] Interview with Neville Greenwood.

England, the Midlands, and London. Operating from modern headquarters in central Manchester, it advanced loans to regular customers once or twice a year. Just over two-thirds of loans were unsecured; the remainder were secured against property or insurance policies. The average loan to private borrowers was £40. Seventy per cent of repayments were made by standing order or by customers visiting the office. Only 30 part-time collection agents were employed at that point.[26] The company had a turnover of £1.5 million in 1968–9 and its chairman remarked that the small loan business 'was just emerging from its infancy'.[27] He was right. The 1960s witnessed a resurgence of moneylending, with significant numbers of check traders and credit traders becoming involved. This represented a significant change in fortunes for the wing of the credit industry that had, historically, been treated with the greatest suspicion and distaste. Numbers of licensed moneylenders rose after 1957, reaching 2,500 by the late 1960s. Eight per cent of this number had obtained their first licence in the previous decade. Around a third were businesses operated by a single person. They were concentrated in industrial areas, seaports, and London. About 45 per cent were involved in another business, 20 per cent being check traders.

What factors lay behind the resurgence of moneylending? A third of loans were believed to be for 'exceptional outlay, over Christmas or for holidays', and another third were 'to meet outstanding bills during periods of financial difficulties'. This pattern of demand bore strong similarities to that demonstrated by those using pawnbrokers in the 1960s. Around half the loans forwarded on pledges submitted to pawnbrokers were required to 'pay bills', whilst the remainder covered irregular financial commitments such as 'holidays or weddings' or the purchase of 'other durable goods'.[28] But as the numbers of pawnbrokers fell they became more inaccessible to many of the 3.5 million people who lived on council estates by the mid-1960s. As a result, doorstep lending became an increasingly viable alternative.[29] Pawnbroking's decline had begun in the interwar years and it continued steadily after the Second World War. Numbers fell from 2,981 in

[26] Livingstone, *Refuge Securities Limited*, 14–16. *The Times*, 21 April 1970, 3 July 1970.

[27] *The Times*, 24 October 1970.

[28] Committee on Consumer Credit, *Report of the Committee* (London: HMSO, 1971), 29.

[29] James Cronin, *Labour and society in Britain, 1918–1979* (London: Batsford, 1984), 163.

1935–6, to 1,726 in 1948–9, and to 402 by 1968.[30] One assessment is that during the 1940s and 1950s the groups that had previously constituted 'the pawning classes' fell out of 'the habit of pawning or never acquired it'.[31] In 1952, an estimated 400,000 people per annum made use of pawnbrokers. The same investigation suggested total loans of £25 million per annum, at an average of between 12 and 15 shillings each. This figure was dramatically more—perhaps unreliably so—than the figure of £2m for 1966, which was drawn from an analysis of the Census of Distribution by the Crowther Committee.[32] Increasingly, those pawnbrokers who continued in business operated a retail business; often marketing jewellery. This was true in 90 per cent of cases by the late 1960s.[33] The pattern of pawning and the items being pledged had changed markedly from the start of the century. The National Pawnbrokers' Association (NPA) told the Crowther Committee that the welfare state had virtually removed the requirement for week-to-week pledging of 'bundles of clothes'. [34] There had also been significant changes in the items received in pawn: 'articles pledged are now as frequently things like transistor radios and cameras as the clothing and domestic necessities of earlier years'.[35] This development was assisted by legislation increasing the amount that could be lent on pledges from £10 to £50, which was enacted in Northern Ireland in 1955 and across the rest of the UK in 1960. The trade registered immediate shifts in demand. A Middlesbrough pawnbroker recalled that 'the change in our shop was unbelievable. Overnight we acquired a completely new type of customer who had hitherto borrowed from moneylenders at 48% and were only too happy to come to us for 25%.'[36] The NPA claimed that prior to the legislation the numbers of 'unlicensed dock-gate and public house moneylenders' had become 'far more numerous'.[37]

[30] *The Times*, 17 February 1950. NA/PRO: BT250/38. National Pawnbrokers' Association Inc. Oral evidence to the Committee on Consumer Credit, 20 March 1970.

[31] Kenneth Hudson, *Pawnbroking: an aspect of British social* history (London: Bodley Head, 1982), 120.

[32] L. A. Minkes, 'The decline of pawnbroking', *Economica*, New Series 20, February 1953, 21. Committee on Consumer Credit, *Report*, 29.

[33] NA: BT 250/38 Committee on Consumer Credit. National Pawnbrokers Association, 1968–1970. NOP poll.

[34] NA: BT250/38. Oral evidence to the Committee on Consumer Credit, 20 March 1970.

[35] Committee on Consumer Credit, *Report*, 77.

[36] Hudson, *Pawnbroking*, 134.

[37] NA: BT250/38. Oral evidence to the Committee on Consumer Credit, 20 March 1970.

A number of areas were highlighted as being ones in which a visit to the pawnbroker was still an all-too-familiar experience. St Ann's, in Nottingham, provided two local pawnbrokers with a 'bustling trade' in the 1960s, serving as a reminder of the pockets of relative poverty that existed within an increasingly affluent working class. In some regions these pockets were far from insignificant and they reflected sharp divergences in the UK economy. Liverpool was noted for pawning, which had 'a stronger hold there than in any other region'.[38] Glasgow, like Liverpool, stood out amongst UK cities in retaining a strong pawning tradition. A study carried out in 1973 found that unlike 'many other cities, Glasgow has still a flourishing pawnbroking business', which for many 'is either a regular way of borrowing or the first port of call in a crisis'.[39]

However, established moneylenders, such as H. T. Greenwood Ltd or Refuge Securities Ltd, benefited from a demand for loans created by the continued contraction of pawnbroking. It appears that this involved a shift downmarket for them. This was also related to the fact that they lost some established customers as a result of competition from the cheaper personal loans that were offered by the high street banks from the late 1950s.[40] The more active engagement of mainstream financial institutions represented a key shift in attitudes towards personal loans. The courts of equity came increasingly to 'regard money as comparable to the sale of a commodity'. By the early 1970s they were upholding contracts with interest rates 'as high as 120% on short term advances'. Echoing the thoughts of several generations of moneylenders, one financial journalist argued, in 1971, that retailers 'operate on a 30 per cent to 50 per cent profit margin. If the goods are sold within six months the gross rate of return is well above the 48 per cent fixed for moneylenders.'[41]

With pawnbrokers unable to follow former customers to the new estates, it is no surprise to learn that that H. T. Greenwood Ltd first dipped its toe into the waters of doorstep lending on Manchester's Langley council estate. The success of this venture was greatly assisted by a local woman who introduced Greenwoods to over 100 customers within twelve months.[42] We can only speculate about whether or not

[38] Melanie Tebbutt, *Making ends meet: pawnbroking and working-class credit* (Leicester: Leicester University Press, 1983), 176, 167.

[39] Sally Baldwin, 'Credit and class distinction', *The year book of social policy* (London: Routledge and Kegan Paul, 1973), 193.

[40] *The Times*, 12 February 1967. [41] Ibid., 20 March 1971.

[42] Interview with Neville Greenwood.

she may formerly have been the source of loans for those customers she secured for the company. Clearly local knowledge and networks were vital factors once again, and the approach H. T. Greenwood Ltd took was the only one likely to succeed in the risky business of unsecured doorstep lending. However, there was at least one spectacular failure in this respect. One North of England moneylender's office was approached by an Indian man who claimed to have identified a ready market for loans amongst local Asian communities. He offered to operate as the agent for this enterprise and was given a small sum with which to work. As the venture appeared to be successful, his cash limit was increased and other agents were appointed on his recommendation. However, the company had not discovered the Holy Grail, which was the untapped British-Asian market; it had been defrauded. These agents had operated a pyramid scheme. 'Customers' names were entered into repayment books and loans taken out on their behalf. The loans were then 'repaid' with further loans to another set of 'customers'. All the names entered in the loan books were of local Asians, none of whom knew that their details were being deployed in this way. It was only when the company contacted some of their new 'customers' directly that the chicanery was uncovered.[43] The company did not have long-term experience of employing agents and this example helps explain why so many of the well-established credit traders and check traders became the leading players in the doorstep lending sector. The next section of this chapter discusses their entry into the doorstep lending sector.

A NEW BREED OF MONEYLENDER: CHECK TRADERS AND CREDIT TRADERS ENTER THE MARKET

As was seen in the chapter on check trading, Provident and other companies diversified their operations from the early 1960s via the introduction of higher-value vouchers. However, a number of smaller operators took the decision to branch out in a different direction by offering doorstep loans. Those involved recognized a growing preference for cash rather than checks amongst customers, whilst also appreciating the significance of the reducing number of pawnbroker's offices. It is also

[43] Interview with Anonymous Moneylender.

likely that an increasing inability to compete with the Provident—in the check market, led some smaller companies to explore new routes to profitability. However, Provident soon followed in their wake. In 1971, it bought The People's Bank and hoped to rebrand itself as 'Provident—The People's Bank'. It envisaged itself as a competitor to the Trustee Savings Bank that would offer a 'comprehensive range of family and domestic financial services for the whole wide field of present and potential Provident customers'. The company planned to operate this new service from its existing network of offices and hoped that they could be enlarged or 'even moved to better sites than they have at the moment', although what it called a 'marble halls' approach was not envisaged.[44] Personal loans, available via Provident's existing agents, were offered from 1972. Their introduction contributed to an acceleration of turnover growth, from a figure of 11 per cent in 1971 to 54 per cent in 1972. At the start of the 1970s, check traders spoke of a diversification process that was designed to meet the multiplying financial needs of a broadly defined working-class market. In 1973, Provident envisaged an expansion to meet working-class borrowing and saving requirements, noting that half the population still did not have bank accounts.[45] Many of the company's customers began 'to prefer the cash scheme' rather than checks or vouchers, as Provident agents discovered to their cost, because they received lower commission for loans than checks or vouchers.[46] *Credit Trader* explained that some customers wanted 'to shop at Marks & Spencer or C & A Modes, neither of whom accept checks, or buy a set of tyres with 30 per cent off. . . all of which may be beyond their immediate needs'. These customers wanted 'cash, or, in the modern idiom, a personal loan . . . even when the much cheaper alternative of shopping checks' was offered to them. It was 'cheaper' because the check traders' gross margin was divided 70/30 between shopkeeper and customer respectively; once the retailer had paid their discount and the customer had submitted their 'poundage' payment. With a personal loan the customer carried the whole service charge. Nonetheless, demand was healthy and the first set of check traders to introduce doorstep loans reported a threefold rise in turnover

[44] *Investors Review*, 7 September 1973. *Evening Standard*, 20 May 1972. Provident Financial Group, PFG/O0/044, Annual Report, 1972 (henceforth PFG).

[45] Ibid., 7 September 1973. London: Monopolies and Mergers Commission (Henceforth MMC), *Great Universal Stores PLC and Empire Stores (Bradford) PLC: a report on the proposed mergers* (London: HMSO, 1983), 16.

[46] *Shields Gazette*, 5 April 1974.

between 1962 and 1970.[47] One Scottish moneylender reiterated the belief that cash provided customers with flexibility when speaking to the *Sunday Mail* in 1972. He argued that in some cases customers found that a loan taken out to buy a consumer durable could undercut hire purchase rates.[48] However, an investigative report—'Borrowing trouble'—undermined such claims, identifying interest rates of around 150 per cent on loans from the Refuge Lending Society.[49]

Alongside check traders, significant numbers of doorstep credit traders also secured moneylending licences during the 1960s, addressing the rising demand for cash in preference to merchandise. Their diversification proved more controversial than that of the check traders, who had, in effect, offered a substitute for moneylending since the late nineteenth century. For credit traders, moneylending's location 'at the end of the credit line', as the Crowther Committee put it, led to much soul searching and, for some, a loss of commercial status.[50] As was explained in an earlier chapter, credit traders had been engaged in a battle to overcome the negative image attached to the nineteenth-century tally trade. Any progress that had been made was jeopardized by the new association with moneylending. Positions taken up by individual credit traders in the debate were posited on a mixture of their market location, sensitivity to bad publicity, and religious affiliation. Although *Credit Trader* published an article in 1962 offering advice for readers who were considering entering the moneylending sector, subsequent news stories revealed the difficulties many had with this development. In 1970, *Credit Trader* maintained that entry into this field was 'still inhibited by the stigma attached to moneylending'.[51] This stigma had been reignited by media reports, such as one in the *Sunday People* in August 1964, which described an 'ugly new trend in the credit drapery business'. It explained how fierce competition had led more and more firms to become moneylenders, meaning that 'housewives who would normally turn down purchases because they haven't got the cash, now have the opportunity to borrow from the very person who is offering the goods for sale'. This was producing 'women with a secret agony' and, for some, was 'wrecking their homes and their health'. Two London firms were allegedly charging interest at 297 per cent a year. One customer was Mrs O'Hara, recently widowed and the mother of fourteen children

[47] *Credit Trader*, 2 May 1970.
[48] Scottish *Sunday Mail*, 9 July 1972.
[49] *Daily Mirror*, 19 June 1973.
[50] Committee on Consumer Credit, *Report*, 80.
[51] *Credit Trader*, 2 May 1970.

(five of school age). She had a weekly income of £12 15s and was paying £6 10s in repayments for a series of loans from the Church Street Finance Company of Islington. She claimed that she was first offered a loan when she was unable to meet weekly payments for clothing she had bought from the company's drapery wing, Home Outfitters. Such 'touting' was an infringement of the 1927 Moneylenders Act and the company denied it had sanctioned it.[52] However, it had previously been before the courts for similar malpractice and for issuing documentation that failed to accurately indicate interest rates to borrowers.[53] A rival credit draper told the *Sunday People* that 'I had to join in' and that he had been forced into moneylending against his better judgement. He believed that it should be illegal for credit drapers to be able to offer loans but 'if I don't lend money I lose customers to firms who do'. He was lending £8, for which he charged £11 repaid at £1 over eleven weeks and felt this practice lured some customers into 'a permanent state of indebtedness'.[54] London credit traders reacted to the negative media attention, debating a motion that members of the local representative forum be prohibited from offering loans. The resolution argued that any system in which credit trading was allied with moneylending 'was out of keeping with the principles that animated the association and by which the prestige of the credit trade had been established'. The meeting heard that it would be 'a breach of privilege' to use the 'credit customer relationship as a bridge to bring customers into contact with money lending'. After a discussion that witnessed 'a few sparks flying' the gathering 'decisively' rejected 'moneylending-cum-credit trading'.[55] The ability of credit traders to canvass customers created an opportunity for those offering loans to circumvent the 1927 Act and concerns had been aired since the 1930s about this possibility. Unease frequently emanated from the prospect of a customer who had paid a high retail price for merchandise subsequently borrowing expensive money to meet their repayments. For example, in 1933 Glasgow's F. H. Kane Ltd was refused a moneylending certificate because 'the lower Court viewed with concern the idea of a credit draper carrying on business as a moneylender'.[56] The debate in the 1960s fanned out across the country from London. In Bristol, veteran member Harold Walkins threatened to resign from the Retail Credit Federation (RCF) because he was 'fed

[52] *Sunday People*, 23 August 1964.
[53] *Credit Trader*, 15 September 1962.
[54] *Sunday People*, 23 August 1964.
[55] *Credit Trader*, 16 January 1965.
[56] *Scotsman*, 29 July 1933.

up' of reading negative coverage about moneylending in *Credit Trader*. His local association smoothed over the issue, declaring the controversy a matter that 'did not affect those in the Provinces' and noting that Watkins was 'a man of integrity', who 'carried on his business [which included moneylending] on a sensible basis'.[57] London was indeed the focus of the negative publicity and its position in the public's imagination was enhanced by the fictional depiction of the uneasy relationship between credit trading and moneylending featured in Ken Loach's 1965 BBC TV production of *Up the junction*. The obnoxious tallyman, Barny is depicted offering loans in scenes that mirror those depicted in the Nell Dunn book on which the production was based:

H.O. Husband objects . . . they're the best of all because they'll do anything to stop their husbands finding out. After a bit you loan 'em ten pound at the rate of seven shillings in the pound to be paid back in ten weeks—So there you are, collectin' twenty-seven bob a week. Then if after five weeks they're a bit short you say 'All right love. I'll help you out, I'll tell yer what I'll do. I'll lend yer another tenner.' So you give 'em another tenner, subtract what they still owe yer from the first ten—say it's five with another thirty-five bob on top fer the interest and they usually give yer five bob—'You've been good to me'—and all that. Then you walk out of the flat leavin' them three pounds and they've got to pay you twenty-seven bob fer the next ten weeks—oh it never ends.[58]

Tom Chirnside, whose family were long-standing credit traders and active Presbyterians, believed that the 1960s represented a crossroads for credit traders: 'You've either got to go merchandise or you've got to go check trading and moneylending.' With many in the RCF taking the latter option, Chirnside eventually terminated his firm's membership. He felt that by going over to moneylending 'you get the wrong customers and . . . I think it is immoral the charges they had to make'. The latter, he reasoned, were imposed because of the bad debt incurred in dealing with customers 'who don't pay their bills' and 'don't have a bank account because the bank don't want them'. However, he also revealed operational factors that influenced his decision. In the 1930s, when many firms were functioning on a shilling a week minimum collection basis, the Chirnsides adopted a two-shilling-a-week policy. This symbolically placed them a cut above other credit traders and Chirnside reflected that: 'I could almost say I was a bit snobbish about our type of credit trade. Some of the folk who did check trading—check trader's customers—are

[57] *Credit Trader*, 6 February 1965.
[58] Nell Dunn, *Up the junction* (London: Virago, 1988), 105.

not the same type.' Just as consumers might wish to signal a certain status by consuming at particular shops or by using particular forms of credit, so the Chirnsides and others like them reflected on their position as credit retailers and carefully selected the areas of the market in which they wished to operate. Somewhat symbolically, Chirnside counted the family of the actress Thora Hird—well known for her portrayal of solid and respectable working-class characters—amongst his clientele. Chirnside also acknowledged the fact that his company's location, Lancaster and its hinterland, did not present the opportunities for moneylending presented within London, Liverpool, or Glasgow. Those credit traders who did move into the doorstep lending market felt that many who opposed their decision were motivated by religious considerations.[59] Whilst Chirnside's strong Presbyterian beliefs left him with moral objections to moneylending, it was Catholic members of the RCF who were most commonly associated with the opposition to moneylending.[60] As is demonstrated below their position paralleled that of those Catholics who, from the 1960s, promoted credit unions as an alternative to moneylending. Attitudes towards moneylending were not, however, confined to the religious scruples of particular individuals. Even large public companies, such as GUS and Phillips, could not be persuaded by the management of their doorstep credit trading subsidiaries (Alexander Sloan and Midorco House respectively) that their future lay in personal loans rather than merchandising.[61]

Despite these qualms, many credit traders had taken the leap into direct lending by the late 1960s. As a result, in some areas the majority of moneylenders were also credit traders. In Tower Hamlets during 1969, for example, 16 of 19 licensed moneylenders were credit drapers.[62] Some of those making the switch encountered problems from long-standing customers. Michael Lilley, of Kings in Chester, recalled that the company had to take care not to affront regular users. He recalled that '50 per cent of all the customers you dealt with wouldn't do moneylending. If you faced them with it, you'd lose 50 per cent.' He described the vouchers that the RCF began to market in 1972 as 'a godsend' because it allowed credit traders who were departing the

[59] Interview with Tom Chirnside (retired credit trader. Born 1916. Interviewed 16 August 2002).

[60] Interview with Lilley and Greenwood.

[61] *Consumer Credit Association News,* June 1985.

[62] NA: BT 250/91, Committee on Consumer Credit, Evidence from Councils on moneylending and pawnbroking, 1969.

merchandising sector to retain old customers who were unwilling to take up personal loans: 'You go along with the voucher and they don't see that as money they see that as a piece of merchandise . . . So you were still able to supply the customer who wouldn't borrow money.'[63] The tie-in between merchandising and moneylending was formalized in 1978, when the RCF merged with the National Personal Finance Association to form the Consumer Credit Association (CCA). Provident and other former check traders subsequently joined this new trade association.

'BUY ON RISING SOCIAL INEQUALITY': DOORSTEP LENDERS AND THEIR CRITICS

By the late 1970s and early 1980s personal loans were becoming the core activity for Provident, Cattles, and other major check and credit traders. In 1979 the value of personal loans issued by Provident was greater than that of its checks and vouchers.[64] Vouchers and merchandise sales, however, still retained a strategic importance. As the Consumer Credit Act 1978 prohibited doorstep canvassing of personal loans selling merchandise, which could then be purchased via a loan, remained a common method of getting a foot in the door. In 1996, 70 per cent of turnover for the Cattles' subsidiary Shopacheck Financial Services was through unsecured cash loans averaging £150. The remainder was achieved via a combination of voucher sales, and through Ewbanks Mail Order Ltd, and Teleplan. Ewbanks supplied catalogue credit via agents who collected payments at customers' homes, while Teleplan rented television and video sets, paid for via cash slots attached to the television. Both companies provided opportunities for Cattles to market loans.[65]

The Consumer Credit Act also included 'truth in lending' clauses that brought a higher than ever profile to the APRs charged by companies providing short-term loans. From October 1980, APR rates had to be clearly stated on all agreements with a set formula being employed in their calculation. In 1981, the Monopolies and Mergers

63 Interview with Michael Lilley, veteran credit trader and former chairman of the Consumer Credit Association.

64 Monopolies and Mergers Commission, *Trading check franchise and financial services* (London: HMSO, 1981), 90.

65 Cattles PLC, *Annual report and accounts, 1996* (1996).

Commission calculated that typical APRs for bank loans ranged from 20 to 23 per cent, credit card rates were up to 31 per cent, hire purchase rates were as much as 57 per cent, whilst those from the doorstep lenders ranged from 65 per cent to 756 per cent. Like the moneylenders of 1900 and 1927, the CCA argued that APR did not compare like with like, and had a 'distorting effect' when applied to short-term loans that were costly to collect and attracted significant administrative expenses.[66] The short-term loans most often required by their customers attracted massive rates of interest: a £10 loan, repaid over 13 weeks at £1 per week represented an APR of 659.87 per cent. The moneylenders were piqued by the fact that some competitors could mask the real cost of credit involved in their repayment systems. They resented mail order's ability to escape APR regulations by advertising 'interest free credit' because the same price was paid whether a customer paid in instalments or by one payment. The 'truth in lending' requirements emerged at a time when the costs of the already expensive home collection system were rising. High inflation was one factor; another was the spiralling unemployment that increased bad debts throughout the consumer credit industry. H. T. Greenwood Ltd reported that 23 per cent of its customers were out of work in 1985 and that prior to that, unemployment had not been a major concern in the company's recent history.[67] In 1983, Harry Skelton of Eccles District Savings and Loans reported that high unemployment had brought 'thousands of applications for reduced payments' and led to many bankruptcies amongst moneylenders.[68]

Despite the costs, doorstep lenders attracted large numbers of customers; there were an estimated 3 million by the early 1990s.[69] Why so? One major reason were the shifts in both economic direction and government policies brought about by the Conservative administration elected in 1979. The proportion of Britons living in poverty, or its margins, thereafter rose from 22 to 28 per cent. Rising unemployment was the biggest factor in this development, but there were increases in the number of low-paid jobs and reductions in some benefits.[70] It was reported that the proportion of low-income households using credit rose

[66] Monopolies and Mergers Commission, *Trading check franchise*, 91–3.

[67] *Consumer Credit News*, May–June 1983. [68] Ibid.

[69] Rowlingson, *Moneylenders and their customers*, 4.

[70] Janet Ford, *Consuming credit: debt and poverty in the UK* (London: Child Poverty Action Group, 1991), 7; David Vincent, *Poor citizens: the State and the poor in twentieth century Britain* (Harlow: Longman, 1991), 202–4.

from 22 per cent to 69 per cent between 1980 and 1989.[71] A further factor was the rise in lone-parent families, which were usually headed by a female. During the 1980s their numbers rose from 0.8 m to 1.2 m.[72] This brought the gendered nature of poverty and low-income money management into sharp focus once again. There were other echoes of former times: one Belfast interviewee, Penny, narrated the disturbing story of her mother's long struggle to make ends meet between the 1940s and 1980s. She was hampered by the fact that she had ten children and a husband who gave only half his modest wage—he was a 'bin man'—over for housekeeping. Penny remembered that as the family grew bigger 'my mother then started to go and get loans' which were used 'to feed us and keep something on our feet'. Eventually she 'got really heavily into debt, and we noticed that my mother was very agitated'. By this point, Penny had a young family of her own, but her mother begged her to take out a loan in her name because her moneylender was not allowing her an extension on her credit. Penny reluctantly did this, but shortly afterwards received a knock on the door from the collector when her mother had not paid the instalments as promised. Her mother ended up 'taking a nervous breakdown', leaving an adult son to negotiate reduced payments with her many creditors.[73]

Thus, whilst in the early 1970s Provident envisaged moving upmarket with a more affluent customer base, within ten years the company had dramatically reconsidered its strategy and was, if anything, more associated with poverty than had ever been the case. By the 1990s financial journalists were urging private investors to purchase shares in the company and its rivals in order to '[b]uy on rising social inequality'. By that point, Provident had one million customers and its soaring share price saw it hover on the edge of the FTSE 100, with a market valuation of £1 billion.[74] Approaching these developments from a contrasting perspective, social scientists were increasingly probing the concept of financial exclusion, speculating about the precise numbers of low-income consumers, and others with records of debt, who were

[71] Janet Ford and Karen Rowlingson, 'Low-income households and credit: exclusion, preference and inclusion', *Environment and Planning*, 28 (1966), 1345.

[72] Richard Berthoud and Elaine Kempson, *Credit and debt: the PSI report* (London: Policy Studies Institute, 1992), 182.

[73] Interview with Penny (born 1940. Mother of four. Husband a labourer. Raised as a Protestant, converted to Catholicism on marriage).

[74] *New Statesman*, 16 August 1996. For similar advice on Cattles see *Money Observer*, June 1998.

being defined as 'sub-prime' borrowers by mainstream lenders. The term sub-prime had crossed the Atlantic from the USA. In UK terms, it came to include the customers of doorstep lenders, pawnbrokers, and newer entrants to the market such as sale and buy-back outlets, like the Cash Converters chain, and rental purchase shops, such as Brighthouse (formerly Crazy George's). But the sub-prime sector also targeted products at those who were excluded from main stream credit due to their poor credit record or history of bad debt.[75] The housing market crash of the early 1990s, and the negative equity associated with it, extended this sub-market. The house price correction of the early 1990s also signalled the end of the credit boom of the 1980s and led mainstream financial providers to engage in a 'flight to quality'.[76] The personal finances industry was increasingly able to segment the market by its use of more sophisticated computerized credit-scoring techniques and risk assessments. This profiling militated, for example, against those who lived in council or housing association accommodation.[77] In 2006 this group represented 74 per cent of doorstep lender's customers; a figure that had not changed much from the 71 per cent of home-collected credit customers holding council house tenancies in 1981.[78]

By the opening of the twenty-first century an estimated 7 per cent of UK households (1.5 million) had access to no financial products at all and a further 20 per cent (4.4 million) were deemed to be on the margins of financial services.[79] Many of these people were in the D/E social groupings: 58 per cent of doorstep lender's customers were drawn from this sector of society, despite it representing only 25 per cent of the total population. Over half (55 per cent) of the sector's clientele were unemployed/unwaged in 2001. In 1981, Provident told the Monopolies and Mergers Commission that unemployed applicants were not accepted for its doorstep credit services.[80] But more recent findings indicate the extent to which it was subsequently obliged to move downmarket. Not surprisingly, the income levels of Provident

[75] Sharon Collard and Elaine Kempson, *Affordable credit: the way forward* (Bristol/York: Joseph Rowntree Foundation, 2005), 1.

[76] Ford and Rowlingson, 'Low-income households and credit', 1346.

[77] Ford, *Consuming credit*, 74–5.

[78] Competition Commission, *Home Credit Market Inquiry* (2006), 54. <http://www.competitioncommission.org.uk/rep_pub/reports/2006/index.htm>, accessed on 12 December 2006; Monopolies and Mergers Commission, *Great Universal Stores PLC*, 30–1.

[79] S. Collard, E. Kempson, and C. Whyley, *Tackling financial exclusion* (London: The Policy Press, 2001), 1.

[80] Monopolies and Mergers Commission, *Great Universal Stores PLC*, 19.

customers in 2006 were demonstrably lower than the national average: 44 per cent had an annual income below £13,000, compared with 22 per cent of the general population.[81] In 1989, five out of ten loans were thought to be to make ends meet, rather than to facilitate a particular consumer purchase, and there was little evidence of any subsequent change in that dynamic thereafter.[82]

The high street banks were uninterested in the small loans that were required by many low-income consumers. Whereas 86 per cent of all doorstep loans in the late 1980s were for sums under £250, only 1 per cent of bank loans were for that amount.[83] As a result, the high street banks' penetration of working-class markets remained far from complete. In 2006 only 52 per cent of doorstep borrowers were estimated to have a basic bank account, 41 per cent had a full service bank account, and 24 per cent had a post office card account.[84] The first and last of these options had particular limitations on their uses. In 1988, a potential alternative for low-income families on benefits was introduced in the form of the Social Fund, which provided interest-free loans for essential items. However, its limited impact was indicated by the fact that in 1996 Provident's total lending was double that of the Social Fund. Partly this was the result of rationing: over one million applicants were turned away by the Social Fund during 1993/4, for example, despite meeting all the criteria, because the budget was exhausted.[85] Moreover, although they were interest free, Social Fund loans had unpopular features. Repayments were deducted directly from benefits, restricting the borrower's ability to juggle weekly finances. It was criticized as slow and bureaucratic and early applicants reported being 'demeaned' by the process. In 1991, one woman bitterly remarked: 'I am angry that I have been refused help from the Social Fund and I must seek a loan from the Provident who charge very high interest.'[86] Some believed that the introduction of the Social Fund provided a fillip to illegal lenders. In 1988 Newcastle councillor Tony Flynn explained that because it offered loans, for furniture and clothing, instead of grants, which had formerly been the case, it placed greater financial pressure on low-income family budgets and created a 'loan shark's charter'.[87] The

[81] Competition Commission, *Home Credit Market Inquiry* (2006), 54.
[82] Berthoud and Kempson, *Credit and debt*, 89. [83] Ibid. 88.
[84] Competition Commission, *Home Credit Market Inquiry*, 55.
[85] Ford and Rowlingson, 'Low-income households and credit', 1345.
[86] Ford, *Consuming credit*, 45–6.
[87] *Consumer Credit Association News*, March 1988.

Child Poverty Action Group's journal was also concerned by the fact that Social Fund loans would increase debt because people were to be forced to compete for loans from a cash-limited pot.[88]

Although low-income borrowers were frequently met by supply-side difficulties associated with financial exclusion and the limitations of the Social Fund, there are also demand-side explanations for the growth of doorstep lending since the 1960s. As was the case with previous generations, who had used the tallymen or check trader, borrowing from doorstep lenders was seen by many as a form of enforced saving, with the weekly knock on the door imposing discipline. It was, in effect, a resource for managing poverty or low incomes. There were no default charges for missing payments, which was a regular occurrence for many borrowers.[89] The ability to miss a payment, although no doubt frowned upon by their agent, meant that, unlike with Social Fund loans, borrowers had some financial flexibility in weeks when there were other calls on their hard-pressed cash. Moreover, unlike the Social Fund, a hallmark of doorstep lenders was their ability to approve loans and deliver cash swiftly to applicants with few enquiries about the purpose of the loan. Customers' experience of this aspect of their relationship with doorstep lenders often differed markedly from encounters when they were interviewed for Social Fund loans. The latter carried echoes of the poor's alienation from the Means Test in the 1930s.[90] It has also been argued that many of the doorstep lenders' customers simply did not consider other options, with patterns of credit that had been traditionally used within families being continued from one generation to the next, usually from mother to daughter.[91] Faced with the option of either filling in a detailed Social Fund application or having a Provident agent fill out a more straightforward form for them, many borrowers opted for the second, more costly option.

The gendered nature of demand in this market was met with a feminization of the agency workforces who marketed and collected loans for the large-scale moneylenders. Many female agents established strong relationships with customers. It was these connections that made the greatest contribution to regular favourable customer responses about doorstep lending. In the early 1990s, Karen Rowlingson found that the

[88] Theresa Hinton and Mark Dunn, 'United we stand—credit unions: a positive response to debt', *Poverty*, 69 (Spring 1998).

[89] Rowlingson, *Moneylenders and their customers*, 6.

[90] Vincent, *Poor citizens*, 77.

[91] Ford, *Consuming credit*, 38.

image of moneylending amongst customers was far removed from its popular representation. Her study uncovered that many relationships between moneylenders (or their agents) and borrowers were commonly 'built on friendship rather than fear' and centred on a 'women's economy'. A number of Rowlingson's respondents held greater concerns about bank managers and the unknown costs that would incur if they fell behind with a loan from that source. One explained: 'We have had a bank loan a couple of years ago now. And it was awful. We were paying £80 a month it was, which we are paying now. But if we left it one month, we used to get a letter and they'd add another 25 quid onto that and interest on you if you don't pay it... It was horrifying.' Another respondent summed up her decision to use a moneylender with the phrase: 'The devil you know is better than the devil you don't.' Rowlingson's sample also frequently articulated a broad understanding of the high costs they paid for their loans:

> I do think it's a lot on top. Like, I said, £160 what he said was available at the moment. I'm sure that was £240 odd, you know, to pay back. It's a lot of interest again. And some people, like maybe even me this year, will have to have it because of the grandchildren really. You have to have it and you're paying all year then and before you know it it's Christmas again.

Rowlingson's final respondent neatly summed up how doorstep lenders' customers calculate their decision to take out a loan from a very weak position in terms of consumer choice or power:

> There's not piles and piles of paperwork before you get an answer—and usually it's a refusal [from a mainstream lender]. The agent is very friendly. If for whatever reason you can't pay him on the Friday, he doesn't mind calling back on the Saturday. Minus wise there's the interest, but you can't do much about that.[92]

The female-centred nature of doorstep borrowing was maintained after Rowlingson reported. In 2006 it was estimated that 69 per cent of the doorstep lender's customers were female.[93] Rowlingson's study may have surprised some with its revelations about the almost 'cosy' image of relations between doorstep borrowers and moneylenders, but Avram Taylor more recently offered a historical

[92] Rowlingson, *Moneylenders and their customers*, 8, 83, 95.
[93] Competition Commission, *Home Credit Market Inquiry*, 54.

perspective on how these relationships were commercially manipulated, focusing on the central factor that agents were paid by commission on turnover and were financially motivated to ensure that their relationships became long-term and personally profitable ones.[94]

Rowlingson's study was part of what can be dubbed a culturalist turn taken by social policy experts investigating credit in low-income communities in the mid-1990s, which has remained influential in recent years. Those taking this approach looked beyond the institutional structures involved in the process of financial exclusion and into household 'custom and practice in regard to financial management'.[95] This led to a growing awareness of an element of self-exclusion, by low-income consumers, from mainstream financial systems. Evidence was discovered, for example, that some individuals cancelled bank accounts when they became unemployed, exhibiting a desire for a greater grip on cash flows. Bank accounts presented unwanted opportunities to become overdrawn and engender penalty charges. A preference for cash transactions was, thereafter, demonstrated.[96] It was also noted that the product offered by moneylenders on the doorstep was seen by many as cash rather than credit. One moneylender's customer, interviewed as part of Rowlingson's study in the early 1990s, explained that her husband 'won't have any credit cards, he won't have anything on HP'. When he wanted something 'he likes to pay for it there and then, so he hasn't got to think that's got to be paid for'.[97] Of course, it was paid for with borrowed money from a doorstep lender, but in his mind the routinized collections became part of weekly budgeting rather than debt repayments. This paralleled many of the rationalizations of credit use in the early twentieth century when mail order customers or users of Provident checks defined their borrowing strategies as being weekly payments to a friendly agent's 'club'.

Whilst insights into doorstep lenders and their customers became increasingly sophisticated from the 1990s, the critique of the sector

[94] Avram Taylor, *Working class credit and community since 1918* (Basingstoke: Palgrave Macmillan, 2002), 44.

[95] Ford and Rowlingson, 'Low-income households and credit', 1347.

[96] Elaine Kempson, *Outside the banking system* (London: Policy Studies Institute, 1994), cited in Ford and Rowlingson, 'Low-income households and credit'; Collard, Kempson, and Whyley, *Tackling financial exclusion*, vi.

[97] Rowlingson, *Moneylenders and their customers*, 76.

did not decline. Lobbyists, such as the umbrella group Debt on Our Doorstep, became highly influential voices in the debates surrounding new emotive terms such as 'predatory lending', which were increasingly deployed in the campaign for tougher credit controls. According to a report for the New Economics Foundation, predatory lending 'not only devastates individual families and households. It is systematically stripping the wealth and assets of some of the country's poorest neighbourhoods.' It is, in short, 'one of the worst excesses of the free market economy'.[98] The authors called for statutory ceilings rates on loans and support for more affordable forms of credit, principally credit unions. This lobby secured a number of victories. Amongst these was Church Action on Poverty's success in getting the Church of England to sell its shareholding in Provident Financial in 2001.[99] However, the most notable success was the launch of a Competition Commission inquiry into Home Credit in 2004, following a so-called super-complaint, launched by the National Consumer Council (NCC), alleging lack of competition and unwarranted high costs amongst doorstep lenders.

Consumers certainly paid more for these forms of credit. In 1989, Berthoud and Kempson reported that the top income group paid only 60 pence per week for each £100 they borrowed, whilst the poorest paid £1. But they also acknowledged the higher costs of lending to the latter group. These included losses incurred in lending to 'risky markets', the fact that administrative costs made up a larger proportion of smaller loans, and the expensive collection systems determined by the nature of the market. They concluded that there are 'genuine reasons why small loans cost more, but without direct data about each element of these costs it is not possible to draw a line between genuinely high costs and excessive profits'.[100] Whilst the Consumer Credit Act of 1978 contained a clause allowing courts to examine 'extortionate credit bargains', only a tiny number of individual cases were brought before the courts subsequently and they had minimal impact. The Competition Commission inquiry which began in 2004 represented arguably the most likely method to probe this matter adequately. To carry out its task, it decided that APR was a weak measure when applied to this form

[98] H. Palmer and P. Conaty, *Profiting from poverty: why debt is big business in Britain* (London: New Economics Foundation, 2002), 3.

[99] Interview with Alan Thornton of Church Action on Poverty, 2 June 2004.

[100] Berthoud and Kempson, *Credit and debt: the PSI report*, 98–102.

of credit and replaced it with the total charge for credit or TCC. It subsequently identified a lack of price competition. It partly explained this by pointing to customers' insensitivity to price and their tendency to value other attributes of the product, such as home collection, more highly. However, it estimated that customers were paying a total of around £100m per year—or £9 in every £100 loaned—over what they might be expected to part with in a competitive market. Particular criticism was also aimed at the doorstep lenders' practice of marketing top-up loans. As one loan neared completion, it was common practice to offer a new loan, with part of the sum lent being used to terminate the previous loan. In effect, this involved 'expensive' money being borrowed to pay for previous 'expensive' money. The Competition Commission maintained that on a £100 loan £10 more was paid on a top-up loan than if a customer was instead offered a separate loan to run parallel to the first one.[101] However, the Commission's proposals disappointed campaigners because they did not include the desired ceiling on annual interest rates. The Commission accepted arguments that any 'external imposition of a ceiling on interest rates (as exists in some countries) is likely to close down existing avenues of commercial credit to the poor and increase the likelihood of their using illegal extortionate credit'.[102]

Thus, the fear of the loan shark precluded capping, despite the strongest campaign against moneylending charges since the 1920s. It was true, that doorstep lenders were reluctant to take on the very poor, including the long-term unemployed and many single parents.[103] This meant that what can be dubbed a sub-sub-prime market, with many of the features of the illegal lending that took place in the early twentieth century, continued to operate a century later. One of its features was the involvement of an increasingly visible violent criminal element. The final section of this chapter explores this area, which although relatively small, has held a great deal of practical and symbolic importance. In practical terms, its existence was a major stumbling block for potential legislative reform of the much larger legal moneylending market. Its symbolic significance lay with the fact that it provided the sinister and disturbing images of moneylending that dominated mainstream depictions of the activity.

[101] Competition Commission, *Home Credit Market Inquiry*, 6, 83.
[102] Ford, *Consuming credit*, 100.
[103] Rowlingson, *Moneylenders and their customers*, 4.

'AS FAR AS THEY'RE CONCERNED I AM AMERICAN EXPRESS': THE RISE OF THE LOAN SHARK

Taylor believes that the affectual element of street lending diminished slowly after 1945. This process is said to have involved the replacement of local gendered networks, centred on female street lenders, with male loan sharks, often from outside the neighbourhoods in which they operated.[104] The seizure of benefit books, as security for loans, was crucial in this development. Those engaged in this practice included some licensed lenders, as well as those on the unregistered fringe of the market. In 1962 Lily Boulton and her brother Dennis Constable from Edmonton, North London, and Great Dunmow, Essex, respectively, were both fined £15 for taking borrowers' family allowance books and cashing them in at the post office.[105] Whilst the post-war welfare state provided new opportunities, such as this, for unscrupulous lenders the practice was not new. Similar activities were prevalent in 1897, when it was revealed that ex-servicemen's 'pension papers' were being deposited in large numbers with moneylenders in Portsmouth and Oldham.[106] The introduction of state pensions in 1908 provided new opportunities to moneylenders and pawnbrokers to take pension books illegally as security for loans. In Southampton's docklands, for example, they became a form of collateral, which was taken by local street lenders as an alternative to wedding rings.[107] These securities reduced the requirement for trust involved in the borrower–lender relationship at the fringes of the market.

Taylor discovered traces of loan sharking in Newcastle from 1969, but noted that the term was not employed there until 1977.[108] As has been outlined already, the term crossed the Atlantic and was deployed in the moneylending controversies of the 1920s. It was also used in Glasgow during the 1960s. But it does appear that it only entered common usage throughout the UK in the early 1980s at which point both government and industry bodies shone a spotlight on illegal lending. Taylor defined

104 Taylor, *Working class credit*, 59.

105 *The Times*, 16 March 1962.

106 Select Committee on Moneylending (1897–8), evidence of Thomas Farrow, 18 May 1987.

107 Tebbutt, *Making ends meet*, 100; Nancy Sharman, *Nothing to steal* (London: Kay and Ward, 1977), 36, cited in Vincent, *Poor citizens*, 92.

108 Taylor, *Working class credit*, 62.

a loan shark as a lender who is involved in agreements that are not legally recorded, where both parties are aware that the transaction is illegal, and where violence is understood to be a potential consequence.[109] He acknowledged, however, that this definition incorporates a large proportion of the illegal lending that took place prior to 1960. Taylor also noted that by the 1970s much of this lending was cross-gendered with male lenders providing loans to female customers, who were often single parents. This, he believed, replaced 'gendered affectual networks', involving elements of emotional ties, centred on informal female-to-female lending. Less attention is paid, in Taylor's analysis, to the fact that the affectual relationships involved in street lending prior to the emergence of the modern loan shark had, by the 1970s, been taken on by the female agents employed by Provident Financial, Cattles, and other large companies. They appropriated working-class credit networks in a fashion that echoed the process carried out by the mail order companies in previous generations when they commercialized the draw clubs that were familiar to working-class consumers. The Provident agent replaced the elderly lady down the street who in the past had 'obliged' a neighbour in return for a little 'interest', as was the case in Liverpool's Ship Street in the 1950s.[110] As Provident, Cattles, and others commercialized this market, those they deemed as too great a credit risk were left to deal with new types of illegal lenders. In our discussion of mail order it was noted that one mail order executive coined the term 'credit orphans' to describe low-income consumers who had formerly been customers of his company's agents. By the 1980s and 1990s, they had no access to catalogue credit because the number of agents willing to take them on and police their repayments was declining. This was due to factors such as the polarization of council estates, with the more affluent buying their council homes or moving away from the least attractive estates. As Taylor described it—adapting the sociology of Philip Abrams, and Anthony Giddens—the traditional neighbourhood in which diffuse trust and reciprocity existed largely disappeared in the late twentieth century. Taylor offered the example of mail order agents who, by the 1990s, were declining credit requests from their neighbours: as ties based on locality 'no longer offer a sufficient basis, in themselves, for trust'.[111]

109 Taylor, 59. Taylor draws upon Peter Reuter, *Disorganised crime* (Cambridge, Mass.: MIT Press, 1986), 88.

110 M. Kerr, *The people of Ship Street* (London: Routledge and Kegan Paul, 1958), 195.

111 Taylor, *Working class credit*, 43–4, 175.

A similar point can be made for illegal lending and the most recent study suggests that 'the traditional old fashioned moneylender' has come to play a minimal role in this market.[112] Loan sharks filled the breach. Rising unemployment, in the early 1980s, was a watershed in this respect. In 1983, the National Association of Citizens' Advice Bureaux reported that the 'loan shark menace' had been increasing for eighteen months, particularly in 'inner-city areas where the unemployed and single parents resorted to moneylenders'. Tactics employed by loan sharks to ensure repayment included parking vans marked 'debt collection' outside borrower's homes and throwing bricks through their windows.[113] Violence, the seizure of benefit books, and the involvement of criminals were increasingly seen as hallmarks of loan sharking. As we have seen, evidence from Glasgow and Liverpool suggests that criminals have had a long involvement in moneylending. However, the available information indicates that criminal involvement in Glasgow's illegal lending market became more sustained in the 1960s. One possibility is that there was a connection with developments surrounding the legalization of bookmaking. It is likely that the decline of illegal bookmakers, following the legalization of off-course betting in 1960, led some of the more ruthless street bookmakers to seek out alternative illicit sources of income. It was seen, in the last chapter, that observers in the early twentieth century frequently made a link between male lending networks and gambling. This relationship was also noted by those investigating illegal lending and loan sharking in the USA during the 1960s and 1970s. Illegal bookmakers were ideally placed to make their finances work in an additional market by providing borrowers with the funds to take a punt. One such individual was operating from the Earl of Warwick pub, in London's North Kensington, in 1969. He 'took bets on grey hounds after the bookies have shut' and deployed 'strong arm tactics on non-payers'.[114]

Another possible explanation for the high visibility of loan sharking in Glasgow is that it had a strong heritage in the city and that it was 'discovered' in 1967 only because the *Daily Record* launched a campaign

[112] DTI, *Illegal lending in the UK*, 69. [113] *The Times*, 11 July 1983.

[114] John Seidl, 'Upon the hip: a study of the criminal loan shark industry' (Unpublished Ph.D., Harvard University, 1968); Ivan Light, 'Numbers gambling among Blacks: a financial institution', *American Sociological Review*, 42/6 (December 1977), 892–904; NA: BT 250, Committee on Consumer Credit. Correspondence with newspaper advice bureaux, 1969.

against 'The Age of Violence'. This followed in the wake of the local press coverage of the 'reappearance' of Glasgow's street gangs in 1965 and subsequent national press attention in the following year.[115] It was felt that illegal moneylending had metamorphosed into an extremely unpleasant form:

> Illegal moneylending in Glasgow is not a new problem. For years moneylending rings have operated successfully in the docks and larger works and factories, but without violence. Only in the last 3 years have gangs of unscrupulous thugs resorted to terror tactics, even charging higher interest rates. Gone are the gentle hints to pay up. In are the knife and the razor. The moneylenders are not interested in the original loan. They thrive on extortionate interest rates. Family allowance, pension and National Assistance books are held by the thugs as security. The payee must sign each money order in the book but this can be done in advance before the book is given to the moneylender. The victim can even endorse the back of the orders allowing someone else to collect the money. Every Friday and Saturday public houses are used as 'agencies' for the gangs. Teams of 'hard' men wait outside post offices and labour exchanges, their presence, itself, a threat to the victim to pay.[116]

The dockland area was described as having been a 'hive of illegal moneylending for years'.[117] Their unfortunate customers included 'Mrs X', a housewife who had to find £10 bail when her husband faced criminal charges. She met a pub moneylender 'who was all smiles', when providing her with £10 for which she was to pay £2 interest each week until such time as the principal was paid. When her husband was subsequently jailed, she was told that 'something nasty would happen' if she missed any payments and it was 'suggested' that she hand over her family allowance book. When she did miss two payments she was assaulted in front of her children. In desperation, she turned to prostitution, which eventually provided the cash to pay off her debt.[118] In other cases, threats were reportedly followed by grotesque actions, such as the case of a man who was nailed to his front door and that of a prostitute whose breasts were slashed.[119] In the most serious case, in November 1967, Jimmy Boyle, described as the 'enforcer who killed

[115] James Patrick, *A Glasgow gang observed* (London: Eyre Methuen, 1973), 20. My thanks are due to Andrew Davies for this reference and for countless others.

[116] *Daily Record*, 15 November 1967.

[117] *Daily Record* n.d., 1967. Cutting in NA/PRO, BT 250/89, Consumer Credit Committee. Miscellaneous evidence from members of the public and others, and general correspondence about evidence.

[118] *Daily Record*, 17 November 1967.

[119] Ibid., 15 November 1967.

for £7 debt' was sentenced for the murder of William Rooney who was said to be indebted to Boyle and another man.[120] In his autobiography, Boyle denied committing the murder and also maintained that the 'crucifixion story', involving the man being nailed to the door, was untrue. He critiqued media coverage of his case and others, arguing that 'most of what they printed was nonsense'. There was little violence involved, argued Boyle, because there 'was very little problem with people refusing to pay back, as it meant that if they didn't, they couldn't go back again' to that moneylender. Although Boyle also noted that lending money 'did attract other criminals who wanted to borrow, and it was usually them who would give the problems in refusing to pay back and so the Heavies were brought in to act as "minders"'.[121]

Another ensnared by the combined media and police interest in Glasgow's illegal lending was the dapperly-dressed Thomas McMenemy, who told journalists assembled outside the court trying him for illegal lending that: 'I've nothing to blame myself for. My customers came to me in the pub for help. I charged 4s a week interest in the £, and they were glad of it.' His operations covered the Rutherglen Road, Oatlands, and Gorbals districts.[122] An unnamed individual, employed as part of a three-man collection team by a loan shark between 1959 and 1964, explained their modus operandi to a journalist. He revealed that collectors 'didn't care how the debt was paid' and their prime concern was for their 2s 6d in the pound commission. He reported how they 'took family allowances or anything we could get our hands on. We weren't angels. Quite a few people got sore faces because of it. But that is nothing compared with what is going on today.' He was reportedly 'sick' because 'women and their families are being terrorised', weapons were being used 'all the time', and at the murder of Rooney 'because he wouldn't make a small debt'. He claimed that in one area alone 'there are at least six big illegal moneylenders at work', and that they 'all have their hardmen to make sure the money is paid'.[123] If these claims are accurate, it appears that competition in the loan sharking market contributed to the levels of violence in Glasgow, because it undermined Boyle's theory that borrowers were forced to repay because any default would remove future opportunities to obtain loans.

120 Ibid., 4 November 1967.

121 Jimmy Boyle, *A sense of freedom* (London: Pan Books Ltd, 1977), 156, 160, 141.

122 *Daily Record*, 12 December 1967.

123 Ibid., 17 November 1967.

Media attention led to the creation of a special police squad, dubbed the 'racket busters', which made the unlikely claim that it had driven 'hoodlum moneylenders' off the streets.[124] Its swoops also sucked in a number of moneylenders whose methods were akin to those witnessed earlier in the century, suggesting that even within the illegal lending market there was a hierarchy of risk that produced different enforcement patterns. Boyle was probably accurate in his suggestion that it was those living chaotic, criminal lifestyles that were most likely to default. So the illegal market paralleled legal lending, by charging higher interest both because risks were greater and because those applying for loans could not access cheaper credit. Additionally, violence—or its threat—became a further method of enforcement.

In 1967 James McDonald, a 37-year-old father of six from Nitshill, claimed he became a moneylender after winning £150 at the dog track. He charged 2s 6d per week for each pound borrowed, suggesting it was more cost effective to take a loan from the one-man operator than from those paying commission to collector-enforcers. It was also safer: the police reported that McDonald did not use violence.[125] In the same year 38-year-old Allan Leslie of Kinning Park told a court that he 'was only lending money to locals to help them out', after winning '£348 on the pools two years ago'. The stipendiary magistrate retorted acerbically: 'It's the old, old story. Everybody seems to be winning money on the pools, dogs, horses.'[126] Females were also involved. Elizabeth Douglas a 36-year-old mother of seven, with official weekly income of £7 national assistance, lent one woman £2 and had received over £39 in interest with the £2 still outstanding by the time of her arrest in 1967. She had been fined £40 for the same offence the previous year and was defended—perhaps coincidentally—by the same high-profile solicitor who represented McMenemy.[127] In a story headed 'The "good deeds" of a woman loan shark', another case was reported that involved Isabella Stewart. A cleaner from Bridgeton who earned £5 per week, she had twenty-six family allowance books in her home when it was raided by police. Stewart told the court that people 'who could not pay their rent came to see me. I would take them to the factors and would pay to prevent them being put out of their homes.' She maintained that her business was financed by a £700 bequest from her father.[128] The

[124] *Daily Record* n.d., 1967. Cutting in NA: BT 250/89.
[125] *Daily Record*, 29 November 1967. [126] Ibid., 30 November 1967.
[127] *Daily Record* n.d. 1967. Cutting in NA/BT 250/89. [128] Ibid.

Crowther Committee on Consumer Credit was sitting at this point and, noting the Glasgow press coverage, approached the *News of the World*'s John Hilton Bureau for further information on loan sharks. As the Bureau had received 'very few letters about it compared with other areas of consumer credit', it appealed to readers for information. Seventy letters were received in response, but they contained nothing paralleling the experience on Clydeside.[129]

The city was also to come to stand out from the perspective of the moneylending companies, in that muggings of their collectors became a problem in the city during the early 1980s. Over half the thirty attacks that took place on collectors working for H. T. Greenwood Ltd between 1980 and 1983 occurred in the city. The company, and others, subsequently 'redlined' Glasgow's high-rise flats.[130] It is possible that this provided more customers for the loan sharks. The fact that the most ruthless illegal lenders were by this point finding clients amongst the city's spiralling numbers of heroin addicts suggests a connection with the robberies of doorstep collectors. Strathclyde's trading standards officers also discovered direct links between loan sharks and drug peddling in the 1980s. They noted that the modus operandi of the Glaswegian loan shark had changed little since the 1960s. Cases involved 'stabbings, beatings, assaults of a very personal nature and threats of violence to members of the debtor's family, including to their children'. Once again, single parents were amongst the most vulnerable. Loan sharks identified in the late 1980s were operating in Paisley, Bridgeton, and Springburn. Resulting prosecutions ended the operations of some loan sharks, only for others to step into the breach. However, it was felt that forcing illegal lenders to be more circumspect about their activities reduced their customer base.[131]

To the annoyance of the CCA, its 850 members were increasingly referred to as 'loan sharks with exorbitant rates of interest' during the 1980s. It felt the term was used by those who had no understanding of how 'an APR is calculated'.[132] At least one trading standards officer agreed that APR 'cannot be used to define a loan shark', but added

[129] NA: BT250/101, Committee on Consumer Credit, Correspondence with newspaper advice bureau.

[130] *Consumer Credit Association News*, July/August 1987, PFG/05/073 Company strategy review: H. T. Greenwood, 1990.

[131] S. Bolchover et al., 'Investigating the loan sharks', *Trading Standards Review*, 98/1 (1990), 18–22.

[132] *Consumer Credit Association News*, March 1988.

that he considered some licensed lenders—including those who did not care for their customers and regularly renewed loans—were deserving of the sobriquet.[133] In 1983, Michael Shanks, Chairman of the NCC, also registered his concerns about relending to pay off the first debt. This was leading to real problems for many families according to trading standards officers. Shanks argued that moneylenders who had encouraged families into a 'mesh of debt from which they find it impossible to extricate themselves have rightly been exposed by the media'. This quote is noteworthy in that it suggests that the NCC was implicitly reliant on the media to slap the wrists of any moneylender exploiting the inequality between themselves and borrowers. This stance reflects the political climate surrounding consumer protection in the early 1980s, which has been described by Matthew Hilton as one in which government was only ready to listen to 'arguments for greater choice and less protectionism'.[134] The CCA, in a meeting with the NCC, responded to Shanks, telling him that reputable lenders did not offer loans to people struggling with existing repayments. At the same meeting, the Director-General of Fair Trading, Sir Gordon Borrie, also welcomed the high profile the media was giving to the 'loan shark'. His own definition of the term included 'any moneylender who takes advantage of the inequality of bargaining power that normally exists between a moneylender and a debtor'. Concerns on his list included the holding of benefit books as security; causing distress or humiliation to a debtor by presenting false legalistic documents to insinuate that legal criminal proceedings were about to ensue; and renewing loans without making the debtor aware of the financial implications. This last point was said to apply 'particularly to immigrants'. The CCA could not, Borrie maintained, expect the reputation of their trade to flourish unless they more effectively exposed the loan sharks amongst licensed lenders, and he held up the prospect of interest rate caps on their business.[135] As a result, the CCA and its members became the subject of regular scrutiny. Like the RCF before it, the CCA's response was to throw itself into public debate, opining that only in that way would it become recognized as 'a professional trade body' that was part of the campaign 'to drive out illicit lending'. In 1988 its Director, Michael Lilley, appeared on a host

[133] *Consumer Credit Association News*, November 1985.

[134] Matthew Hilton, *Consumerism in 20th-century Britain: the search for a historical movement* (Cambridge: Cambridge University Press, 2003), 292.

[135] *Consumer Credit Association News*, January–February 1983.

of BBC TV programmes, including *Panorama, Watchdog, Kilroy*, and *Daytime live*, and later recalled one interview 'on a windswept council estate in Bradford, answering questions which were as tough as the dogs barking in the background'.[136] At a local level, CCA members were encouraged to act against their regular instinct, which was to avoid publicity, by engaging with trading standards officers, Citizens' Advice workers, and others. Such interactions were intended to enable these groups to see, in the words of one moneylender, that he did not have 'a bolt through the head, stitches, crowbar—you know, the usual'.[137] As this quote illustrates, the common usage of 'loan shark' to describe moneylenders ensured that early twentieth-century images of the Jewish 'Shylock' were replaced with ones centred on violent criminals. Possibly the most memorable and shocking of these was the vicious loan shark Tansey from Ken Loach's film *Raining stones* (1993). Tansey is seen first as a character in the background, harassing his debtors as they come out of the post office with their benefit money. He subsequently buys the debt that the unemployed protagonist Bob has incurred, with an unseen 'loan company', to pay for his daughter's Holy Communion dress. Bob's wife, Anne, is shockingly confronted by the loan shark and his henchman in her own home. Her surprise is shared by the audience who were also unaware that Bob had borrowed money. The scene is disturbing, due to Tansey's violence and the cascade of intimidating physical and sexual threats that rain down on the sobbing Anne. The couple only escape Tansey's clutches when he is accidentally killed after Bob has confronted him outside a pub: an outcome that was not the regular denouement in relationships between real-life debtors and loan sharks. Bob's subsequent confession of his part in the loan shark's death is met with his priest's memorable phrase: 'Fuck Tansey! May God have mercy on his soul.'[138] With such dramatic depictions of loan sharks, it was important from the CCA's perspective that it battled to focus attention on illegal lenders: 'On every council estate in the land', its journal noted in 1988, 'there's an unlicensed lender who is probably conducting his business in a violent manner, taking advantage of those who cannot borrow from the legitimate industry'. It claimed that the 'CCA is seeking to terminate the activities of loan sharks'.[139] However,

136 Ibid., March 1988.

137 Interview with anonymous Northern Ireland moneylender 1.

138 *Raining Stones* (Director: Ken Loach), Channel Four Films, 1993.

139 *Consumer Credit Association News*, March 1988.

as was the case with the Moneylenders Act 1927, government policy in the 1980s had unintended consequences that provided potential custom for illegal lenders. In 1985 trading standards officers felt that clauses in the Consumer Credit Act, making it simpler to prosecute loan sharks who took benefit books as security, might 'have had the effect of increasing the element of violence', as illegal lenders used this method of enforcement rather than taking the risk of being caught in possession of incriminating evidence.[140]

In the cases of those who were prosecuted, the CCA was critical of the punishments meted out. In 1988 it highlighted the case of Paisley loan shark Michael Browne. Browne was fined £300 for sixty-two cases of lending without a licence. The CCA pointed out that with such a small fine he could 'afford to return to crime' and asked would he 'be caught next time?'[141] Its view was prescient: Browne was still active two decades later when he received a seven-year sentence for repeatedly slashing a woman in the face because her boyfriend owed him money.[142] Other loan sharks, active in the 1980s included 'Tommy', from Manchester's Wythenshawe estate, whose 'minder' was known as 'The Beast'.[143] Whilst Tommy and 'The Beast' were going about their business, the operational practices of others reflected the 'she usurers' of earlier decades. Shirley told a journalist in 1988, that 'I wouldn't call myself a loan shark. I am providing a service for the people who can't get it anywhere else.' This involved 'an instant injection of £200 over a cosy cup of coffee in the customer's own home'. Shirley only lent to women, as 'men would probably use violence against her when threatened to repay'. Rather than use violence, she 'blackmails those who do not make regular payments. Her powerful weapon is to threaten to make a scene in front of the borrower's neighbours and husband.' However, her husband 'also goes along with her, waiting in the car, to serve as "back-up" when dealing with awkward customers'. Her illegal business, which had grown out of a mail order agency, enabled her to move to the 'stockbroker belt'. She explained that young mothers, 'wanting the best for their children', were her best customers: 'As far as they're concerned, I am American Express.'[144] Lyn Boyd, a founder of Newcastle's Cowgate Credit Union, presumably had 'Shirley' rather

[140] *Consumer Credit Association News*, November 1985.
[141] *Consumer Credit Association News*, March 1988.
[142] *Guardian*, 21 February 2006.
[143] *Consumer Credit Association News*, March 1988.
[144] *Guardian*, 27 January 1988.

than 'Tommy' in mind when she was quoted as saying that the credit union was reluctant to wage war on the local 'loan sharks' because they provide a 'service' in 'an area which has been evacuated by all the legitimate institutions . . . loan sharks are seen as helpful, albeit in an expensive way'.[145] It, therefore, proved difficult for the authorities to gather information on illegal lenders from their customers. Whilst for the customers of Tommy, this could be put down to fear, for those of Shirley it was as much due to her customers' reluctance to see a scarce credit source curtailed.[146]

In 2004, the Department of Trade and Industry set up pilot schemes in Birmingham and Glasgow to tackle loan sharks. They unearthed disturbing evidence of the plight of those borrowers deemed too great a risk by legal lenders. Kim Cornfield, aged 52 from Redditch, was jailed for two years for assaulting a heavily pregnant woman who had failed to make sufficient repayments to him. Cornfield had also threatened to beat up dozens of other vulnerable single mothers and to burn down their homes, as well as making demands for 'sexual favours' as 'payment in kind'. Modern technology allowed him to add a further weapon to the loan sharks' traditional armoury: threatening text messages such as, 'U'll be sorry you messed with me' and 'Ur going to have the crap beaten out of u', were dispatched to debtors. Over a two-year period he advanced £18,000, on which he expected a £70,000 return. In July 2005, the equally repulsive Mark 'Arnie' Johnson, from Birmingham, received a sentence of three years and nine months. His activities included bullying elderly and disabled borrowers and he was alleged to have dangled a man, by his legs, from the balcony of his flat. Some £500,000 was recovered from his estate following his subsequent death in prison.[147] The clients of Glasgow loan shark Gerard Laws included 'single mums, alcoholics and the mentally ill', some of whom had been his 'clients' for twenty years. He operated from the Argosy Bar, where he spent up to six hours daily despite being a teetotaller. Undercover police recorded up to eighteen people a day approaching him. He charged 25 per cent a week interest and some loans were said to have an annual interest rate of 11 million per cent.[148]

In 2006, the first major analysis of illegal lending estimated that 165,000 UK households, or 0.44 per cent of adults, made use of illegal

[145] *Consumer Credit Association News*, March 1988.
[146] Ford, *Consuming Credit*, 87.
[147] *Guardian*, 21 February 2006.
[148] *Scotsman*, 18 August 2006.

moneylenders.[149] It was suspected that this under-represented the full extent of activity. Three per cent of all households, a total of 850,000, were in locations that legal lenders refused to serve on safety grounds.[150] Use of illegal moneylenders was most substantial in areas with the highest indices of multiple deprivation. These districts had been increasingly redlined by legal lenders and were most prominent in Scotland and the North of England. Credit exclusion rates peaked at 5.5 per cent in Scotland, where Glasgow was hardest hit. In Wales, pockets of Swansea and the Rhondda valley were identified as most vulnerable to illegal lenders. In England, Liverpool contained 'some of the most deprived and ghettoized communities within which illegal lenders appear both active and well known'.[151] In the South of England, credit exclusion rates stood at only 1.5 per cent, but Newham and Tower Hamlets in London, and parts of Portsmouth and Plymouth, were areas deemed at risk from illegal lenders. More generally, those living in tower blocks had been redlined by legal lenders, due to problems of gaining entry and ensuring security.[152] Ironically, however, improvement to tower block security made them less fertile territory for loan sharks, because it became trickier to pay an unannounced visit.[153] Significantly, areas with high levels of illegal activity were 'predominantly white', a factor reflecting different cultural traditions in terms of lending practices that will be probed in the next chapter.[154] The customers of illegal lenders discussed in the survey differed somewhat from moneylenders' customers in general. They were much more likely to be on benefits, particularly disability benefits, and to have criminal convictions, mental health problems, alcohol or drug addictions, and county court judgements against their name. Linked to the final issue was the fact that although this group of borrowers had broadly similar credit requirements to those using legal doorstep lenders, a significant minority borrowed to fund drink or drug habits. This assessment tallied with the insights into the subterranean Glaswegian subcultures of the 1960s described in Boyle's autobiography.[155]

CONCLUSION

These depressing findings illustrate that demand for expensive credit in the UK's low-income districts was a persistent feature of the twentieth

[149] DTI, *Illegal lending in the UK*, 5. [150] Ibid. 37. [151] Ibid. 42.
[152] Ibid. 30, 39. [153] Ibid. 31. [154] Ibid. 41.
[155] Ibid., 31, 44–6; Boyle, *Sense of freedom*.

century. Neither economic progress nor legislation removed relative poverty or the financial crises that trail in the wake of family breakdown, ill-health, or unemployment. To the dismay of anti-poverty campaigners, several aspects of the expensive services of the doorstep lenders continued to be appreciated by customers into the twenty-first century. Borrowers welcomed the discipline imposed on them by weekly collections and the ability to miss payments without incurring penalty charges (the costs of this service were, of course, factored into the original fees). Customers also demonstrated elements of obligation to these lenders that were further fostered by their knowledge that mainstream financial institutions had no interest in them. Whilst the media frequently conflated the term loan shark to include legal and illegal lenders, moneylender's customers were also reported to be aware of the distinction and were keen to remain within the legal sector and to avoid the disciplinary measures on offer in the illegal system, which they knew often centred on intimidation and violence.[156] Reflecting the campaigners of the 1920s, such as Dorothy Keeling, anti-debt campaigners in the final decades of the twentieth century became ever more critical of doorstep lenders and eager to provide low-cost or mutual alternative lending institutions for low-income consumers. Like Keeling, they looked overseas for an alternative. They found their answer in community credit unions and advocated them vociferously. However, as we shall see in a later chapter their ability to make an impact in the UK has been limited.

It was the doorstep lenders who best understood the needs of the low-income consumer. They continued to offer the products that most suited those requirements. However, they did so at a price that siphoned precious finances from the family pot; a factor that was all the more serious when the method became a habitual part of weekly expenditure, rather than an occasional factor in crisis management. The Competition Commission ruling, in 2006, that lack of competition in the doorstep lending sector had resulted in borrowers being overcharged provided the first data indicating the extent to which the weak bargaining position of borrowers was reflected in their purses. Anti-debt campaigners continue to press for a cap on the APR associated with doorstep lending. Their views, and those reflected in media coverage of doorstep lending, are somewhat removed from those held by many social scientists working on this issue. The latter believe that a ceilings cap would result in the

[156] DTI, *Illegal lending in the UK*, 78.

withdrawal of Provident and others from its riskiest customers, leaving them increasingly vulnerable to loan sharks. There are echoes of the debates from the 1920s in this argument. Then, powerful stereotypes of Jewish usurers helped cloud elements of the discussion. In recent decades imprecise use of the term loan shark has conflated and confused the role of different types of lender in a market that was, and remains, more complex than much press coverage would suggest. In the 1920s, many of those who supported a rates cap hoped that it would remove moneylenders from the equation. Social workers, and others with more experience of back-street lending, feared that it would simply deepen its subterranean nature. The sequel to the 1927 Act was the reduction of registered moneylenders, but there is no evidence to suggest that numbers of illegal lenders dipped, and some suggestions that violence became more commonplace.

The moneylending sector—more than any of the other branches of the consumer credit industry whose history is examined herein—revolved around the imposition of external discipline on borrowers. From the legal lenders, this came in the form of regular visits and pressure to repay loans and involved a range of elements from reciprocity and obligation through to the threat to refuse future credit or to take court action. These enforcement methods were applied to consumers who, for the most part, had few other lines of credit and limited income. For those who made up what we have labelled the sub-sub-prime market, with whom the doorstep lenders were unable or unwilling to do business, there was the prospect of the harsher forms of discipline associated with illegal lenders of all types, from Shirley who lent to single mums and used old-fashioned threats of exposure to neighbours, through to extremely violent loan sharks such as Michael Browne who preyed on alcoholics and drug addicts. Whatever happens in the future in respect to the legislation of this market, it is clear that government must do whatever is in its power to avoid creating the conditions in which loan sharks multiply.

6

Formal and informal co-operative credit

Perennial concerns about the expense of the credit channels examined in previous chapters propelled a search for low-cost, mutually based alternatives. As a result, a number of co-operative or mutual credit institutions emerged alongside the range of commercial alternatives that were available to nineteenth- and twentieth-century working-class consumers. Mutual activity ranged from the significant contribution made by the co-operative movement through to credit rotation societies that were organized by small groups of consumers to meet relatively modest financial needs. The latter groups emerged organically from within working-class communities and were formed to meet a variety of consumption requirements, whilst the co-operative retail societies were involved, somewhat reluctantly initially, in the provision of vast quantities of consumer credit.

Although the founding principles of the co-operative movement stood squarely opposed to the concept of indebtedness, the retail wing of the movement found itself unable to operate without establishing instalment payment schemes. The first part of this chapter examines the extent to which co-operative retailers provided an alternative to expensive doorstep credit, via the introduction of mutuality clubs in 1923. As has already been indicated, the Women's Group on Public Welfare championed these mutuality clubs during the Second World War. The Trades Union Congress also placed its faith in the co-operative movement, believing that 'with every extension of these predominantly working class organisations the need for other organisations to protect the consumer against the evils inherent in private enterprise will diminish'.[1] However, the philosophical and economic underpinnings of

[1] London: MSS 292/660.77/1 TUC General Council Research Department, *Scheme for a Consumers' Advisory Council* (20 December 1937), cited in Matthew Hilton, *Consumerism in 20th-century Britain: the search for a historical movement* (Cambridge: Cambridge University Press, 2003), 151.

co-operative thought acted as a brake on the development of innovative credit sales and somewhat limited the movement's ability to land a disabling blow to high-cost commercial credit. Co-operatives were risk averse when it came to credit. They had one eye on anticipated reproaches from influential co-operators who proffered regular critiques of indebtedness, and the other on protecting members' dividends, which were threatened by potential bad debt. There were also demand-side factors limiting the extent to which co-operative credit was taken up. These included the greater choice available to users of Provident checks who could shop around, whilst mutuality club members could use their local co-operative only. Most importantly, co-operative stores operated credit rationing by limiting credit to members with healthy share balances in the society. Thus, whilst mutuality clubs came to have an extensive presence in working-class credit networks, many consumers were excluded from their use. Prevalent amongst the excluded were those without the ability to make regular savings. The co-operative movement's adaptation of the Provident check system was successful, but its attempts to adopt the mail order catalogue in the 1940s and 1960s ended in failure for reasons explained below.

Also explored in this chapter is the extent to which a mixture of unofficial mutuality and entrepreneurialism amongst some members flew in the face of co-operative philosophy. Those involved undermined co-operative principles, by making their 'Co book' and credit account available to family, friends, and neighbours who were themselves blacklisted or unable to amass healthy share capital in their local co-operative store. Those lending out their 'Co book' were rewarded via the increased dividends they amassed through the additional sales recorded against their account number. The practice was an example of the important role of the dividend and its quarterly contribution to family finances, albeit one that was not welcomed by those co-operative idealists who felt that high dividends inflated prices.

The resourcefulness and mutuality of those involved in this unsanctioned use of 'Co books' emerged from a cocktail of instrumental and altruistic motives. Rotating savings and credit associations, or ROSCAs, emerged for similar reasons. ROSCAs included the slate or loan clubs that operated from many pubs, and the female-centred draw clubs that operated throughout the UK. These informal societies did not wield the constraint imposed by threats of county court action, which commercial companies could employ, or the non-payment of dividend which the retail co-operative could impose. The absence of economic or legal sanction was potentially problematic, but these credit rotation societies replaced them by the powerful force of social connectedness within the groups involved, which as will be seen, was a powerful method of enforcement. For this reason, and others, ROSCAs have had a long-term presence in the UK. They received new life, and new formats, as important resources for a range of immigrant groups in between the 1950s and 1970s. These groups faced difficulties in achieving creditworthiness in both the economic and cultural measures of that term. Like their white counterparts before them, they responded to limited income or financial exclusion by creating mutual credit institutions. This chapter explores the successes and failures of all these forms of co-operative credit.

THE LIMITS OF MUTUALITY: CREDIT AND RETAIL CO-OPERATIVES

Co-operative retail societies came to represent a serious alternative to commercial credit operations. Initially, however, they were ill-prepared philosophically and, to a lesser extent, structurally to respond to consumers' increasing demand for instalment facilities. As late as the 1950s, they remained wedded 'to a moral understanding of consumption that placed a premium on thrift and anathematized hedonistic, profligate spending'.[2] Co-operatives had traditionally appealed to thrifty workers, who budgeted carefully and eschewed indebtedness. Rule 21 of the Rochdale Pioneers stipulated that all sales be on a cash basis; and as the movement headed towards the twentieth century activists continued to identify 'dependence on credit as incompatible with both co-operative idealism and respectable behaviour'.[3] One key co-operative text from this period maintained that 'the credit system of this country is only second in its demoralising influence to the drinking customs of the people'.[4] As a result, there was strong reluctance to fashion the credit options that were necessitated by the vicissitudes of the working-class family economy. Despite this reluctance, and frequently expressed concerns that prudent cash customers were subsidizing the purchases of

[2] Peter Gurney, 'The battle of the consumer in postwar Britain', *Journal of Modern History*, 77/4 (2005), 1976.

[3] Paul Johnson, *Saving and spending: the working-class economy in Britain 1870–1939* (Oxford: Clarendon Press, 1985), 126.

[4] A. H. D. Ackland and Ben Jones, *Working men co-operators* (London, 1984), 13, cited in Johnson, *Saving and spending*, 131.

unthrifty instalment buyers, credit became widespread throughout the co-operative movement. By 1886, 54 per cent of English co-operative stores offered goods on credit, a figure that rose to 82 per cent in 1911.[5] Retail managers realized that denying credit for groceries during periods of economic downturn reduced customer loyalty. Groceries, however, were not the only items that members wished to buy on instalment. By 1911, a number of retail co-operatives were tentatively offering credit through hire purchase or draw clubs. Their combined total turnover in that year was £67,056. This development had not originated in any form of pro-credit campaign by co-operative ideologues; it resulted from members' demand.[6] The emergence of draw clubs represented something of a compromise, as they were a 'halfway house between credit and cash'. In theory, the clubs were organized to ensure that the co-operative society received full payment for all goods before members received them, with one week's draw club money being received and one member's merchandise being released every seven days. In practice, the 'bulk of such clubs' came to 'permit all final drawing being made at a much earlier stage of the club'.[7]

The co-operative movement took a great leap forward with the introduction of the mutuality club by the London Co-operative Society in 1923. Significantly, this development took place at a time when what Paul Johnson and others have described as co-operation's previous social exclusiveness was being diluted by rising membership. It is notable that a survey of 45 Scottish societies, operating mutuality clubs in 1930, reported that 37 believed they helped 'poor members'.[8] The appearance of the clubs came at a point when retailers, in general, were being forced to address growing consumer demand for instalment options.[9] Mutuality clubs bore many of the hallmarks of the check trading system. Collectors visited members at home to receive the twenty instalments on the coupons or vouchers (as they were known, rather than checks) acquired for use in the local co-operative store. Home collection was a further indicator of the interwar penetration of the co-operative

[5] Johnson, *Saving and spending*, 133. [6] Ibid. 136–7.

[7] E. Topham and J. S. Simm, *Mutuality club trading* (Manchester: Co-operative Union, 1931), 8.

[8] Johnson, *Saving and spending*, 142; National Co-operative Archive (Manchester), John Downie, *Mutuality: Scotland's experience* (Manchester: Co-operative Union, 1930), 5.

[9] Melanie Tebbutt, *Making ends meet: pawnbroking and working class credit* (Leicester: Leicester University Press, 1983), 170.

movement into less affluent working-class homes, where there was a recognized requirement to impose similar disciplinary patterns to those exerted by commercial credit organizations. Mutuality clubs enabled co-operative societies to exploit the same levels of community knowledge, and patterns of gifting and obligation that had served the check traders, credit traders, and mail order companies. The first collectors were 'almost invariably members of the society, who started with a humble "book" of about a score of persons with whom the would-be collector was acquainted'. In 1926, a leading co-operator recognized that the movement would benefit from the 'goodwill and support' that was given to any organization providing goods on credit.[10] Evidence of this emerged from the experiences of the many collectors who 'professionalised the original spare-time employment into a full-time business'.[11] A poundage charge, akin to those levied by the check traders, was not applied to mutuality clubs at first.[12] Some societies were unwilling to levy collection charges on principle, whilst others saw their absence as 'a first-class piece of propaganda for co-operative trade' and an 'inducement to purchasers to abandon private trade credit clubs'.[13] As the scheme matured a 'moral question' was debated as to whether or not 'the more thrifty or more fortunately placed members' of co-operative societies should be expected to pay higher prices to 'help their less prudent or poorer fellow-members by taking a share of the cost of collection of mutuality club payments'.[14] Most societies decided in favour of the 'thrifty' and poundage fees, ranging from 6d to 1s in the £, were introduced. The latter rate was commonplace by the 1960s, although the Economist Intelligence Unit noted that if the payment of dividends to members was taken into account the collection charge amounted to around 1d in the £.[15]

In 1934, *Credit World* expressed commercial traders' concerns about mutuality clubs. It noted that those co-operative members fortunate enough to belong to societies not charging poundage were making credit purchases 'at the net cash price, less a cash rebate of from 7 to over 8 per cent', when the dividend was factored in. It consoled itself with the knowledge that the clubs were not being extensively advertised

[10] Manchester: National Co-operative Archive (hereafter NCA), S. Foster, *The utility of the 'deferred payment' system in societies' drapery and allied departments* (1926), 4.

[11] Topham and Simm, *Mutuality club trading*, 9–10.

[12] *Credit Trader*, 21 August 1926.

[13] Tebbutt, *Making ends meet*, 16.

[14] Ibid. 14.

[15] Economist Intelligence Unit, 'Check trading', *Retail Business*, 71 (1964), 47.

and were 'not known to the general public'.[16] One reason for this was continuing unease about credit within the movement. In 1923 *Co-operative News* reported one vocal activist's response to the new clubs: 'organised credit is not mutual self-help. It is not mutual aid and it is not co-working, it is not Rochdale co-operation. It is mutual thriftlessness, mutual beggar-my-neighbour, mutual help towards bankruptcy.'[17] The Co-operative Union's annual congresses also debated the moral and economic rationale of the system on several occasions during its early years and there was a pamphlet war between 'enthusiastic advocates' and 'unflinching opponents of the Mutuality Club'. The fact that it increased turnover led to its growing acceptance. This was made apparent at the Congress of 1930 when the President, H. J. May, was barracked for stating that the clubs 'were enabling people to draw dividend on debt'.[18] May's perspective was held widely enough, however, to ensure that large sections of the movement remained 'untouched by the mutuality club' at this time, despite evidence of its marked impact. By 1933, 600 collectors were engaged in the London area alone and turnover had risen from an initial £24,500 to £1.3m. Each member was offered credit up to a limit of £5.[19] In Scotland, mutuality clubs were said to have achieved an annual turnover of £611,884 by 1931, with bad debts at under £600.[20] The discipline enforced on members by collectors' visits was described in 1931, in language mirroring that of the commercial doorstep credit companies: 'The habit of regular weekly payment is quickly acquired by members of a mutuality club, if the collection is regular and punctual, and the follow up of laggards is prompt and efficient.'[21] The co-operative movement has left few records of the scale of mutuality club trading, but in 1961 the Census of Distribution indicated that they had an annual turnover of around £40 million. This equated to two-thirds that of the total turnover of the independent check traders and was roughly equivalent to that of the Provident Clothing and Supply Co. Ltd.[22]

Given the financial advantages of mutuality clubs, particularly the fact that purchases contributed towards a member's dividend, the question

[16] *Credit World*, February 1934. [17] *Co-operative News*, 23 January 1923.

[18] NCA: The Co-operative Union, *Congress proceedings* (Annual: The Co-operative Union Limited, Manchester), 1926–30; Topham and Simm, *Mutuality club trading*, 1; *Scotsman*, 10 June 1930.

[19] *Credit World*, July 1935.

[20] NCA: Downie, *Mutuality: Scotland's experience*, 3.

[21] Topham and Simm, *Mutuality club trading*, 17.

[22] Economist Intelligence Unit, 'Check trading', 43.

of why they did not outperform the independent check traders arises. Critics of the latter, such as the Women's Group on Public Welfare, were highly disparaging of their role in the working-class economy. They categorized the use of check trading as 'wrong spending' and believed that the mutuality clubs offered a more equitable form of credit.[23] As was explained in an earlier chapter, the private check offered greater choice to users who could seek out prices or merchandise to suit their budget and taste. Provident hammered this home to customers from as early as 1926.[24] Prices were often higher at co-operative stores than at privately owned competitors. This was partly the result of higher-quality merchandise, but members' demand for high dividends were frequently blamed for forcing up prices and pushing non-members into the hands of private traders.[25] There were further barriers relating directly to credit use by members. One was the widely observed requirement that credit applicants had to have a 'continuous income' and 'complete or substantial financial backing for their credit in the funds of the society'.[26] This investment in the co-operative society represented a hidden charge for credit, one which excluded large numbers of working-class consumers with limited or no opportunity to save. Hence Johnson's suggestion that co-operative credit be viewed 'more as a drawing upon saving than as a borrowing'. This important distinction was not lost on early twentieth-century working-class consumers and ensured that, in contrast with other methods of instalment payment, 'a certain respectability was not easily undermined' by the individual's use of co-operative credit.[27] Another 'effective rule' in many societies stipulated that unless all short-term credit accounts 'are settled by the quarter or half year end, such balances when paid shall not rank for dividend'. This was facilitated through a 'Dividend Stopped on Debt Account' book.[28] In 1969, the Co-operative Union told the Crowther Committee that societies had

[23] Women's Group on Public Welfare, *Our towns, a close-up: a study made in 1939–42 with certain recommendations* (London: Oxford University Press, 1943), Appendix on clothing clubs.

[24] Bradford: Provident Financial Group (hereafter PFG), PFG/04/151, 'There is no Mutuality Club about our System', Draft and proof leaflets.

[25] Johnson, *Saving and spending*, 130.

[26] Topham and Simm, *Mutuality club trading*, 7.

[27] Paul Johnson, 'Credit and thrift and the British working class, 1870–1939', in J. Winter (ed.), *The working class in modern British history* (Cambridge: Cambridge University Press, 1983), 154.

[28] F. S. Smith, *Credit trading in retail co-operative societies* (Manchester: Co-operative Union, 1928), 11–12.

'the right of lien upon money held by the society in the name of the member, should debts remain unpaid'. This was a significant advantage, 'not shared by competing traders'.[29]

Although these rulings excluded many from the co-operative commonwealth, evidence from Belfast suggests that many consumers whose finances did not permit them to build up a financial stake in their local co-operative retail society nevertheless found the means through which to use its credit facilities. Their resourcefulness would not have met with the Rochdale Pioneers' approval. A regular theme in the Belfast interviews was accounts of unofficial use of co-operative 'books' to buy clothing on credit.[30] Staff at the York Street co-operative department store were fully aware of this practice. Lily, who worked there before her marriage in the 1930s and again in the 1960s, explained that people 'who didn't have the money to buy . . . would've come in and got maybe their Sunday coat or something like that'. They were able to do so because 'there was a lot of that lending of books'. Staff turned a blind eye to the practice. In Lily's view 'it had nothing to do with us. No, as long as they had the book—the share book . . . it was a blue book. It was like a bank book and you opened that and you seen how much money she had in it—and that was OK.' Lily allowed goods to be taken away, once she was satisfied that that book recorded capital to the value of the goods being purchased on credit.[31] Another interviewee, Mary, explained that those lending out their book did not always act entirely altruistically: 'If you had a co-op book and you lent it to me, the reason you lent it . . . it was you got the dividend. You got the benefit of me using your book.'[32] Whilst some of this activity was of a casual nature, a number of women ran a lucrative business in either lending their co-operative book out or in taking orders from 'customers' for co-operative merchandise. Lily remembered one member who regularly came in to buy merchandise that she would then resell at a 20 per cent mark-up, collecting the money on a weekly basis.[33] Those allowing their

[29] London, National Archives (hereafter NA): BT250/40, Committee on Consumer Credit, Parliamentary Committee, Co-operative Union Ltd., Memorandum dated 4 March 1969.

[30] This was the document in which a member's transactions with the Co-operative were recorded.

[31] Interview with Lily (born 1920. Widow and retired shop assistant. Mother of two. Deceased husband was a milkman. Protestant. Interviewed 11 September 2002).

[32] Interview with Mary (born 1913. Retired library assistant/shop worker, mother of seven and wife of a slater. Roman Catholic. Interviewed 2 December 2002).

[33] Interview with Lily.

co-operative credit facilities to be used in this way had an incentive to ensure timely repayment. If their accounts were not paid up by the end of each quarter they did not receive their dividend. The pressure they placed on those they had obliged had a knock-on effect in many other areas of the working-class economy. Agnes grew up in the Sandy Row area of Belfast in the 1930s in a household with limited income, partly due to her father's disability. She remembered her mother borrowing a neighbour's co-operative book, but 'when the co-quarter came it was desperation, trying to get the money to pay the co-op'.[34] This presented opportunities for street moneylenders at the end of each of the co-operative's quarterly cycles. Mary, who moved to the Ardoyne district when she married in 1938, recalled that 'people were going crackers to get the money at the end of the thirteen weeks, which meant then that they went to moneylenders to pay that back'.[35] According to Lily, others could only meet the payments by skipping other bills: 'nobody paid anybody—but their milkman, their breadman and what they owed in the Co.'[36] Despite this assessment, Trevor, who worked as a bread delivery man on either side of the Second World War, recalled many customers who did not pay him during the period of financial juggling that preceded the dividend pay-out. He described the 'Co' as a 'curse' because he would be told: 'Trevor, I'll not be able to pay you this week; it's the "Co" quarter.' At one point, he 'lost a good customer', who was lending her 'Co' book to another of his customers who 'went up to the Co and got a pair of sheets . . . and walked straight down til the pawn'. He told the women who had lent the book: 'you're only encouraging that woman; you shouldn't give her your book'. The result was 'she stopped dealing bread with me over that'.[37]

This unofficial use of co-operative credit facilities and its impact on other credit networks is a further indicator of the power of communal ties in enforcing repayment. It is also a reminder of how instrumentalism and altruism were inextricably linked in the hard-pressed finances of many working-class families. For some, a generous gesture was rewarded by an increased dividend, whilst for others possession of a financial stake in the local co-operative presented an opportunity for systematic

[34] Interview with Agnes (born 1923. A retired shop worker and mother of five. Her husband had been an electrician. Interviewed 22 February 2003).

[35] Interview with Mary. [36] Interview with Lily.

[37] Interview with Trevor (born 1914. Retired bread delivery man/trade union official. Widower with one son. Protestant. Interviewed 10 January 2003).

cash accumulation. The informal systems described above also suggest the limitations of co-operative retailers as sources of credit for low-income consumers. They demonstrate that those social investigators who championed mutuality clubs as substitutes for costly commercial credit were poorly informed about the co-operative's credit granting procedure. Despite the Women's Group on Public Welfare's positive views on the potential of co-operative credit, the movement struggled to come to terms with the explosion of 'easy credit' that was the foundation stone of the consumer society. As was the case with other aspects of the co-operative movement's post-war performance, its response to spiralling demand for credit was inadequate. Although co-operative membership rose from 9.7 million members in 1946 to 12.5 million in 1958, the movement responded slowly to changes in market structure and demand. Peter Gurney has related how it fell behind its competitors in sales of the prized items that were the 'symbolically charged commodities' of the affluent society.[38] Organizational hurdles were created by the fact that the movement remained fragmented, with a lack of integration between its wholesale and retail wings and high levels of local autonomy, 'at a time when private enterprise was marshalling its forces into specialised, nationally controlled units'.[39] These issues were explored by the Co-operative Independent Commission Report, which was set up in 1955 to examine the movement's problems. It found that the 'inhibition towards giving credit was seriously restricting trade', leading customers to turn elsewhere.[40] Gurney argues that the issue of credit continued to be problematic for a movement 'that had traditionally addressed its appeal to the better-paid, respectable stratum of workers who understood the importance of financial planning for both individual families and the wider class'.[41] The Commission found that the movement had 'only 7% of the national trade in furniture and household durables' and that 'its share has failed . . . to grow significantly'. Whereas the hire purchase debt of its largest multiple shop competitor, which was GUS, stood at £41.9m in 1956, the combined hire purchase and mutuality club debt of the entire co-operative movement was said to be only £15.7m.[42] Hire purchase packages were introduced by co-operative retailers in the 1950s

[38] Gurney, 'The battle of the consumer in postwar Britain', 960.

[39] J. Birchall, *Co-op: the people's business* (Manchester: Manchester University Press, 1994), 147.

[40] Ibid. 148.

[41] Gurney, 'The battle of the consumer in postwar Britain', 975.

[42] Co-operative Union, Co-operative Independent Commission Report, (Manchester: Co-operative Union, 1958), 50.

that were designed to meet demand for consumer durables, particularly television sets, but internal critics argued that these innovations emerged too slowly.[43]

Rising demand for new credit options occurred at a time when many co-operatives lost customers due to council rehousing programmes that relocated entire working-class communities. It was estimated that the Glasgow retail co-operatives lost up to 200,000 customers with the movement of families to new towns such as East Kilbride, Glenrothes, Cumbernauld, and Irvine from the late 1940s.[44] The historians of the Scottish co-operative movement recorded that many of the former tenement homes of co-operative members were taken by 'commonwealth citizens' who had 'no particular co-operative tradition behind them'.[45] On the new estates, small shop units often only became available a generation after the first tenants had set up home. This provided potential opportunities, in the intervening years, for the co-operative movement's competitors, such as mail order catalogues.

Financing consumer credit, particularly hire purchase schemes for costly consumer durables, brought increasing pressure on co-operative budgets. This was one of many factors behind the demise of the cash dividend in the post-war period. The average dividend paid in 1946 had been 8.5 per cent, but it dropped to 4 per cent in 1963 and the entire movement had abolished it by 1968.[46] The dividend was also becoming less important for co-operative members who demonstrated a rising preference for cash. By the 1960s, the evidence suggested that for the co-operative shopper 'keen prices were becoming more of an incentive to purchase than the longer term goal of accumulated dividend'.[47] Further verification came in the form of the falling turnover of mutuality clubs. In 1961 turnover was estimated to be £40m; by 1967 it was just under £30m.[48] Co-operative retail societies began winding up their mutuality schemes in this period, a major factor being the labour costs involved in employing collectors. Co-operative retail societies were—like the industrial insurance providers who also began their withdrawal from home collection during the 1960s—finding the

[43] Scottish Co-operative Wholesale Society, Quarterly Meeting Minutes, 13 December 1958, cited in J. Kinloch and J. Butt, *History of the Scottish Co-operative Wholesale Society Limited* (Manchester: Co-operative Wholesale Society Limited, 1981), 333.

[44] Kinloch and Butt, *History of the Scottish Co-operative Wholesale Society*, 338.

[45] Ibid. 338. [46] Ibid. 335 and Table 15.6. [47] Ibid. 336.

[48] NA: BT250/40, Committee on Consumer Credit Parliamentary Committee, Co-operative Union Ltd. Memorandum dated 4 March 1969.

costs of weekly visits too draining on resources.[49] Co-operative doorstep collections were terminated in 1968, which was a blow to customers who remained reliant on the disciplinary aspects of this system to keep them out of debt. Mutuality clubs were replaced either by new styled budget accounts or, for those customers who remained wedded to home collection, by the Provident checks that many co-operatives began to accept.[50] Thus a Provident Shopping Guide for Southampton-Hythe in 1971 listed the Portsea Island Mutual Co-op Society, alongside Millets, H. Samuels, John Collier, and other retailers.[51] This was a remarkable development, given the earlier views of the Women's Group on Public Welfare, but, as is explained in the next chapter, by the 1970s the hopes of those campaigning for equitable credit for low-income consumers had come to rest with credit unions rather than retail co-operatives.

The co-operative movement's involvement in mutuality clubs lasted for almost half a century and pumped vast amounts of credit into working-class homes. In contrast, its attempts to enter the mail order sector were disastrous and represented an important missed opportunity. Whereas catalogue retailers were adept at meeting the requirements of female consumers, who provided the bedrock of the sector's dazzling post-war growth, attracting young female consumers proved particularly problematic for the co-operative movement. Gurney argues that this can be explained partly due to the misguided belief of those within the movement who hoped that an education in co-operative principles 'would dispel the illusory attractions of fashion', from the minds of young females.[52] The failed engagement with mail order retailing was a further significant factor in the failure to adapt to changing female demand and lifestyle. The Co-operative Wholesale Society (CWS) first discussed mail order in 1919, and the extraordinary growth of Great Universal Stores and Littlewoods during the 1930s again concentrated co-operators' minds on the issue. It was not until 1947, however, that the CWS finally took the plunge into the catalogue business.[53] The South-Western area was chosen to pilot the CWS By-Post Service and catalogues were sent to the 86,000 members in the region. All purchases

[49] Laurie Dennett, *A sense of security: 150 years of Prudential* (Cambridge: Granta Editions, 1998), 310–13.

[50] Committee on Consumer Credit, *Report of the Committee* (London: HMSO, 1971).

[51] PFG/04/076 Southampton-Hythe Shopping Guide, 1971.

[52] Gurney, 'The battle of the consumer in postwar Britain', 963.

[53] William Richardson, *The CWS in war and peace 1938–1976* (Stockport: Co-operative Wholesale Society Ltd, 1977), 171.

from the catalogue were eligible for the dividend.[54] The CWS cast envious eyes at the estimated £20m turnover of the mail order sector and believed that much of this trade was with co-operative members. It felt that it had a 'tremendous advantage' in having the names and addresses of 9 million co-operative members. J. T. Evans was appointed to manage the service, having had previous mail order experience at Littlewoods and J. D. Williams. He urged individual societies to acknowledge that the 'ramparts of the Co-operative movement' had been pierced by mail order firms and to see to it that this 'enemy within their gates was eliminated'. Evans anticipated increased membership and turnover, as a result of the mail order venture.[55] His optimism, however, was misplaced. The CWS experiment aroused suspicion from the retail societies who, according to one institutional history, 'did not give CWS mail order enough support to make it work'.[56] Evidence for this is to be found in the pages of *Co-operative News*, where in 1947 one London co-operative employee wrote in to complain that mail order customers would return unwanted merchandise to the stores. In the same year, the Derby Retail Co-operative Society demonstrated its irritation with the mail order experiment. It opined that catalogue retailers would themselves prefer to operate from retail stores than via mail order and that was why companies such as GUS and Littlewoods were extending their high street chains. The following year, *Co-operative News* revealed that 'no C.W.S. effort has met with so much opposition'. The retail societies had demanded that all goods included in the catalogue must also be available to them. They reportedly 'picked over the catalogue' to ensure that this was the case.[57] The system was wound up in 1950, following a 'showdown' between the retail societies and the CWS. The scheme had 'made little progress, despite 'repeated extensions of areas of selling' and 'extensive publicity'.[58] The retail societies feared that the By-Post Service would receive preferential treatment in the allocation of merchandise that was then in short supply, due to post-war austerity and rationing.[59] From the consumer's perspective, the scheme was less attractive than other mail order options. It operated on a purely cash basis, 'with the exception of those societies which were operating

[54] *Credit Trader*, 23 November 1946. [55] Ibid., 7 December 1946.
[56] Birchall, *Co-op: the people's business*, 147.
[57] *Co-operative News*, 1 February 1947; 19 April 1947; 28 February 1948.
[58] Kinloch and Butt, *History of the Scottish Co-operative Wholesale Society*, 341; *Credit Trader*, 22 July 1950.
[59] *Credit Trader*, 7 December 1946.

mutuality clubs', which at that point would appear to have been as few as one in four.[60] The absence of a uniform and straightforward credit system that could have been clearly outlined in the catalogue contrasted tellingly with what was being offered by commercial rivals. In 1960, a second short-lived experiment with mail order was essayed by the Scottish Co-operative Wholesale Society. Within two years 'the retail societies were complaining that the mail order business was under-cutting their own sales—especially in drapery goods' and it was abandoned in 1966.[61]

By the end of the 1960s, hopes that co-operative retailers could provide a viable alternative to more costly forms of commercial credit were rapidly receding. The movement's efforts to enter the dynamic mail order market were a flop, but for four decades mutuality clubs did provide a serious alternative to check traders. The costs associated with the mutuality clubs were also significantly less than those levied by check traders. It was this aspect of the mutuality clubs that attracted favourable comments from campaigners for equitable credit. What they failed to note was that the co-operative retailers operated conservative credit-rationing policies that excluded consumers who were most likely to use higher-cost commercial alternatives. Meanwhile, some consumers were prepared to pay higher collection charges to the Provident for access to a more extensive range of products than those available at the local co-operative shop. The surreptitious use of co-operative credit by those who faced formal or informal barriers that ostensibly prevented them from using it demonstrated the ability of working-class communities to adapt credit institutions for their own ends. In this example, the 'creative' use of the 'Co book' was very much against the grain of discourses about thrift on which the movement was built. Working-class women, in particular, were not content to allow extra-communal organizations, whether driven by dreams of the co-operative commonwealth or the profit motive, to be the sole determinants of their options. Many forms of organic self-help groups emerged from working-class communities. They were designed to give those involved the opportunity to overcome hurdles such as a lack of choice or high costs that they faced in the

[60] *Credit Trader*, 7 December 1946, London: NA/PRO: BT 258/172, Control of Check Trading order 1948: evidence of contravention of Order by those trafficking in checks. Memo on Census of Distribution 1950.

[61] Kinloch and Butt, *History of the Scottish Co-operative Wholesale Society*, 341.

market place. Their story forms the next stage in our analysis of credit and debt in working-class communities.

FROM DIDDLUM CLUBS TO HAGBADS: THE MORAL ECONOMY OF CREDIT ROTATION SOCIETIES

Credit rotation societies of various types have featured amongst many different cultural and ethnic groups. In the UK they have commonly been known as draw or thrift clubs, but anthropologists and economists who have noted their global nature have dubbed them rotating savings and credit associations or ROSCAs.[62] As we have seen, they provided inspiration for a number of UK commercial credit institutions, the most successful being mail order clubs. A number of North American savings and loans institutions also emerged from this trajectory.[63] In the UK, draw clubs have had a long association with working-class communities. Most frequently they were female centred, with one woman collecting small weekly contributions from neighbours or family.[64] The total weekly sum was then made available to one member of the club, the date of each individual's draw from the club being decided by ballot. The schemes often had some flexibility and a member with a sudden financial emergency could ask to receive an early pay-out. The organizer was usually rewarded, either with a small commission or by receiving the first use of the kitty. Draw clubs had different labels in various regions. In Scotland they became known as the 'ménage', in Liverpool they were dubbed 'tontines' or 'the tonnie'. Elsewhere in England they were sometimes known as 'diddlum' or 'diddly' clubs. The latter term reflected the risk that either the organizer might disappear with the funds or an early recipient of the draw could default on their

[62] The classic works on ROSCAs are Shirley Ardener, 'The comparative study of rotating credit associations', *Journal of the Royal Anthropological Institute of Great Britain and Ireland*, 94/2 (1964), 202–29; Clifford Geertz, 'The credit rotation society: a middle rung in development', *Economic development and cultural change*, 10 (April 1962), 241–63.

[63] T. Besley and S. Coate, 'The economics of rotating credit and savings associations', *American Economic Review*, 83/4 (September 1993), 792.

[64] Robert Roberts, *The classic slum* (London: Penguin edn., 1986), 33.

subsequent payments.[65] However, evidence from numerous cultural contexts indicates the social constraint imposed on participants by 'social connectedness', which enables ROSCAs to overcome their inability to enforce debts legally. Non-payment results in the loss of valuable 'social collateral' for the individual concerned.[66] The experience of draw clubs in the UK's working-class communities tallies with that recorded for other cultures. Close ties, such as those described by Ann McGuckin in her historical account of women's lives on Glasgow's Blackhill housing scheme, ensured that payments to these informal clubs were made before any debt to commercial forms of tick. McGuckin describes the ménage as having been 'an attempt to keep the moneylenders at bay' and 'an effective way of preparing for large outgoings at school time, Christmas or for a new baby'. The members' priorities were recalled by one former member: 'you would pay your ménage before your tick'.[67] Draw clubs mobilized communal ties, enabling participants to engage with the credit economy for mutual benefit in its purest form. For this reason, the women of Blackhill, and others like them, placed it at the top of their monetary priorities. It also represented a highly rational response to limited income. Members could have attempted to save individually at home, but this would, as the social anthropologist Shirley Ardener notes in her classic study of ROSCAs, 'withdraw money from circulation: in a rotating credit association capital never need be idle'.[68]

Although draw clubs were frequently operated to provide cash for any number of purposes, they were also regularly linked with a local retailer. Anne-Marie, who during the 1970s was a mother of three, recalled that in Belfast's New Lodge area there were 'hundreds of different wee clubs'. One was arranged with a local chemist:

> We used to go down and negotiate with the chemist and everybody would agree to pay a pound a week and for that pound a week, for ten weeks, you got twelve pounds worth of stuff out of the chemist. Now thirty years ago it meant that you could have gone in and bought stuff that you generally wouldn't be able to afford to buy. You know, like maybe Oil of Ulay creams or maybe stuff for the

[65] Sean Damer, *Glasgow: going for a song* (London: Lawrence and Wishart, 1990), 89; Paul A. Jones, *Access to credit on a low income* (Manchester: Co-operative Bank, 2001), 25; Tebbutt, *Making ends meet*, 50.

[66] Besley and Coate, 'The economics of rotating credit and savings associations', 805.

[67] Anne McGuckin, 'Moving stories: working-class women', in E. Breitenbach and E. Gordon (eds.), *Out of bounds: women in Scottish society 1800–1945* (Edinburgh: Edinburgh University Press,1993), 215.

[68] Ardener, 'The comparative study of rotating credit associations', 217.

baby you know . . . But what you done you paid a pound a week and you got twelve pounds and whoever ran the club got their twelve pounds for nothing.

The chemist accepted clubs on the basis that they had at least fifteen members, so that 'he was guaranteed fifteen pounds a week. That was a hundred and fifty pounds worth of gear he was shifting.' Before taking part, Anne-Marie made sure that she knew, and trusted, everyone involved. As she remembered it, 'down the New Lodge at the time everybody was in at least two wee clubs and there was sort of your own wee clique that was in them.' Although this was a female-centred endeavour, her husband, a scaffolder who had periods out of work due to poor health, was aware of the money flowing into the club, but as he 'got something out of it, a bottle of Old Spice or something like that there [laughs], a soap on a rope, he was happy. You always made sure you got him something to justify your wee pound every week.'[69]

Whilst working-class women used draw clubs to make ends meet, men had an equally long tradition of employing various forms of loan clubs. As was the case with male pawning, much of this activity appears to have been associated with leisure and, appropriately, was often centred on a pub.[70] Money clubs were common in nineteenth-century alehouses, with everyone either drawing their cash at one common point, such as Christmas, or periodically and on the basis of lots.[71] As with diddlum clubs, they carried a risk of fraud, but the moral hazard was greater because pub loan clubs amassed bigger sums of money as they were vehicles for medium-term saving rather than short-term spending. They were the subject of a parliamentary Bill, in 1929, aimed at enforcing transparent accounting and banking procedures on 'sharing out clubs'. In the discussions that followed it was said that these clubs were 'a very large social problem', with public attention frequently 'drawn to an annual crop of defalcations and suicides at Christmas-time', at which point errant treasurers were most likely to be unmasked.[72] The Bill failed and these associations remained popular. In 1949, loan clubs

[69] Interview with Anne-Marie (born 1951. Mature student and mother of seven. First husband a scaffolder; current husband a musician. Interviewed 20 May 2003).

[70] Tebbutt, *Making ends meet*, 34.

[71] John Benson, *British coalminers in the nineteenth century* (Dublin: Gill and Macmillan, 1980), 183.

[72] NA: CUST 49/1215—Slate and loans clubs. Position in connection with Moneylenders Act and Sharing-Out Clubs (regulation) Bill 1931. Letter 2 June 1931—Chief Registrar of Friendly Societies to The Secretary HM Customs and Excise.

came under the gaze of Mass Observation. The organizers of a loan club in a pub in London's East End reported that whilst it was well patronized, success was only guaranteed 'if you know all your members personally'. There were said to be many instances where applicants had required a loan in a rush and 'You can't do that unless you know who you are dealing with', investigators were told. Reports on the meetings of similar clubs emphasized 'the intimate and local character of the groups'. Members were greeted by their Christian names and 'there was a great deal of talk about jobs and families'. Mass Observation captured the views of one 35-year-old docker and father of two about his loan club:

> It's a very good way of saving money for Christmas and holidays. Another fing, John. If you get art of work for long you 'ave got a bit be'ind you. If you got a family like I 'ave, you got to save for 'olidays, and fings. You can't just take it art of the wage packet. I got forty shares, and that mounts up. You got ter keep goin' wiv it though. See, if I mike a bit extra I only spend it 'ere, so I might as well put some by for the time even if we 'ave to go a bit short. Getting together like this is the only way people like us can keep goin' in 'ard times.[73]

The brewers were said to be supportive of these clubs because they brought additional business, whilst club members viewed a brewery's involvement as a safeguard in the event that 'the landlord did a bunk'.[74] Although these clubs were said to be thriving in 1949, it was noted that their membership was ageing. In the post-war years, rising earnings, rehousing, and the extension of financial services for working-class consumers reduced the attraction and availability of loan clubs. They were still reasonably common in the late 1960s, but they were in decline. When the Crowther Committee took evidence from the Brewers' Society, it reported that many of its members no longer allowed loan or slate clubs. Those that did continued to reimburse losses in cases of fraud, in order to maintain goodwill.[75] When *New Society* visited the Alexandra Arms in Enfield, North London, in 1974, it found that its loan club had been functioning since 1926. At its foundation the typical loan, which was between £1 and £2, funded a day at the seaside. Members were allowed to borrow up to the amount that they

[73] Mass Observation Report, 'Mutual aid and the pub', in Lord Beveridge and A. D. Wells (eds.), *The evidence for voluntary action* (London: George Allen and Unwin, 1949), 30–1.

[74] Ibid. 32.

[75] NA: BT250/17, Committee on Consumer Credit. Brewers' Society.

had in savings with the club. Interest of 5 per cent was paid in advance, by an immediate deduction from the sum advanced. Fines were levied on those who missed payments or did not take out a loan in any given year. In 1974, the club paid a secretary and two stewards £1.50 per week for around three hours' work. Any remaining profit, or the 'divi', was distributed to members annually. The landlord explained that as regular customers, borrowers 'have no choice but to repay otherwise they daren't show their faces in here'. The brewers had clearly lost further interest in the clubs than was the case when they gave evidence to the Crowther Committee, telling *New Society* that they were being phased out as 'a matter of policy'. They were, for example, to be found in only 10 per cent of Charrington's 2,000 pubs, in 1974.[76]

Whilst the regulars in the Alexandra Arms had their loan club to turn to, other Londoners were meeting their credit needs via forms of ROSCA that were new to the UK. They were centred on a number of recently formed immigrant communities. ROSCAs frequently represent a response by a 'socially connected group to credit-market exclusion'.[77] This was certainly true of their appearance within the UK's burgeoning communities of West Indian origin, who were forced to satisfy many of their monetary requirements outside the mainstream financial system. To do so, they transplanted informal communal schemes from their homelands. Jamaicans, for example, made use of the 'partner' (or 'pardner') and Trinidadians employed the 'sou sou'.[78] Institutional racism meant that access to financial services, in general, proved problematic for recently arrived black immigrants. The Jamaican High Commission was drawn into a discussion, in the early 1960s, about the extra financial charges that its country people were being asked to pay for a variety of services.[79] It is unsurprising, therefore, that in some British-Jamaican communities as many as one in four reported membership of a partner.[80]

In the early 1960s, the partner was used for a variety of purposes. In providing a major source for the remittances that were dispatched to family in the West Indies, it had functions that were not associated

[76] *New Society*, 18 April 1974.

[77] Besley and Coate, 'The economics of rotating credit and savings associations', 807.

[78] A. Sivanandan, 'From resistance to rebellion: Asian and Afro-Caribbean struggles in Britain', *Race and Class*, 13 (1981–2), cited in Tebbutt, *Making ends meet*, 204.

[79] Frank Villiers, 'The way it was', *Credit Union News*, 6/2 (December 2003), 3.

[80] R. B. Davison, *Black British: immigrants to England* (London: Oxford University Press, 1966), 103.

with the draw clubs. A further important role partners took on was in enabling West Indians to amass sizeable deposits to put towards a deposit on a house. In her sociological study *Dark strangers* (1963), Sheila Patterson reported 'a large number of small cooperative savings associations' in Brixton that were used 'to assist members to achieve their economic goals more rapidly'. Those cited included 'a down-payment on a house, car, or other large purchase, or to send the fare home for a relative'.[81] In instances where their aim was to save towards significant financial commitments partners were often male dominated. Harold Mangar made the journey from Guyana to Ipswich as a young man in 1955 where he managed to secure a position as a trainee engineer. He joined a partner organized by his landlord, Mr Plummer, who was Jamaican. The members, who also included individuals from Barbados, St Kitts, and Trinidad, calculated that because Plummer owned his own home he was unlikely to make off with their hard earned cash. The target of those involved was to follow Plummer's path towards home ownership by raising enough for a deposit on one of Ipswich's less desirable terrace houses, which could be acquired for around £100.[82] As historians such as Chris Waters and Wendy Webster have demonstrated, British identity was racialized in this period and was reconstructed on notions of difference between white and black. The former were characterized 'by the privacy of domestic and familial life' and the latter by 'an incapacity for this and a propensity for "domestic barbarism"'. Webster also describes how black immigrants were viewed as 'rootless and transient' and without any 'domestic or familial identity of life'.[83] In this respect, the use of partners to amass the deposits that facilitated the purchase of a home was extremely significant. The type of racism the immigrants encountered in the consumer credit sector was most notoriously found in the private rental market and this spurred on many black immigrants to seek home ownership.

[81] Sheila Patterson, *Dark strangers: a sociological study of the absorption of a recent West Indian migrant group in Brixton, south London* (London: Tavistock Publications, 1963), 348–9.

[82] Interview with Harold Mangar (born 1937 in Guyana. Retired engineer. Local county councillor and credit union volunteer. Married with two children. Interviewed 14 December 2007).

[83] Wendy Webster, *Imagining home: gender, 'race' and national identity 1945–1964* (London: UCL Press, 1998), xii, 180–1. See also, Chris Waters, '"Dark strangers" in our midst: discourses of race and nation in Britain, 1947–1963', *Journal of British Studies*, 36/2 (April 1997).

Partners also filled functions more commonly associated with draw clubs, providing either a substitute for mainstream consumer credit or a useful addition to it. For example, Patterson's study recited the experiences of Beulah F., a single mother, who used her pay-out from a partner to buy an electric sewing machine so that she could make some money from home dress making.[84] Another survey of West Indian immigrants, published in 1966, suggested that the use of hire purchase and clothing clubs was low amongst Jamaican communities.[85] As well as indicating the relative importance of partners, it is likely that this reflected a lack of cultural fit between credit providers and black Britons. The credit trader's inclination to seek out customers who were 'natives of the district' was discussed above. This operational strategy took on new connotations in post-war urban areas and created a potential credit barrier for immigrant groups. The racial assumptions made in the quasi-anthropological studies of post-war immigrant communities, discussed in Paul Ward's recent study of Britishness, must have been replicated, at street level, in the less academic assessments made by thousands of credit agents/collectors whose previous experience had been solely with the white working classes.[86] It is not clear at what point commercial credit firms in general began to employ significant numbers of agents from immigrant communities. Those that did do so no doubt hoped to gain financially from the new agents' own connections and networks. This was the case in Brixton in the late 1950s, where a number of 'hire-purchase wholesale firms' that operated 'on a considerable scale from door to door' employed 'coloured agents who work on commission in the evenings and at weekends as a sideline to their normal jobs'. Products on offer ranged from 'motor-cycles to radios and oil-stoves to baby clothes'.[87] One agent was a Jamaican-born Brixton woman, Miriam W., who was described by Patterson as ambitious and with a social background 'on the borderline of the lower and the middle classes'. Significantly, she was also organizing a partner.[88]

A typical partner had between 5 and 20 members, paying £1 to £5 per week into it. The organizer did not 'receive any formal payment for this service, but he would normally receive a gift from the recipient of the jackpot each week'. Despite the use of the masculine pronoun

[84] Patterson, *Dark strangers*, 310. [85] Davison, *Black British*, 96.
[86] Paul Ward, *Britishness since 1870* (London: Routledge, 2004), 51.
[87] Patterson, *Dark strangers*, 241. [88] Ibid. 317.

in this sentence, it was women, like their counterparts in draw clubs, who were most frequently involved in 'throwing pardner'. The gender divide demonstrated between draw and pub clubs, in terms of the size of weekly contributions, was also evident in the partner with weekly payments in the early 1960s said to range 'up to several pounds, especially in the case of men' and as has been seen this was evidently the case for those partners that facilitated house purchases.[89] The view of various contemporary observers was that, ultimately, the partner 'may prove unsuitable for export'.[90] Another conclusion was that 'given greater familiarity with banks and savings accounts, and the continued high incidence of theft from fellow-lodgers or tenants which is reported in Brixton, such associations may well fade away after some years'.[91] In respect of the latter point, the case of a Jamaican woman who, in 1956, sued a man to whom she had unwisely entrusted her £37 partner pay-out was cited.[92] Social connectedness was clearly not foolproof.

However, it remained strong enough over the following four decades to ensure that ROSCAs remained of use to various communities of West Indian origin. In the 1970s, Montserattians were still using what they called 'the box'; a typical grouping having 8–25 members contributing up to £30 a week. Its effectiveness was achieved because potential defaulters were readily traceable, unless they were prepared to sever links with their relatively small community. An implicit sanction lay 'in the fact that the news of such a misdemeanour would be quickly communicated amongst Montserattians in London and transmitted back to the home island'.[93]

Research on credit and ethnic minorities conducted in the 1990s, by Alicia Herbert and Elaine Kempson, noted that whilst credit use in the African-Caribbean community was, 'in many ways, similar to that found in low-income communities generally', communal saving and loan networks remained significant.[94] Their interviewees consistently raised suspicions of racism amongst financial institutions, a factor which

[89] Patterson, *Dark strangers*, 349. [90] Davison, *Black British*, 103.

[91] Ibid. 349.

[92] *South London Press*, 3 May 1956, cited in Patterson, *Dark strangers*, 348.

[93] Stuart B. Phillpott, 'The Montserratians: migration, dependency and the maintenance of island ties in England', in J. L. Watson, *Between two cultures: migrants and minorities in Britain* (Oxford: Blackwell, 1977), 110–11.

[94] Alicia Herbert and Elaine Kempson, *Credit use and ethnic minorities* (London: Policy Studies Institute, 1996), 16.

contributed to an element of self-exclusion from mainstream credit, with several individuals ruling out the prospect of making an application. The report cited the comments of one man who believed that 'banks perceive black people as having bad credit'. He felt that 'if I am doing something for myself. . . I don't need to let someone's preconceived ideas about me ruin my chances of going for what I want'.[95] However, another man felt that 'it doesn't matter what colour you are 'cos once it goes on the computer it doesn't identify what colour you are'.[96] Herbert and Kempson broadly agreed with this assessment, but suggested that 'structural racism' was a factor in some of the refusals reported by interviewees. Many black families did not score well on computerized systems that analysed employment status, residential factors, and family status.[97] Partly as a result of such factors, partners remained common and were 'predominantly used in response to limited access to the high-street credit market'.[98] Their usefulness in this respect has not been confined to members of the black community. Toni, a white woman from Birmingham, explained that she was introduced to the partner by her Jamaican mother-in-law. Her involvement was strongly motivated by the fact that in her late teens and early twenties, when she was employed in a junior clerical job, she had become heavily indebted to store cards and credit cards and had been unable to pay her council tax. County court actions and bailiffs' visits were the sequel to this story and her credit score plummeted. Toni has now repaired her financial profile. She is in a well-paid job, is buying her own comfortable home, and the partner is no longer part of her weekly budgeting.[99]

Whilst using the partner Toni and her husband had been engaged in relatively modestly paid employment. This was the classic profile for the partner user in the 1990s. The weekly contributions of between £10 and £25, which were made by the 10 to 12 members of the average partner, were a barrier to those who were not in full-time work.[100] By this point, remittances had ceased to be a factor driving engagement in partners. Instead pay-outs were used 'to purchase consumer items, holidays and other "luxuries" and to finance deposits on homes'.[101] There was also evidence that the erosion of community-based trust, which has been

[95] Ibid. 34. [96] Ibid. 22. [97] Ibid. [98] Ibid. 33.

[99] Interview with Toni (born Birmingham, 1968. Officer manager, mother of three, and married to a school caretaker. Interviewed 3 June 2005).

[100] Herbert and Kempson, *Credit use and ethnic minorities*, 30–1.

[101] Ibid. 33.

described for the 'traditional' white working class by Avram Taylor, may also be a factor for the second and third generation of West Indian communities.[102] A number of Herbert and Kempson's younger interviewees were reluctant to join partners, having heard stories about the trust amongst members collapsing. Barbara, a single mother from Brixton, said: 'I don't like the idea. I have had friends who have used it before but think that the arrangement is dicey.'[103] The conclusion was, therefore, that the majority in the UK's Afro-Caribbean communities preferred to use high street credit and that partners were used primarily by those in low-paid jobs. For this group, they were used in tandem with mail order catalogues and hire purchase. The partner represented a substitute for cheap cash loans. Use of the partner generally terminated when either they could 'get a loan more easily elsewhere or when they started to live on benefit'.[104]

ROSCAs were also deployed amongst British-Muslim communities. They included the 'kuri', prevalent amongst those from India's Kerala region, and the bond committees ('kameti' or 'kommitti') used by Pakistani and Punjabi families. Research conducted in Oxford in the early 1990s indicated that weekly payments in the latter schemes were usually £25. Members decided the order in which funds were made available, timing this to coincide with weddings, holidays in the Indian subcontinent, or other expensive episodes in the family life cycle. Similar social pressures to those that underpinned repayments in the Glaswegian ménage in the 1930s operated in Oxford in the 1990s. One interviewee remarked that 'if I was in a bank, I could miss paying in for a week or two if I wanted to spend the money on some unnecessary thing. But I cannot do that with the Kameti.'[105] They also performed an important social function. Studies carried out in Manchester, during the 1970s and in Oldham two decades later, reported that they were a key site of socialization amongst Pakistani communities. They were organized by key individuals, such as shopkeepers, and were highly successful because their members often

[102] Avram Taylor, *Working class credit and community since 1918* (Basingstoke: Palgrave, Macmillan, 2002), 43–4, 175.

[103] Herbert and Kempson, *Credit use and ethnic minorities*, 32.

[104] Ibid. 36.

[105] Shaila Srinivasan, 'ROSCAs among South Asians in Oxford', in Shirley Ardener and Sandra Burman (eds.), *Money-go-rounds: the importance of rotating savings and credit associations for women* (Oxford: Berg, 1995), 199–204.

originated from the same Pakistani village.[106] In contrast with the ménage, diddlum club, or partner, the kameti and kuri had greater male involvement. This reflected the bigger sums involved and their greater importance as social institutions, as well as the fact that men were responsible for family finances.[107] In contrast, Somali women often conceal their involvement in the 'hagbad' from their husbands. In the early 1990s payments to them were between £25 and £100 a month. Pay-outs were arranged by the organizer, whose reward was a small gift for her children from each week's recipient.[108] Women-only bond committees were also discovered in Oldham's Pakistani community in the 1990s and were 'probably associated with the increasing economic independence of women within the community'. This freedom was exhibited by the fact that members felt that they could spend their lump sum on clothing or jewellery for themselves. The latter did, however, represent an investment that could be liquidated in the event of a family financial emergency.[109] The option of pawning was not entertained by the Pakistani community, nor was the use of doorstep lenders. Instead, an alternative source of borrowing came from the foreign exchange agents who began operating within these communities in the 1960s. They lent money, without interest, for remittance to family in Pakistan, their profit being realized via manipulation of the exchange rate at which the currency was offered.[110]

ROSCAs proved particularly attractive to Muslims because Islamic doctrine contains 'strong moral and legal interdictions against the taking of interest'.[111] This was reported to be a factor in the low incidence of high street credit use, reported during the 1990s, amongst Oldham's Pakistani community.[112] This community made use of interest-free

[106] Prina Werbner, 'Taking and giving: working women and female bonds in a Pakistani immigrant neighbourhood', in Sallie Westwood and Parminder Bhachu (eds.), *Enterprising women: ethnicity, economy and gender relations* (London: Routledge, 1988), 188, 194; Herbert and Kempson, *Credit use and ethnic minorities*, 60.

[107] Herbert and Kempson, *Credit use and ethnic minorities*, 57.

[108] Hazel Summerfield, 'A note on ROSCAs among Northern Somali', in Shirley Ardener and Sandra Burman (eds.), *Money-go-rounds: the importance of rotating savings and credit associations for women* (Oxford: Berg, 1995), 209–15.

[109] Herbert and Kempson, *Credit use and ethnic minorities*, 60–1.

[110] Ibid. 54.

[111] Martin Lewison, 'Conflicts of interest? The ethics of usury', *Journal of Business Ethics*, 22 (4 December 1999), 334.

[112] Herbert and Kempson, *Credit use and ethnic minorities*, 41.

credit from corner shops run by co-religionists. However, interviewees pointed out that the sums involved were very small and that this facility was considered as the community's traditional way of provisioning the household rather than signalling limited income. Delayed payments were a function of trust rather than poverty.[113] This option was no longer available to most working-class communities. Corner shop tick was commonly reported in 1950s surveys and it even featured in the first episode of *Coronation Street*, in 1960, where the new shop owner is given advice on tick by its former proprietor and is instructed that offering tick gets 'some folk' spending twice as much in the shop than they would otherwise do.[114] However, the practice had largely disappeared by the 1990s and Avram Taylor ascribes this to factors such as the decline of trust, which made shopkeepers unwilling to offer credit and led to countless variations of signs reading 'Please do not ask for credit, as refusal only offends'. Taylor also argues that the stigma associated with public requests for credit, which potentially demonstrated that the individual concerned was unable to manage money, grew greater in the affluent society.[115] This embarrassment was not confined to the white working class. Herbert and Kempson's study revealed that Bangladeshi shopkeepers were less content to allow tick than their Pakistani counterparts. Customers of the former group used it less, citing the embarrassing nature of public requests for repayments as a powerful deterrent.[116] Members of the Bangladeshi community also used high street credit more regularly than those of Pakistani origin.[117] It was felt that this did not demonstrate any difference in the 'depth of religious belief between the two communities', but that it 'reflected the lack of alternatives to high-street credit in the Bangladeshi community'. In particular, they had no equivalent to the bond community, which was described as having the 'same function as a credit union' for British Pakistani communities. Foreign exchange agents were also less frequently used.[118]

Herbert and Kempson argued that the failure to develop a ROSCA amongst Bangladeshi communities led to the appearance of unlicensed moneylenders.[119] Like other illegal lenders they harassed borrowers and

[113] Herbert and Kempson, 52–3.
[114] Granada Television Ltd, *Coronation Street*, 9 December 1960.
[115] Taylor, *Working class credit*, 101.
[116] Herbert and Kempson, *Credit use and ethnic minorities*, 80.
[117] Ibid. 68. [118] Ibid. 58, 79. [119] Ibid. 79.

seized personal documents, such as passports, as security.[120] Rather like the customers of the UK's illegal lenders, in general, the Bangladeshi community was reluctant to speak about this issue. Moreover, the depiction of illegal lending in Monica Ali's successful novel *Brick Lane* was one of the issues that mired the book in controversy. It features the ironically named Mrs Islam, who 'practices usury'. A friend of the protagonist, Nazneen, explains to her that one borrower who had not made her last payment had 'to come up with it next time, plus extra interest as punishment', otherwise Mrs Islam's 'sons will break her arm'. Nazneen's husband, Chanu, subsequently borrows from Mrs Islam, but does not inform his wife of the costs and tells her only that 'It's between friends . . . She is doing me a favour. I knew her husband.' They become involved in seemingly endless payments until Chanu decides 'that crook has had enough'. However, 'after a persuasive visit from her sons', he agrees to continue paying 'fifty pounds per week'. On another occasion, Mrs Islam pressurizes Nazneen to increase the size of payments, combining low-level intimidation, laments about her health, and comments about how she will bequeath much of her money to the mosque, as a tactic through which to ensure Nazneen's submission to her.[121] The characteristics of this fictional relationship are strikingly similar to those described in an earlier chapter by Johnny, who explained the dynamics of illegal lending amongst Belfast Catholics during the 1950s. There too, lenders exploited communal and religious identity to emphasize bonds of trust and heighten borrowers' strong sense of obligation. This behaviour is what Taylor has described as a manipulation of the norm of reciprocity in circumstances in which the exchange taking place was far from equal.[122] Mrs Islam describes herself as follows: 'I do all these things for my community and I expect no thanks . . . If someone is sick, they come to me. If someone's husband runs off, they come to me. If a child needs a roof, they come to me. If someone has no penny for rice, they come to me. And I give. All the time, giving.'[123] Some inhabitants of the real Brick Lane objected to its literary depiction. Mrs Islam's character may have been amongst aspects of the novel that did not appeal to them, but Herbert and Kempson's work indicates that she was not simply engendered in Ali's imagination.

[120] Ibid. 81.

[121] Monica Ali, *Brick Lane* (London: Black Swan, 2004), 128–9, 231–2, 271, 305, 308.

[122] Taylor, *Working class credit*, 65.

[123] Ali, *Brick Lane*, 308.

CONCLUSION

A variety of organic mutual credit institutions offered alternatives to high-cost commercial credit during the period under review. They did so in localities and time periods that ranged from Robert Roberts' Edwardian Salford to late twentieth-century immigrant communities. Their existence demonstrated both the resourcefulness and agency of working-class individuals. It also evidenced, once again, the ability of peer monitoring to create and maintain powerful credit networks, centred on neighbourhood and community. In recent decades, ROSCAs have been most strongly associated with those immigrant groups where a sense of communal identity remains powerful, but they remained common in areas, such as Merseyside, where the 'traditional working class' retained a strong presence. However, it is clear that all the various forms of ROSCA occupied a niche market and that at no time did they represent a serious challenge to the commercial credit providers. Moreover, by necessity they excluded the unemployed and others not in full-time work from their ranks. The inability of these groups to make regular contributions to the ménage or partner prevented their inclusion and placed economic limitations on mutuality. Their financial insecurity meant that they could not be trusted to pay their way by other members of the communal group. Instead they were left to turn to high-cost lenders whose credit charges reflected the risk that was involved in taking on their business.

The retail co-operatives were also socially exclusive, eliminating those who did not have the ability or inclination to leave funds resting in their local society. Despite this, mutuality clubs represented the most successful source of co-operative short-term consumer credit in the UK between the 1920s and the 1960s. The system's turnover was equal to that of the Provident in the late 1950s, but the slow decline of the co-operative movement had brought the system to a close by the following decade. By that point, idealistic eyes were turning towards a new form of co-operative credit and saving institution that promised to offer an equitable rival to moneylending, hire purchase, and other commercial credit channels. This was the UK credit union, which was born in the early 1960s. Like the new-style ROSCAs of the period, the West Indian community featured strongly in the credit union story. Credit unions, like the partner, were a further response to the high financial costs placed in the way of this community on their arrival in post-war Britain. Several of the original credit unions emerged from partner groupings and the credit union movement was, in essence, an attempt to marry the potential of organically developed ROSCAs to nationwide co-operative organization and idealism. Pioneers of the movement hoped that this powerful combination might produce a financial Holy Grail: a socially inclusive equitable savings and loan institution that would fatally damage high-cost commercial lenders. An account of their struggles to bring this about provides the final chapter in this analysis of credit in the UK's low-income communities.

7

Renewed hope for mutuality: credit unions

Since their arrival in the UK in the 1960s, credit unions have been championed as an alternative to expensive commercial credit and a panacea to the money problems of the poor. The traditional community credit union operated on a co-operative basis, being managed by volunteers who were elected by the credit union's members. Those who joined were entitled to apply for loans once they had demonstrated an ability to save. This enabled them to establish an element of trust within the credit union; a feature further enhanced by volunteers' knowledge of members. Each credit union set out to reward members for their thrift via an annual dividend, financed through any profit that had been made.

Writing in 1998, the journalist Polly Toynbee highlighted the 144 per cent annual interest rates that were attached to an average loan from Provident Financial and urged the recently elected Labour government to 'sow the seed-corn to set up a nationwide network of credit unions'. She asked what 'bank offers the community service of the credit union in Lewisham?' Toynbee explained how a grandmother had knocked on the door of a credit union committee member at 10.00 p.m. on Christmas Eve with a desperate, but successful, request for a £50 loan. 'Imagine he was James Stewart,' wrote Toynbee, 'whoever this Christmas wept over the re-released It's a Wonderful Life will understand what this is all about: little people banding together to fight off the depredations of the ruthless big financial institutions.' She invited readers to imagine that 'every single community had its own credit union', and how it would create 'a sense of community' and 'draw local people together'. In conclusion, Toynbee argued that if government really 'cares for the poor, then credit unions are what they should go for', because they represented 'extraordinarily good social value for money'.[1]

[1] *Independent*, 19 January 1998.

The case for credit unions was, however, far from incontrovertible. First and foremost, membership levels in Britain had lagged far behind those in North America and, closer to home, in Ireland. Second, and overlooked by Toynbee's piece, the 1990s had witnessed rising disquiet about British credit unions. Much of the initial idealism associated with the movement had been punctured and a number of academics and credit union insiders argued for a more instrumental, less idealistic approach to credit union extension. This approach was shaped by the knowledge that the impact of credit unions in low-income communities had been marginal and uneven. Credit unions in England, Scotland, and Wales had only 325,000 members in 2000, representing just over 0.5 per cent of the total population. Scotland had the widest uptake of credit unions, with 136 unions and 40 per cent of the total British membership. Wales and England had 46 and 512 respectively, with over 50 per cent (275) of those in England in the North.[2] This contrasted with much higher diffusion rates elsewhere. In another part of the UK—Northern Ireland—267,000 people, or 16 per cent of the population, were members. In the Republic of Ireland, the USA, and Canada, the respective figures were 45, 30, and 20 per cent.[3] The British membership total was all the more disappointing because throughout the 1980s and 1990s there was significant national and local government spending on credit union promotion and development. As much as £15m per annum was spent in each of these decades: an investment which should, in the words of the academic Paul Jones, have made 'a considerable difference to the economic vitality of the movement'.[4] It had not done so and Jones's voice was part of a growing chorus raising concerns about the credit union movement's limited impact. Although Toynbee was unaware of this in 1998, she had caught the emerging mood by the time she returned to the issue the following year:

For this negligible progress, a lot of money has been spent. Some £20 million a year has been poured in by local and central government and European social funds. And yet the total assets of all community credit unions are still only £36 million. (That suggests they might have done more good if they had just handed the £20 million out each year.) There is something about the word 'community' that ought to ring alarm bells. The credit union story is just

[2] Registry of Friendly Societies, *Report of the Chief Registrar 2000–1* (London: HMSO, 2001), 9, 36, 16. The figures for credit union numbers are for November 2001.

[3] HM Treasury, *Credit Unions of the Future Taskforce report* (London: Treasury, 1999).

[4] Paul A. Jones, *Towards sustainable credit union development* (Manchester: Association of British Credit Unions, 1999), 6.

one example of the sort of misguided good intentions that have plagued social policy for years, offering the poor high-minded good ideas that none of the rest of us would bother with . . . the only thing that binds the inhabitants of the worst estates together is their desire to get out. Yet social planners get amazingly sentimental about 'bonding', wanting poor people to get together in ways the rest of us rarely have time, energy or inclination to do . . . There's a danger that in the name of something called 'community' we keep expecting the least able, with the fewest resources and the least support, to do magically energetic things in their spare time.[5]

How did this pessimism emerge and why did the British credit union movement fail to mobilize 'community'? In the following discussion, its modest achievements will be contrasted with the successes of the movement in Northern Ireland. By the late 1980s a Northern Irish Catholic was 300 times more likely to be a credit union member than the average Briton.[6] It will be demonstrated that membership growth in this case was not straightforwardly organic, from within local communities. In the late 1950s and early 1960s, the Catholic Church actively promoted credit unions throughout Ireland. Moreover, two decades later, the Orange Order provided a similar role in Protestant communities facilitating a second spurt of credit union growth in Northern Ireland. Although the British credit union movement was born very shortly after its Irish counterpart, it was unable to mobilize trust and create the common bonds on which the successful Irish credit unions operated. Mid-twentieth-century Britain had no equivalent to the Orange Order or the thriving Irish Catholic parish. Credit unions also faced strong competition for the savings of the more affluent consumers whose membership was required to build up the financial assets of individual unions. As a result, like retail co-operatives before them, British credit unions operated in a niche market. It was, moreover, a much smaller one. They were unable to develop services that catered to the very particular needs of the least affluent groups, and their worthy campaign to provide serious competition to expensive doorstep lenders and other companies operating in the 'sub-prime' market proved largely quixotic. However, the failure of the British credit union movement in this respect was not unique: its counterparts in late twentieth-century Ireland and North America, and in early twentieth-century Germany,

5 *Guardian*, 8 February 1999.

6 Richard Berthoud and Teresa Hinton, *Credit unions in the United Kingdom* (London: Policy Studies Institute, 1988), 25.

were all unable—or in some cases unwilling—to provide savings and loans institutions that were socially inclusive.

This discussion will look first at the roots of credit unions in nineteenth-century Germany and their subsequent uptake in North America. It then examines their arrival in Ireland, where the Catholic Church was of fundamental importance to their widespread adoption in the 1960s. A similar process will then be outlined for the 1980s and the Orange Order in Northern Ireland. In Britain the credit union movement found no such organic common bond around which it could coalesce. Notably, the majority of early credit unionists were from Britain's West Indian and Irish Catholic communities. This chapter explains why that was the case and also suggests that this underscored the 'otherness' of credit unions, from a British perspective, and contributed to the movement's inability to secure a mass working-class membership. A further factor in this failure is addressed in an analysis of the fissures that developed amongst UK credit union activists, between those with altruistic or instrumentalist agendas. The chapter concludes with a discussion of 'new model' credit unions and assesses their chance of success from the historical perspective on working-class patterns of credit use that has been proffered in these pages.

'YOUR OWN SELVES AND CHARACTER MUST CREATE YOUR CREDIT': THE EMERGENCE OF THE INTERNATIONAL CREDIT UNION MOVEMENT

Credit unions trace their origins back to the co-operative principles of the Rochdale Pioneers and to two Germans, Frederick Raiffeisen and Herman Schulze-Delitzsch, who founded separate co-operative credit institutions in 1848 and 1864 respectively. 'Your own selves and character must create your credit', Schulze-Delitzsch told members of his people's banks, as they were dubbed, and they were asked to demonstrate an ability to save before they were granted a loan.[7] This founding principle was to create a significant barrier to credit union membership for the poorest groups in every society in which people's

[7] J. Caroll Moody and Gilbert C. Fite, *The credit union movement: origins and development 1850–1970* (Lincoln: University of Nebraska Press, 1971), 5.

banks were instituted. In fact, 'the predominantly urban Schulze-Delitzsch's credit co-operatives deliberately discouraged the very poor from joining'.[8] The movement's English publicist, Henry W. Wolff described them, in 1910, as 'a middle-class movement', an assessment illustrated by his membership analysis of Schulze-Delitzsch's original credit union. Craftsmen and small retailers were its most regular patrons.[9] Schulze-Delitzsch envisaged his system as a pragmatic one, rather than an experiment in reforming moral character, and his vision of self-help was secular in concept.[10] In contrast, Raiffeisen felt that the Christian principle of brotherly love should underpin his co-operative banks. As a result, they were staffed by volunteers. Only those employed as cashiers were remunerated for their efforts.[11] The rural location of Raiffeisen's institutions represented a further contrast with Schulze-Delitzsch's co-operatives. The former were usually centred on a parish with a population of fewer than 3,000.

Despite the fact that by 1909 the combined membership of these co-operatives was 2.2 million, Tim Guinnanne has pointed out that little 'is known about the basis for their success . . . beyond their backer's assertions'.[12] They operated on the principle that local co-operatives were better suited to meet the needs of certain categories of borrower than larger financial institutions. Their rationale was that that those living and working in close proximity build up insights into neighbours and the co-operative bank could 'harness this information on borrowers where formal institutions could not'.[13] By avoiding the costs of data collection, these co-operatives were able to provide cheaper loans. Guinnane reports that critics of the Raiffeisen system suggested that the involvement of rural elites in the supervision of loans provided opportunities for social control. He believes that these credit societies thrived because they attracted individuals who provided 'crucial monitoring and expertise', and because a variety of people were involved—including 'those with infrequent credit needs, those with substantial savings to invest', and 'perhaps those who merely thought they could profit from

[8] Tim Guinnane, 'Thy neighbor's keeper: the design of a credit cooperative with theory and a test', *Quarterly Journal of Economics*, 109/2 (May 1994), 507–8.

[9] Henry W. Wolff, *People's banks: a record of social and economic success* (London: P. S. King & Son, 1910), 82–3.

[10] Moody and Fite, *The credit union movement*, 5. [11] Ibid. 11–12.

[12] Tim Guinnane, 'A failed institutional transplant: Raiffeisen's credit co-operatives in Ireland, 1894–1914', *Explorations in Economic History*, 31/1 (1994), 38.

[13] Ibid. 45.

their neighbour's economic success'.[14] Involvement in a managerial role did, however, provide opportunities for paternalistic assessment of spending practices. Raiffeisen felt that by itself money 'will improve nothing' and of much more importance was 'education in the use of funds' to bring about improved conditions. Loans were, therefore, only offered for productive purposes.[15] The copious pragmatic and idealistic possibilities offered by credit unions led to their diffusion in other parts of Europe and in North America. It was their arrival on the latter continent that was to have the greatest influence on developments in Ireland and Britain. Alphonse Desjardins, a Quebec-based Catholic journalist, developed an interest in mutual credit institutions in 1897 following a period reporting on legislative debates about usury. Fired with zeal to provide a cheaper alternative to moneylenders, he established La Caisse Populaire de Levis in 1901. As well as encouraging 'economy and financial responsibility among members', it aimed to 'combat usury . . . provide capital for local individual enterprises; and to help borrowers achieve economic independence through self help'.[16] Desjardins forged a strong alliance with the French-Canadian Catholic Church to promote his credit institutions, which, like Raiffeisen, he organized at parish level. The Jesuit organization Ligues du Sacré Coeur was very influential in this respect, operating as a conduit of information amongst Catholic elites and ensuring the involvement of clergy at a local level. Desjardins argued that a caisse populaire was 'a parish institution which necessitated the direct and active support of the curé'.[17] Once the curé had been incorporated, he could be relied upon to attract the participation and skills of the local elite. Historian Ronald Rudin believes that the parish elite became involved through a mixture of humanitarianism and self-interest: 'In addition to providing services for the poor, however, the petit bourgeoisie also wanted something from them as well, namely recognition once again of French-Canadian clergy, professionals, and small businessmen as legitimate leaders.'[18] Rudin argues that the growth of French-Canadian credit unions resulted partly from the petit bourgeoisie's response to their loss of power to the state

[14] Ibid. 39 n. 1, 58.

[15] Cited in Rory McLaughlin, 'Credit union in Northern Ireland: a historical and social analysis', unpublished Ph.D. thesis (University of Ulster, 2003), 80.

[16] Moody and Fite, *The credit union movement*, 21.

[17] Ronald Rudin, *In whose interest? Quebec's caisses populaire, 1900–1945* (Montreal: McGill-Queen's University Press, 1990), 17.

[18] Ibid. 26.

and corporate capitalism. The philosophical underpinnings of the caisse populaire, particularly its aim of providing material and moral uplift to the working classes, also neatly dovetailed with the Catholic Church's emerging thinking on social action. Desjardin's concept offered a practical expression of the Papal encyclical *Rerum Novarum*, issued in 1891, which represented the Church's response to economic inequality.[19] It attacked socialism and what the Church felt were the excesses of liberal individualism, whilst urging the greater participation by all in the ownership of private property. It identified the state's role as a minimalist one and in this context reminded more affluent Catholics of their responsibilities to those less fortunate than themselves.[20] The influence of this instruction was seen in the exhortation of one of Desjardin's colleagues to his peers: 'Let us descend into the homes and workshops of our brothers who labor for a living . . . Let us establish caisses populaires everywhere that we are able.'[21] Through the energies of Desjardins and the backing of the Church caisses populaires made steady inroads across Quebec. By 1920, 2 per cent of the French speaking population were members, a figure that reached 15 per cent in 1945 when around 200,000 Quebeccers were members.[22] However, as was the case in early twentieth-century Germany, in 'both urban and rural Quebec, the poor were largely conspicuous by their absence from the membership rolls of the caisses', as their leaders 'had difficulties devising policies that served the best interests of the needier Quebeccers'.[23] They met with least success in urban areas. In Montreal the local caisse included only 5 per cent of its potential membership in 1945. Its limited outreach was a result of the inability to deliver financial products tailored to low-income budgeting, as well as weaker bonds of trust amongst a relatively unstable, transitory, urban population; the more limited importance of parish identities in such a locality; and the greater availability of alternative financial products.[24]

However, it was the successes of the caisses populaire rather than their limitations that reverberated most clearly and facilitated the diffusion of the movement across the Canadian border into the USA. In 1909, Desjardins assisted a group of French-American Catholics in Manchester, New Hampshire, to follow his example. He was also an

[19] A. P. Quinn, *Credit unions in Ireland* (Dublin: Oak Tree Press, 1999), 6.

[20] Charles E. Curran, *Catholic social teaching, 1891–present: a historical, theological and ethical analysis* (Washington, DC: Georgetown University Press, 2002), 9.

[21] Rudin, *In whose interest?*, 26. [22] Ibid. 27–8. [23] Ibid. 143.

[24] Ibid. 36.

architect of the Credit Union Enabling Act, passed in Massachusetts in 1909. This created the fundamental apparatus for credit unions in the Anglophone world and underscored the co-operative element of the movement. It stipulated that credit unions be based upon a membership that shared some form of common bond: examples were a parish or workplace. All members were entitled to vote at meetings to appoint the credit union's officers and to direct policy. Managerial posts were to be held in a voluntary capacity only and a significant proportion of annual surpluses were to be returned to members as a dividend.

The initial growth of credit unions in the USA was sluggish and the movement was greatly indebted to the enthusiasm, persistence, and financial muscle of the Jewish department store owner, Edward Filene. He was reputed as a progressive employer and philanthropist. Like others involved in credit unions Feline shared a desire to achieve equitable credit arrangements for workers, but he stated that a further motivation was to 'fight an age old prejudice that all Jews were usurers'.[25] Filene's financial nurturing finally bore fruit in the decade following his formation of the Credit Union National Extension Bureau in 1921. By 1934, there were 2,500 credit unions in 19 states.[26] Significantly, this growth spurt occurred once Filene had reduced his vision of what could be achieved. In the early 1920s he argued that 'it is time to quit wasting time trying to organize credit unions among poor Appalachian mountaineers and concentrate on workers in the industrial centers'. He concluded 'that by the very nature of credit unions their benefits were confined mainly to workers with jobs because members had to have money to invest and means to repay loans'. The 'hardcore, unemployed poor' did not need loans, but grants or jobs instead.[27] A preference for workplace credit unions over community-based ones emerged as a consequence of this approach: a development that coalesced with Filene's paternalistic employment practices. In 1953, the new national body, the Credit Union National Association (CUNA), described its function as the 'cooperative pooling and use of credit and financial resources of average salaried income groups'. Thus it became 'principally a middle-class movement'.[28] On this basis, growth in the USA was impressive. By the late 1980s, one in five adults belonged to a credit union, with a strong bias toward the white middle classes. Almost four in every five credit unions had a common bond centred on a workplace

[25] Moody and Fite, *The credit union movement*, 46–50. [26] Ibid. 82.
[27] Ibid. 355. [28] Ibid. 308.

and most loans were offered to the 'credit-worthy' rather than the 'credit-needy'.[29] In Canada, the creditworthy white middle class also dominated the movement.[30] The total numbers of credit unions in the USA peaked at almost 24,000 in 1969. Thereafter, an emphasis was placed on mergers and increasingly sophisticated financial products that made credit unions serious rivals to banks. In the process, the size of the potential common bond was increased from a parish or single workplace, up to a whole state.[31]

The social action agendas of the early pioneers were not entirely eradicated. Credit union extension featured in the American government's anti-poverty programme of the 1960s. Over 400 new community credit unions were established to 'wipe out poverty' between 1964 and 1969.[32] However, their fortunes suggested that Filene's dictum on Appalachian mountaineers was still appropriate four decades later. By 1975 the assault on the summit of poverty had faltered and half the newly created credit unions had folded. As few as 35 of the 400 remained in 1999. A significant problem was that these credit unions were imposed from above by CUNA and government, rather than emerging organically from within black, Hispanic, and poor white communities. Once initial funding had dried up, skilled development workers were laid off and suitable volunteer replacements were elusive.[33] Their members frequently lacked the self-confidence and independence to sustain the union or to address the issue of long-term capitalization. The collapse of so many community credit unions created a crisis of confidence within CUNA about their prospects and led to the formation of a breakaway organization, the National Federation of Community Development Credit Unions (NFCDCU) in 1974.[34] The two organizations came to embody the tension within the credit union movement between instrumentalist and idealist philosophies. It was a tension that, as will be seen shortly, was replicated in Britain. Next, however, we track the diffusion of credit unions across the Atlantic from North America to Ireland.

[29] Berthoud and Hinton, *Credit unions in the United Kingdom*, 7–8.

[30] Teresa Hinton and Mark Dunn, 'United we stand—credit unions: a positive response to debt', *Poverty—Journal of the child poverty action group,* 69 (Spring 1988).

[31] H. Black and R. H. Dugger, 'Credit union structure, growth and regulatory problems', *Journal of Finance*, 36/2 (1981), 529–38.

[32] Hinton and Dunn, 'United we stand'.

[33] C. F. Robinson and A. Gibson, *Credit and the war on poverty: an analysis of the credit union programs of the Office of Economic Opportunity* (Chicago: Woodstock Institute, 1993), cited in Jones, *Towards sustainable credit union development*, 89.

[34] Hinton and Dunn, 'United we stand'.

'VALIANT SOLDIERS OF CHRIST': CATHOLIC SOCIAL ACTION AND THE IRISH CREDIT UNION MOVEMENT

The modern Irish credit union movement emerged in the 1950s, but attempts were made to transplant Raiffeisen-style credit co-operatives to Ireland in the late nineteenth century. The system was championed unsuccessfully by the agricultural co-operative pioneer Sir Horace Plunkett. Historical explanations of this failure have centred on the lack of engagement by influential members of Irish rural society. One plausible explanation for their lack of involvement was that in adopting Raifeissen's system of unlimited liability, these co-operatives deterred the more affluent who would have been liable for any failed co-operative's debts.[35] But the lack of support from key parties was partly the result of Plunkett's critique of the Church's anti-modernity, set out in his book *Ireland in the new century* (1904).[36] Thus, unlike Desjardins, Plunkett failed to rally the support of the Catholic Church. Raking over the failure in 1931, the Plunkett Foundation concluded that:

> Ireland has not produced a large class of persons capable of and willing to run a local credit society with success. It is noteworthy that priests and schoolmasters—classes possessing comparative leisure, education and detachment, to whom the movement in other countries looks to largely for its local leaders—have not come forward in any considerable number. When they have, it has usually meant a successful society.[37]

This was in marked contrast with events in the 1950s, when 'local leaders' were at the forefront of the spectacular growth of Irish credit unions. Enthusiasm for credit unions was indebted to the growing importance of Catholic social action in Ireland, following the papal encyclical *Quadragesimo Anno*. Irish Catholic responses to the earlier *Rerum Novarum*, in contrast, had been muted.[38] Published as the Great Depression began to bite, in 1931, *Quadragesimo Anno* highlighted the

[35] Guinnane, 'Thy neighbor's keeper', 510.

[36] P. Bolger, *The Irish co-operative movement: its history and development* (Dublin: Institute of Public Administration, 1977).

[37] Plunkett Foundation, *Agricultural co-operation in Ireland* (London: Routledge, 1931), 385.

[38] Louise Fuller, *Irish Catholicism since 1950: the undoing of a culture* (Dublin: Gill and Macmillan, 2002), 69.

dangers of state power and urged 'valiant soldiers of Christ' to 'strive according to the talent, powers, and position of each to contribute something to the Christian reconstruction of human society'.[39] The stirring of Irish Catholic social action in the 1930s led to Irish credit union pioneers looking towards the appropriately named Irish-Canadian Jesuit Monsignor Moses Coady, from the St Francis Xavier University (Antigonish, Nova Scotia), rather than Desjardins, as the individual to lead them into a promised land of co-operative credit. Coady founded a credit union in 1933 as part of a broader welding of Catholic and co-operative social action.[40] He described economic co-operation as 'the ultimate in justice' and as 'an organisation for world society that permits charity and the practice of mercy, for the performance of which the Divine Master promised eternal life'. Whilst involvement in co-operation held spiritual advantages there were also worldly material rewards. According to a colleague, Coady's ideas developed in response to an outbreak of 'violent industrial strife' in the Cape Breton area in the 1920s and 1930s, 'when troops were mobilised for almost every strike' and the 'Red International was sung in May Day parades'. Through the St Francis Xavier University Extension Department's adult education classes, 'people were shown an alternative to the revolutionary techniques of industrial conflict and class war'. These included 'credit unions, and co-operative housing groups'.[41] The Antigonish form of co-operation offered the Church in Nova Scotia a response to the industrialization and labour unrest that had unsettled it.[42] At an international level it presented the Church with a tool in its ideological response to communism and in 1938 Coady's ideas received the formal blessing of Pope Pius XI.[43] Coady's efforts reinvigorated the Church's role in propagating the credit union gospel at both the diocesan and international level. Jesuit networks were particularly influential in spreading Coady's message. Father John Sullivan, an Irish-American Jesuit, oversaw the foundation of the Sodality Credit Union in Kingston, Jamaica, in 1941 and by

[39] *Quadragesimo Anno, Encyclical of Pope Pius XI on Reconstruction of the Social Order,* 15 May 1931, in Claudia Carlen (ed.), *The Papal Encyclicals 1909–1939* (Wilmington, NC: McGrath Pub Co., 1981), 415–43.

[40] The Extension Department, St Francis Xavier University, *The social significance of the co-operative movement,* Anigonish (Nova Scotia: Extension Department, St Francis Xavier University, 1963), 14.

[41] Ibid. 30.

[42] M. R. Welton, *Little Mosie from the Margaree: a biography of Moses Michael Coady* (Toronto: Thompson Educational Publishing, 2001), 10.

[43] Quinn, *Credit unions in Ireland,* 42.

1959, 65,000 Jamaicans were credit union members. The concept moved beyond the island's Catholic population and by 2004 around one-third of the population (755,000) were members.[44]

The Irish Catholic Church had historically intervened in the credit transactions of its members, as was seen in our discussion of moneylending. It is no surprise, therefore, that it was central to the rapid diffusion of credit unions in the late 1950s and early 1960s. It was particularly important in establishing the common bond—which was often centred on the parish—that brought diverse social groups together as savers, borrowers, and—importantly—as skilled volunteers. As was the case in Quebec, many of these volunteers were well-educated professionals with the confidence and ability to get fledgling credit unions off the ground. In Ireland, a number of highly motivated groups and individuals with strongly Catholic backgrounds created a groundswell of support for the movement. These Irish credit union pioneers shared, with Desjardins, a desire to re-energize the Catholic moral and social hierarchy. The 1950s was a decade of social and cultural change, with a 'widespread rejection of the conditions of rural life which had been characteristic of most western European countries since the turn of the century . . . happening in Ireland'.[45] A significant factor was the availability of comparatively well-paid work in Britain, prompting renewed high levels of emigration. The Church lamented the fact that young emigrants' faith would be tested by Protestant and materialistic British society. Bishop Cornelius Lucey of Cork, a leading campaigner against emigration, held the view that the 'rural [Irish] home always has been, and still is, the best place in which to bring up a family'.[46] The Church hierarchy was also awash with an exaggerated fear of communism that owed much more to events on mainland Europe than those in Ireland. On a more practical level, the 1950s were punctuated by a number of episodes during which successive Irish governments took tentative steps towards challenging the Church's authority on a number of social policy issues.

Credit unions were promoted as part of a package of measures to promote community development and rural self-help by Muintir na Tire, which was founded in 1931 by Father J. Hayes.[47] Another group of pioneers coalesced around Nora Herlihy, a former novice nun who

[44] Jamaica Co-operative Credit Union League, *The credit union story* (Kingston: Jamaica Co-operative Credit Union League, 2004).

[45] Fuller, *Irish Catholicism since 1950*, 45. [46] Ibid. 46.

[47] R. O'Connor, O. McCarthy, O. and M. Ward, *Innovation and change in Irish credit unions* (Cork: Centre for Co-operative Studies, 2002).

became a Dublin teacher, civil servant Seamus MacEoin, and bakery worker Sean Forde. Herlihy's employment in inner city Dublin allowed her to witness 'at first hand the effects of poverty and homelessness in the community'.[48] She was inspired by Coady's vision and believed that the first problem to overcome 'was to convince people that between the market capitalism of the money sector and the promised utopia of socialism there was a third way, the co-operative way'.[49] Several of the individuals working with Herlihy followed Coady's Antigonish path towards education and fulfilment, by enrolling on the evening diploma course at University College Dublin co-ordinated by the Jesuit Father Edward Coyne. Lucey contributed to the course, in the years before he became Bishop of Cork, lecturing on the relationship between 'Victorian Rochdale co-operative principles' and 'Christian social teaching on human dignity'.[50] On such principles the first Irish credit unions were established at Donore Avenue, Dublin, in 1958, and at Dun Laoghaire, and Clones, the following year.[51] By 1962, 136 credit unions had been formed, with 29 in the Dublin area alone. Loans were provided for 'bikes, clearing old debts, Christmas gifts, building garages, car insurance and tax, doctors' bills' as well as 'first holy communion and confirmation outfits'.[52]

Progress was not totally unproblematic. The combination of the paternalistic trends in credit union philosophy, plus the differences in social status between many volunteers and members occasioned difficulties. One area where this occurred was on the issue of 'productive loans'. In 1962, Herlihy explained that borrowing should be for 'any purpose which, in the best judgement of the credit committee, promises to be of real benefit to the borrower. The purpose is important and must be stated on the loan application.'[53] A regular grumble amongst members was that this principle led to loans for holidays being judged unproductive: 'you might have wanted to go on a holiday, or whatever, but you couldn't put down "holiday", you might have to put down

[48] Anthony P. Quinn, 'Irish credit unions: a success story', *History Ireland*, 9 (Spring 1995), 35–6.
[49] A. T. Culloty, *Nora Herlihy: Irish credit union pioneer* (Dublin: Irish League of Credit Unions, 1990), 34.
[50] Anthony P. Quinn, 'Irish credit unions: a success story', *History Ireland*, 9 Spring 1995), 34–5.
[51] Culloty, *Nora Herlihy*, 26–7.
[52] Credit Union League of Ireland, *Question Time* (Dublin: ILCU, 1962), 17.
[53] Ibid. 6.

furniture for the house or something', recalled one County Derry man.[54]

Applicants faced interviews with the loan committee, which did not appeal to those who either wished to maintain financial privacy or were uncomfortable dealing with those of higher social status. These occasions provided an arena in which lifestyle, spending choices, and—most significantly—a family's financial situation were exposed to unwelcome scrutiny. At such moments, discomfort could be enhanced by the local connections and knowledge that made the common bond—and the credit union—effective. Bridie, a mother of six from a Dundalk council estate, recalled how she and her husband left one credit union following a rejected loan application. Her husband was temporarily unemployed, and this was known to a woman working in the credit union: 'she knew he was not working and we found out later that it was her who told them we might not be able to pay off the loan and so we were refused'. Her characterization of those managing the credit union reflected a keen sense of social distinction that made her uneasy, particularly when she was struggling to repay a loan: 'there was Mr Coburn, he was a councillor, and Jim McGee, he was a builder; anybody who had a bit of backing, you know, a bit of money really ran it'. She recalled awkward encounters with one loan committee member: 'you would think the money was coming out of his pocket; you would think he was paying you personally. He would be very rude when you were being interviewed for a loan. Nobody on the estate liked him, although he would not say a word about your credit union businesses outside the credit union.' It is likely that these experiences were functions of Bridie's low income and of the official's need to scrutinize her ability to repay. The tone of her narrative altered appreciably when she went on to describe a more prosperous period in which she entered the labour market and increased family finances. She and her husband were then able to utilize the credit union to finance a car purchase and she 'did not mind, then, the local people who were in the credit union—I mean the staff, the directors—knowing my business. I didn't even mind being seen going into the building; the credit union became more popular—everybody was in it and didn't mind who knew.'[55]

54 University of Ulster/Newry credit union history project. Interview conducted by student Mary Frances with Dan, 26 October 2004.

55 University of Ulster/Newry credit union history project. Interview conducted by student David Cunningham with Bridie, 20 October 2004.

Class tension could, therefore, bubble to the surface in circumstances such as those outlined by Bridie, endangering the ability of credit unions to attract a diverse membership. Here the Church played a vital role, providing a strong element of communal identity where social and economic differences might have fundamentally weakened the common bond of a nascent credit union. Thus it provided more than the philosophical underpinnings for the Irish credit union movement. The hierarchy put its weight behind the concept and, at a local level, parish priests often facilitated their creation and represented the physical embodiment of the trust that was needed for a mutual saving and loan scheme. The Dundalk Credit Union, for example, was launched in 1967 by Father Frank Donnelly. He subsequently deployed his personal influence to convince a reluctant bank manager to provide the loan that established the credit union in bigger premises.[56] Individuals further up the Church hierarchy also made symbolic contributions. Bishop Lucey attended the first AGM of Ballyphehane Credit Union, founded in Cork City during 1960, and commended its work 'in these days of so called easy payments'. His speech attracted local and national media coverage that assisted the establishment of six further credit unions in the Cork area in the following two years.[57] Reverend Paddy Gallagher became the first President of the League of Credit Unions of Ireland in 1960. His Christmas message to the movement in 1964 was that each local credit co-operative 'will certainly fulfil the demand of Christ to feed the hungry, clothe the naked, help the sick and relieve untold stress'.[58] A philanthropic tone also emerged in regular references to the credit union's mission to provide an alternative to 'unscrupulous moneylenders' who were making it difficult for 'ordinary people to achieve any kind of economic independence'.[59] The potential influence of the Catholic Church was assisted by high levels of religious observance: a survey conducted in 1974 indicated that over 90 per cent of Catholics in the Republic attended mass at least once a week.[60] These attendance levels ensured that large numbers fell within the

[56] Dundalk Credit Union Limited, *21 years serving the people of Dundalk* (Dundalk, 1988).

[57] Culloty, *Nora Herlihy*, 74.

[58] *Irish Credit Union Journal*, 1/3 (December 1964).

[59] Dundalk Credit Union Limited, *21 years serving the people of Dundalk* (Dundalk, 1988).

[60] S. J. Connolly, '"The moving statue and the turtle dove", approaches to the history of Irish religion', *Irish Economic and Social History*, 31 (2004), 20.

common bond represented by the parish, whilst also providing a pool of confident, educated, and influential volunteers. Dundalk's credit union, for example, was able to call upon the Louth County Council's accountant to act as treasurer.[61]

Development was also aided by the competitive and legislative environments in which credit unions emerged. Ireland in 1960 was still a very rural society, with limited financial services outside the larger conurbations. The emergence of credit unions also coincided with the economic modernization associated with Sean Lemass, who was sympathetic towards the movement. As Minister of Industry and Commerce, he set up a Committee on Co-operative Societies, which sat from 1957 to 1963. It recommended the Credit Union Act, 1966, which simplified credit union registration, gave statutory recognition to the credit co-operative concept, and enabled credit unions to make unsecured loans.[62] On these strong foundations the Irish League of Credit Unions (ILCU), as the governing body was renamed in 1972, became a major actor in Ireland's personal finance market. By 1986, there were 564,000 credit union members in the Republic of Ireland.[63] The figure rose to 1.8 million, or around 40 per cent of total population, in 1999.[64] Much of its latter growth was related to the success of the Irish economy. Levels of private saving rose and the credit unions, which sometimes offered dividends of up to 10 per cent, often provided 'higher interest rates than would have been available from banks'.[65] Altruism may have been the midwife present at the birth of the Irish credit union movement, but instrumentalism watched over it as it reached middle age.

'IT IS ANYTHING BUT A CATHOLIC ORGANIZATION': CREDIT UNIONS IN NORTHERN IRELAND

Credit unions were taken up with equal enthusiasm amongst Catholic communities in Northern Ireland, where additional factors assisted growth. The Catholic middle class was swollen as a consequence of the opportunities created by the Education Act, 1947. This saw the

[61] Dundalk Credit Union Limited, *21 years serving the people of Dundalk.*
[62] Quinn, *Credit unions in Ireland*, 21.
[63] Berthoud and Hinton, *Credit unions in the United Kingdom*, 11.
[64] Quinn, *Credit unions in Ireland*, xxix.
[65] Ibid. 86–7.

emergence of significant numbers of confident and articulate individuals, many of whom were involved in the civil rights campaign of the 1960s. The credit union movement offered Catholics a vehicle for financial empowerment in the years immediately preceding their push for greater political and civil rights. Prominent amongst the youthful activists was John Hume, who had trained for the priesthood before returning to Derry to become first a schoolteacher and then a successful politician. Hume was a member of the Knights of Columbanus, a Catholic men's lay organization with a strong interest in social action based on *Rerum Novarum* and in the 'material well-being of Catholics in business and corporate life'.[66] In 1960, the local branch of the Knights heard a presentation on credit unions from Derry priest Father Anthony Mulvey.[67] Derry Credit Union was established thereafter by a handful of individuals who placed a total of £8 10s into its coffers. This was overseen by Hume in his role as treasurer. Although membership reached 200 in the first year, the credit union did not have permanent offices until 1968. By 1974, it had 8,200 members, was Ireland's third largest credit union, and had extended loans totalling £5m. Membership rose further to 12,500 in 1990.[68]

Catholic communities in Belfast were equally receptive to the credit union bug. Amongst the first was Clonard in West Belfast, which emerged in 1962. It involved the Redemptorist priests based at Clonard Monastery who had received advice from members of their order in Limerick, who had help found its credit union. Once again, lay enthusiasm followed in the wake of clerical initiative. In this case, the Clonard Confraternity was involved. A similar pattern lay behind the formation of Newington Credit Union, in North Belfast, during 1968. Its foundation was instigated by Father Breen of Holy Family parish, who had encountered credit unions in Tipperary. The parish newsletter advertised a preliminary meeting, attended by 300 people, at Holy Family School. Members of the management board recalled that the Church provided the trust element that encouraged people to place their savings at the disposal of the credit union, or to take out loans with it. The Newington volunteers included schoolteachers, an architect, and several civil servants who lived in the leafier parts of the parish. Within

66 Fuller, *Irish Catholicism since 1950*, 8–9; S. J. Connolly (ed.), *The Oxford companion to Irish history* (Oxford: Oxford University Press, 2nd edition, 2002), 304.

67 Culloty, *Nora Herlihy*, 91.

68 *Derry Journal*, 2 February 1990; *Belfast Telegraph*, 3 September 1974; McLaughlin, 'Credit union in Northern Ireland', 163.

a year it had 500 members, although its office at Holy Family School was only open on Friday evenings. By 2000, they were operating six days a week from a former bank building and employing several staff, including a Chief Executive Officer. A sizeable proportion of its 7,000 members—an estimated 30 per cent—were on benefits. This example suggests credit unions in Northern Ireland provided a service for at least some of those on low incomes.[69]

However, whilst the social depth of the credit union movement in Northern Ireland was impressive, it was initially far less successful in diffusing through the Protestant community. Credit unions were widely associated with the Catholic Church and the affiliation of those based in Northern Ireland to the ILCU, rather than to a British credit union body, encouraged this association in Protestant minds. Although there is evidence that some Catholic French-Canadian credit union pioneers did seek to exclude applicants of other faiths and cultural traditions, there is no evidence of similar sentiments in the Irish context.[70] Hume attempted to spread credit unions throughout Northern Ireland. After his election to the Northern Ireland parliament in 1969, he sponsored legislation simplifying credit union registration and highlighting their existence. Other initiatives included an address to Protestant women in East Belfast, where Hume's rhetoric was received politely, but bore no fruit. Meanwhile, Derry Credit Union reportedly had significant numbers of Protestant members in its first decade, but rising sectarian tensions led to Protestant migration across the river Foyle and out of the union in the late 1960s and 1970s.[71] Elsewhere, various attempts were made to build an inclusive credit union membership. Newington Credit Union's name was selected to provide a cross-community appeal, although its first location in a Catholic school effectively undermined that goal. A perusal of pamphlets produced by individual credit unions at various points reveals that they often included encouraging messages from local Protestant Church leaders and statements that credit union ideals were Christian, rather than specifically Catholic. The souvenir brochure marking Keady Credit Union's twenty-first anniversary, in 1988, included letters of support from various local Protestant ministers, but the antennae of any Ulster Protestant reader would have honed in on the account of the Catholic priest's role in its formation and management.

[69] Interview with senior officers, Newington Credit Union, Belfast, 10 February 2004, *North Belfast News* (23 October 1999).

[70] Rudin, *In whose interest?*, 11.

[71] Culloty, *Nora Herlihy*, 92.

They may also have spotted the announcement for the local cinema's screening of *The Little Flower*, the 'authentic story of Lourdes', which was eclectically juxtaposed with an advert for Deirdre's Take Away.[72]

In interviews carried out with a number of those involved in Irish credit unions in the 1960s, the role taken by the Catholic Church was often downplayed. Father John, a County Louth priest, argued that 'the Church didn't give any significant support' to credit unions. He explained that his own involvement as a founder of one credit union, in the 1960s, was due to the fact that priests were 'handy' for recruiting people. He felt that he had 'recruited an awful lot of the original members of the credit union not because I was a Catholic priest, but because I happened to be a Catholic priest [*sic*], that was all. I just was interested in credit unions.'[73] Like the other credit union volunteers who were interviewed, it seems highly likely that Father John's analysis was framed in the context of the violence that had broken out in Northern Ireland a decade after Irish credit unions had first emerged. He, like other interviewees, appeared concerned that credit unions might be labelled sectarian because they had drawn most of their membership from the Catholic community and had the support of the Church. One interviewee, from Country Down, was at pains to make clear that 'our credit union has both sides of the house involved'.[74] In a separate interview, another founding member of the same union said 'one of the things that worries me about the credit union in Ireland—it is wrongly dubbed a Catholic organization. It is anything but a Catholic organization.'[75] Similar protestations were accepted in a recent doctoral thesis, which denied any central role for the Catholic Church in the rise of the credit union movement.[76] This claim is inaccurate. Nine out of ten credit unions in the Republic of Ireland base their common bond on community rather than workplace. Much of the growth of Irish credit unions can be described as organic, but the seeds were sown by Catholic clergy and influential lay groups. Once credit unions were formed in

[72] Keady Credit Union, *Keady Credit Union Ltd.: 21 years caring for you* (Keady, 1988).

[73] University of Ulster/Newry credit union history project. Interview conducted by student Elizabeth McGuckin with Father John, 26 October 2004.

[74] University of Ulster/Newry credit union history project. Interview conducted by student Lorraine Cole with Founder Member 2, Warrenpoint, Burren and Rostrevor Credit Union, 26 October 2004.

[75] University of Ulster/Newry credit union history project. Interview conducted by student Mary Burns with Founder Member 1, Warrenpoint, Burren and Rostrevor Credit Union, 23 October 2004.

[76] McLaughlin, 'Credit union in Northern Ireland'.

various localities it is clear that a diffusion process took place, in which the role of the Church was arguably less conscious and the element of organic development stronger.[77] A failure to attract large numbers of Protestants to the credit union movement was inevitable in a society where tensions between them and their Catholic neighbours were on the rise. Trust between members is fundamental to the formation of credit unions, and in Northern Ireland during the 1960s and 1970s precious little of that valuable commodity existed between different religious denominations.

By the late 1970s credit unions appeared to have reached their optimum number amongst Northern Ireland's Catholic communities. There were 78,660 members in 1976 and 122,860 ten years later, but this increase was achieved primarily by growth within existing unions.[78] The impact of credit unions did not go unnoticed across the sectarian divide. In 1976, the County Armagh Orange Lodge investigated the possibility of founding a credit union. However, 'the main problem for Orange Brethren and their families was the close connection of many Irish League credit unions with local Parishes in the Roman Catholic Church, the presence of many Priests on their Boards of Management, usually as Chairmen, and the fact that all their surplus funds were invested in Dublin'.[79] As a result, no action was taken and many Protestants continued to perceive credit unions 'as an exclusively Roman Catholic enterprise'.[80] That attitude persisted until the late 1980s, at which point credit unions began to appear amongst Protestant communities. One of the first was Loughside Credit Union in North Belfast. Located barely ten minutes' walk from Newington Credit Union, it was a world away in terms of the sectarian landscape of 1980s Belfast. Another early example, Shaftsbury Credit Union, in Belfast's Sandy Row district, was established in 1987.[81] Nonetheless, suspicion lingered that credit unions were Catholic institutions. On 12 July 1990, with the area outside the Shaftsbury Credit Union's office milling with visitors for the annual Orange parade, one founder

[77] A. A. Horner, *Geographical diffusion in Ireland: the example of credit unions 1958–1982* (Mannheim, 1984), cited in Yvonne McCool, 'Idealist or instrumentalist: an investigation into the changing nature of credit unions in Northern Ireland', unpublished MBA dissertation (University of Ulster, 1997).

[78] Berthoud and Hinton, *Credit unions in the United Kingdom*, 11.

[79] <http://www.armaghorange.org.uk/credit.htm>, accessed 23 March 2007.

[80] *Belfast Telegraph*, 15 August 1989.

[81] Ulster Federation of Credit Unions (UFCU), *Member's Book*, n.d., 2.

remembered that 'some of the Orangemen were gonna burn us out 'cos they thought we were Catholics . . . people just had to be educated to the fact that credit unions were for everybody'.[82] Education followed, with the Orange Order giving its seal of approval to credit unions. They spread rapidly from the late 1980s, in a fashion resembling what had taken place in Catholic communities in the 1960s.

Although the new wave of credit unions had contacts with their ILCU-affiliated neighbours, they opted to remain distinct from that organization. They sought 'a credit union movement that would have a distinct Ulster-British identity'.[83] Members of the South Belfast Community Council approached the British-based National Federation of Credit Unions (NFCU) in 1985, asking for its assistance. Ironically, the NFCU was itself composed largely of Catholics. The Northern Ireland branch of the NFCU was soon bigger than the British one and in 1995 broke away to found the Ulster Federation of Credit Unions (UFCU). Many of its members, like the 1,000-strong Frontier Credit Union in Newry, have their offices at the local Orange hall. This institution was clearly providing the common bond, networks, and trust that the Catholic parish had provided in the nationalist community. According to Orchard Credit Union (Armagh):

> The credit union ideal of mutual assistance is also a central ideal in Orangeism. A Brother who saves with the Credit Union has the assurance that he will be helping another Brother who has need of a loan. Since the Bicentenary we are all conscious of the religious, cultural and political dimensions of Orangeism. Now Orange Credit Unions are adding another dimension of financial security so that our people may go forward with confidence.[84]

During the 1990s, the UFCU was the fastest growing sector of the credit union movement in Ireland and the UK. In 2002, 69 of the 185 credit unions in Northern Ireland were affiliated to that body.[85] The growth achieved by the ICLU and the UFCU make clear the value of a strong point of allegiance in the formation of successful credit unions. As their respective common bonds, centred on the Catholic parish and the

[82] University of Ulster/Newry credit union history project. Interview conducted by student Niki Girvan with founder member of Ulster Federation of Credit Unions, 28 October 2004.

[83] Ulster Federation of Credit Unions (UFCU), *Member's Book,* 2.

[84] <http://www.armaghorange.org.uk/credit.htm>, accessed 23 March 2007. Capitalization as in the original.

[85] Department of Enterprise, Trade and Investment, *Report of the Registrar of Credit Unions for the year 2002* (London: DTI, 2002).

Orange Order, crossed socio-economic divides they had the ability to create institutions that brought savers and borrowers together. In the rest of the UK, attempts to create socially diverse credit unions were much less successful and the movement struggled to make a significant impression.

'THE POOR MAN'S BANK'? CREDIT UNIONS IN BRITAIN

As was the case in Ireland, credit unions in Britain had a false start. The potential benefits of such organizations were first trumpeted in the 1890s by Henry W. Woolf in a series of publications on European people's banks and by his membership of the 'propagandist body', the Agricultural Banking Association.[86] But Woolf was disappointed by the response of potential allies in his campaign, finding himself 'pooh-poohed incredulously' when he delivered a paper on co-operative banking at the Co-operative Congress.[87] Thomas Farrow, the vociferous anti-moneylending campaigner, also staunchly advocated the transplantation of Raiffeisen's system to Britain and sat on the Agricultural Banking Association. In 1904 he moved from advocacy to action, placing advertisements in the national press seeking capital for Farrow's Credit Bank Ltd. This bank was to be a national 'movement to supplant the 60 per cent usurer' and provide such 'facilities and advantages as are afforded by the People's Banks on the Continent'. It was registered under the Industrial and Provident Societies Act, 1883, and monitored by the Chief Registrar of Friendly Societies. Shares were valued at £1 each and investors were promised a 5 per cent return per year and the opportunity to appoint a committee to run the bank. Loans were available at interest rates of around 10 per cent, backed by 'promissory notes' and 'substantial sureties' and Farrow promised to 'make character . . . a valuable financial asset'.[88] By 1907 the bank had fifteen branches across England, offering customers a Thrift Account and an Anti-Usury Department.[89] In 1908 its own publication, *People's Bank Gazette* hailed Farrow's initiative as the 'first successful English people's bank'. Later that year it declared that its 'gospel of thrift' had only reached the fringes of its

[86] *The Times*, 26 February 1984.
[87] Henry W. Wolff, *Co-operative banking: its principles and practice* (London: King, 1907), 7.
[88] *The Times*, 12 May 1904. [89] Ibid., 20 January 1921, 21 August 1908.

potential market. It noted proudly that 'working men and women who have not hitherto dared to enter the portals of a Bank, have hastened in with their shillings and half-crowns'.[90] Two years later, it reported on the formation of a bank for and managed by women, claimed to have over £500,000 on deposit in its various savings accounts, and revealed an expansion programme that included branches in Cardiff, Dublin, and Glasgow.[91] However, the bank came to an ignominious end in December 1920, presenting depositors at its 73 branches—most of whom were 'small tradespeople and persons of limited means'—with an unwelcome Christmas gift. *The Times* lamented the fact that it had not conducted business on 'recognised banking principles', and it was subsequently revealed that over the previous nine years the bank had lost over £1 million, whilst laying claim to liquidity. Farrow was imprisoned for four years for false accounting. It appears that the fraud was an ill-considered act to keep the institution alive, rather than an attempt at personal aggrandisement.[92] It was to be another four decades before Raiffeisen's principles were put into action again in Britain.

It has been observed that support for the credit union movement which emerged in Britain during the 1960s was strongest in areas where 'traditional communities' remained.[93] Whilst this is true, particularly in regard to the west of Scotland, the creation of the British credit union movement owed much to new entrants to those communities. These included West Indians and Irish Catholics who drew upon experiences in their homelands. The former were motivated by obstacles placed in their path by traditional financial institutions and, as was explained in the last chapter, this also encouraged them to introduce various informal mutual financial co-operatives to the UK. In 1962, the West Indian Standing Conference discussed the financial problems they were encountering, and credit unions were suggested as a palliative. One of those involved later recalled that British credit unions were 'born of adversity' because West Indians 'were often charged higher rates of interest, and asked to pay larger deposits for houses or flats, than the host community'.[94]

[90] *People's Bank Gazette*, February 1908; July 1908.

[91] *The Times*, 3 August 1910.

[92] *The Times*, 21 December 1921, 22 June 1921; *Scotsman*, 30 August 1934.

[93] Iain Crowe, Gerraint Howells, and Kathy Pick, *Support for community based credit unions* (Sheffield: Faculty of Law, University of Sheffield, 1993), 3.

[94] Frank Villiers, 'United Kingdom: the first ten years of credit unions in Britain', in *Report of the 3rd International Conference on Co-operative Credit* (London: International Co-operative Alliance), 131.

Marcus Collins has written cogently on the experience of male West Indian immigrants in Britain from the 1940s to the 1960s. Affronted by their depiction as wild, hedonistic, and rootless individuals, Collins suggests that they sought to represent themselves 'as threatened, not threatening, sinned against, not sinning, deskilled, not unskilled' and to contradict 'white portrayals of them at every point'. Ultimately, they responded in a 'comparatively undemonstrative manner' by beginning 'to reject assimilation as an undesirable and in any case unobtainable goal' and to 'fashion a masculinity at once respectable and black'.[95] Their involvement in credit unions could certainly be interpreted as being closely related to this cultural dynamic. These self-help institutions had no British heritage, offered independence from the institutional racism of British financial concerns, presented those involved with the chance to amass respect, and were a vehicle through which to support the families that British popular culture assumed they had abandoned. West Indians played an extensive role as members, volunteers, and leaders of the burgeoning credit union movement. Factors such as race, their minority status, and common experiences of unsatisfactory treatment from the mainstream financial sector must all have helped build a common bond amongst them. However, it is a strong possibility that their high visibility in the developing movement exacerbated the otherness of credit unions in the minds of white Britons. During the 1980s Paddy Bailey, the Jamaican who had become President of the World Council of Credit Unions concluded that this was a contributory factor in the stuttering development of UK credit unions.[96] In this respect it was significant that the one other group who most readily joined the nascent credit unions were those from Irish Catholic backgrounds. For them the institution was not alien and they had greater levels of social interaction with the growing Afro-Caribbean community, with whom they shared the '"twilight zones" of British cities and towns'.[97]

Bailey's familiarity with British credit unions began with his involvement in the formation of Hornsey Co-operative Credit Union by members of a Baptist church in 1962. The leading role in its emergence was taken by Frank Villiers, who had come to Britain to pursue a

[95] Marcus Collins, 'Pride and prejudice: West Indian men in mid-twentieth-century Britain', *Journal of British Studies*, 40/3 (July 2001), 393, 417–18.

[96] Interview with Martin Logan, credit union volunteer and historian, Manchester, 10 November 2006.

[97] Enda Delaney, *The Irish in post-war Britain* (Oxford: Oxford University Press, 2007), 120.

management course. The group used model rules from the Jamaica Co-operative Credit Union League, but faced objections from the Registrar of Friendly Societies because the existing legislative framework stipulated that mutual societies could not advance unsecured loans. This restriction had limited earlier attempts to form mutual loan clubs. An investigation of moneylending in the 1930s reported the existence of 'Money Societies' that were organized under the Friendly Societies Act 'to provide credit facilities to workingmen and to compete with commercial lenders'. It revealed that they 'correspond roughly to credit unions in America', but had not been 'highly successful'. Like 'many other co-operative credit enterprises', the authors continued, 'a number failed because of lack of experienced managers'. In other cases, 'finding the restrictions by the Registrar of Friendly Societies too binding' they 'registered as moneylenders, thus going over to the enemy'. Those that continued on their original basis offered loans over three to four years that were secured by two or three guarantors.[98] The length of these agreements indicates that the members of these institutions were relatively affluent and that they operated in rather a limited market. Giving evidence before the Select Committee on the Moneylenders Bill in 1925, H. W. Bagwell of the City of Leicester Permanent Money Society revealed that 'we absolutely discourage anything like small loans such as £1; we do not encourage even £5'. His lack of interest in such business was reflected by a total ignorance of the number of Leicester's registered moneylenders.[99] By 1967, only eleven such institutions were registered with a total membership of 8,223.[100] Friendly Societies had more of an impact, but they also offered only secured loans. For example, in 1967 the Royal Liver lent £250,000 and Liverpool Victoria £100,000 to members using insurance policies as security.[101]

The Hornsey Credit Union reluctantly agreed to the modifications to its rules suggested by the Registry and became operative in 1964. This meant that loans for sums exceeding a member's savings had to be guaranteed against those of another member, limiting the latter's ability to take a loan of their own. Within a year, Hornsey had 200

[98] Dorothy Johnson Orchard and Geoffrey May, *Moneylending in Great Britain* (New York: Russell Sage Foundation, 1933), 150–1.

[99] Select Committee on Moneylending (1924–5), evidence of HW Bagwell, 25 (June 1925), col. 1752.

[100] NA: BT 250/12 Committee on Consumer Credit. Registry of Friendly Societies, 1969–70.

[101] Ibid.

members and assets of £2,000.[102] In 1967, together with four other unions in London, it founded the Credit Union League of Great Britain (CULGB). They were soon joined by unions in Bradford, Leeds, Huddersfield, Manchester, and Glasgow. By 1974, the CULGB had 48 affiliated unions and 39,000 members, 65 per cent being from West Indian backgrounds.[103] The movement was also beginning to attract media attention. In 1970, the *New Statesman* reported that British credit unions had a long way to travel before reaching the membership rates of the USA and Canada. It noted that security for loans in North America was through 'character of the member' and this 'reliance on independent judgement and integrity' had been rewarded with a default rate of only 1 per cent of annual turnover.[104] In the same year, the *Guardian* interviewed Father Kevin Felix, a West Indian sociology graduate, about the Bradford credit union he had established in 1968. He felt its main objective was 'to spread and teach the virtue of thrift' and to 'educate the members in the proper use of money'. This union offered free legal and financial advice, and consolidated multiple hire purchase agreements into one low-interest loan—in order to 'set a pattern for better management in future'.[105]

A number of Jamaican 'partners' were converted into credit unions as the movement extended. One was Camberwell Credit Union, which traced its origins to a partner that operated from the late 1960s until 1972 when it registered as a credit union. By 1993 it had 2,300 predominantly Afro-Caribbean members and assets of £600,000.[106] Harlesden Credit Union also evolved out of a partner in 1971. Three years later it had 526 members, including many who were Irish. Its multicultural make-up also included an Indian-born treasurer, with experience of a credit co-operative gained in his homeland. Most frequent loans in Harlesden were for 'house repairs, school clothes, consumer durables or return trips to the West Indies or Ireland'. One Afro-Caribbean member reflected the ideals of the movement when he said the 'credit union is not only about money, it's helping to educate one another, trusting and treating each other like brothers'.[107]

[102] R. B. Davison, *Black British: immigrants to England* (London: Oxford University Press, 1966), 103 n. 2.

[103] Villiers, 'United Kingdom: the first ten years of credit unions in Britain', 131–2.

[104] *New Statesman*, 27 August 1970.

[105] *Guardian*, 22 August 1970.

[106] Herbert and Kempson, *Credit use and ethnic minorities*, 34.

[107] *New Society*, 18 April 1974, 122.

Western Credit Union, founded in 1970, was the first CULGB affiliate with no West Indian members and the first in Scotland. It was established in Glasgow's Drumchapel area, largely through the actions of painter and decorator Bert Mullen. He learned of credit unions from newspapers sent by Irish relatives and subsequently received advice and support from both Hume and Villiers.[108] The Catholic parish hall was Drumchapel's first base, but overtures were made to the local Church of Scotland and the United Free Church of Scotland and offices were sought in a secular location. It later became Drumchapel Community Credit Union and in 1991 had 650 members—many of them on benefits—with £164,000 in savings.[109] Along with Dalmuir, Newarthill, Mosshill, Johnston, and others in west central Scotland, Drumchapel became part of Britain's most successful credit union region. In 1997, Scotland had 10 per cent of Britain's population, but 40 per cent of credit union members. It was home to over one in five of Britain's credit unions and 47,402 of the total 220,000 members, meaning that credit union membership rates were around twice the British average. Of the 115 Scottish credit unions, 101 were community credit unions with a total membership of 20,700.[110] The relative success of the Scottish movement had a number of potential explanations. Scotland's stronger tradition of mutual and co-operative activity was one. Others included its strong cultural links with Ireland, effective leadership, strong support from local government, and the fact the physical proximity of many credit unions amplified mutual support and co-operation.[111] This relative success, and frustration with the lacklustre performance in England and Wales, led to the formation of the Scottish League of Credit Unions (SLCU) in 1993. The emergence of the SLCU represented a further fissure in the British credit union movement that, from the outset, failed to agree upon common philosophical or organizational structures.

Ironically, given the Northern Ireland experience, one report described the splits in the British credit union movement as having 'the appearance of a sectarian squabble'.[112] The origins of this 'squabble'

[108] *Drumchapel News*, 43 (October 2005).

[109] Catriona Burness, *The people's bank: Drumchapel community credit union* (Glasgow: The Union, 1991).

[110] R. Donnelly and A. Haggett, *Credit unions in Britain: a decade of growth* (Oxford: The Plunkett Foundation, 1997), 25.

[111] Ibid. 29.

[112] Berthoud and Hinton, *Credit unions in the United Kingdom*, 128.

lay in the emergence of the Wimbledon Credit Union, which, like Hornsey, was registered in 1964. Its common bond was based on the Parish of the Sacred Heart, whose members were 'anxious to set up a community fund to assist young families in the area where accommodation was expensive and credit difficult to obtain'.[113] The motivations of those involved were as much spiritual as economic. The parish was run by Jesuits and, as was the case in Derry, the Knights of St Columba were involved in recruiting volunteers. These included barristers and solicitors, and Edward Sammons, a teacher at Wimbledon College.[114] He was instrumental in the foundation, during 1967, of the National Federation of Credit Unions (NFCU). Other credit unions involved in it included several established by members of Catholic parish elites in Brighton, Leeds, and Leicester.[115]

A number of sources, including *Credit Union News*, indicate that the NFCU's relationship with the CULGB was uneasy.[116] There were philosophical and personal differences between the two groupings. Villiers later claimed that the relationship became uneasy when CUNA International, the body that oversaw international credit union development, indicated that it wished to recognize CULGB as the 'sole representative body for credit unions in Great Britain'.[117] Villiers suggested that the NFCU's operations 'were somewhat unorthodox' and that it was unwilling to conform to CUNA International's requirements.[118] The CULGB was more receptive to advice and funding from the international credit union movement, which was dominated by the North Americans.

Both British bodies viewed credit unions as financial organizations through which a community could be built or re-energized, but the NFCU was the more idealistic. Its manifesto was introduced by Reverend Eamon Casey, who had been dispatched to Britain as part of the Irish Catholic Church's efforts to minister to emigrants. He was on the progressive wing of the Church and became an active campaigner on the issue of homelessness, co-founding the charity Shelter in 1966.[119] Casey

[113] Crowe, Howells, and Pick, *Support for community based credit unions*, 52.

[114] See obituary for founder member Edward Sammons,<http://www.owa.org.uk/ted_sammmons.htm>, accessed 20 January 2007; *Credit Union News*, 6/1 (March 2004).

[115] NA: BT250/106 Committee on Consumer Credit. Credit Unions. Letter from the National Federation of Credit Unions (30 May 1970).

[116] *Credit Union News*, 6/1 (March 2004).

[117] Ibid.

[118] Ibid., 6/2 (December 2003).

[119] Fuller, *Irish Catholicism since 1950*, 216.

argued that credit unions 'provided the means to help man in the right use of credit and money; they show him the way to make credit serve the purpose of his existence rather than rule it'. Thus money and credit were 'far from being gods themselves' and could 'contribute towards man's service of God'.[120] From this theological well, the NFCU drew inspiration and nurtured an idealistic approach that advocated small credit unions, believing them to foster a strong common bond, active participation, empowerment, and self-help. The NFCU outlined a complex agenda for credit unions. It suggested that they should enhance service, thrift, security, interdependence, and community. Casey argued that as the movement was developing 'at a time when a sense of community is all too often lacking', it could 'help restore community to our society and so enrich its individual members'. The provision of inexpensive loans could relieve the stress and exploitation from those whose 'life is one of financial struggle'. By encouraging saving it could promote thrift, a virtue that 'seems to have disappeared amongst the young'. Casey felt credit unions needed to be 'adapted to fit in with the British temperament' and would, therefore, 'develop through small individual groups in which personal contact could be maintained between members, rather than in terms of larger units, which although financially stronger must by their nature be impersonal'.[121] Casey was aware of the rapid growth of large credit unions in his homeland, but his manifesto outlined the case for what many now believe to have been a fundamental flaw of British credit unions. The academic Paul Jones, for example, argued in 1999 that this philosophy 'seriously held back the growth and the economic viability of credit unions in Britain', leaving many of them 'struggling even to make ends meet'.[122]

Although there were differences at leadership level, the idealist approach most commonly associated with NFCU was also deeply ingrained amongst the majority of small community credit unions affiliated to CULGB, which became the Association of British Credit Unions Ltd (ABCUL) in 1984. ABCUL maintained formal financial and organizational links with the North American movement and took on an increasingly instrumental approach, viewing credit unions as financial facilities that should be extended as broadly as possible: they should not simply be 'the poor man's bank'. CUNA encouraged ABCUL to

[120] Edward Sammons, *Credit unions in Britain* (London: National Federation of Credit Unions, 1967), 4.

[121] Ibid. 4.

[122] Jones, *Towards sustainable credit union development*, 2.

develop a stronger business model that reflected its own experience in the USA. This involved prioritizing the development of occupational credit unions, which were both simpler to launch and less draining on central resources.[123] The multiplication of organizing bodies concerned the Registry of Friendly Societies. In 1994 it asked how such a small movement could sustain ABCUL, NFCU, and the SLCU.[124] The variety of bodies and their shifting degrees of instrumentalism and idealism complicated the movement's relationship with government and, many have argued, limited its growth. But the movement also offered regular criticisms of the state's tepid response to the emergence of credit unions and its failure to construct a more workable legislative framework in which they could develop. The Credit Union Act, 1979, was designed to alter that. Many saw it as the movement's moment of opportunity and it ushered in an era of optimism. In retrospect, however, that was actually a very inopportune moment to relaunch credit unions in the British market.

'AN ACORN FROM WHICH A VERITABLE GROVE OF CREDIT UNION TREES WILL GROW': CREDIT UNIONS AFTER THE 1979 ACT

In discussing the lacklustre growth of British credit unions, activists consistently lamented the government's slow response to the movement's appeal for legislation equivalent to that passed in the Irish Republic and Northern Ireland during the 1960s. As has been explained, legislation on provident societies prevented credit unions from advancing unsecured loans.[125] In 1972, Labour MP John Roper attempted to steer a private member's Bill through Parliament to overcome this and to legally recognize credit unions as financial entities. Conservative ministers, as well as civil servants, were unconvinced of the need for legislation. They suggested that the existence of only 47 CULGB-affiliated credit unions, with 22,140 members, demonstrated minimal demand for the institution. It was argued that the Trustee Savings Bank already occupied the market niche to which credit unions laid claim. Roper was

[123] Berthoud and Hinton, *Credit unions in the United Kingdom*, 22.

[124] Registry of Friendly Societies, *Report of the Chief Registrar of Friendly Societies* (London: HMSO, 1994), 9.

[125] *Credit Union News*, 6/2 (December 2003).

not diverted from his mission, and with the support of the National Consumer Council (NCC), lobbied successive governments. The NCC wrote to MPs, in 1976, arguing that credit unions had the potential to provide unsecured loans to low-income consumers at modest cost. The NCC's initiative stemmed from its interest in the work of the US academic David Caplowitz and his concept of 'consumer detriment': a model which outlined how the poor's deficit of educational and financial capital meant they were unable to obtain value in consumer exchanges. The self-help ethos of credit unions suggested an ideal vehicle for financial education and empowerment.[126] The NCC provided the secretariat for the Credit Union Steering Group, which triumphed when the Credit Union Act was passed in 1979.[127]

The Act recognized credit unions as specific bodies that could provide unsecured loans, supervised by the Registrar of Friendly Societies. Members were allowed to borrow up to £5,000 above the amount of their savings with the credit union. Interest on loans was set at 1 per cent a month on a reducing balance, producing an APR of 12.68 per cent. Members faced a maximum savings limit of £2,000, a figure subsequently raised to £5,000. The dividend paid to members was capped at 8 per cent. In practice, many community credit unions were unable to achieve the levels of financial liquidity at which a dividend could be paid and those that were able to do so usually paid at a rate between 1 and 3 per cent. The Act also made partners and similar informal financial associations illegal and obliged them to convert to credit unions.[128]

The measure was welcomed warmly. The *Observer* trumpeted it as 'an acorn from which a veritable grove of credit union trees will grow'. It described credit unions as an 'invaluable help in providing credit for low-income borrowers, many of whom have no bank account and would otherwise be driven into the uncaring and expensive arms of tallymen, money-lenders or pawnbrokers'. It noted that 'because of the "common bond" concept, credit unions have an extremely good track

[126] NA: T 233/2990, Registration of Credit Unions, Memo from J. Unwin to Mr Kelly, 3 September 1973, Notes for meeting with Mr John Roper MP to be held on 11 November 1973; *The Times*, 15 July 1977.

[127] D. Caplowitz, *The poor pay more: consumer practices of low-income families* (New York: Free Press, 1967 edition). On the NCC and credit unions in the 1970s see Matthew Hilton, *Consumerism in 20th-century Britain* (Cambridge: Cambridge University Press, 2003), 282.

[128] HM Treasury, *Credit Unions of the Future Taskforce report*; Berthoud and Hinton, *Credit unions in the United Kingdom*, 18–19.

record': 'it seems, people just don't welsh on debts secured on the savings of friends and colleagues'.[129] The Act's timing was, however, inauspicious. Credit unions were engulfed swiftly by an unfortunate pairing of economic recession and credit boom and their growth was unspectacular. For a number of years, the main clearing banks had been competing with the TSB, the Giro Bank, and building societies to attract 'unbanked' blue-collared workers. Whereas in 1969 only one in three adults had a bank or building society account, by 1979 that had risen to three in four.[130] The financial journey of these individuals towards the banks was greatly assisted by major employers' growing preference to pay wages directly into banks.[131] A further important development saw the traditional divisions within consumer credit markets—through which banks had been primarily responsible for personal loans, building societies for mortgages, and finance houses for hire purchase—erode slowly between the 1950 and 1970s. In the 1980s this erosion turned to landslide as the Thatcher government finally ended post-war credit controls and enacted a number of measures that liberalized personal finance markets, stoking a rapid rise in consumer credit use. A variety of measures, such as the Building Societies Act, 1986, that allowed those institutions to offer personal loans and credit cards, encouraged further market diversity and growth. Credit card numbers rose from 11.6 to 29.8 million between 1980 and 1990, whilst outstanding consumer credit grew from 8 per cent to 15 per cent of consumer expenditure between 1979 and 1989.[132]

Importantly, therefore, British consumers had a much wider range of financial products available to them than those on offer to their predecessors in 1960s Ireland, or early twentieth-century Canada. Many financial institutions offered higher interest rates on savings and lower rates on loans than those offered by credit unions. This was a significant factor given that credit unions had to attract healthy savings balances to facilitate their lending function. In any case, community—already weak in the 1960s according to Casey and the NFCU—was even less robust by the time the Thatcher government took power, and the search for the form of workable common bond that had been so effective in Ireland resembled the quest for the Holy Grail. Other credit institutions that

[129] *Observer*, 5 February 1979.
[130] Berthoud and Kempson, *Credit and debt*, 14.
[131] *The Times*, 4 November 1975.
[132] Berthoud and Kempson, *Credit and debt*, 46–7.

relied on community networks were experiencing decline. As outlined in an earlier chapter, mail order companies that had for decades been heavily reliant on the sociability of hundreds of thousands of part-time agents, who received only small financial rewards to assess customers' creditworthiness and collect instalments, reported diminishing average agency sizes. If trust and community solidarity were much harder to drum up when a little profit was to be made, what chance the selfless voluntarism implied by credit union philosophy?

Whilst some aspects of credit unions' operating climate were not favourable, others were more positive. Modest growth was assisted from the mid-1980s via the formation of agencies designed to promote and support credit unions. The accompanying rhetoric, which consisted of calls to citizenship, community, thrift, and self-help, proved sufficiently broad to appeal to local politicians on the left and right. The first credit union development agency was established in 1984 in Glasgow. The Birmingham Credit Union Development Agency followed in 1987, and within five years was supporting 25 credit unions with 8,000 members.[133] There were thirteen similar schemes by 1988. Despite this backing, the Policy Studies Institute (PSI) reported, in 1989, that there were only 35,000 British credit union members.[134] The following year, financial problems saw ABCUL announce a number of redundancies, suggesting that the movement was in reverse. Its President cited the transient population on estates and a lack of 'community spirit' in Britain as contributory factors.[135] By 1994, the NCC was less ebullient about credit unions than it had been during its 1970s campaign, identifying a number of problems in the sector. Amongst them was the issue of well-intentioned, but flawed, top-down intervention. It concluded that successful British community credit unions had emerged organically, rather than being imposed from above.[136] A common bond of some sort had to pre-exist and it could not be created around loose concepts such as 'the community' or 'poverty', as part of national or local government anti-poverty agendas. Such strategies frequently led to credit union failure and dealt a demoralizing blow to morale in the community concerned. For example, in 1999, the 100-strong credit union on Bradford's Canterbury Estate was forced to close when around

[133] National Consumer Council, *Saving for credit: the future of credit unions in Britain* (London: National Consumer Council, 1994), 15.

[134] Berthoud and Hinton, *Credit unions in the United Kingdom*, 2.

[135] Crowe, Howells, and Pick, *Support for community based credit unions*, 49–50.

[136] National Consumer Council, *Saving for credit*, 12.

half those taking out loans were unable to repay them. Community development worker Shahnaz Bochari feared that residents would turn to 'loan sharks'.[137] The high bad debt ratio suggested that the formation of this credit union represented a triumph of hope over pragmatism.

Efforts to highlight funding of credit union development as part of its anti-poverty strategies were also counter-productive, according to the NCC, creating a stigma that deterred the recruitment of more affluent members on whose savings the economic buoyancy of credit unions depended.[138] Research, published in 1999, suggested that many volunteers felt that the label 'poor man's bank' was harming the movement. One volunteer commented: 'the perception of local authorities, community workers, and churches that credit unions are poor people's banks, and only form part of anti-poverty strategies, is really unhelpful.' Another said that 'not only is it patronising, it encourages people to exclude themselves from credit unions. Who wants to declare themselves as poor?' Asked whether the credit union's purpose was to 'get rid of the loan sharks', another said, 'No credit union can get rid of loan sharks.' Whilst another felt that this sentiment was 'a myth used by the media'.[139] The evidence suggested that this was indeed the case. Assessing possible connections between potential users of moneylenders and credit unions in 1989, the PSI concluded that: 'it appears that credit unions do not generally replace other forms of credit'.[140] This assessment was supported by the fact that companies such as Provident Financial had not been driven out of Dublin despite the city's extensive credit union network. Research, conducted in the 1980s, indicated that moneylenders were still used heavily in Ireland and that measures to control their activities would 'be fruitless unless accompanied by action to increase the disposable income of the poor'. Of the moneylenders' customers surveyed, over half had four or more children and only 10 per cent were employed. Less than 4 per cent had a loan from the credit union at the time of the study. The authors concluded that 'respondents turned to moneylenders in the context of few alternative sources of credit, the easy and fairly ready availability of credit from this source and an established pattern of using this form of credit among their family and friends'. In addition, they were 'considered poor risks for

137 *Bradford Telegraph and Argus*, 5 November 1999.
138 National Consumer Council, *Saving for credit*, 12.
139 Jones, *Towards sustainable credit union development*, 64–6.
140 Berthoud and Hinton, *Credit unions in the United Kingdom*, 120.

conventional forms of credit'. The costs of moneylenders' loans were 'not of great significance to the low income borrower' because they often did 'not have sufficient information to evaluate the true costs of different types of credit' and because their need 'is frequently so great that it over-rides a consideration of the costs of credit in the short-term'. Despite the widespread diffusion of credit unions in Ireland, the report noted that many low-income areas remained without one. It urged funding for development in such localities and identified cases in Cork and Waterford where debts to moneylenders had been renegotiated by credit unions. This was described as a 'labour-intensive' exercise and repayments sometimes had to be assisted by the St Vincent de Paul Society.[141] More recently, in Belfast, which is equally well served by community credit unions, one moneylender articulated a very relaxed attitude towards their presence even though 80 per cent of his customers were members:

> I think they're a good thing. I'm in a credit union myself. I think it seems to be a separate market. People will have their credit union accounts—they might borrow the money for their holiday from a credit union and maybe borrow the spending money from me. They'll always be going along to the credit union on a Friday night. They'll be going to get their loans at Christmas, but . . . people get caught short, they mightn't have the money for the oil that Friday . . . they like to have you there for that. So, no, I don't think they're conflicting.[142]

It might be assumed that individuals involved in this crossover had reached their credit limit with their credit union, necessitating recourse to the much more expensive product offered by the moneylender. A report by the Competition Commission in 2006 also suggested that Irish credit unions have had a marginal impact on moneylenders. It estimated that 6 per cent of the UK population used home-collected credit, as opposed to 5 per cent in the Republic of Ireland. Significantly, Provident Financial reported that 42 per cent of its Irish customers were credit union members. Rather frustratingly, however, the Competition Commission was unable to determine whether the slightly cheaper cost of a Provident loan in the Republic of Ireland was in any way attributable to the presence of credit unions. Other potential explanations included the Republic's 200 per cent cap on interest rates and the fact that Provident's Irish customers exhibited lower levels of bad debt

[141] Mary Daly, *Moneylending and low income families* (Dublin: Combat Poverty Agency, 1988), vii, 14–15, 102, 119.

[142] Interview with anonymous Northern Ireland moneylender 2.

than their British counterparts, which enabled the company to reduce charges.[143]

The weaker diffusion of community credit unions in Britain provided even less competition for moneylenders than in Ireland. In 1997, a study by two of the most influential advocates of the 'social' aspects of credit union development calculated that limited asset accumulation in the majority of community credit unions left them unable to employ full-time staff. Without them, credit unions offered a limited service to members.[144] The mix of full- and part-time, and paid and voluntary, staff was linked by the Registry of Friendly Societies, with the important issue of 'stewardship'. Surveying developments between 1979 and 1994, it cited this as of core importance in the success or failure of a credit union.[145] The reporting requirements of the 1979 Act placed great pressure on the volunteers who were tasked with filing annual financial reports. The Act introduced fees for registration, eating into dividends and introduced professional auditing procedures. There were widespread complaints from volunteers of being 'paperworked to death'. By 1982, twelve credit unions had closed, including several that had originated as Jamaican partners.[146] Of the 812 credit unions that registered between 1979 and 2000, 115 subsequently folded.[147]

In 1994, the NCC questioned the ability of volunteers to carry out the numerous complex tasks involved in credit union management. The average credit union had between seven and fifteen elected volunteers on its Board or Management Committee. This group established a Credit Committee, of between three and seven members that met weekly, and a three-strong Supervisory Committee that convened periodically to oversee operations. Volunteers also had to be found to act as President, Treasurer, Assistant Treasurer, Education Officer, Membership Officer, Insurance Officer, and Credit Control Officer. There were also routine tasks to be carried out by collectors, tellers, and cashiers,

[143] Competition Commission, *Home credit market enquiry* (London: HMSO, 2006), 78.

[144] Pat Conaty and Ed Mayo, *A commitment to community and place: the case for community development credit unions* (London: Policy Studies Institute, 1997).

[145] O. Clutton-Brook, *Credit unions in GB: a review of the years 1979–1994* (London: HMSO/Registry of Friendly Societies, 1996).

[146] Mick Brown, Pat Conaty, and Ed Mayo, *Life saving: community development credit unions* (London: New Economics Foundation and National Association of Credit Union Workers, 2002), 9.

[147] Registry of Friendly Societies, *Report of the Chief Registrar 2000–1* (London: HMSO, 2001), 9.

which were taken up by paid staff when a credit union's finances—and philosophical disposition—permitted.[148] Unsurprisingly, this extensive workload stretched volunteers' resources. For example, in 1994, four of the five NFCU affiliated credit unions in Salford were reported to be struggling for this reason, and their governing body was forced to introduce more central control.[149] The motivations of volunteers varied. Many exhibited the beliefs espoused by Casey: one from Northern Ireland felt that the credit union 'instilled a sense of pride, a sense of saving, a sense of community in the members'.[150] One English volunteer became involved for reasons that echoed those of the socially orientated mail order agents in earlier generations: 'It was a cheap way of socialising for me in the beginning. It went on from there. I got a taste for it.'[151]

In the late 1980s, the average credit union in Northern Ireland was four times the size of its British equivalent, with 1,240 members as opposed to 280.[152] The failure of British credit unions to expand their membership restricted the services they could offer. A certain level of assets was required if a credit union was to hire full-time staff to facilitate extensive opening hours, or to acquire attractive premises. In interviews, veteran Irish credit union volunteers regularly discussed the symbolic importance of the union's office in reinforcing trust and confidence. A founder member of a County Monaghan union said: 'the premises in York Street represented the first time we owned a premises. So that was a statement, in its own way. It was saying—the credit union is here to stay . . . it represented to the people in the town that the credit union is not a fly-by-night organization. We're bricks and mortar.'[153]

Many small British credit unions were unable to offer a dividend to members. This inhibited their ability to attract the savings of more affluent individuals and to accumulate the financial assets that would enable them to extend lending.[154] The offer of a return on savings had to be dangled because, unlike many credit union activists, potential

148 Berthoud and Hinton, *Credit unions in the United Kingdom*, 37–8.

149 NCC, *Saving for credit*, 16.

150 University of Ulster/Newry credit union history project. Interview conducted by student Mary Burns with Founder Member 1, Warrenpoint, Burren and Rostrevor Credit Union, 23 October 2004.

151 Berthoud and Hinton, *Credit unions in the United Kingdom*, 39.

152 Ibid. 26.

153 University of Ulster/Newry credit union history project. Interview conducted by student Kate Loughran with Founder Member Castleblaney Credit Union. 17 October 2004.

154 Berthoud and Hinton, *Credit unions in the United Kingdom*, 31, 118.

members saw the institution as a financial service rather than a social one. This was underlined by the Belfast oral history interviews, which produced greater evidence of instrumental attitudes towards credit unions than of altruistic behaviour. Credit union participation was not particularly marked amongst the sample, probably due to its age profile. Many of the Protestants, in particular, had been close to or beyond retirement age when credit unions first appeared in their communities in the late 1980s. Those older interviewees who did report membership articulated a negative response to the fact that credit unions expected members to take out an interest-bearing loan rather than withdraw their savings. In a reversal of the normal pattern of intergenerational credit use, Mary was introduced to a credit union by her daughter. In her twenty-eight years of membership she had not taken a loan. When she needed cash, Mary accessed her savings account, even though 'they don't like you to draw your own money out'. When doing so, her daughter repeatedly told her: 'Mummy, they don't like you doing that.' 'But that's just the way I do it', Mary remarked. Her rationale was 'I don't like borrowing . . . I'd prefer just to draw what I need myself.' For her, the mutuality of the credit union came second to careful money management. Rather than viewing the credit union as a promoter of thrift, she felt that paying interest on a loan whilst having savings to draw upon represented profligacy.[155] The four youngest interviewees in the Belfast sample had all experienced credit union membership, but they demonstrated a range of attitudes towards it. Two provided testimony on credit union membership that was as dispassionate as that from Mary. Patrick, a west Belfast Catholic, explained that he had formerly been a member of his local credit union, had obtained a loan to buy a car, and had saved £1,200. He then decided 'I don't think I need the credit union anymore.' This was because he felt 'the interest was rubbish. See the interest works both ways: there's small interest on loans, so obviously it's small on the money you have in it. So I closed my account with the credit union and moved it to the bank.'[156] Joan, a north Belfast Protestant had an even more clinical flirtation: 'We joined the credit union to enable us to go to my sister's house in England, but we paid that off quickly and we haven't been back to it

155 Interview with Mary (born 1913. Retired library assistant/shop worker, mother of seven and wife of a slater. Roman Catholic. Interviewed 2 December 2002).

156 Interview with Pat (born 1948. Boilerman. Three children—one deceased. Roman Catholic. Interviewed 10 September 2002).

again.'[157] Anne-Marie, a Catholic, was much more engaged with the movement's ideals. She felt that 'you were part of something, that when your money was going in somebody else was getting it'. Anne-Marie believed that 'credit unions are very, very popular in west Belfast' and 'everybody I know would go to a credit union before they'd go to a bank'. She measured their success via the material improvements she saw around her: 'all my daughters, all my sons, all my neighbours, all my brothers and sisters; every single thing they have in their homes has all been bought through the credit union. New kitchens, double glazing, everything.'[158] Ironically, the one other particularly positive testimony on credit unions was from Moneylender 2, himself a member, who was cited above.[159]

Mary's testimony corresponded with evidence collected by the PSI in 1989. It noted that as members were expected to save before they were granted a loan, and were then asked to leave their savings in place, they were being asked to borrow their own money. They compared the costs of a £250 loan from a credit union with one from a bank or building society and found that they were not very much cheaper when these factors were taken into account. This was a strong deterrent for those with access to mainstream credit.[160] Interviews with Irish credit union volunteers produced frequent complaints of the difficulties of getting members to take out loans. A founder member of one credit union in County Down was aware that he could 'probably get a better deal elsewhere but it's going into the community. It's there for the community.' But ordinary members did not share his outlook: 'Unfortunately, and we're not alone in this—other credit unions are in the same boat—we cannot get people now to borrow as much as they did.'[161]

This particular issue was not the prime concern of many of the small British credit unions that struggled to survive. Their main problem was to attract sufficient savings to finance their lending function. Cowgate

157 Interview with Joan (born 1960. Mature student, care home worker and mother of three. First husband a labourer; current husband a taxi driver. Protestant. Interviewed 10 April 2003).

158 Interview with Anne-Marie (born 1951. Mature student and mother. First husband a scaffolder; current husband a musician. Interviewed 20 May 2003).

159 Interview with anonymous Northern Ireland moneylender 2.

160 Berthoud and Hinton, *Credit unions in the United Kingdom*, 118–19.

161 University of Ulster/Newry credit union history project. Interview conducted by student Mary Burns with Founder Member 1, Warrenpoint, Burren and Rostrevor Credit Union, 23 October 2004.

Credit Union was established in Newcastle, in 1985, in an area with unemployment rates of 93 per cent and large numbers of single-parent families. The only sign of economic development in Cowgate at the time, according to the journal *Poverty*, was 'the number of loan companies whose offices now ring the estate'. Concern about rising debt led the Citizens Advice Bureau to consult residents about forming a credit union. As a result, twenty-one residents set one up in 1985, each paying a £1 registration fee. Once they had saved £1 for ten weeks they were eligible for a loan of up to £25 over and above the amount they had saved. Subsequent advances rose to a figure set at £50 over the value of the member's savings. By 1988 there were 200 members. Notably, the 'vast majority' of its volunteers were female, reflecting 'that the responsibility for household budgeting, and consequently any household debt lies with women'.[162] Cowgate Credit Union's gender profile was typical of countless community credit unions in deprived areas. In 1988, the PSI found that the females made up 70 per cent of volunteers in the poorest credit unions.[163] Several researchers felt that the reason credit unions were 'struggling to rebuild community spirit' was due to a gender divide that produced a lack of male involvement.[164] This assessment was shared by Beatrix Campbell in her influential study of Britain's 'dangerous places', *Goliath* (1993). More recently, the SLCU stated that the typical profile of a volunteer 'is a 55+ year old lady, who has reared her family, has sound knowledge of her community and a strong commitment to it'.[165] Conversely, males predominated amongst the movement's hierarchy. In the late 1980s, they represented 42 per cent of members, but 67 per cent of leaders.[166] In part, this reflected the demand for certain skills and time.

Researchers noted that community credit unions offered potential financial and social empowerment for women struggling to manage on limited budgets, often without the co-operation of their husband or partner. This aspect of them was demonstrated by evidence, collected in the mid-1990s, from a credit union in north-west England that involved black and white women: 'The good thing is, I can get a loan

162 Hinton and Dunn, 'United we stand'.

163 Berthoud and Hinton, *Credit unions in the United Kingdom*, 64.

164 Barbara Lewis, 'Credit unions: past, present and future', *European Journal of Marketing*, 16/3 (1982), 59.

165 <http://www.scottishcu.org/view_company_info.asp?fld_company_info_id+4>, accessed 7 March 2007.

166 Berthoud and Hinton, *Credit unions in the United Kingdom*, 41.

for the first time in my life, without asking him [her husband] first, and I don't have to grovel to a bank manager.' The enormous potential for personal development gained from acting as volunteer was outlined by another woman: 'before I joined a Credit Union I was miserable as sin because I had a few problems. I used to sit at home all day feeling sorry for myself and fat and ugly. Now I've got something to look forward to . . . I'm needed here and I'm good at the work I do. Nobody has ever said that before.'[167] The *Poverty* article about Cowgate ended on an equally upbeat note, declaring that there was 'hope of ending widespread indebtedness on the estate' and that 'Cowgate has regained some of its lost spirit and identity'.[168] The postscript to this article was less cheery, however, as in 1999 membership had dwindled to only 40.[169] The debates and fissures amongst the various credit union organizations must have appeared rather elevated and theoretical when viewed from the perspective of Cowgate's volunteers. Experience there, and in countless other community credit unions, indicated that the movement had failed to develop a workable model that could serve Britain's low-income communities. A rising tide of opinion believed that new ideas and approaches were necessary if credit unions were to succeed in Britain and a number of parties began advocating new proposals in the 1990s.

'WE NEED TO BE A BUSINESS': NEW MODEL CREDIT UNIONS

At the start of the twenty-first century Cowgate Credit Union ceased to exist. It was incorporated into Moneywise Newcastle Credit Union, founded in 2003 through an amalgamation of twelve unions that united 4,500 members.[170] This development was part of a radical reinvention of credit union organization that coincided with the arrival of Tony Blair's government. Credit unions were jokingly referred to as the only unions that Blair appreciated and his administration undertook a number of initiatives designed to facilitate their growth.[171] A Treasury

[167] A. Rimmer, 'Power and dignity: women, poverty, and credit unions', in C. Sweetman (ed.), *Gender and poverty in the North* (Oxford: Oxfam, 1997), 32.

[168] Hinton and Dunn, 'United we stand'.

[169] <http://www.moneywise.org.uk>, accessed 1 April 2007.

[170] Moneywise, Newcastle Credit Union, Publication No. 5 (January 2007).

[171] *Guardian* (Money supplement), 20 November 1999.

Taskforce, established in 1998, was midwife to several major policy decisions. These included the complete removal of the upper limit on the size of a common bond. One intention of this measure was to encourage mergers. A potential golden scenario was envisaged, in which larger well-resourced unions linked up with smaller community credit unions to secure their financial futures. This enabled Cowgate's tiny membership to become part of the Moneywise Credit Union, which had a common bond that included all Newcastle's council employees and any resident of the city.[172] This form of joint residence/workplace common bond was highly encouraged. Central to these developments was the academic Paul Jones, who worked closely with ABCUL to develop new strategies. Amongst the most important new proposals to emerge, from a manifesto prepared by Jones in 1999, was a call for greater levels of objectivity and market analysis to be placed at the heart of decision making. This approach was designed to replace what many felt had been the ideological concerns that had driven the movement previously. Visions of community empowerment that involved credit unions adopting a 'small is beautiful' mantra were flawed, according to Jones, and had produced limited growth. Moreover, he questioned the value of what had been achieved in the small community credit unions: 'A credit union with a hundred members is not, for example, doing anything for the social goals of the 19,900 people within its common bond, most of whom may be facing exclusion from low-cost financial services.'[173] Jones provided detailed evidence that community credit unions had frequently encountered financial or other problems. He also demonstrated that a membership of 200 appeared to be a plateau beyond which they rarely progressed. In 1997, 297 credit unions had fewer than this figure.[174] Measurement criteria devised by Birmingham's Credit Union Development Agency revealed that only four community credit unions in England and Wales were self-sufficient and economically viable in that year. The remaining 344 relied on grants for their existence.[175] In Jones's view, a 'credit union run by a group of tired and burnt-out volunteers, fearful of the consequences of not giving every ounce of their energy to the credit union, is not doing a great deal for the social goals of these volunteers either'.[176] He noted that the low growth of credit unions had been acknowledged increasingly, but that it

[172] Moneywise, Newcastle Credit Union, Publication No. 5 (January 2007).
[173] Jones, *Towards sustainable credit union development*, 3.
[174] Ibid. 11–13. [175] Ibid. 25. [176] Ibid. 3.

was either 'glossed over or submerged within an assumption that credit unions were going through some "passing phase" '.[177] Jones cited credit union workers in support of his perspective. Speke Credit Union in Liverpool was established, in 1989, to meet financial needs in a deprived area. Its chairperson explained that 'for many years, the credit union just struggled and limped along with burnt out volunteers'. In 1996 it secured annual funding of £90,000, enabling it to employ four full-time staff and move into a former bank building in the main shopping area. Three years later, it was still 'nowhere near being sustainable or viable'. Its income 'would not cover the costs of the rent, never mind the wages of the workers'. Its chairperson's conclusion tallied with Jones's view: 'We've got to get away from this image of being a "poor man's bank", at the moment it's mostly the least economically active people in Speke who are members of the credit union and it just doesn't work. We are a community service, but what we need to be is a business.' It hoped to achieve this by extending the common bond to include those who worked in the area, thereby building financial assets.[178]

Spurred on by Jones's report, ABCUL stepped up its campaign of encouraging larger credit unions and mergers. This led to a fall in the number of credit unions. Between 2003 and 2004, for example, numbers fell from 847 to 779.[179] It was increasingly argued that a virtuous circle had to be created, involving larger unions with more members and higher turnover which, in turn, would enable the employment of suitably qualified staff, better marketing, and the establishment of more attractive and accessible offices in high street locations. Only via this option, it was maintained, would community credit unions be able to stand on their own feet, as economic and social entities. Significantly, it was anticipated that membership growth would emanate from more affluent groups rather than the financially excluded. The aim was to offer more business-like credit unions, which placed less stress on self-fulfilment and the creation of 'community' on low-income estates, and more on the simple extension of membership and basic financial services. Advocates of this policy believed that it would produce more practical results. From their perspective, the credit union movement was not and could not become a panacea for poverty or for the decline of community. However, if it could increase its scale and scope and

[177] Jones, *Towards sustainable credit union development*, 6. [178] Ibid. 78.

[179] Peter Goth, Donal McKillop, and Charles Ferguson, *Building better credit unions* (Published by the Policy Press for the Joseph Rowntree Foundation, Bristol, 2006), 3.

introduce a wider range of simple savings and loans schemes, it could offer products that provided a new element of competition to doorstep, and sub-prime, lenders.

Thus pragmatists felt that a potential spin-off from larger membership and asset accumulation would be an increased ability to take greater risks in lending, in order to target more financially excluded individuals. As history has demonstrated, through the examples of the Schulze-Delitzsch credit co-operatives in the early twentieth century, North American credit unions in the middle of the century, and British unions in recent decades, saving was and remains difficult for the most financially challenged families. Credit co-operatives' emphasis on their members' ability to save before granting a loan proved to be an exclusionary practice. However, in 2005, a number of credit unions began to leave what *Credit Union News* called their 'comfort zone', by moving away from savings requirements and share loan ratios into 'capacity based lending'.[180] This venture was supported by a Growth Fund of £36m (administered by the Department of Work and Pensions), announced in the government's 2004 Pre Budget Report. Its aim was to facilitate affordable personal loans to people living in areas of 'high financial exclusion'.[181] As a result, a number of larger credit unions began to experiment with capacity-based lending as an alternative to using a savings ratio to define how much a member could borrow. Members were asked instead to 'prove ability to repay' by making a number of deposits in a savings account, allowing the credit union to gauge what repayment levels they could meet. In another break with traditional credit union philosophy those unions adopting this approach began using credit referencing services. Moneywise Newcastle Credit Union was amongst those that adopted this practice. This was partly driven by its decision to introduce 'Key Loans', which were aimed at 'borrowers caught up in high interest costs from doorstep lenders who may not have the ability to save for the six weeks requirement'. At the end of 2006 it had a total of £60,000 on loan to 220 people in this category. A member of staff, previously employed as an unsecured loans officer with a building society, had responsibility for interviewing applicants.[182] This type of lending had greater attendant risks, and in

180 *Credit Union News*, 8/3 (November 2006).

181 Department of Trade and industry, *Illegal lending in the UK,* 85 n. 44<http:/www.dti.gov.uk/files/file35171.pdf>, accessed 6 December 2006.

182 Moneywise, Newcastle Credit Union, Publication No. 5 (January 2007).

December 2005 the government granted credit unions powers to charge higher interest rates. The measure more than doubled the maximum APR associated with credit unions, to 26.7 per cent.[183] Whilst this was still a long distance from the rates associated with doorstep lenders it further reflected the difficult symbolic choices the movement had to take if it was to even begin to offer a real alternative to them.

CONCLUSION: IT'S A WONDERFUL LIFE OR NEVER NEVER?

Policy decisions on credit union development, which emphasized a need for a more professional approach and the adoption of appropriate business models, set a strong agenda for credit union growth at the outset of the twenty-first century. But great uncertainty surrounded their ability to become inclusive of those social groups who were still paying dearly for their credit products. The second of the two Polly Toynbee articles cited at the outset of this discussion appeared the more apposite. Life in Britain's deprived areas did not resemble *It's a Wonderful Life*. It was much more akin to the community depicted in Tony Marchant's TV play *Never, Never*. Screened by Channel 4 in 2000, it dealt with doorstep lending and credit unions and featured the ironically named John Parlour (played by John Simm) as, in Marchant's words, 'a benign loan shark'. Parlour charms his way into the living rooms of his customers, who include a single mum, Jo (Sophie Okonedo). In a modern twist on the doorstep lender as Lothario, the two characters become lovers and are involved in setting up a credit union, after Parlour becomes unemployed. He loses his job because Jo secretly arranges for him to be mugged for his collection money: her desperate pragmatic search for cash being juxtaposed with Parlour's own cynical business ethics. The bleak story does contain moments of warmth and humour but, as one reviewer remarked, the plot is distant from anything that Ken Loach might have offered, in its exploration of 'working class ignorance, venality and incompetence'. It features poor quality volunteers and borrowers who defraud the communal venture, including one who disappears to Spain with her loan.[184] Marchant

[183] Department of Trade and Industry, *Illegal lending in the UK*, 69.
[184] *New Statesman*, 13 November 2000.

thought that it 'seemed quite timely to explore the difference between [to show] setting things up that are supposed to be for the social good but in turn the conflict between that and the need to be a financially successful entity'. Channel 4's Head of Drama believed that Marchant 'doesn't let the viewer off at all and you're left with painful realisations. But when Tony's writing is working at that level you feel like you're engaging in a strong moral dialogue—which would have been more apparent in a whimsical way in a Frank Capra movie, but he's far cleverer at manipulating the whimsy out of it.'[185] In an interesting denouement, the other volunteers become disaffected or are jettisoned by the ambitious Parlour, as he uses his entrepreneurial abilities to force through his vision of a larger credit union. He relocates the organization from the estate, expands the common bond, and moves into a derelict bank by skilfully accessing local authority funding. In the final scene, Parlour regains his role as financial gatekeeper to Jo, who is once more in need of loan to cover a family crisis. Their final relationship mirrors the hierarchical one they had at the play's commencement: a conclusion that is not Capraesque. It was a television production which certainly reflected the deep unease felt by many credit union idealists about the road on which the movement was travelling.

Despite the deep penetration of UK banks and other financial providers in contemporary Briton, millions of consumers remain outside the target market of mainstream financial services and constitute a large sub-prime market. Doorstep moneylenders serve the needs of many in this category, dwarfing credit unions in both scale and scope. It is in this context, that activists have been urged not to think of credit unions primarily as a tool of anti-poverty strategies. Instead they should be re-imagined, it is argued, along the lines of the nineteenth-century co-operative movement's creation of services for a broad spectrum of members. But as was explained, in the previous chapter, the co-operative's movement's provision of consumer credit facilities was socially exclusive. Whilst the new model credit unions have created imaginative foundations on which credit unions could grow, some basic problems remain. The movement is still beset by fissures at an organizational level, with a mixture of philosophical and geographical differences remaining. The number of organizing bodies actually increased on either side of the millennium, reducing the opportunity for the movement to speak with one voice. Although the NFCU was wound up in 1997, it was succeeded by ACE

[185] *Observer*, 22 October 2000.

(Access to Credit Unions for Everyone). In 2007, it had 46 affiliates and its website explained that it was particularly interested in working with smaller credit unions.[186] The Association of Independent Credit Unions emerged and quickly disappeared, to be replaced in 2004 by UKCreditUnions. Its affiliates 'range from small church based credit unions to large employee based credit unions'. In 2007, 63 were listed on its website. They included some of the pioneers of the movement, such as Divisview Credit Union (Belfast), Moss Side and Hulme Credit Union (Manchester); and some new model credit unions, such as Cash Box Credit Union (facilitated by Tameside Council), and Thorne Credit Union (created by the General and Municipal Boilermakers' Union for its members in 1999).[187] The National Association of Credit Union Workers (NACUW) was founded in 1992 and was deeply committed to the fight against doorstep lenders.[188] Its formation was influenced by developments in the USA. It was inspired not by CUNA, but by the NFCCU that, as was explained above, broke away from CUNA in 1974, due to disaffection with the latter's business-centred model.[189] In a report prepared with the New Economics Foundation in 2002, the NACUW disputed Jones's view that there had to be a trade-off between the social and economic objectives of credit unions, with a more affluent membership being a prerequisite for sustainability. The report argued that such a 'trade-off was neither desirable nor inevitable' and that experience in the USA demonstrated 'how to achieve a streetwise balance of both social justice and business development goals'.[190] The report did, however, like Jones, articulate a more clearly developed business plan. This centred on a scheme to take a 10 per cent share of the doorstep lenders' market within a five-year period. It believed that 160,000 new members could be secured if the government provided the finance to create a network of 100 community development credit unions.[191]

It is telling that almost half a century after the formation of the British credit union movement, this analysis follows so many others by concluding that the future of the credit union movement remains uncertain. Can it move beyond its current tiny niche in the consumer credit market? Will it mount a realistic challenge to doorstep and other sub-prime lenders? What does history tell us? It suggests that the model

[186] <http://www.acecus.org>, accessed 26 March 2007.

[187] <http://www.ukcu.co.uk>, accessed 25 March 2007.

[188] Brown, Pat, and Mayo, *Life saving: community development credit unions*, Appendix E.

[189] Ibid. 12. [190] Ibid. 11. [191] Ibid. 7.

that ABCUL is currently advocating has been successful in numerous other financial markets. Critically, however, those advances were made in periods when financial services were extremely limited in comparison with those on offer in contemporary Britain. Ironically, of course, many low-income consumers remain excluded from that sophisticated market and have, so far, not been accessed by credit unions. History also tells us that credit co-operatives, from nineteenth century Germany through to modern-day Ireland, have been unable to resolve the credit problems of the poorest groups in society. Perhaps Moneywise Newcastle Credit Union's Key Loan programme, and others like it, can offer greater competition to doorstep lenders and more cost-effective borrowing to their customers. It is clear, however, that there is a long road to travel before the 220 Key Loan's customers in Newcastle match the number of customers in the area using doorstep lenders. Currently the credit unions 'appear to be serving a different universe' than the doorstep lenders, and the vast majority have 'yet to build enough scale to serve high-risk borrowers through cross-subsidy by their better-off customers'.[192] This does not have to remain the case; 42 per cent of Provident Financial's customers in the Republic of Ireland are believed to be credit union members. This figure must, however, send mixed messages to the credit unions. In the context of their widespread diffusion, Irish mutual credit institutions have attracted those who would be labelled financially excluded in the UK, and yet they have been unable to eradicate the market for doorstep lending. As generations of commercial creditors have discovered, the most efficient way to reach these consumers and to obtain repayment is by dealing with them on their doorstep. The next stage of credit union development may well involve experiments with not-for-profit doorstep collection and the Joseph Rowntree Foundation was seeking to fund research in this area in 2006.[193] The findings of any relevant research should be very interesting because our final lesson from history is that doorstep credit creates obligation, reciprocity, and a method of payment enforcement. How much more would that be the case if the service were mutual and cheaper than the commercial alternatives?

[192] Department of Trade and Industry, *Illegal lending in the UK*, 86.
[193] Ibid. 87.

Conclusion

Easy terms remain elusive

This study has taken an innovative approach to the topic of working-class consumer credit. It has introduced evidence from a number of important previously unexplored sources and provided the first fully nuanced discussion of a number of significant forms of lenders: those whose operations took them deep within working-class communities. The opportunity to probe the archives of significant companies, such as Provident Financial and the leading mail order retailers, together with the files of the Crowther Committee, deepens our understanding of important aspects of working-class credit. Together, these sources have enabled this study to follow the tallyman, and the check trader, out of the nineteenth century, through the twentieth century and beyond. Their history became part of a complex and controversial story of moneylending that is explained above, in the detail that its significance deserves. The check traders, tallymen, and the doorstep moneylenders who inherited their mantle have operated in significant markets. Provident, alone, has served over a million customers in virtually every year since the 1930s. The relationship between the business models of the doorstep credit companies has been compared with those of the mail order sector, which proved even more successful. Its success was based on a variety of factors. Amongst these were the convenience of catalogue shopping and the diversity of merchandise offered. But much of the sector's dynamism lay around its capture of female social networks. Its agency system provided the most utilized form of consumer credit for millions of women in the twentieth century. Its informality was particularly important for females, who faced cultural and legal barriers when attempting to secure hire purchase agreements in their own name.

The role of co-operative credit, in various guises, receives detailed treatment herein for the first time. The scale and scope of the co-operative movement's mutuality clubs, viewed by many as the equitable alternative to the doorstep credit firms, were analysed. But mutuality clubs represented a niche product, serving those who both wished and could afford to keep cash balances retained at their local co-operative store. Other consumers demonstrated a preference for the more costly commercial service of the Provident, because its checks could be utilized at a large number of independent retailers. In the 1960s, with the co-operatives declining, credit unions were envisaged as an equitable alternative to the most expensive modes of commercial credit. However, they were relatively unsuccessful in Britain where the credit union model proved unable to include those consumers who came to be labelled as the sub-prime market.

At various points over the past century, those using the methods of commercial borrowing studied above were seen by outsiders as feckless or dupes. Those accusations owed much to the gendered nature of a market that was dominated by the money concerns of female household managers. This study rejects any notion that low-income consumers, as a body, were generically careless or incapable of making rational selections. They took decisions from the limited choices that were available to them, making the most of their constricted agency. One example of this was the repeated appearance of informal credit and savings bodies, from diddlum clubs in Edwardian Salford to bond committees in 1970s Oxford. We have also observed that instrumental motives drove individuals to become involved in formal and informal credit networks. Their engagement ranged from earning a little commission as a catalogue agent, perhaps to pay for Christmas gifts, through to more calculating involvement in the business of debt when lending out surplus cash to less fortunate neighbours or workmates. The more affluent working-class users of check traders, and credit traders (the 'cream' as one credit trader called them), also exercised their choice from the 1960s onwards. With increased disposable income, thcy had less requirement of the external discipline that the home-collected credit providers had imposed on their parents and grandparents. They also encountered increased lending options, provided by an increasingly diverse and liberalized mainstream financial service industry.

Each of the commercial creditors examined in the study met success by relying on informal credit assessment via local collectors or agents. Weekly calls for payments then provided an effective level of enforcement. To the repeated frustration of outside observers, their customers frequently demonstrated an appreciation of these systems (even, in some cases, those of unlicensed moneylenders) focusing on convenience, rather than cost. The reasons for this have been examined and it has been demonstrated that the high levels of sociability between customers and agents proved useful for credit control, and in creating the obligation and reciprocity that maintained the relationship. In the last four decades of the twentieth century there were significant changes in this market. Mail order's traditional agency networks declined and more and more catalogues were sent to individuals who shopped only for their own household needs. Many customers, who formerly accessed mail order credit through an agent, were sieved out of this sector by its increasing use of computerized credit scoring. They found themselves excluded from a source of credit that was central to the budgeting of those on limited incomes. Whilst the catalogue lady might no longer be a visitor to their parlour, arriving on the doorstep were the agents of Provident Financial, Cattles, and London Scottish Bank. In the 1960s each of these companies made plans that involved taking their business to a more affluent working-class market, but they found the competition for these consumers increasingly intense as the mainstream lenders began to address their needs. Provident, Cattles, and London Scottish Bank subsequently discovered an alternative new lease of life, as doorstep lenders for the sub-prime market. By the end of the twentieth century, each of these three occupied positions in the FTSE 250: their scale and scope dwarfed the operations of the 'fringe capitalists' whose credit merchandising on the doorstep had been scrutinized in the Victorian county courts. Their success indicated that a tried and tested business model, little changed since the Victorian era (with the important exception of the feminization of agency workforces), remained effective in providing credit to those with low incomes.

This success was deplored by anti-debt campaigners, who viewed doorstep lenders, and others dealing with the sub-prime sector, as 'predatory lenders'. A study by the New Economics Foundation, in 2002, described the business 'as one of the worst excesses of the free market'. It suggested that the adoption of legislative models from Europe and the USA, restricting interest rates and other aspects of consumer credit, would halt those involved in 'systematically stripping the wealth and assets of some of the country's poorest neighbourhoods'.[1] The

[1] H. Palmer and P. Conaty, *Profiting from poverty: why debt is big business in Britain* (London: New Economics Foundation, 2002), 3.

authors of this report were boosted by the Competition Commission's subsequent assessment that a lack of price competition in the doorstep credit market was hitting the purses of consumers who could least afford to pay more than necessary for their credit requirements. However, they did not win the debate about the practicality of an interest rate ceiling. The findings contained herein offer a contribution to that debate. The history of consumer credit legislation suggests that where demand exists it is difficult to legislate it out of existence. The interest rate ceiling imposed on moneylenders in 1927 dramatically reduced the numbers of licensed moneylenders, but it had no discernible impact on the illegal sector. In fact, there is some evidence that violent criminal gangs became involved in the latter area—in Glasgow at least—in the 1930s. This evidence tallies with concerns expressed in a recent Department of Trade and Industry (DTI) report that levels of illegal moneylending in contemporary Britain would rise, were the government to reintroduce a rate cap. This is because legal lenders would end their dealings with those borrowers with the highest propensity to slow payment or default. The DTI claimed that because the UK credit industry is so diverse, it caters for high-risk borrowers and the incidence of illegal lending is actually lower than in other European countries. The French and German levels of illegal lending were respectively estimated to be three and two and a half times those in the UK. One explanatory factor being that price controls on credit in both those countries 'may have precluded the development of a high-cost sub-prime sector'.[2]

Further insights into the difficulty of crafting protective legislation on consumer credit have emerged during the course of this study. It has been seen that numerous methods emerged that were designed to evade various legislative measures. The development of voucher sales by check traders in the 1960s, for example, provided a means to sidestep hire purchase controls. Evidence of the difficulty of finding a one-size-fits-all legislative model can also be observed in the recent development of a diverse range of products available to the 'sub-prime' market. Included in this category is a re-energized pawnbroking sector that is now centred on three large companies, offering services that include cheque cashing, loans, and the purchase of merchandise, which can be bought back within twenty-eight days for a service fee. This business mirrors that of the Cash Converters chain which offers a parallel

[2] Department of Trade and Industry, *Illegal lending in the UK*, 5, 25<http://www.dti.gov.uk/files/file35171.pdf>, accessed 6 December 2006.

range of services. A further addition in many local shopping centres is Brighthouse (formerly Crazy George's), a company with Australian origins that had over 100 branches in the UK by 1996. It specializes in offering high-cost furniture on instalments, with sales usually tied in to expensive insurance cover. It tried to establish itself in France in 1996 but encountered widespread protest, led by the Socialist Party leader and future Première Lionel Jospin, who denounced the company for its 'exploitation of poverty'. Although it had broken no French law, its three stores were temporarily closed by the Finance Minister and the company, then a subsidiary of Thorn EMI, abandoned its plans for Gallic expansion.[3] The remit of this monograph did not include an attempt to probe various historical European attitudes towards the forms of consumer credit described herein, but it would make for an intriguing study.

In contrast to Crazy George's reception in France, Provident successfully exported its product to Poland, Hungary, the Czech Republic, and Slovakia in the last decade. It also has a long history of successful operation in the Republic of Ireland despite that country's extensive credit union membership. Its prices in Ireland are slightly lower than in Britain, suggesting that credit unions can have some impact in that respect. However, it must be concluded that, in Britain, the historical business models of the doorstep lenders are adapted better to the needs of low-income consumers than those of credit unions. This is because the latter asked members to save before a loan is granted, which proved impractical for many poorer consumers. Thus, importantly, the agent/doorstep collection model continues to work. In that context the Joseph Rowntree Foundation's announcement of funding for research into a not-for-profit doorstep credit service is very interesting. This proposal arrives at a point when the doorstep lending model is itself shrinking, as new products emerge. These include credit cards, with higher than average interest rates, aimed at those in the 'sub-prime' sector who are home owners; mostly those who have exercised their right to buy their former council homes. Hence the trend is for companies such as Provident to shift away from its riskiest borrowers. The DTI report suggested that a new credit hierarchy of preferred options amongst sub-prime borrowers has emerged and is topped by sub-prime credit cards, followed by mail order, the Social Fund, doorstep moneylending (or

[3] Palmer and Conaty, *Profiting from poverty*, 15; *Société*, 9 November 1996; *Daily Telegraph*, 12 November 1996.

pawnbroking), and finally loan sharks.[4] The tactical decision taken, by Provident and others, to abandon the riskiest borrowers will presumably increase the market for the illegal loan sharks. It appears, therefore, that doorstep moneylenders are edging away from the cross-subsidy models, by which they have traditionally charged their more reliable patrons prices above the 'natural' market rate in order to subsidize debts they incurred in dealing with riskier borrowers. Ironically, this is at a time when credit unions are still struggling to conjure up their own cross-subsidy model that will finally enable their brand of not-for-profit lending to make significant inroads into Britain's low-income communities.

Unfortunately, the evidence from our historical analysis suggests that cheap credit remains elusive for the depressingly large number of families who still have to manage on limited budgets. Society has come to terms with the concept of easy terms, but unfortunately the liberalization of credit that accompanied the great leap into the consumer society has not produced a simple solution for the economic problems of the poorest groups. For them, easy terms remain elusive.

[4] Department of Trade and Industry, *Illegal lending in the UK*, 32, 80.

Index